D1238749

On Concepts and
Classifications of
Musical Instruments

MARGARET J. KARTOMI

On Concepts and Classifications of Musical Instruments

THE UNIVERSITY OF CHICAGO PRESS
Chicago and London

MARGARET J. KARTOMI *is professor and chairperson in the Department of Music at Monash University in Australia. She is a specialist in organology and in the music of Southeast Asia.*

The University of Chicago Press, Chicago 60637
The University of Chicago Press, Ltd., London
© 1990 by the University of Chicago
All rights reserved. Published 1990
Printed in the United States of America
99 98 97 96 95 94 93 92 91 90   5 4 3 2 1

Library of Congress Cataloging-in-Publication Data

Kartomi, Margaret J.
    On concepts and classifications of musical instruments / by
Margaret J. Kartomi.
        p.   cm.—(Chicago studies in ethnomusicology)
    Includes bibliographical references.
    ISBN 0–226–42548–7. —ISBN 0–226–42549–5 (pbk.)
    1. Musical instruments—Classification.   I. Title.   II. Series.
ML460.K36   1990
784.19'012—dc20

                                                90–31361
                                                    CIP
                                                    MN

∞ *The paper used in this publication meets the minimum requirements of the American National Standard for Information Sciences—Permanence of Paper for Printed Library Materials, ANSI Z39.48-1984.*

To Mas Dris

Contents

Illustrations

Acknowledgments

Many people have contributed to this work, either through their published writings, correspondence, or conversation. I had some especially stimulating discussions with Stephen Blum and Jamie C. Kassler, both of whom also read or commented on parts of the manuscript. I also benefited greatly while writing the drafts of this book from critical comments sought from and so readily given by Judith Becker, Howard Mayer Brown, Ter Ellingson, Oskár Elscvhek, Ellen Hickmann, Timo Leisiö, Adrian McNeil, Thomas J. Mathiesen, Harold Powers, Amnon Shiloah, Ruth Stone, Sumarsam, Bell N. Yung, and Hugo Zemp. One of the most perceptive and helpful critics of a late draft of this book was my daughter, Karen.

Data for some chapters were based on fieldwork carried out by my husband, Dris, and myself in parts of Sumatra and Java on grants from the Australian Research Grants Scheme, using equipment loaned to us by the Department of Music, Monash University. My thanks are due to many field informants who gave me much of the information for this book. A visiting professorship in the Music Department of the University of California, Berkeley, gave me the time to complete work on the manuscript and the opportunity to benefit from comments given by Berkeley colleagues Bonnie C. Wade and Richard Crocker as well as graduate students James Mannheim and Zhang Wei Hua. Zhang Wei Hua kindly prepared the Chinese characters used, translated parts of some Chinese texts, and prepared transliterations of Chinese terms. Wang Ying-fen also translated parts of some contemporary Chinese texts. Discussions with graduate students of Monash University's Department of Music—Manolete Mora, Aline Scott Maxwell, Ashley Turner, and Gregory Hurworth—were enlightening, and all four kindly agreed to provide some field data for certain chapters. Poedijono, also of the Monash Department of Music, contributed through interviews some Javanese classification schemes that he learned in childhood. Monash University's Faculty of Arts provided the funding to bring the draft to final-copy stage, and Gary Swinton and Sue Tomlins of the Monash Geography Department's Drawing Office prepared the charts and drawings. The Press Syndicate of Cambridge University, the Trustees of the British Museum, Ruth Stone, Catherine Falk, and Adrian McNeil provided or gave permission for the reproduction of some illustrative material already in print.

To all these people and to others whom I have not mentioned, I should like to acknowledge a debt of gratitude.

Prologue

This book presents and explains how various of the world's cultures classify their musical instruments and instrumental ensembles, together with the concepts of instrument upon which the schemes are based.

The expression *concept of instruments* refers to the dominant or competing views in a society of the meaning and significance of instruments as cultural phenomena, including the hierarchical ratings of instruments. For a particular classification scheme, a taxonomist normally selects only part of the relevant culture's broad concept of instruments, or what we may call the taxonomically operative concept of instruments. For example, the selected conceptual data on which, say, a Dutch writer bases a classification of Javanese gamelan instruments would naturally be different from the concept on which a Javanese musician would construct a scheme, although both may initially select from the same pool of Javanese ideas about the ensemble. The Dutch writer would unavoidably view things in a partly Eurocentric way in the light of his or her own musical and educational background, while the Javanese musician, if totally unexposed to primary or secondary foreign influence, would base his or her classification on a Javacentric concept.

Whatever the authorship of a scheme, the choice of instruments included in it and its principles or characters of division and its resultant categories and steps are all largely determined by the classifier's view of the significance of instruments. Indeed, a classification is fully comprehensible only in the context of its creators' or adherents' concept of instruments, which in turn may form part of even broader concepts—for instance, of music, of knowledge of the cosmos, or of human existence. Some Tibetan and Hellenistic writers, for example, classified the instruments of their respective cultures within a comprehensive system of thought that included the classification of musical knowledge itself, and this in turn was conceived of as part of an even broader religious ontology.

In fact, then, the classifications may often be seen as abstractions or terse statements of ideas and beliefs that are held about the social, musical, and other functions of instruments and ensembles at a particular point in time, and these ideas and beliefs may in turn be part of even wider complexes of views about the nature of music, science, art, knowledge, the world, or the cosmos. In some cases a concept or classification of instruments may illustrate universality; in others, the particularity of an individual culture and its social structures. Classifications tend, of course, to change over time, though in many cultures the data showing how change occurred are not readily available. Moreover, in the case of schemes separated from us by a long expanse of time or some other impediment, the associated cultural data are not always available. Sometimes all but the bare bones of a classification are lost, in which case the scheme is not susceptible to such interpretation.

In attempting to explicate these hypotheses about the nature of classifications of instruments and ensembles, we shall need in the course of this book to ruminate about how and why human beings think taxonomically at all. In so doing we shall examine theories of classification, including the various formal cognitive structures resulting from the process of classifying, and define some of the terminology used in taxonomical discourse. The basic data will be derived from case studies that I have drawn together from various cultures.

The study of taxonomical organology, then, has two separate but related aspects. On the one hand it includes the creation and application of classificatory schemes and on the other the broad human concepts or complexes of concepts (or the selected taxonomically operative aspects of them) in which the schemes are born and proceed to function. The two aspects involve different research methodologies—the one more formal and systematic and the other more humanistic and sociological. Together they may be visualized as occupying opposite ends of a continuum in which an investigator operates. To gain some balance, future interpretative studies in taxonomical organology need to close the gap between the two approaches. It is the latter, human end of the continuum that has been most neglected to date.

An examination of a society's classification schemes and the rationale behind them (where available) can give us not only an insight into the relevant culture itself but also a greater understanding of our own, for the study of contrasting cultures can—paradoxically—be an exercise in self-knowledge or consciousness-raising. Though the ethnographic and critical study of musical instrument taxonomy throughout the world is still in its infancy, the last few decades have seen the development of many relatively new ways of classifying instruments. Recently several organologists have moved independently in similar methodological directions, while others have persisted in the old paths. It is therefore timely to make interpretative or critical analyses of the terminology, structure, basic concepts, logical status, and history of various schemes, both for their own sake and more particularly for the light they may throw on past and present trends in the concepts and classifications of instruments. All known schemes, including those representing a major conceptual or methodological shift, are characterized by their continuities with the classificatory ideas, structures, and techniques of the past.

In some cultures data are available with which to trace something of the intellectual history of taxonomical organologies. Sometimes, on the other hand, an organology assumes a somewhat ahistorical, positivist character, especially when it has focused primarily on morphological and acoustic characters, as it did in the valuable systematic work of Mahillon in late nineteenth-century Europe and in the eclectic classifications devised by Yang Yin-Liu in twentieth-century China. At other times instrument classification research has emphasized its human face, as in Needham and Robinson's perceptive exposure of the concepts and beliefs associated with Chinese instruments and classification from ancient times (see chap. 4).

Clearly we need to become more conscious of the ways in which people think in different cultures as well as how they organize and explain ideas, including how they think, organize, and explain things taxonomically. Folk, or traditionally transmitted, taxonomies have more to recommend them than the average Western musician or musicologist might expect. Certainly they tend to be more in tune with the manner in which people think and behave than some of the classification systems promulgated by scientists and philosophers in societies characterized by literary transmission.

Not all cultures have classifications of instruments. If we define the term *musical instrument* in the usual (though admittedly limited) way as "implements used to produce music, especially as distinguished from the human voice" (Webster's Third New International Dictionary, 1976 ed.), where *music* is defined according to its specific meaning in the relevant cultural context, then a few cultures may be isolated as having no musical instruments at all. These cultures have the materials and technological skill to make instruments but for various reasons choose not to. They include the Veddas of Srilanka, the Andaman Islanders of the Bay of Bengal, the

Todas of southern India, the Yami of Botel Tobago (south of Taiwan), the Fuegians at the southern tip of South America, the Lapps, the Celtic inhabitants of the Isles of Aran (Ireland) and the Outer Hebrides (Scotland), and the now extinct full-blood Tasmanian Aborigines of Australia (verbal communication from Gregory Hurworth). If we wish to define sounding body movements (such as clapping) as musical instruments or if we regard instruments as extensions of the human body or even if we adhere to a theory that the practice of clapping eventually developed into the use of instruments such as clapsticks, as did Sachs (Sachs 1940, 26), then a case could be made to include classifications of sounding body movements (corpophones, Olson 1986, 5) in a scheme. However, the line is usually drawn short of this; and in the great majority of classifications discussed in this book, corpophones are not included.

Nor do all cultures classify instrumental ensembles. Members of some cultures do not have ensembles at all. Others have them but classify only individual instruments. In some other cultures, ensembles are the most important object of organological classification. One might object that a classification of an ensemble should really be called an act of instrumentation and that it is basically different from a classification of instruments. Instrumentation, however, implies a process by which a composer selects a group of instruments and sets or orchestrates them for the purposes of a particular work. That is not the intended meaning here. If a group of people identifies with a particular ensemble of instruments and then proceeds to subdivide it into smaller units, say, for a practical musical purpose, then they are indeed classifying it. For example, the classical rock music ensemble of the 1960s breaks down for practical performing purposes into six main vocal and instrumental categories: lead vocal, backing vocals, drums, bass guitar, rhythm guitar, and lead guitar, with keyboards serving as an optional extra category. This is a classification of an ensemble.

Among the cultures or subcultures that prefer to classify instrumental ensembles rather than single musical instruments are the T'boli and the Mandailing peoples. Sometimes a particular ensemble is seen as representing the musical identity of a certain group vis-à-vis the identity, say, of a neighboring group that has a slightly different classification of instruments. The division of an ensemble may be based on such matters as the musical function of instruments, their order of entry in ensemble playing, and the portability of instruments (as in Minangkabau, West Sumatra). In the absence of a score or other set of directions, the practical requirements of group musicianship need to be spelled out for ensemble players; and the resulting set of taxa may be interpreted as a classification of the instruments or of the players' roles in the ensemble in question.

For the purposes of this book there could be no question of collecting together or referring to all the classifications of instruments and ensembles throughout the world, or even a high proportion of them. Reference is made to a number of written schemes in Western culture from Hellenic, Hellenistic, Roman, and Byzantine times until the contemporary period. A diachronic account is also given of schemes that are transmitted partly by literary means in the Arabian area, India, Srilanka, China, and Japan, as well as Tibetan schemes reserved for a monastic context and some contemporary schemes in Java and Japan. Orally transmitted schemes from 'Are'are, Dan, Hausa, Kpelle, Finnish, Javanese, Mandailing, Minangkabau, and T'boli cultures are also dealt with. Excluded is a vast amount of material that we know exists but has not yet been gathered. For many regions we lack the classificatory data about whole cultures or groups of cultures, past and present. Not one South American scheme, for example, has been referred to. For other regions we have some data about schemes in contemporary use but no evidence of the way in which they evolved and changed in the past. In yet others we have data on the dominant schemes but not on the divergent or alternative ones, which we know normally exist in a culture. The present selection of schemes is inevitably based on a limited amount of available data gleaned from a relatively small number of cultures.

This book, therefore, is but a preliminary introduction to the study of concepts and classifications of instruments and ensembles. It is far too early to write "the definitive work" on the subject. The fact that we are unable in the present volume to refer to more than a small part of the potentially relevant material draws attention to the need for the massive collection of data on these classifications and associated concepts in the cultures and subcultures of the world, past and present. It is to be hoped that this preliminary book will stimulate field-workers and library researchers studying musical cultures to collect data on the concepts and classifications of instruments and ensembles. I hope it will eventually result in the systematic cross-cultural study of the data gathered.

The present volume will be of interest to students of organology, classification theory, musicology, and music, and perhaps also to those interested in the sociology of art. If it can serve to interest others in the diverse ways in which instruments are conceived of and classified, and encourage them to collect more data and take the study further, then its publication will have been worthwhile.

PART ONE

On the Nature of Classifications of Musical Instruments

In Part I, I shall pose such questions as why do human beings classify and what are the various structures in which we do so. I shall attempt to clarify the somewhat confused terminology of the taxonomy of instruments in preparation for the use of these terms and abstract classificatory constructs in the discussions about established schemes from various cultures characterized by literary transmission (covered in Part II) and certain cultures characterized by oral transmission (covered in Part III).

The cultures discussed in this study were chosen on the grounds of the availability of data on our topic. Naturally, less information was available on the societies depending on oral transmission than on those with a history of literary transmission. Moreover, it is probable that some of the literary classifications of instruments originated in oral tradition.

The main reason for distinguishing between societies that are mainly or partly oriented toward literary transmission and those that depend on oral transmission is not that the classifications of instruments produced in the former are essentially different from those found in the latter. Although classifications of instruments in societies marked by literary transmission do have some characteristics that differ from schemes in cultures characterized by oral transmission, as will become apparent in the following chapters, the main reason for the distinction is that concepts and classifications of instruments in societies characterized by literary transmission are much more substantially documented over time, permitting a much more diachronic approach to their study. The lack of historical data in the orally transmitting societies is, however, somewhat compensated for in many cases by the availability of detailed musical, ethnographic, and other synchronic data that can be elicited through fieldwork or other methods of observation and deduction.

O N E

Any Classification Is Superior to Chaos

We classify because life in a world where nothing was the same would be intolerable. It is through naming and classification that the whole rich world of infinite variability shrinks to manipulable size and becomes bearable.

Stephen Tyler, *Cognitive Anthropology*

To classify groups of objects such as musical instruments is a fundamental principle of human thinking. Except for a few human groups who do not use any musical instruments at all and societies that have no separate category of instruments, cultures around the world have developed their own formal or informal ways of classifying instruments or ensembles. A few of them are examined in this book.

Although we have no way of knowing how established classifications originated, we can speculate about the needs giving rise to them. Human beings seem to require the intellectual security offered by classifications of a large body of data, whether it be ideas, flora, fauna, kinship groups, or musical instruments. The desire for rational structure—like its opposite, the urge for spontaneous expression—is an attribute of being human. Classification is needed, then, partly in order to grasp, remember, and teach others the diversity of species. It results from the desire to simplify and understand. "Any classification is superior to chaos" (Lévi-Strauss 1966, 15). The security proffered by a classification scheme helps us to comprehend an intimidatingly large or profound body of knowledge. We feel that we are more able to control the items contained in the scheme and to use them with confidence.

Conversely, the schemes that we habitually use affect the way we perceive the world and understand it. In the case of musical instruments this includes the way in which we create and respond to music itself. For example, a Western composer who adheres to the traditional European classification of instruments into strings, winds, and percussion writes and orchestrates works in a very different style from, say, a contemporary

3

composer who habitually thinks of instruments as comprising categories based on their timbres. Similarly a listener, performer, or analyst adhering to the former classification would perceive and appreciate certain musical works differently from a listener, performer, or analyst who had the latter classification in mind.

Human beings obtain aesthetic satisfaction from the act of classifying, or from re-creating a classification from memory, as I have noticed many times during field trips in Sumatra, Java, and elsewhere. To construct a classification is somewhat like drawing a fine geometrical design. To draw a family tree or to classify a ritually important instrumental ensemble is to elicit the same kind of perceptual and cognitive pleasure as we draw from viewing a work of visual art or reaching an elegant resolution of a mathematical or music-compositional problem.

Which distinguishing characteristics are chosen to construct a classification scheme depends mainly on the cultural assumptions and the purpose of the classifier or classifying culture. To a Westerner devising a close scheme (i.e., a grouping having a substantial number of steps), the morphological elements that influence the sound production will seem very important, largely because of the traditional acoustic and morphological bias of the dominant Western concept of instruments. Thus the distinction between single and double reeds is found in virtually every modern Western classification. To the Batak peoples of North Sumatra, on the other hand, this character of division is simply not important enough to be chosen for classificatory purposes, though the Batak do recognize the validity of the distinction in that they make and use both single- and double-reed instruments. To them the important character of division of a reed wind instrument is its size or material, as evidenced by the names given to the types of reed winds they use. For example, the Toba Batak distinguish between "big reed wind instruments" (*sarunei bolon*) and "small reed wind instruments" (*sarunei na met-met*), while the Mandailing Batak distinguish one of their reed pipe categories according to its material, calling it a "bamboo reed wind instrument" (*sarunei buluh*). To the Rejang people of coastal Bengkulu (Sumatra), on the other hand, the ceremonial function is the significant character of division, which explains why they have named one of their reed pipes—the *sarunei nenet*—after its function of accompanying the ritual *nenet* dance. The chosen characters of division are culture-specific.

What is it that determines the length or number of levels or paradigmatic sections of a classification, and how important is the symmetry of a scheme? Classifications ruled by the method of logical division have considerable capacity for vertical or lateral expansion, as the case may be. A classification with a limited aim tends to come to an end when it has fulfilled the primary purpose for which it was intended. A scheme may be quite extensive and systematic, but its adherents will normally not add categories just for the sake of intellectual completeness or symmetry. Occasionally, when an author is concerned to treat a large group of instruments relatively systematically by logical division, the resulting classification may have a large number of steps of close division and a relatively symmetrical arrangement of categories at each step, as in the case of Galpin's schemes of 1910 and 1937 (see chap. 11). However, despite the undoubted aesthetic element involved in constructing a classification, I have found little evidence to suggest that this element includes symmetry for its own sake. Downward schemes which move from the general to the particular) discussed in this volume generally have irregular or asymmetrical structures. Indeed Hornbostel and Sachs made a special point of rejecting schematic symmetry in their scheme (1914, 10).

The taxonomically operative concepts of instruments in some cultures, however, are not easily bent to simple linear classification. One widespread misconception about the classification of musical instruments is that it necessarily takes the form of single-character, downward logical division. That this view was held in at least part of the United States in 1987 was found to be the case in a limited test carried out by James Mannheim, a graduate student at the University of California, Berkeley, who asked some passersby, including some music students, how they would classify musical instruments. Some instinctively answered the question by: "Oh, you mean like large and small? It depends what you want to use the instruments for. If I wanted to put them on the walls of my house, I would classify them by large and small." The idea of selecting a single, consistent character of division to serve a limited classificatory purpose was there. Other informants mentioned the old strings-winds-percussion grouping or the traditional strings-woodwinds-brass-percussion scheme, while others divided instruments into categories such as "ones you hit, ones you blow, ones you scrape." Most had heard these singular classificatory ideas at school and they had stuck.[1] As applies in most cultures, the popular notion of classification was tradition-bound and based exclusively on the method of logical division.

Classifications, however, are not immutable constructs that occur "naturally" in the form of downward logical division, even though hidebound tradition may regard them as such. Sometimes a scheme—even the dominant scheme in a culture—may aim at showing relationships between various ideas in a more comprehensive and nonlinear fashion than logical division allows. When two or more simultaneously operating parameters are taken into account, the resulting classification takes the form of a paradigm (e.g., in a dual-axis form), a multifaceted diagram or list, or a mandala. As we shall see, a paradigm is often gapped in structure, rarely taking symmetrical form, while a mandala (Sanskrit *mandala,* literally meaning "circle"), one of humanity's oldest classification devices (Hall 1984, 15), usually assumes the shape of a circle or a square within a circle divided into a number of symmetrically arranged parts. Several examples of classification of instruments by paradigm are discussed in this book. The Chinese, Indian, and Javanese schemes presented in figures 4.1, 4.2, 5.1, and 7.6 are presented in mandala form.

It is surprising initially to discover that the classification of instruments and ensembles in the many cultures of the world has been so neglected in musicology, and especially in ethnomusicology. A reason is not difficult to find, however. The number of ethnomusicologists is small and the amount of information available is vast, and ethnomusicologists have so far directed their attention to other priorities, such as a close description of musical instruments, styles, and behaviors. The total number of person-hours of ethnomusicological research engaged in before the 1970s was quite small and the amount of basic research remaining to be carried out throughout the world is still enormous.

Nevertheless we need to consider why it is that most ethnomusicologists have neglected to compile these data. A considerable amount of information on instruments has been collected, but this has been limited mostly to physical descriptions. The discipline has insisted that its members try to elicit indigenous musical terms and concepts when collecting field data and to reject Western preconceptions in the attempt to comprehend native categories. Yet field-workers are still not properly conscious of the need to gather and study the taxonomical data and related concepts in the cultures they study. Instead of searching for native categories in the field, most ethnomusicologists have automatically fallen back on what they learned at school as being the "objective" ways of classifying instruments.

Why do many field-workers lack this awareness? Why do ethnomusicologists, who normally insist on using indigenous terms and concepts wherever possible, content themselves with the use of European schemes when they classify a non-European or nonmainstream European group of instruments? Some ethnomusicologists say they avoid thinking about classifying instruments altogether because they regard classification as a desiccated, formalist kind of study that they would prefer to leave to some systematician or other. As I have noted, however, classifications are often synopses or terse accounts of a culture's, subculture's, or individual's deep-seated ideas about music and instruments, as well as, in some cases, philosophical, religious, and social beliefs. In fact taxonomical organology is far from being a dry, clinical study and is better not approached in a purely formalist fashion.

Admittedly the study of indigenous instrument taxonomies has not been totally neglected. Some anthropologists have called for the development of "ethnoclassification" studies and a few field-workers have searched for certain kinds of native categories of musical instruments. For example, Ames and King went to great pains to collect indigenous terms and concepts for their book on African musical instruments (see Ames and King 1971, x), but even they used a foreign scheme instead of a locally derived one for their main classification. They pointed out (1971, 60) that Hausa musicians divide instrumentalists (and hence instruments, as Stone noted for the Kpelle [1982, 89]) into two categories: drummers (drums) and blowers (blown instruments), relegating players of stringed instruments (lutes) to the drum category because lutes are regarded as having a similar performing action. Yet when it came to high-level classification they chose to divide Hausa instruments into the four Hornbostel and Sachs categories rather than the two Hausa ones or the categories of some other local scheme.

Kunst also sought out indigenous categories, dividing the instruments of the Central Javanese gamelan into five categories partly by using indigenous terminology (Kunst 1949, 247). But he did not succeed in eliciting Javanese cognitive categories for this purpose in toto and instead imposed mostly Western concepts and categories on the data he had collected; for example, he designated a category of instruments according to what he believed to be their musical role, that is, playing what he called "the nuclear theme." As an examination of recent Javanese treatises shows, contemporary Javanese musicians do not use Kunst's classification but prefer their own schemes. Another study of Kunst's—of the instruments of Nias (1939)—also imposed the Hornbostel and Sachs scheme on the data collected, as did Sárosi's work on Hungarian instruments (1960) and a number of projects by other authors.

Some other scholars have either modified the Hornbostel and Sachs scheme or reversed the direction of classification from downward (i.e., moving initially from the general to the particular levels of division) to upward (i.e., moving from close inspection of the details of an instrument upward to higher-level division); for example, Elschek did both in the development of his so-called typological method of classification (1969b). Other musicologists imposed on their data the traditional European division of instruments into strings, winds, and percussion. Yet others developed their own individual classifications, including Galpin in 1910 and 1937, Schaeffner in 1932, Dräger in 1947, Reinhard in 1960, Yamaguchi in 1969, Hood in 1971, Ramey in 1974, Sakurai in 1980, and Lysloff and Matson in 1985.

Our knowledge of the world's classifications of instruments and ensembles, especially in the mainly orally transmitting cultures of the world, then, is very sketchy and incomplete. A few scholars have collected some data, however. Zemp was one of the first ethnomusicologists to attempt to elicit and publish an indigenous, orally transmitted classification of instruments, which he did in the case of the Dan people of West Africa (1971). In addition, van Thiel gave an outline of a classification used by the Ankole people of Africa (1977), Leisiö reconstructed a classification used by the Finns (1977), I elicited classifications among the Mandailing as well as the Javanese and the Minangkabau (see below), Turner presented a classification by the Petalangan Malay (in a forthcoming dissertation, Monash University), Stone elicited one for the Kpelle (1982), Simon for the Batak (1985), and Mora for the T'boli (1990). Almost no research, however, has been carried out on the orally transmitted classifications of instruments to be found in the many other cultures and subcultures of the world, including urban popular-music subcultures such as those that produced rock and roll and "heavy metal."

In Lévi-Strauss's opinion (1966, 40) the reason why research into indigenous classification developed so late in such fields as biology, botany, and anthropology is that ethnologists have "often been prevented from trying to find out about the complex and consistent conscious systems of societies they were studying by the assumptions they made about the simpleness and coarseness of 'primitives'. It did not occur to them that there would be such systems in societies of so low an economic and technical level since they made the unwarranted assumption that their intellectual level must be equally low" (Lévi-Strauss 1963, 42). Thus, scholars have been responsible for "many errors and misunderstandings, some of which have only recently begun to be rectified. [They] could have been avoided had the older travellers been content to rely on native taxonomies instead of improvising entirely new ones" (Lévi-Strauss 1966, 44). "And it is only just beginning to be realised that the older accounts which we owe to the insight of . . . [a few] rare inquirers . . . do not describe exceptional cases but rather forms of science and thought which are extremely widespread in so-called primitive societies. We must therefore alter our traditional picture of this primitiveness" (Lévi-Strauss 1966, 42).[2]

Similarly, writers who have applied Western categories to non-Western instrumentaria are responsible for such "errors and misunderstandings." Yet all "outsider" students of a culture are automatically responsible for a degree of distortion in what they write about it, however hard they may try to abide by native categories, being unable to overcome all the effects of their upbringing and the assumptions inherent in the very language they use for communication.

Doubtless all writers on non-Western musics in the nineteenth and early twentieth centuries were influenced by the assumptions referred to by Lévi-Strauss, though the difficulties involved at that time in long-distance travel and recording techniques ensured that very few music ethnologists were really working in the field and extremely few were collecting field data on musical instruments and ensembles (as opposed, say, to working on non-Western music recordings of instrumental music performed at the Paris World Exposition in 1889). More importantly, however, the primary aim of studying and writing about non-Western music in that era of comparative musicology was to compare it with Western music, in addition to which authors wrote for an entirely Western and musically conservative readership. Thus they naturally classified instruments in a "scientific" Western fashion rather than in native categories. The assumption that it was correct to use Western categories for the study of a non-Western instrumentarium was so deeply ingrained that it remained virtually unquestioned among ethnomusicologists until the late 1960s; and vestiges of it are still dominant in the minds of many, perhaps most, Western-trained musicians and musicologists to this day.

Clearly, cognitive schemes never develop in a vacuum, which is the reason why classifications of instruments tend to express their creators' cultural assumptions. As we shall see from the various case studies below, however, different cultures select different elements from their total concept of instruments to serve as criteria for division; for example, some emphasize specific elements of performance practice, others reflect more general religious or social ideas, while yet others combine both general and specific social and/or musical aspects. When properly established over time, classifications serve the purpose of enabling members of a culture to recognize fundamental musical, social, and other relations between the instruments contained in the scheme or, if so inclined, to formulate new myths or theories about them. Conversely, the schemes devised reflect previously formulated concepts or theories about the respective instruments, whether in cultures that are primarily oral or those that are primarily literary in their transmission.

What are the essential differences between cultures chiefly oriented toward oral transmission and cultures characterized by literary transmission? In view of the distinction made between them in the present study, it is necessary to discuss the relevant terms and concepts for a moment.

As Finnegan pointed out in her book on oral poetry, "the meaning of the term 'oral' is far from self-evident; it is a relative and often ambiguous term. . . . 'Oral' poetry essentially circulates by oral rather than written means; . . . its distribution, composition or performance are by word of mouth and not through reliance on the written or printed word" (1980, 16). If an initially oral communication later becomes a written one, 'does the fact of its having been recorded in writing make it no longer oral?' ' . . . The relativity and ambiguity are part of the nature of the facts, and to try and conceal this by a brief definition would only be misleading" (Finnegan 1980, 22). Oral culture and written culture, Finnegan submits, should be viewed as the ends of a continuum ranging from the nonliterate through the partly literate to the mass literate, for even mass literate cultures normally have some orally created and transmitted communications. The basic point, then, is the continuity of oral and written literature in literate societies. There is no deep gulf between the two. They shade into each other, and Finnegan points to innumerable cases of poetry that has both oral and written elements.

The term *oral literature* as used by Finnegan and others has been criticized on logical and normative grounds by Ong, who likens it to speaking of a horse as an automobile without wheels (1971, 291), encouraging us to view "oral composition as a sort of unwritten writing" (Sweeney 1987, 9) and to regard oral composition as being inferior to written composition. Composition in an orally oriented society does not differ in kind from that in a print culture (Sweeney 1987, 12); all human discourse is by nature formulaic. In both kinds of societies compositions are created "with a set of given themes, schemata, or models," which allow structure to be brought into what otherwise would be meaningless chaos (Sweeney 1987, 12). Therefore no purpose is served by trying to explain away a "society's discourse . . . purely in terms of the 'nature' of orality, . . . to reduce the complexities involved to a simple dichotomy between orality and literacy. While it cannot be denied that even a minimal amount of literacy has a very considerable effect upon thought processes, it must be emphasized that 'literacy' is not some undifferentiated condition" (Sweeney 1987, 69), nor does the advent of literacy in a culture necessarily mark the end of social homeostasis or result in other cognitive or psychological change. At this stage, at least, no case of change in the structure of classification as the result of the coming of literacy can be documented.

Like Finnegan's cases of poetry with both oral and written elements, classifications of musical instruments are sometimes both oral and literary in their transmission. For example, the eight-category Chinese classification of instruments according to material (the *pa yin*) is part of both oral and written culture. As Needham and Robinson indicate (1962, 142), this ancient scheme was arrived at only gradually and in oral tradition. It is believed to have existed from the twenty-third century BCE in the time of the legendary Emperor Shun. However, the evidence also indicates that a similar four-category scheme based on the materials from which the instruments were made coexisted with the eightfold scheme in the ancient period. The *pa yin* classification was written down many times in the middle ancient period and even in the late historical period. It was conceived in oral tradition but was transmitted over the centuries both orally and in written form.

We can only rarely speak of purely oral or purely written cultures. Some peoples communicate certain information only orally (e.g., classificatory schemes) and other information only in writing (e.g., poetry).

In the rural Mandailing culture of North Sumatra, village scribes do commit some of their legendary poems and family trees to writing, yet they never write down their classifications of instruments or ensembles, and they rarely document anything else. Indeed, Mandailing culture as a whole is essentially oral. Traditionally it has not depended on writing, making only limited use of the written word for a small number of specific purposes, and this remains the case in most villages today. As is indicated in chapter 13, four properties of the taxonomies of instruments and ensembles are observable in the culture: (1) there is a plurality of schemes, one of which is regarded as being the most representative of the culture and is indeed symbolically the richest; (2) there are parallels between the main classification and other spheres of Mandailing thought such as cosmology, social organization, and the history of clan settlements in a village; (3) there is a closer classification of the prestigious instruments than of the lesser ones; and (4) single-character division and multifaceted, paradigmatic division are used. These four characteristics also apply in differing amounts of detail to classifications in cultures that transmit largely by literary means, such as in China, Tibet, India, and Europe, where the available data on instrument classifications date back many centuries.

The reader might argue, on the other hand, that to write a classification down makes it different, in that it gives it greater potential for stability, longevity, and rigidity than an oral scheme possesses and possibly a degree of autonomy from its original purpose. For example, an ancient scheme may eventually acquire a modern, nationalist purpose, as the ancient four-category Indian scheme arguably has in recent times.[3] One might also argue that to write a scheme down lends it the prestige of the literati. But even if all this was true, and true for many cultures, it would still not demonstrate that there are substantial differences between orally and literarily transmitted schemes per se.

Despite the problems outlined above, it seems necessary for present purposes to retain the expressions *oral orientation* and *literary orientation* as working terms. As long as we regard the two categories as the ends of a continuum, the usefulness of the distinction remains. The fact is that we need to employ different research methods when eliciting data about classifications in cultures with an oral as opposed to a literary orientation, which is a good reason for retaining the terms. Research into classifications in orally oriented cultures requires fieldwork, while research into schemes transmitted in the literary mode necessitates library research.

Closely related to the distinction made between classifications in oral and literary transmission is the difference between what may be called culture-emerging and observer-imposed schemes. A gulf lies between classifications that emerge from within a culture or subculture, whether expressed in oral or written form or both, and classifications that are conceived—in fact imposed—by an insider or outsider musician, scholar, or museologist, usually in written form. For centuries, biologists, botanists, and other scholars have called this distinction "natural" versus "artificial" classification. A natural classification is one "into which things fall, as it were, of themselves" (Kaplan 1964, 50); it is one that carves at the joints, as Plato said:

> Its naturalness consists of this, that the attributes it chooses as the basic classification are significantly related to the attributes conceptualised elsewhere in our thinking. . . . A natural grouping is one which allows the discovery of many more, and more important resemblances than those originally recognised. Every classification serves some purpose or other. It is artificial when we cannot do more with it than we first intended. The purpose of scientific classification is . . . to disclose the relationships that must be taken into account, no matter what. (Kaplan 1964, 50)

A culture-emerging, or natural, classification is sometimes so informal that it can hardly be called a scheme. In such a case its uncodified terms have to be elicited by an observer. It is actually a reconstructed model of an ordering of data in the minds of members of the culture.

Culture-emerging schemes tend to reflect the broad ideas or the identity of the culture that produced them, including in some cases ideas about such matters as performance practice, the ways sounds are produced, the other arts, philosophy, religion, social structure, the social uses of particular musical instruments and ensembles, or combinations of two or more of these. Artificial, or observer-imposed, schemes, on the other hand, are frequently based on the goals of an individual investigator, whether scientific, museological, or other; for example, schemes may be limited to morphological aspects or to acoustic detail.[4]

Both kinds of classification may aim to include all or a selection of the instruments of a culture under their rubric, but the culture-emerging kind may be limited to the instrumentarium of a particular village, which originally developed the scheme it uses in order, say, to facilitate its own practical music making or ritual procedures, as in the case of the Minangkabau culture.

Classifications of instruments naturally differ in their structure and content from other forms of communication such as myths, proverbs, riddles, rituals, dramas, spells, hymns, prayers, chants, and sacred laws. Classifications express in condensed form, either by single-character or multifaceted division, a culture's or subculture's concept of what instruments are and mean in their musical, social, or musical and social context. In this respect the genre that orally transmitted classifications most resemble is the proverb, which expresses in terse form a statement that may be rich in cultural implications and embody observations about the nature of life and human conduct. Classifications least resemble the myths and legends, for unlike myths and legends, classifications do not depend on stock formulas or other repetitive devices. Like a proverb, a classification is a highly compressed form of expression that may nevertheless be pregnant with cultural meaning.

In contrast, written classifications that have been imposed on a society by a scholar or museologist are like clinical diagnoses, terse in form and in most cases essentially systematic rather than richly symbolic. They are also broad in scope, as are some schemes that emerge from a cultural tradition. This is not, of course, to say that schemes imposed by individuals never reflect some of the values of the society in which they are created. For example, the scheme of the museologist Mahillon (1893) arguably expressed the contemporary rationalist emphasis on "objective" thought, as may be deduced from its reliance on fixed acoustic and morphological characteristics rather than on historical, social, and performance-oriented properties of instruments, properties which are by nature highly variable. However, schemes developed by individuals usually represent a single train of thought or intent rather than directly reflecting the broad musical or symbolic base of a culture or subculture as a whole or aspects of it.

Of course the division between so-called natural and artificial classificatory types is not absolute. Some writers want to have the best of both worlds and have succeeded to a degree in achieving it. For example, when the Chinese Manchu-period scholar Chu Tsai-Yü and the contemporary Indian musicologist Deva (1980) produced their own individual classifications of instruments, each first borrowed from their respective culture's mainstream classificatory traditions for the uppermost level of their scheme and then proceeded to add their own classificatory steps, thus combining the culture-emerging with the observer-imposed type of scheme. In this way their classifications acquired both the aura of national identity and the desired degree of scientific accuracy and intricacy.

Clearly we need to collect many more data about both culture-emerging and observer-imposed classifications. As will become apparent in the following chapters, we know much more about the observer-imposed schemes of a very few cultures, especially those of nineteenth- and twentieth-century Western societies, than about the many culture-emerging schemes of societies in the rest of the world. We have tended to value highly classifications transmitted in the literary mode while neglecting orally transmitted schemes that emerged naturally from a culture and to have remained largely unaware of the fact that the most common aspect of the transmission of classifications of instruments around the world is that it has been oral. If we succeed in collecting a broad sample of the world's classifications of instruments, we shall then be in a position to draw some comparative conclusions about the nature, purposes, and types of classification of instruments in the various kinds of societies. This book is intended as an initial step in that direction. How best to effect the comparison across the cultures once sufficient data have been collected, however, will be a methodological problem that we shall have to ponder for some time to come.

TWO

On the Methodology of Classification: Taxonomies, Keys, Paradigms, and Typologies

> ... what the Kaluli data show are that cultural knowledge is neither a map nor a summation of a group of taxa but rather the creative ability to organize and think about natural historical and zoological processes in ways consistent with socially structured beliefs about the world.
>
> Steven Feld, *Sound and Sentiment*

Despite the considerable contributions of organologists to the study of musical instruments around the world, the theory of classification in organology is still in its preliminary stages of development, partly because scholars have been working somewhat in isolation, both from each other and from the developments in classificatory thinking in some other disciplines. In the following discussion it will be useful to borrow terms from authors in the fields of cognitive anthropology and biology, where the theory of classification is more advanced and terminologies are more rationalized.[1]

Before we discuss the various kinds of classification, it is necessary to define the basic term to be used. What, then, is a classification? It is a scheme that organizes knowledge about selected entities from a chosen domain, grouping them in one or more steps (stages of subdivision) into sets of classes. Thus, classification may minimally be defined as "assignation to a proper class."[2] As has been mentioned, a basic distinction is made between classifications that are observed to emerge naturally from a culture over time and those that are imposed artificially or manipulated intellectually by the observer for a specific purpose. The former is likely to take a broad semantic domain or concept of instrument into account, while the latter may arbitrarily select a limited number of characters of division (distinguishing features) to serve the particular purpose at hand. There are two structures of classification in each case. Culture-emerging, or natural, schemes may take the form of *taxonomies*, which apply one character of division at each step, or of *paradigms*, which apply more than one principle of division at each step. Scholar-imposed, or artificial, schemes may take the form either of *keys* (tree diagrams), with one character per step, or of *typologies,* applying more than one character or facet (sharply defined aspect) per step. Thus, taxonomies and keys are unidimensional, and paradigms and typologies are multidimensional. As we shall see, the details of the schemes and the semantic domains to which they belong vary widely in differing kinds of societies. "Each classification is attached to a semantic domain which is organized around numerous features of meanings . . . no two cultures share the same set of semantic domains, . . . nor do they share the same methods of organizing these features" (Tyler 1969, 11). In the case of natural classifications, the task of the scholar is to discover these semantic domains and their methods of organization, avoiding the imposition of his or her own preconceptions. In the case of artificial schemes, on the other hand, the observer has consciously constructed the scheme for a particular systematic purpose. The former usually emerge in oral transmission, though they may eventually be written down, while the latter are virtually always transmitted in literary form.

The four main classificatory procedures vary in the directions of their cognitive processes. Taxonomies and keys are both based on downward classificatory thinking, paradigms are based on the horizontal and vertical intersection of facets, and typologies involve upward thinking. Paradigms may sometimes be presented in mandala form, as in the case of the multidimensional Chinese and Indian classifications (figs. 4.1, 4.2, and 5.1).

Not only individual instruments but also ensembles may be classified in a culture. Some cultures habitually classify ensembles in addition to or in preference to individual instruments, which they may see as being philosophically incomplete in comparison to ensembles, which may be seen as symbolizing social groupings or ranks or simply as reflecting the usual musical practices. Ensembles are normally divided into taxonomies by single- or multiple-step division or into paradigms.

TAXONOMIES AND KEYS

A taxonomy consists of a set of taxa or groupings of entities that are determined by the culture or group creating the taxonomy; its characters of division are not arbitrarily selected but are "natural" to the culture or group. A taxonomy normally uses the method of logical division, which "logically" applies one character per step and proceeds downward, metaphorically speaking, from a general to a more particular level. However, it may be less regular than that, loosely adopting the method of logical division but applying more than one character in one or more steps. It may also be partly incomplete or nonsymmetrical (see fig. 2.1).

A taxonomy may superficially resemble a key if the taxonomy is presented in the form of a branch diagram or a tree, to use an analogy found in Indian, Arab, European, and some other cultures. However, the formal resemblance between a taxonomy and a key is superficial. A key imposes an order on a body of data; it does not discover the order underlying it (Tyler 1969, 11). A key is an arrangement of dichotomous oppositions in several steps based on the method of logical division. Thus, the plus ($+$) and minus ($-$) signs in figure 2.2 mean the presence or absence of the relevant features as determined by the characters of division, which in this case are the presence or absence of a boss and of a wide rim in the case of gongs.

The characters governing a key may be selected quite arbitrarily for a limited classificatory end, but most commonly they enable us readily to identify a specimen in a body of objects that are similar in one respect or other. Like an index (which is the simplest form of catalog, as it lists objects in alphabetical order or other arbitrary sequence), a key may serve to locate objects in a collection or to identify specimens by means of deduction. Hence keys do not work well if more than one character (or at most two) is considered simultaneously. Keys are artificial constructs that impose arbitrary structure on a body of objects and normally have a limited purpose of serving as an index of items in a collection; they are therefore used mainly by curators and collectors.

As Mayr explains (1982), modern biologists have largely rejected keys. Identification by means of a key may result in an unsatisfactory or even ridiculous answer because specimens in each division need not have anything in common except the chosen character (e.g., if a piano is classed with a shawm because they share the character of being painted black).

MUSICAL INSTRUMENTS			
PERCUSSION	WINDS	STRINGS	
		BOWED	PLUCKED

FIGURE 2.1 Sample taxonomy of instruments

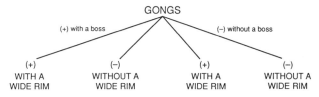

FIGURE 2.2 A key or tree diagram

Thus, keys and other artificial classifications may actually obscure real relationships. Of course, such problems may partly be avoided by applying a succession of carefully weighted characters at each step of division. But a priori weightings give a scheme a static, inflexible character, which can cause further illogicalities to arise in some of its divisions. Moreover, the larger the number of steps of division, the more difficult it is to maintain a consistent and symmetrical logical structure. Natural classifications, with their a posteriori weightings of a number of characters, avoid the danger of deriving absurd groupings altogether, because they group together only those specimens that appear empirically to be essentially related.

The structure of a key or a taxonomy, then, depends on the number of steps delineated, the number of classes distinguished at each step, the number of characters governing each step, and the degree of symmetry of the scheme. A *step* is a stage of subdivision of a class. A *class* or *division* created by a step may be broken down into smaller units termed *categories* and *taxa*. *Category* means "rank or level in a hierarchical classification; it is a class, the members of which are all the taxa to which a given rank is assigned" (Mayr 1982, 207–8). A *taxon* on the other hand has the more restricted meaning of "a group of organisms [entities] of any taxonomic rank that is sufficiently distinct to be worthy of being named and assigned to a definite category" (Mayr 1982, 207–8).[3] Thus, it is useful to reserve the term *categories* for classes distinguished at the highest or most abstract level or step and *taxa* for classes at the lower step or steps. A *character* is the distinguishing feature of a step of division. Depending on the step it governs, a character may range from the most abstract or general to the quite specific.

A classification with only one or several steps is termed a *broad* scheme as opposed to one with several steps, which is referred to as *close*. If a scheme is symmetrical, it views all instruments with equal thoroughness; that is, it asks the same question or series of questions about all instruments in each category, even if at times these questions yield nonsensical or nonexem-

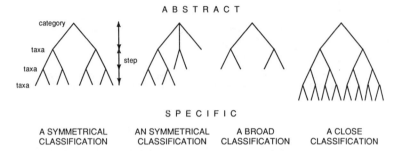

FIGURE 2.3 Examples of downward classification

plifiable answers (as in Galpin's first scheme [1910], discussed in chap. 8). Hence asymmetrical classifications have close subdivisions in some taxa and relatively broad ones in others (see fig. 2.3).

In strict logical division, all categories and taxa are mutually exclusive; that is, they do not have any element in common. If in addition they are jointly exhaustive, then they must contain all members of the partitioned class. As a result, borderline cases, or cases of entities that can equally well be accepted or rejected as members of more than one class, are bound to occur. This disadvantage can be overcome by adopting a logical theory that allows for inexact classes in analyzing the relationship between mathematical and perceptual propositions (Koerner 1979, 691). However, the problem is usually resolved by allowing dual or multiple class membership for the one entity, as in a scheme that permits beaten stringed instruments such as tube zithers and pianos to be classified either as chordophones (a stringed category) or idiophones (a self-sounding category).

This kind of problem is irrelevant in the orally transmitted schemes discussed in Part III of this book, as their users are normally quite unconcerned about matters of logical perfection.

PARADIGMS AND TYPOLOGIES

It is of course very limiting to allow the application of only one character of division per step, given the multidimensional nature of objects such as musical instruments. Frequently a culture or an observer discriminates relationships between facets that intersect at two, three, or more levels rather than one at a time.[4] This is so especially in cultures that are rich in lexemes, for example, the 'Are'are. A *lexeme* is defined as a label of a cognitive category having several levels of meaning; its range of reference may be quite complex, especially if it refers to a long history of changing or expanding usages over time. Sometimes, therefore, it is necessary to group by multidimensional division, using paradigmatic or typological structures. These two methods may also be called "classification by faceted grouping," to use Ramey's expression (1974). *Facet* or *feature*, referring to the sharply defined aspects of an entity, have a similar meaning to *character* but a different logical status and therefore replace the term *character* in this context. Alternatively the phrase *grouping by inspection* may be substituted for *faceted grouping*, as in the case of Mayr's survey of biological classification methods (1982).

Paradigmatic grouping and typological grouping, then, differ from classification by logical division in that the classes are derived from the simultaneous intersection of several facets or dimensions. Hence they are logically incompatible with taxonomies and keys. A paradigm is normally a natural, culture-emerging phenomenon, whereas a typology is always the construct of the observer. In constructing a paradigm we isolate the dimensions in simultaneous intersection. In a typology, on the other hand, all the available data are first scanned and then grouped into categories that apply to multifaceted intersection. These categories may be called *variants* and *types*. Typological thinking moves from the observation of particular details to their groupings at more general or abstract levels of knowledge; that is, it results in upward classification. Since both typological and paradigmatic thinking are based on multidimensional intersection, their diagrammatic representations take on a similar form.

Figure 2.4 is a schematic representation of a classification that is deducible or "emerges naturally" from observations of musical practices in the T'boli culture of the southern Philippines (Manolete Mora, personal communication 1987). Since some of the instruments are played only solo and others only in ensemble, it is necessary to include both solo instruments and ensembles within the one scheme. As the T'boli characteristically apply three main dimensions in simultaneous intersection, their mode of classificatory thought in this instance has to be recognized as being paradigmatic. Alternatively the same material can be presented in two separate schemes, as in figures 15.1 and 15.2. To do so, however, is relatively unwieldy and breaks up the unity of T'boli classificatory thought. One advantage of paradigmatic presentation is that it clearly indicates what is and what is not done in the culture. Hence the empty cells in the T'boli paradigm tell us, among other things, that the T'boli never play their lute and fiddle ensemble in the "strong" musical style, they never play

	Solo instruments		Ensembles		
NAWA "played with the breath"	FEU: KEYOTUT: FLENDEG: S' LOLI: KUMBING:	(reed winds) (" ") (flutes) (") (jew's harp)			LEMNOY "gentle" musical style
T'DUK "played with the fingers"	DWEGEY: S' LUDOY: HEGELUNG:	(fiddle) (zither) (lute)	SETANG (zither with two players)	SEGUYUN (lute and fiddle)	
TEMBOL "played by beating"	KLUTANG: S' LAGI SOTU: KLINTANG: T' NONGGONG SOTU: MEDEK DOL:	(percussion beam) (gongs) (gong chime) (drum) (stamping trough)		SEBELANG (gongs, drums, sticks and gongchimes)	MEGEL "strong" musical style

FIGURE 2.4 Three-dimensional paradigm of T'boli instruments and ensembles

their gong, drum, and stick ensemble in the "gentle" musical style, and instruments "played with the breath" are always played singly, never in ensemble.

Technically, the existence of empty cells in this scheme means that it is an "imperfect paradigm," for a "perfect paradigm" would comprise only filled boxes. For an example of a perfect paradigm see figure 2.5, which shows a domain of eight lexemes divided in three dimensions (A = a1, a2) (Kay 1966, 22).

Perfect paradigms rarely occur in the cognitive systems of a culture (Kay 1966, 21). Paradigmatic thinking in a "folk" scheme such as the T'boli one evolves in informal communication over long periods of time and is applied in a largely intuitive fashion. Hence there is no pressing need to fulfill all the theoretical possibilities of a scheme within the rules established by the culture. Lack of logical completeness in paradigms, like imperfect logical division in taxonomies, is not, of course, to be regarded as a sign of inferior-quality classification. In this context, logical completeness and symmetry are not values in their own right. Logically complete

	a1	a2	
c1	L1	L5	b1
c2	L2	L6	
c1	L3	L7	b2
c2	L4	L8	

FIGURE 2.5 A perfect paradigm

schemes would in any case be tiresome and misleading as they would in some instances have to include elements having little or no significance in the culture.

As has been mentioned, paradigms sometimes take the form of a mandala, as in Sumarsam's classification of the gamelan (see fig. 7.6). Like this Javanese scheme, the ancient Chinese and Indian classifications shown in figures 4.1, 4.2, and 5.1 happen to fall most readily into mandala form, which is perhaps not surprising in view of the common Tantric Buddhist and Hindu history of Java, India, and China and the importance of mandalas in Tantric thought. "Mandala designs, both simple and complex, of satellites arranged around a center, occur with such insistence at various levels of Hindu-Buddhist thought and practice that one is invited to probe their representational efficacy. . . . Cosmological schemes of various sorts in Tantric Hinduism and Buddhism have been referred to as mandala" (Tambiah 1985, 252).

Mandalas are one of the oldest classification devices known. They usually take the shape of a circle or a square or both in one and are comparable to a matrix in mathematics. Their basic purpose is to show the relationship of various ideas or facets to each other in a comprehensive, nonlinear fashion. Mandalas are particularly useful when dealing with dissimilar pairs or clusters of activities that intuition indicates are related but which have not been previously associated, linked, or combined into a comprehensive system (Hall 1984, 15).

Paradigmatic classification has only recently begun to be recognized in ethnomusicology (e.g., see Zemp's paradigms for the 'Are'are culture [1978, 43]) and its existence may therefore be more widespread than is generally surmised. Ethnomusicological field workers, in particular, need to raise their awareness of paradigmatic thinking and to collect and collate the data cross-culturally.

Like paradigms, typologies are "multi-dimensional forms of arrangement organised by class intersection. . . . In a paradigm, the entities to be classified (e.g. folk taxa) provide the necessary contrasts from which . . . defining attributes are derived; in a typology, this process is usually reversed" (Conklin 1964, in Tyler 1969: 107). In a typology, the particular aspects of the entities to be classified are inspected and these attributes are then assembled on the basis of which taxa may be constructed at consecutively higher levels of generality. The only case of the use of typologies to classify musical instruments so far encountered is in the recent work of the Czech scholar Elschek, though his approach was foreshadowed by the work of Hood and others.

The typological diagram shown in figure 2.6 resembles a paradigm in its structure, yet it was constructed on the basis of typological, upward classificatory thinking. The designations A.1. and A.2. represent clusters of variables elicited by Elschek in his detailed study of many specimens of European willow-bark flutes. The typological diagram in figure 2.6 has been derived by the present writer from the synoptic chart (Elschek 1969a, 33) of "types" of willow-bark flutes (see chap. 12).

The eight variants are distinguished according to three intersecting attributes: whether they are open or stopped flutes, whether they have a regulatable end duct for pitch change, and according to the various shapes of the ducts. At a higher level the variants are classed into types, which Elschek termed A, B, and C. A *type* is defined as a group of specimens linked by similarities of internal structure; it may also be defined as a model with variable realizations, or simply a group of variants that are related in some way at a higher level. Typologists such as Elschek recognize that the items they study are subject to constant change. Thus, they may also build this factor into their definitions and define a type as a group of specimens related not only by aspects of internal structure but also by similar degrees or kinds of change (see chap. 12).

The typological method, which aims at grouping objects into types (a bundle of attributes, Conklin 1962, 108), is a method for the scholar who wishes accurately to order a mass of observed detail about a body of data in order to construct increasingly abstract categories, which are called variants, types, and groups of types.

Parts II and III of this book discuss many examples of the four methods of classification discussed in this chapter.

	← SHAPE OF DUCT →				
	lengthened duct	obliquely cut duct	obliquely rounded out duct	plain duct	
without regulatable duct	A.1.	A.2.a.	A.2.b.		open
	B.2.	B.3.a.	B.3.b.	B.1.	stopped
with regulatable duct at lower end		C			

FIGURE 2.6 Three-dimensional typology of European willow-bark flute

THREE

Cognitive Directions: Downward and Upward Grouping

The shift from downward to upward classification [in biology] (together with the associated methodological and conceptual changes) was slow, gradual and irregular, as has been true for nearly all scientific 'revolutions'.

Ernst Mayr, *The Growth of Biological Thought*

To our present knowledge, most classifications of instruments around the world take the form of downward logical division; that is, they move mainly by single-character steps from a more abstract to a more specific level. We know that horizontal classification of instruments by simultaneous, multifaceted intersection occurs in some—especially orally oriented—cultures, but as yet we know corporately only of a few examples of such paradigms. Upward classificatory thinking based on the detailed knowledge of a body of specimens and the building of increasingly more abstract classes may also be a mode of spontaneous taxonomical thinking in some cultures, but if so, we know very little about it.

How does vertical classificatory thinking occur? Do we tend to generalize before or after acquiring a close knowledge of the objects of generalization? Lévi-Strauss suggests that we begin to think at the specific level and then move to the general: "animals and plants are not known as a result of their usefulness; they are deemed to be useful or interesting because they are first known" ([1962] 1966, 9). The implication is that there is a tendency to generalize or to develop general categories *after* obtaining a close knowledge of species. On classifying we first compare aspects of well-known specimens with each other and then group them according to empirically or intuitively chosen principles. Once the most abstract level of a classification has been reached by upward thinking (e.g., the classification of all instruments into the beaten and the blown categories), the abstract level may then serve as a framework for and stimulate one's memory of the body of specimens on which it is based. Thinking, of which classifying is one form (albeit not perhaps its most stringent form); "admits of degrees, and a way of thinking can degenerate imperceptibly into a way of remembering . . . a mnemotechnic procedure is less trouble to operate than a speculative one, which in turn is less exacting than a device for communication (Lévi-Strauss [1962] 1966, 67).

Eventually, some adherents or inheritors of a classification scheme may come to think of its specific categories as being of secondary importance; certainly specific categories are more difficult to remember than general principles. They may then proceed to transmit the scheme to others by presenting the easier, more general categories first, without bothering to think through or pass on the detailed reasoning that originally came to distinguish the lower levels of classification. After becoming accustomed to a downward scheme, they may either forget or disregard the detailed lower levels of classification and transmit the reduced scheme—that is, the highest level only—to future generations. The social determination of cognition will mitigate in favor of the stability of the scheme over time, or at least until someone seriously questions its rules or devises an alternative scheme, which may or may not replace it.

Of course it is not possible to show that the scenario just described is a typical course of classificatory thinking in a society or group or that there are in fact such typical courses of taxonomical thinking. In fact the early stages of classifying cannot be a simple matter of straight, unidirectional thinking. Within the dialectical process of deepening our understanding of something—including the process of classifying—we continually move back and forth between the specific and the general levels; thought processes oscillate between the upward, downward, and lateral modes. Possibly some established schemes that do not concern themselves with the accurate details of specimens did in fact originate at the uppermost level. The ancient Chinese scheme *pa yin* concerns itself with the highest level only (although a scheme by Chu Tsai-Yü begins with the *pa yin*, moves in a downward direction in deference to tradition, and then proceeds upward (see chap. 4)). Perhaps the *pa yin* never included more than its present eightfold division. Alternatively, its eight classes could represent a reduced version of a larger scheme that began its development at a low level and moved upward to an attractively simple eightfold division while the lower levels were forgotten. We shall never know, of course. However, merely to think about this scenario is a useful assignment, especially for Western musicians and organologists, who have to date been almost totally dominated by downward classificatory thinking by logical division.

Westerners also have a cultural bias in favor of classifying instruments as "logically" as possible, where instruments are conceived of—theoretically at least—as fixed, static objects.[1] In desiring organization, which we may define as "a matter of following or not following the rules" (Bloch 1977, 280), we tend to judge a scheme by its adherence to rigid principles and to feel dismay when loose ends or ambiguous categories arise. Of course it is neater and easier to remember and apply a key, which by definition contains a minimal amount of ambiguity. But if we adopt a concept of instruments that takes full cognizance not only of their propensity to change in time but also of the depth of their musical and cultural meaning, some departures from strict logical division can only be expected. Normally perfectly logical schemes cannot begin to match the complexity of musical practice.

The loose ends in some schemes may in fact be usefully interpreted as unwittingly preserved elements of historical change. To illustrate this point, let us consider an imaginary single-step scheme incorporating diachronic data as in figure 3.1, where A originally was a general term for instruments in an orally transmitting culture but over time narrowed in meaning to denote percussion instruments made of wood, skin, or both, as distinguished from stringed instruments, named B, and wind instruments, called C.

Let us suppose that due to culture contact the people in question learned the new techniques of how to work metals in addition to wood and skin, and that A further narrowed in meaning to denote only keyed percussion instruments made of bronze or wood (see fig. 3.2, which shows a two-step scheme incorporating diachronic data). Then, for practical musical purposes, a new term—E—evolved, also at the second step, which was applied exclusively to bronze keyed percussion, and a class called D

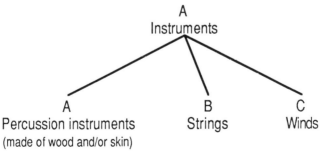

FIGURE 3.1 A single-step classification

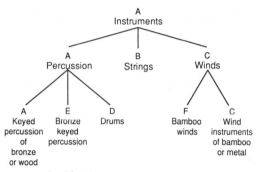

FIGURE 3.2 A two-step classification

was allocated to instruments, made of wood and skin, or drums. Similarly, let us suppose that at the second step (or third level) of division, the wind category C included both bamboo and metal instruments. Later, C was subdivided into two classes with the creation of a new class called F, which was reserved for bamboo wind instruments only. Meanwhile the knowledge of all these changes was lost in the transmission of the scheme from one generation to another. An investigator appearing in the field centuries later would be presented with the problem of having to try and explain why the lexemes C and A had two or three different meanings, to say nothing of the problem of trying to account for the nonexclusivity of categories A and E as well as F and C at the third level of division. Here we have a case of a scheme unable logically to accommodate changes in instruments and terminology. By deduction, the investigator could, of course, propose that the structure of the scheme and the levels of meanings of the terms were interpretable in the light of historical change. With supporting historical data, a convincing explanation of the scheme could be put forward in terms of the processes of culture contact and consequent transplantation and adaptation of skills from an outside culture. A real-life example similar to this imaginary case is Leisiö's reconstruction of a Finnish classification of instruments, which is discussed in chapter 18.[2]

In contrast to Western organologists, who, as we have noted, have been dominated by the method of downward logical division, scholars and practitioners in the discipline of biology moved away long ago from reliance on this method in their classifications, adopting in its stead an upward approach to grouping based on detailed inspection. How and why did this happen? In 1982 Mayr traced the history of biological systematics in a way that is useful to organology and other systematic disciplines that similarly conceive of their objects of classification as being variable or changing entities. In Europe we first have evidence of the use of logical division over two thousand years ago in Plato's writings. The method was properly expounded in the writings of Aristotle, reached its full importance among Aristotle's followers, and was taught to all who attended school between the Middle Ages and the late eighteenth century.

Of course the long-standing use of this downward-grouping method is probably universal: certainly it is found independently in many parts of the world, especially—but not only—as applied to kinship relationships. Mayr (1982, 150) highlighted its simplicity by illustrating its use in a parlor game well-known in Western culture, where someone is asked to guess the identity of an object chosen in his absence. "Is it alive?" might well be the first question. If the answer is no, the possibilities are divided into two classes, and the next question is asked. The continual splitting of the remainder into two or more parts by dichotomous division eventually leads to the correct choice. In terms of Aristotelian logic, the largest class is divided by deduction into two subclasses called *species,* which in turn become genera at the next lowest level of subdivision, and are again subdivided into species and so on.

Although Aristotle intended the method of logical division to be applied only to static inanimate objects and not to living biological specimens, which are characterized by a high degree of variability, it dominated classifications of both animate and inanimate entities for the two thousand years of Western scholarship after his death. To Plato, variable phenomena reflected a limited number of fixed forms and essences, as they were called by the Thomists in the Middle Ages. Downward classification was coupled with essentialist Platonic philosophy, which emphasized the regularity and constancy of nature (and later, according to Christian dogma, of Creation). Hence its adherents saw variation among specimens not as historically explainable phenomena but merely as imperfect forms of the underlying "essence."

Because Aristotle advanced different methods in his earlier writings on logic and in his later works on biology, scholars from the time of the Renaissance to the present have been uncertain about what his real principles of classification were (Mayr 1982, 150). Aware of the complex aspects and variability of specimens, Aristotle ridiculed the idea of classifying biological specimens in an elaborate, downward-oriented, logically based hierarchy, was interested in species rather than genera, and chose to classify at the lower levels of generality by the method of detailed inspection. But his followers were misled by his use of biological examples in his writings on logical divisions; and they applied its principles even in their biological classifications.

Not until the seventeenth and eighteenth centuries did the philosophy of essentialism begin to be widely rejected. Between the publications of the botanist Adanson in 1763 and the naturalist Darwin in 1859, downward classification was gradually replaced by upward, multifaceted classification based on *population thinking*, which recognizes the importance of individual specimens, stresses their uniqueness, rejects the idea of the typical individual,[3] and sees classes as populations of changing individuals. "As the history of systematics has proven over and over again, satisfactory classifications—classifications based upon a critical evaluation of all the evidence—can be constructed only by those who have a thorough knowledge of the group concerned" (Mayr 1982, 195).

Adanson, as Mayr pointed out, was the first biologist openly to question the method of logical division and thus to begin to loosen "the paralysing grip of essentialism" (Mayr 1982, 87). "Downward classification became more and more unsatisfactory as European botanists and zoologists were inundated by the avalanche of new genera and families from the tropics" (Mayr 1982, 190). Specimens began to be viewed empirically in their variable forms and as holistically as possible, in relation to their changing environment. The empirical, upward method of classification is now "by and large the method employed by every modern taxonomist, at least in the initial stages of the classifying procedure" (Mayr 1982, 192).

Mayr distinguishes two subfields of taxonomy: (1) microtaxonomy, "the methods and principles by which kinds of organisms (objects) are recognized and delimited," and (2) macrotaxonomy, "the methods and principles by which kinds of organisms (objects) are . . . arranged in the form of classifications" (1982, 146). Microtaxonomy, then, begins with the study of the concrete individual object, which is inspected in as many of its aspects as possible. Essentially similar objects may then be grouped into taxa of increasingly higher degrees of generality. Microtaxonomy is the basis of one of the two main multidimensional classification methods, namely, upward classification by inspection and empirical (or a posteriori) grouping (Mayr 1982, 192), a method that in the past has sometimes been termed *natural classification*. As has been noted, Ramey (1974) called it "classification by faceted grouping." Upward classification is the process of grouping individuals into categories of individuals, these categories into more general categories, and so on. It starts at the bottom, sorting species into groups of similar species and combining these groups into a hierarchy of taxa (Mayr 1982, 192; Eysenck 1972). Downward classification by logical division begins with the most general or abstract level observed and moves downward to the less general or more specific. It rests, in theory at least, on a priori ideas as to what is important.

Chapters 11 and 12 will trace the beginnings of a shift toward multifaceted classification in the work of a number of twentieth-century organologists who have desired to study instruments in all their complexity. The increasing realization that instruments are not just static objects but are products of human culture and therefore resemble living organisms and are subject to continual change both in their parts and as a whole has impelled some scholars to group them typologically on the basis of detailed inspection. As the essentially ahistorical concept of instruments as fixed, unchanging objects began to be replaced by an appreciation of the dynamic qualities of the culture surrounding and comprising musical instruments, organologists began to radically reassess their research methodology. Thus, some scholars saw the variant and the type rather than the taxonomical category as the basic classificatory units upon which hypotheses about the history of the instruments could be constructed. "Variants are not mere deviations from some assumed basic organization: with their rules of occurrence *they are the organization*" (Tyler 1969, 5).

On the one hand, then, recent organological studies have tended to become more and more particularist, as we shall see, postponing the study of higher-level categories until a larger number of reliable data have been accumulated. On the other, organological research has begun to move toward serious consideration of methodological matters; and this has included the beginnings of the cross-cultural study of concepts and classifications of instruments.

PART TWO

Classification in Societies Oriented toward Literary Transmission

Part II investigates concepts and classifications of instruments in societies that transmit their schemes in literary form or partly literary form, which facilitates the diachronic study of their development.

All the societies discussed have a literary tradition that is at least a millennium old. The oldest and longest-lasting known classification is the Chinese *pa yin* scheme, which possibly dates back to the third millennium BCE and survives to this day. The major ancient religions of South Asia all have their own specific classifications of instruments, though the main Hindu scheme, which is about two millennia old, is by far the dominant one. Early Arab and monastic Tibetan schemes date back to the first millennium CE. Java's literary tradition stretches back well over a thousand years but only recently have classifications of instruments emerged there from oral tradition, thus producing a documented case of a culture in transition from the oral to the written classification of instruments. The region with the largest amount of surviving information about our topic is Europe. The origins of the dominant tripartite classification of instruments in Europe and the West date back to Greece in the third century BCE, though the first full-blown statement of the scheme was not made until the third century CE.

Between them the cultures oriented toward literary transmission have produced and preserved many treatises and other sources over the centuries. Together they give evidence of the constancy of change and occasionally of major shifts in taxonomical thought, for example, shifts from schemes based on the music theory to those based on, or largely based on, the musical practice of a given period, or shifts of preference from one type of instrument to another. In many cases the data may be found to illustrate the coexistence of several schemes in a society at one time. Some classifications demonstrate the broad convergence of social, religious, or other extramusical ideas with the strictly musical, while others are conceived by individual scholars having a limited scientific, musical, or other theoretical purpose in mind. Examples of schemes partly influenced by religious or social ideas are the Hellenistic scheme of Aristides, the Sung dynasty Chinese court ensemble classifications, and to a lesser extent the Tibetan monastic scheme. However, religious beliefs and social constructs are peripheral to many of the written schemes, including those of Java, the Arab world, Europe, and even India (in which each of the main religions is nevertheless associated with its own classification of instruments, but in each case the schemes are based mainly on music-acoustic or morphological characters).

As we shall see in the following chapters, the direction of classification in cultures characterized by written transmission is mainly downward, and the dominant form is a key (or tree diagram), or logical division. A recent trend in the West favors upward classification by inspection or a combination of upward and downward classificatory activity. A few ancient schemes are in paradigm or mandala form. However, they probably originated in oral culture, and some changed in later centuries to the form of downward division or (in a few Chinese cases) to downward-then-upward division, and some twentieth-century schemes added extra levels governed by mode of sound excitation and aspects of morphology. In several cases, modern reformulations of antique schemes combined ancient constructs with more recent Western classificatory ideas, retaining the old ideas for purposes of emphasizing national or regional color and respect for tradition. The most widely used character of division in the cultures oriented toward literary transmission is the mode of sound excitation. Other characters include morphology, national character, and the material of which an instrument is made.

Continuities and Change in Chinese Classifications

Sonorous are the bells and drums. Brightly sound the stone-chimes and
 flutes.
They bring down with them blessings—rich, rich the growth of grain!
They bring down with them blessings—abundance, the abundance!
               A prayer in the *Shih ching* (The Book of Poetry)[1]

The earliest known principle by which the Chinese classified musical
instruments or sources of sound (*yin*)[2] was according to the materials of
which they were made. The choice of character was based on the link in
the sphere of cosmological thought and ritual between these materials and
the seasons, the winds, the abundance of grain, and, by extension, human
welfare, wealth, and political power.

Possibly dating back as far as the twenty-third century before our era,
this principle of classification has remained influential to this day. It is by
far the oldest and longest-lasting known character of instrument classification in the world. Its extraordinary persistence is largely due to the
prestige it derived from being part of the mainstream tradition of
philosophical thought and the literary transmission of schemes derived
from it since the ancient period.[3] Possibly other ancient schemes based on
different characters of division once coexisted with it in the oral tradition,
but if so they have remained unrecorded.

The sources are unclear about the history of development of the *pa
yin*, but it is widely believed that in the time of the legendary Emperor
Shun (2233 to 2188 BCE) a classification based on the kinds of materials
predominantly used in the construction of the various kinds of instruments already existed. At one time the Chinese divided instruments into
four categories (fig. 4.1), as recorded in the *Yo chi* (Record of ritual music
and dance), a book compiled from sources of the Chou period (ninth to
fifth centuries BCE). Eight instruments of "music" were mentioned: bells,
drums, pipes, flutes, ringing stones, leather, shields, and axes. Only four

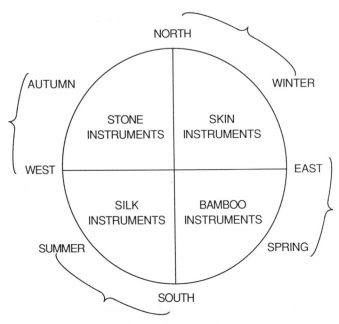

FIGURE 4.1 The association of the Chinese four-category scheme with the directions and the seasons (based on Needham and Robinson 1962, 153–55)

"sources of sound" occur here, namely metal, skin, bamboo and stone. Elsewhere in the *Yo chi* it is more clearly stated that instruments are the four sources of sound, and they are listed in the order of metal, stone, silk, and bamboo instruments (Needham and Robinson 1962, 145).

In another passage of the same source, mention is made of the eight sources of sound: "Dancing is that by which one regulates the eight sources of sound, and thereby conducts the eight winds" (Needham and Robinson 1962, 145). However, it was not the eightfold but the fourfold division of instruments that predominated in the *Yo chi*. Perhaps the fourfold and the eightfold schemes were equally popular at that time. In any case, "it is clear that the eightfold Chinese classification of sounds was arrived at only gradually" (Needham and Robinson 1962, 142). The linking of the eight winds to the sources of sound was frequently referred to in the *Yo chi*, and it is this correlation that gives the clue to the development of the four sources of sound into eight (Needham and Robinson 1962, 148). This Chinese scheme is known as the *pa yin* (the "eight [sources of] sound") (fig. 4.2). In Emperor Shun's time it is

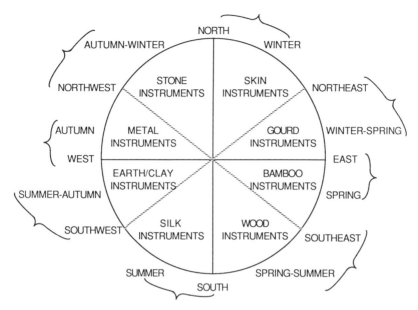

FIGURE 4.2 The association of materials and the *pa yin* with the directions and the seasons (based on Needham and Robinson 1962, 153–55)

believed to have been presented in the following order: instruments made of metal (*chin*), stone (*shih*), silk (*ssu*), bamboo (*chu*), gourd (*p'ao*), clay (*t'u*), leather (*ko*), and wood (*mu*).[4]

However, the *Chou-li* (Programs of Chou) presented the *pa yin* in a different order. This anonymous treatise, which was compiled from earlier sources in about the second century before our era, referred to the *pa yin* as "the eight (sorts of) sound (deriving from instruments made of) metal, stone, clay, leather, silk, wood, gourd and bamboo" (Robinson 1980, 78). The same order of presentation of the *pa yin* was given in the *Tso chuan* (Tso commentary), which was attributed to Tso Chiu-Ming and was probably compiled in the fourth century before our era (see Legge, 1880 V: 18).

The concept of instruments lying behind the *pa yin* was based on ideas about the nature of sound, which included the concept of *chi* (subtle matter, emanation, human breath, spirit) and the idea that sounds were portents, prognostic aids,[5] and manifestations of the equilibriums and disequilibriums of nature and political power. In fact, the concept of *chi* "moulded Chinese thinking from the earliest times, just as form and matter dominated European thought from the age of Aristotle onwards" (Needham and Robinson 1962, 133). It was used in the context of sacrifice to the ancestors, who were thought to be attracted to return to earth by the sounds of instruments as well as prayers and the aroma of food cooking (see the prayer at the head of this chapter). The *chi* were believed to rise up or descend from heaven and their "intermingling to produce wind, wherewith heaven makes music. . . . All were signs and symbols of those great climatic processes on which the life of the ancient Chinese people depended, balancing ever between flood and drought. Such was the environment which brought forth their organic philosophy' (Needham and Robinson 1962, 133).

The meaning of the term *chi* changed and became more precise in time. In the *Tso-chuan,* mention was made of six *chi* called *yin, yang,* wind, rain, brightness, and darkness (Needham and Robinson 1962, 134). The concept of the *Yin* and the *Yang* comprised a conglomerate of opposites, such as high/low, heaven/earth, and male/female. In the *Chou-li* it was said that the *yin* tubes could predict good or bad luck. The term could also apply to something that could be "piped off." Early references were made to "the shaman-musician piping off his own *chi* through bamboo tubes in an attempt to alter the processes of Nature—of heaven's *chi*—by sympathetic magic," which is a reminder of the story of Tsou Yen (fourth century BCE) blowing on his pitch pipes for the benefit of the crops (Needham and Robinson 1962, 134–35). Moreover, the Chinese believed that one could determine the morale of one's enemy by the divinatory humming through tubes (Needham and Robinson 1962: 138).[6]

The reason why the materials of instruments were important was not, as one might first expect, their influence on the timbre of sounds produced, though the Chinese have long been highly sensitive to the timbre of instruments as well as to the sympathetic magic of sound vibration by which kings were believed to attain political and moral power. According to the interpretation of Needham and Robinson, it had to do with the idea that instruments made from each of the eight materials each controlled one of the dances performed at ritual mimes, which in turn could induce one of the eight winds. Thus the materials of instruments were indirectly related to humankind's control of the winds and the weather. Music and instruments were part of the calendrical system and the seasons as well as the welfare of the state.

In most of the archaic reference works the eightfold classification of instruments was correlated with the eight directions or sources of wind as well as the eight seasons (Needham and Robinson 1962: 153–154). The eight categories were usually exemplified by the ringing stone, bell, lute or zither, flute and pipe, tiger-box, drum, reed organ, and globular flute. Stone instruments were associated with the northwest and autumn-winter, metal instruments with the west and autumn, silk-stringed instruments with the south and summer, bamboo instruments with the east and spring, wooden instruments with the southeast and spring-summer, skin instruments with the north and winter, gourd instruments with the northeast and winter-spring, and earthen instruments with the southwest and summer-autumn. If the order of the seasons and the points of the compass seem a little peculiar, this may be due to the fourfold classification having been expanded into an eightfold scheme. For in the fourfold scheme, stone had been associated with the west and autumn, silk zithers with the south and summer, bamboo pipes with the east and spring, and skin drums with the north and winter (Needham and Robinson 1962, 153–55). The four-category scheme actually linked the instruments to the directions and the seasons much more directly than the eight-category one.

> First, autumn is the season when the *Yang* forces of nature are in retreat, and bells or metal slabs were the instruments sounded when a commander ordered his troops to retire. In winter there occurred one of the most solemn ceremonies of the year, when the sun was assisted over the crisis of the solstice by the help of sympathetic magic. The primeval instrument, the drum, was essential to this ceremony, and there could be none more fitting to announce the sun's renewed advance than the drum which also sounded the advance in human conflict and battle. In spring when men desire trees to bud and crops to grow, the most potent instrument would naturally be one made of bamboo, a plant of such vitality that it remains green even in winter. The various types of bamboo, then, through which men's *chhi* causes a similar *chhi* in Nature to respond, were the instruments of spring, and even in the orthodox eightfold classification the other vegetable substances, wood and gourd, were associated with this season. Finally, in summer when the silkworms are fattening on mulberry leaves, or spinning their cocoons, it was appropriate to play an instrument whose strings were of silk. Moreover, summer was the time when drought was to be feared, and the zithers which accompanied rain-making songs were believed to be excellent implements of magic. The association of the instruments with the points of the compass was no less straightforward. If autumn is the season of decline, the west is its direction, whereas spring and the east are contrary. Similarly, the north and winter must be associated with cold, and the south and summer with heat. (Needham and Robinson 1962, 155–56)

Another aspect of the speculative nature of the ancient Chinese schemes was their link to discussions about the total number of instruments in existence. In Emperor Shun's time, the total given was eight hundred, a figure arrived at on numerological grounds. The number eight had simply been multiplied by a hundred and the result bore no relation to the number of existing instruments (Gimm 1966, 548). In the Warring States period (around the fourth century BCE) the total count of instruments diminished to five hundred, a figure calculated by multiplying the "five tones" (*wu yin*), by which was meant the relative pentatonic pitches do re mi sol la, by a hundred. Yet at most a hundred kinds of instruments are known to have existed before the Ch'in period (about 250 BCE) (Gimm 1966, 548). The total number of three hundred instruments given in the T'ang dynasty (from 618 CE), however, bore some relation to the number used in musical practice, for the sources show that about two hundred different kinds of instruments existed during the middle of the T'ang dynasty.

CLASSIFICATION OF ENSEMBLES PLAYING COURT RITUAL MUSIC

Throughout the middle ancient and late historical periods, the *pa yin* continued to be used to exemplify the dominant philosophy and cosmology of Confucian and pre-Confucian China. The scheme was applied instruments used in court ritual music, which "could educate people, regulate society, strengthen government, and exist above all in harmony with nature" (Yang Yin-Liu 1980, 260).

Court ritual music (*ya-yüeh*) lasted over two thousand years, from the first Ch'in dynasty (221 to 206 BCE) to the last Ch'ing dynasty (1644 to 1911). By the T'ang dynasty (618 to 907), not just instruments but also music itself was classified. Besides the court ritual music, which was divided into a simple taxonomy consisting of outdoor chime ensemble music and indoor chamber song, there were four other categories: popular, foreign, banquet, and theatrical and *ch'in* (zither) music. The classification of music was paralleled by the classification of ensembles, which were distinguished according to the main levels of power in the court. The court hierarchy was symbolized by the spatial arrangements of instruments in the ensembles (see Kishibe 1980, 251–52), which were related to the four directions and to the four divisions of social ranking, thus creating a paradigm. This paradigmatic classification actually served as a terse statement of social relationships.

Thus, the music chime ensembles were subdivided into (1) those reserved for emperors and arranged on all four sides of a square; (2) those reserved for lords and arranged on three sides (east, west, and north) of a square; (3) those intended for ministers and arranged on two sides (east and west); and (4) those used for lower officials and arranged on one side (north). Indoor chamber song ensembles were distinguished from outdoor music chime ensembles by the fact that the former included two-stringed and wind instruments and the latter all the court instruments except the strings. A very complex arrangement of an ensemble that was claimed to have played the music of the emperor and was arranged around the sides of and inside a square is illustrated in the early Yüan dynasty encyclopedia *Wen-hsien t'ung-k'ao* (A comprehensive investigation of documents and traditions) by Ma Tuan-Lin (c. 1245– c. 1325).[7]

The individual instruments were classified according to the traditional eightfold scheme. The categories were listed as follows: metal instruments, such as bells and bell-chimes; stones and stone chimes; wooden instruments, such as the struck woodbox and the tiger-shaped, notch-backed wood-block scraped with a bamboo whisk; earthen instruments, such as the struck clay bowl and the ocarina; leather instruments, such as the various barrel drums; bamboo instruments, such as the end-blown and transverse flutes as well as the panpipe; instruments made of gourd, such as the large and small mouth organs; and instruments with silk strings, such as the long seven-stringed zither (Yang Yin-Liu 1980, 251). This ordering of the *pa yin* differed from all those previously mentioned but it still kept the traditionally important metal and stone instruments used for rituals in first and second place.

MUSICAL PRACTICE CONFRONTS THE PA YIN

Distinctions made in the T'ang dynasty between court, popular, foreign and other music remained current in the Sung dynasty (960–1279). However, scholars were finding it difficult to fit previously unclassified instruments such as bone flutes, leaf-reed oboes, and conch-shell trumpets into the rigid *pa yin* scheme, which by now had lost much of its cosmological meaning and was conceived of as a taxonomy rather than a paradigm. Beginning in the sixth century many foreign musical instruments were adopted by the Chinese, and the expanded instrumentarium posed new classificatory problems. Ma Tuan-Lin, for instance, who grouped a large inventory of instruments into the *pa yin* categories in his above-mentioned encyclopedia, found that some instruments could not logically fit into the eight categories and was therefore forced to create a ninth category, which he termed *pa yin chih wai,* meaning "not falling under categories one to eight." Remarkably, each of his nine categories was then subdivided into three according to whether the instruments were played in ceremonial, foreign, or popular music contexts (Pian 1967, 17–18). This classification, which moved downward and then upward, had a structure resembling a classification by the Sung dynasty scholar Wang Ying Lin. Three centuries later, two schemes by the famous Ming dynasty musicologist Chu Tsai-Yü took a similar form (fig. 4.3).

The fact that Ma Tuan-Lin tried to match the ancient theoretical scheme to modern practice and found it inadequate for his purpose was a

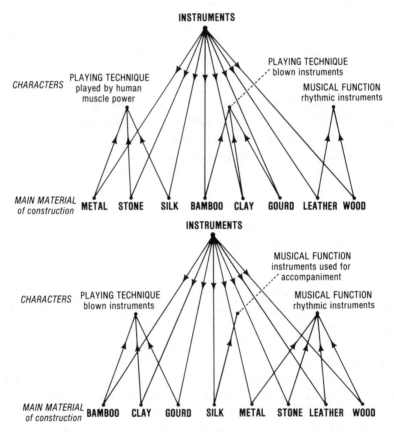

FIGURE 4.3 Two classifications of instruments by Chu Tsai-Yü: *top,* from his treatise on the essential meaning of the standard pitch pipes; *bottom,* from his collected works on music and the pitch pipes

sign of the times. Interest in performance practice was growing, as was reflected in the production of performing manuals for the *ch'in* (Liang 1972: 311). Moreover, instruments were actually beginning to be classified, though not rigorously, according to mode of sound production. Thus the chapter headings in the Sung dynasty encyclopedia *Yü-Hai* (Jade Sea) compiled by Wang Ying Lin suggested a threefold categorization of instruments into wind, percussion, and strings.[8] Wang Ying Lin also classified instruments according to the *pa yin* and then subsumed its eight categories by upward classification into three, thus adopting a downward-then-upward classificatory structure.

In his scheme, instruments given the highest status—those made of metal or stone—were said to "lead" a middle group of instruments made of silk, bamboo, gourd, and clay; the lowest status was given to instruments made of leather and wood. Bamboo instruments were rated higher than in previous classifications mentioned. Wooden instruments received a low rating because of their nonmelodic function; they could not produce the "five tones" (degrees of the pentatonic scale system) or the "twelve fundamental pitches" but served merely to mark musical rhythm.

Several centuries later, a quite different hierarchy was presented in a subgrouping of the *pa yin*. In this, bamboo instruments rose further in status. No longer were they listed last as they had been in the *Chou-li* and the *Yo chi* but were now in second place. However, metal instruments were still given the highest rating in the *T'ung-ya* (Comprehensive refinement) by Fang I-chih. In view of the prestige afforded to metal instruments, it is telling that the word *chin* means "gold" as well as "metal" in Chinese.

In one famous Ming period source, bamboo pitch pipes were given first place in a presentation of a *pa yin* grouping (see the second scheme in fig. 4.3b). The author—Chu Tsai-Yü (1536 to 1611)—saw great significance in the bamboo pitch pipes, giving a precise account of their measurements and acoustic qualities. "In your humble servant's respectful opinion, of the sounds (from musical instruments made) of the eight (kinds of material) those (made by instruments) of bamboo must be taken as the chief."[9] Furthermore, "of the sounds of bamboo, those of the standard pitch-pipe flutes (*lü-kuan*) must be taken as the chief" (Robinson 1980, 78).

During the third century before our era, the old bamboo humming tubes became known in China as pitch pipes and were used as the standard for the tuning of instruments. Though bamboo pipes can produce sounds of only approximate or inconstant pitch due to the variability of the blowing force of the player and the quantity of moisture in the tubes, they were used as pitch standards over the millennia mainly because of the magical significance of the numbers used to determine the lengths of the pipes (Robinson 1980, 78–79). For instance, a set of twelve pipes was traditionally seen as symbolizing the dualistic nature of existence, with the six longer pipes being influenced by the "warm, active, male emanation" and the six shorter ones being affected by the "cold, passive, female emanation" (Robinson, 80). As Chu Tsai-Yü mentioned, in ancient times bamboo pipes were also related to certain propitious times of the year or day, to ethos theory, and to the harmony of the state.

Chu Tsai-Yü had an exceptional understanding of early Chinese thought about instruments and music, but he classified instruments in a way that combined characteristics of contemporary musical practice with the orthodox eightfold scheme. He was interested in the way a player produces sound as well as the musical function of instruments, and he used these two factors as characters of division at the second step of two classifications that he presented (see fig. 4.3). Like his predecessors Ma Tuan Lin and Wang Ying Lin, he first classified the instruments in downward fashion into the eight sources of sound. Then he proceeded to move upward, grouping the eight classes into three higher categories. In his treatise entitled *Lü-lü ching I* (The essential meaning of the standard pitch pipes), instruments made of metal, stone, and silk (i.e., beaten and plucked instruments) were grouped together because they all use human muscle power to produce tones, while instruments made of bamboo, clay, and gourd (i.e., wind instruments) were subsumed into one category because they all use human breath to produce tones, and instruments made of leather and wood (i.e., beaten instruments) were grouped together because they are used by players to produce rhythmic accents of the music (Gimm 1966, 547). Thus two characters—mode of sound production and musical function—were used at the second step.

A different threefold classification of the eight *pa yin* categories was presented by Chu Tsai-Yü in his *Yo-lü ch'üan-shu* (Collected works on music and the pitch pipes, vol. 12, pp. 5–66). Here he used a similar downward-then-upward classification, grouping wind instruments made of bamboo, clay, or gourd into one class, silk-stringed instruments "used for the accompaniment of singing" in another, and rhythmic, or beaten, instruments made of metal, stone, leather, or wood in the other (Gimm 1966, 547), thus using playing technique and musical function as characters at the second step. Again, simple logical division was eschewed because it could not represent his theory or concept of instruments in practical music making. Chu Tsai-Yü's classifications are remarkable for their successful combination of tradition and contemporary musical needs as well as their use of downward-then-upward structure.

Thus the *pa yin* is marked by its persistence over the millennia. Its eight parts were faithfully preserved, but not their order of presentation. The French Jesuit missionary Father Amiot (1718 to 1793), who lived in China, mentioned the *pa yin* in his *Mémoire sur la musique des chinois tant anciens que modernes,* written in 1777. He presented it in yet another order: leather, stone, metal, clay, silk, wood, bamboo, and gourd. This, he wrote, was the accepted order of the time, which differed from the most ancient order. By then, metal had lost its first place in the scheme.

We can only guess the reasons for the varied order of the presentation of the *pa yin* categories. The differences were probably due to changes in the hierarchy of preferred materials or instruments for various numerological, religious, or theoretical reasons. In Chu Tsai-Yü's case, the chosen order was apparently due to his theoretical concerns of the moment, including his interest in the ancient religious associations of the pitch pipes and his focus on the acoustics and playing action and musical function of these instruments.

CLASSIFICATIONS IN CONTEMPORARY CHINA

Recent writings by Chinese theorists and encyclopedists also mention the *ba yin* (Pinyin spelling) as a matter of course. For example, two recent sources introduce the eightfold scheme as being the orthodox grouping used in ancient China: they are the *Cí hài* (Dictionary), which was published in Beijing in 1980, and the *Zhongguo yinyue shiliao* (Historical sources on Chinese music), which was published in Taiwan in 1975. Both publications present the eightfold scheme in what is believed to be the most ancient order, namely, metal, stone, earth, leather, silk, wood, gourd, and bamboo, where bells (*zhong, ling*) are allocated to the metal category, stone chimes (*qing*) to the stone category, ocarinas (*xün*) to the earthen category, drums (*gu*) to the leather category, zithers (*qin se*) to the silken category, wooden bowls (*zhu, wu*) to the wooden category, mouth organs (*sheng, yu*) to the gourd category, and pitch pipes (*guan*) to the bamboo category.

Some modern Chinese music historians have begun to criticize the traditionally accepted interpretation of the ancient literature concerning the eight sources of sound, emphasizing that it is not a clearly stated theory but that it occurs in a variety of somewhat contradictory sources that have a legendary quality about them. In the view of the music historian Yang Yin-Liu, references to the *ba yin* in the ancient sources are too obtuse for later readers to be certain even of the exact meaning of the term and associated sphere of thought in ancient times. "We must reserve judgment," he wrote, "about the legendary sources, which present the *ba yin* as a system of classifying instruments according to the eight different materials of which they are made" (1980, 13). He quotes two conflicting sources to prove his point. In the *Shang shu,* which is one of four ancient sources edited by Confucius (551 to 429 BCE), Yi Su wrote, "I would like to hear six temperaments, five tones, eight sounds," a statement that does not really tally with one by Emperor Shun, who is reported to have referred to the "three years, four seas, and eight sounds, where the eight sounds reach harmony."

Yang Yin-Liu's understandable doubts may be one reason why a number of contemporary Chinese organologists have replaced the *ba yin* in their publications with new classifications derived from aspects of practical music making. This questioning of the *ba yin* accompanied the acceptance of influences from Western organology. Because Western instruments are in widespread use in modern China, the new schemes include both Western and Chinese instruments, including keyboards.

An example of a new scheme can be found in the *Cí-hài* (Committee of Editors 1980b), which divides instruments at the first step into four categories by means of two characters, one being mode of sound excitation and the other morphological. The first category is headed "percussion," where the sounds are said to originate from the beating action of the player; fifty-six kinds of instruments are included here. The second category is headed "wind instruments," where the sounds are said to "originate from the vibrating air inside its body"; forty-two kinds of instruments are included. In the third category, "stringed instruments," the sounds are said to be "produced by friction on the strings"; fifty-six kinds of instruments are included. In the fourth category, "instruments possessing keyboards," the specimens are distinguished solely by their possession of keyboards; there are nine entries.

At the second step, the percussion instruments are subdivided into two categories distinguished according to the mode of sound excitation. The categories are (1) idiophones, such as cymbals, gongs, wood-blocks, and triangles; and (2) membranophones, such as the Chinese drums *tang-gu, ban-gu,* and *yü-gu* and the Western timpani. Chinese wind instruments are subdivided into two categories: (1) those with reeds, such as the common shawm (*sona*), mouth organ (*sheng*), and small shawm (*guanzi*); and (2) those without reeds, such as the vertical flutes (*dong xiao*) and the transverse flutes (*dizi*). Western wind instruments are also subdivided at this step into two categories according to the main materials of which they are (or once were) made. These are (1) the woodwinds, including oboes, bassoons, and flutes (which formerly, it is explained, were made of wood and now usually of metal); and (2) brass instruments, including trumpets and trombones. Stringed instruments are subdivided into three categories: (1) those plucked by the fingers or by plectra, such as the lute (*pi'pa*) and the Western harp; (2) bowed instruments, such as the two-stringed fiddle (*er hu*) and the violin; and (3) struck instruments, such as the dulcimer (*yan-qin*). Finally, instruments with keyboards are exemplified by such instruments as the piano, pipe organ, accordion, celesta, and keyboard mouth organ.

This close, two-step classification of Chinese and Western instruments in tree diagram form has echoes of several European schemes. It resembles Galpin's classifications in its emphasis on keyboards at the first step, and it is like Mahillon's and Hornbostel and Sachs's schemes in its division of percussion instruments into idiophones and membranophones at the second. It is remarkable in that it divides stringed instruments into the plucked, bowed, and struck varieties, and is even more remarkable in that it uses a different character of division for Chinese, as opposed to Western, instruments. It contains a rare example of the use of a character which distinguishes by cultural group or nationality.

Also in tree diagram form is a four-category scheme presented in a chapter on instrumental music in the *Minzu yin-yue gailun* (Survey of national music) (Committee of Editors 1980a, 249ff.). According to this source, at least two hundred instruments are used in China today; but the statistics are incomplete. The instrumentarium is divided according to the principle of performing technique into the "pulled" (*la*), "played" (*tan*), "blown" (*chui*), and "struck" (*da*). Pulled instruments, which include bowed and plucked strings, are presumably so called because their performing technique resembles the action of pulling. In this case, the term *pulling* is ascribed to the action of bowing across strings as well as the action of plucking strings. Played instruments, on the other hand, simply signify "fingered" keyboards such as pianos. Blown instruments (mostly exemplified by woodwinds) are subdivided according to morphology into those without reeds, such as the transverse and vertical flutes (*dong xiao*), those with reeds, such as the small shawm (*guanzi*) and the common shawm (*sona*), and those with free reeds, including the various kinds of mouth organ (*sheng*). The pulled instruments are subdivided into plucked and bowed strings according to the mode of exciting sound. At another step they are subdivided according to playing position, including those held vertically like the *pi'pa*, those that lie flat such as the zithers without bridges (*qin*) and the zithers with bridges (*zheng*). The 'struck' instruments (i.e., those that "play the rhythm") are exemplified by the drum, gong, cymbal, and wood-block.

Like the other modern tree diagram scheme, this three-step scheme cannot, of course, claim to be perfectly logical, because it applies two characters (morphology and mode of sound excitation) at the second step. However, its characters of division—mode of sound excitation, morphology and playing position of the instruments—would seem to be eminently suited to the prevailing performance-centered concept of instrument prevailing in contemporary China.

CONCLUSION

This outline of some of the main movements in China's history of instrument taxonomy shows above all the remarkable tenacity of the eightfold *pa yin* scheme, which classifies on the basis of the material from which an instrument is made. It appears to have developed gradually from various fourfold schemes during the ancient period. Both the eightfold and the fourfold classifications began as paradigmatic constructs: they were cosmological statements about the "sources of sound," which were seen as being indirectly related to the seasons, the directions of the winds, and political power and human welfare.

The early ideas about instruments were based on the elemental belief in the "breath" or "spirit" that enabled sounds and instruments to serve as manifestations of nature as well as prognostic aids, performing magical services that could benefit the harvest, divine the enemy's morale, and so on. Instruments made from the eight materials each controlled one of the dances performed at ritual mimes that in turn could summon one of the eight winds.

In the middle ancient and late historical periods, the *pa yin* continued to be used to class individual instruments. In addition, court ritual ensembles were classified paradigmatically according to social class and the directions. Spatial arrangements of instruments in four main ensembles symbolized the court hierarchy. As in Java, ensembles were also divided by simple taxonomy into those played outdoors and those performed indoors.

Throughout the centuries, theorists faithfully preserved the eight categories of the *pa yin* but not their order of presentation; reasons for the varied order of presentation have mostly been lost in the mists of time. Occasionally a clue appears in the literature, however, and sometimes we can piece a hypothesis together from various sources to explain a particular order. It is the prestigious metal and stone instruments that usually appear in first and second place in presentations of the *pa yin*. Instruments in the metal category are important not only because of their implied material value and magic craftsmanship but also because of their great importance from ancient times in religious and military ceremony. Stone instruments also have superior ritual status. Leather and wooden instruments, on the other hand, have mostly been listed last or nearly last in the literature on the *pa yin*. One Ming dynasty source mentioned that wooden instruments were rated low because of their rhythmic, rather than melodic, function, in that they were not linked to the "five tones" and the "twelve pitches." Bamboo instruments have mostly been listed last; but the magic significance of the numbers used to determine the length of pitch pipes eventually gave them great importance, as correct pitch standards were considered crucial to the welfare of the state. Moreover, as theorists became more interested in acoustics and precise measurements of pitch, the bamboo pitch pipes rose further in status. Such was the theoretical importance of the pitch pipes that in one Ming dynasty source the bamboo category actually headed the *pa yin*.

In some sources, however, the order of the categories does not seem to imply a hierarchy at all. For example in the ancient scheme of thought that related each instrumental category or source of sound to a specific compass direction and season, each class was assigned a highly respected ritual use. In any case, where the hierarchies exist they are mostly related to cosmology or music theory, not to musical practice. Indeed, the sum of the evidence suggests that the order of categories of the eightfold scheme *pa yin* bears little relation at all to practical music making.

The age and prestige of the *pa yin* have ensured that virtually every Chinese instrument taxonomist has referred to it or used it as the basis for classification. By the time of the T'ang dynasty, however, it had lost many of its cosmological connotations and had become a taxonomy of single-step, downward division. Governed by an interest in performance practice,

T'ang, Sung, and Ming scholars grouped the *pa yin* taxonomy upward into three more general categories governed by mode of sound production and performance technique. In the Sung dynasty, some scholars found difficulty in trying to fit new foreign instruments made of bone, leaf, or shell into the eightfold scheme, and one scholar at least created a ninth category for miscellaneous instruments.

In contemporary China, cognizance is still taken of the *pa yin,* but mostly either to note its past usage or to question its past interpretation. Some current classifications exclude such obsolete instruments as stone chimes. Most schemes take tree form. Common characters of division are mode of sound production, and morphological attributes such as the possession of keyboards. Western instruments are sometimes classified in the same scheme with Chinese instruments. In this case different characters of division are applied to European and Chinese instruments at the same step. These modern schemes represent part of the centuries-old shift from a theoretical to a performance-centered concept and classification of musical instruments in China.

LIST OF CHINESE TERMS (CHINESE CHARACTERS PREPARED BY ZHANG WEI HUA)

ban-gu	板鼓
chin	金
ch'in	琴
Cheng Ti (emperor)	成帝
chi	气
Ch'ien han-shu	前汉书
Cí-hài	辞海
Chou	周
Chou-li	周礼
chu	竹
Chu Tsai-Yü	朱载堉
Chung-kuo Yin-yueh Shi-kang	中国音乐史纲
chui	吹
Confucius	孔子
da	打
dizi	笛子
dong xiao	洞箫
er hu	二胡
Fang I-Chih	方以智
gu	鼓
guan	管

guanzi	管子
ko	革
la	拉
Lao Tzu	老子
Líng	铃
lü-kuan	律管
Lü-hsüeh hsin-shuo	律学新说
Lü-lü ching I	律吕精义
Ma Tuan-Lin	马端临
Ming	明
Minzu yin-yue gailun	民族音乐概论
mu	木
pa'o	匏
pa yin, ba yin	八音
pa yin chih wai	八音之外
pi'pa	琵琶
qin	琴
qing	磬
San xian	三弦
Shang shu	尚书
sheng	笙
shih	石
Shih ching	诗经
Shun (Emperor)	舜
sona	唢呐
ssu	丝
Song, Sonq	宋
tan	弹
T'ang	唐
tang-gu (t'ang-ko)	唐鼓
t'u	土
Tso Chiu-Ming	左丘明
Tso chuan	左传
Tuan An-Chieh	段安节
T'ung ya	通雅
Wang Ying Lin	王应麟
Wen-hsien t'ung-k'ao	文献通考
wu	梧
wu yin	五音
xün	埙

ya-yüeh 雅乐

yang 阳

Yang Yin-Liu 杨荫浏

yin 阴

Yo-fu tsa-lu 乐府杂录

Yo-lü ch'üan-shu 乐律全书

Yü-Hai 玉海

yü-gu 渔鼓

yu 竽

zheng 筝

zhong 钟

Zhongguo yinyue shiliao 中国音乐史料

zhu 筑

Indian and Sri Lankan Classifications from Ancient to Modern Times

By seeing or touching the *veena* one attains *Svarga* and *Moksha;* it purifies a fallen man from sins such as that of killing a Brahmān. The *daṇḍa*[1] is God Siva, the string is Goddess Uma, the shoulder is Vishnu, the bridge is Lakshmi, the gourd is Brahmā, the navel is Saraswathi; the connecting wires are Vasuki, the Jiva is Moon, the pegs are Sun; the *veena* thus represents all Gods and is therefore capable of giving all auspiciousness.

> Sangītaratnākara, 1210–1247 CE, on
> the Hindu-Indian symbolism of the
> *vīṇā*[2]

. . . the drum had its birth from the mouth of Brahmā, timing from his teeth, and song from his tongue.

> J. E. Sedaraman, *Nrtyaratnakaraya,* on
> the Srilankan belief in the divine origin
> of the drum, rhythm, and vocal music

The two main rival ideologies in ancient India—Hinduism and Buddhism—each produced a major classification of instruments. Each lives on to the present day as the dominant instrument classification in India and Sri Lanka, respectively. A third religious ideology—Jainism—also produced its own classifications of instruments, which survive in Jain India to this day.

According to some scholars, India's dominant religion, Hinduism, dates back to the *Véda*s (early Hindu sacred writings) of the Aryans, between 2000 and 1500 BCE (Singh 1979, 19–25); others believe it arose in the pre-Aryan age. Buddhism originated about the sixth century BCE. Jainism, which is "one of India's most ancient *śramaṇa* or non-Vedic religious traditions" (Jaini 1979, 1), adopted regular monastic communal structures from about the fifth century BCE. From ancient times the literature of all three religions has referred extensively to musical instruments. The distinction between each of the religions in India and Sri Lanka today is manifested partly in their traditional classifications of instruments.

A full realization of the diversity of the concepts and classifications of instruments in India and Sri Lanka, however, awaits further research into the indigenous classifications that we can assume exist among minority religious groups, including the various ancestor- and nature-worshiping peoples living in remote areas. This chapter will deal with the classifications of instruments promulgated by some key Hindu, Buddhist, and Jain treatise writers,[3] beginning from the early part of the common era; it will discuss some schemes presented in treatises by Tamil Hindus as well as a few classifications developed by Indian writers in recent decades.[4] Unfortunately, research into treatises on Indian Muslim music has not yet (to my knowledge) made available any data on the formal classification of instruments used in Indian Muslim culture. However, data about the changing taxonomies and status-determined hierarchies of instruments during the Mogul court and the British colonial periods are beginning to be gathered together. Not only did the classical Hindu instrument *vīṇā* become prominent in Mogul court culture beginning in the sixteenth century, but various other instruments rose and fell in status according to the patterns of patronage (verbal communication from Adrian McNeil).

From ancient times the Hindu concept of music and instruments was integrated into the concept of the performing arts as a whole. The arts had their origin in the *Vēdas*, as "is expressly stated in Bharata's *Nāṭyaśāstra*" and other ancient sources (Sastri 1966, 24). Vocal music (*gīta*), instrumental music (*vādya*), and dance (*nṛtya*), the unity of which was demonstrated by their inclusion under the umbrella term *saṅgīta*, were of divine origin and a means of liberation and union with God (*yoga*). Yājnāvalkya wrote (Smriti III.4.115) that "he who knows the truth about *vīṇā* [lute]-play and the science of *śrutis* [micro-intervals], *jāti* (scale patterns) and *tāla* (rhythm) treads an easy path of salvation" (Sastri 1966, 14). As the quotation at the head of this chapter indicates, merely by seeing or touching a *vīṇā* one can attain *svarga* and *moksha* (salvation from the bondage of finite existence). The *vīṇā*'s parts are analogous to the various gods. The instrument symbolizes the divinity of human beings. It has numerological significance[5] and is considered to be the most complete of instruments because it has the fundamental drone within itself (Subramanian 1985, 15).

Certain other instruments have also traditionally been associated with celestial beings (see Sastri 1966, 14, 25), including the strings, drums, and flutes. Similar associations have also been made with the closely related art of dance. The goddess Sarasvati was depicted as playing on the *vīṇā* with two hands and having a book and a rosary in the other two hands, thus symbolising the unity of knowledge, art and devotion.[6] Siva was linked to the drum (*ḍamaru*); and Naṭarāja (an aspect of God Siva) and the Goddess Uma are the deities of dance. Śri Kṛṣṇa was the supreme, divine flute-player and god of congregational dance. He not only performed the *rāsa* dance [dance of the six sentiments] but he also danced on the head of the serpent Kāliya. (Sastri 1966, 14)

In Sri Lanka, the drum was traditionally associated with Brahmā, from whose mouth it is said to have been born.

Legend has it that human beings made certain instruments that imitated those created and played by celestial beings. For example, drums were first created by the sage Svati after having heard the wondrously beautiful sounds caused by torrential rains beating on lotus leaves in a lake at a time when the god Indra wanted to make an ocean out of the earth. Returning to his hermitage he created drums such as the *mṛdaṅga, pushkara, paṇava, dardura,* and *muraja* (a counterpart of the *dunduvi,* or *dundubhi,* played by the celestial beings), assisted by Visvakarna. He then covered the instruments and bound them with cords.[7]

Associations made between instruments, celestial musicians, and their human imitators suggest the existence in the culture of a classification of instruments based on these links. Such a classification initially seems comparable to that of the Dan culture of West Africa (see chap. 16). Extant traces of this ancient taxonomy, however, suggest that it was much more general than the origin myth classification detected by Zemp among the Dan. Not just one but a number of celestial beings are associated with each of the main instruments in India; in some cases the gods are simply described as being excellent musicians and are not linked to specific instruments. For example, not only the goddess Sarasvati but also Dakṣiṇāmūrti (an aspect of the god Síva) and Syamala (an aspect of the goddess Uma) play the *vīṇā.* And Valmiki, author of the epic *Rāmāyaṇa,* described Prince Rama and the monkey general, Hanuman, as being supreme musicians, without specifying a particular instrument.

The link between origins or parts of instruments and the body, especially the dancing body (whether human or celestial), is part of the concept and classification of instruments in both India and Sri Lanka. This anthropomorphic link is reflected in the idea that the *vīṇā* parallels parts of the human body. For example, frets parallel the human vertebrae, a link that is significant in yogic philosophy (Subramanian 1985, 14).[8] It is also reflected in the Sanskrit lexeme *aṅga*, which literally means "limb of the body" but has also been widely used taxonomically in the sense of "category." This term has been used over the ages in the classification not only of instruments but also of the sciences and other schemes of knowledge, parts of Mahayana Buddhist chant melody, sequential subsections of musical form or durational units, *rāsas* (emotions), dance movements, and so on.[9] While some other cultures classify by analogies such as families or trees, ancient Indians tended to classify by analogy with the parts of the body.[10] They then grouped subordinate levels into categories called "major" limbs and "minor" limbs or, alternatively, "chief," "intermediate," and "lesser" limbs.

THE HINDU CLASSIFICATIONS

The oldest extant classification of instruments in India is one presented in chapter 28 of the famous Sanskrit treatise *Nāṭyaśāstra*, which was attributed to Bharata, or Bharata Muni, but was possibly coauthored by a number of writers sometime between the second century BCE and the sixth century CE (fig. 5.1). Instruments were assigned to the categories of
1. "stretched" (*tata vādya*) instruments, such as the various kinds of *vīṇā*
2. "covered" instruments (*anaddha* or *avanaddha vādya*), such as the various drums
3. "hollow" instruments (*śuṣira vādya*), such as flutes and trumpets
4. "solid" instruments (*ghana vādya*), such as bells and cymbals.[11]
The many varieties and high status of strings and drums in early India were reflected in the fact that they were given first and second place in the scheme. Indeed the treatise gave much more attention to the "stretched" strings and "covered" drums than to the "hollow" and "solid" instruments; the section on flutes, for example, was very brief. The iconographic sources also display a great variety of strings and drums in ancient India (see illustrations in Marcel-Dubois 1941).

All four categories of this scheme were distinguished by the physical (sound-producing) characteristics of the sounding body—either its solidity, its being covered, its hollowness, or its being tense. At the second step of division, each of the four categories was subdivided into a "major limb," or instruments that play the most prominent musical role, and a "minor limb," or accompanying instruments, which were relegated to second place. At the next step, to take an example from among the "major limb" instruments, the *vīṇā* category was subdivided into the bow-harp type

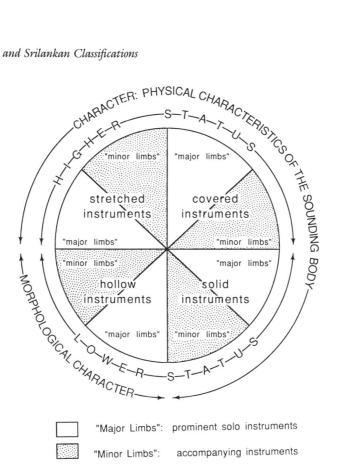

FIGURE 5.1 The four-category Hindu-Indian classification of instruments according to characters of division and status of instruments (based on Nāṭyaśāstra
[Ghosh 1961])

(*vipañcī-vīṇā*) and the short-necked ovoid lute type (*citra-vīṇā*). These
major limb instruments, which played melodic solo parts, were distinguished from the minor limb instruments, including the stringed *ghoṣaka*,
which played a drone. The divisions into major and minor limb instruments in the *Nāṭyaśāstra* read as follows (Ghosh 1961, 161–63):

> 15. Among the wooden (stringed instruments) *Vipañcī* [a *vīṇā* with seven
> strings] and *Citra* [a *vīṇā* with nine strings] are major limbs and *Kacchapī*
> [a one-stringed instrument] and *Ghoṣaka* [a kind of *tānpurā* used as a
> drone] etc., are minor limbs.
> 16. Among the drums, *Mṛdaṅga* [an earthen drum still used in Bengal]
> *Dardura* and *Paṇava* (a drum which was probably made of wood) are
> major limbs, while *Jallarī* and *Paṭaha* (deep-sounding drums) etc., are the
> minor limbs.

ꝰꞮꞐꙀ

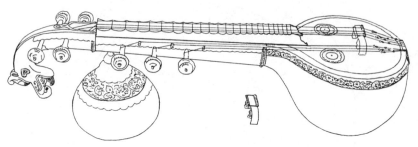

FIGURE 5.2 A Vīṇā

17. [Among the hollow instruments] the flute (*vaṃśa*) has the characteristics of the major limbs [of a performer] and conch-shell and *Dakkinī* [that of] the minor limbs.[12]

Other lower-step characters applied in the scheme included the quality of sounds produced by the instruments, for example, whether drums produce "regular" sounds or "deep and loud" sounds. This distinction possibly refers to a relatively uncontrolled drum sound as opposed to a controlled sound such as is produced on the *mṛdaṅga* and other drums with composite or multiple-layer heads.[13]

The strings and winds were discussed (but not classified) in the treatise in connection with their playing techniques, their accompaniment to vocal music, and their function in the drama. The main musical function of the "solid" instruments was said to be to mark off the time cycle.

This antique Hindu scheme seems remarkably modern, practice-oriented, and far-removed from the religious aura surrounding Indian instruments. The reason for this is presumably that it appeared in the context of a practice-oriented discussion of musical instruments used in the theater. For the *Nāṭyaśāstra* was in fact a practical manual on dramaturgy in which not only instrumental music but also dance, vocal music, the practical layout of the theater and stage, stagecraft, costuming, decoration, ritual for founding a theater, poetics, and the varieties of dramatic characters were discussed. Yet the fact that the scheme gave priority to the *vīṇā* and drums, which were highly valued religiously, means that it was not entirely divorced from the religious sphere.

It is instructive to compare the classification of instruments with the classification of dance. The most detailed classification in the treatise was of the dance movements; it is said to remain the best classification for its purpose to this day (Shastri 1973, 34). Indeed, the Indian propensity to classify by analogy with limbs in general may initially have derived from the traditional classification of dance. The dance classification that appears in the *Nātyaśāstra* is probably among the most complex of antique Indian taxonomies in any field. It begins by distinguishing the chief *aṅga*, or main movements, and then the *upāṅga* ("minor limbs"), or secondary movements, including those of all parts of the face, from the eyebrow to the chin. These minor movements include thirteen movements of the head, thirty-six of the eye as a whole, nine of the eyeballs, nine of the eyelids, seven of the eyebrow, the eight gazes, six movements of the nose, six of the cheeks, six of the lips, seven of the chin and teeth, six of the mouth, four hues of the complexion, and nine movements of the neck. Then there are sixty-four movements of the hand (*hasta*), including five free movements, four winding movements, and a number of wavings and interlockings of the hands all accompanied by the required facial expressions and movements of the eye and eyebrow. This is followed by ten arm movements, five chest movements, two movements of the sides of the body, three belly formations, five movements of the hips, and five movements of the feet. The feet movements include sixteen steps on the ground, sixteen steps leaving the ground, ten combinations of movements below the hips, the standing poses that begin and end all units, and four styles of fighting movements. There are the hundred and eight *karana*s (movements of the hands and feet with corresponding body movements) and their combinations—the thirty-two *angaharas,* each of which is divided into sixteen combination movements.[14] In summary, movements are morphologically divided into those of the head, hands, arms, chest, sides, belly, hips, and feet, plus many combination movements.

The structure of classification of the dance movements in the *Nātyaśāstra* is somewhat similar to the structure of its classification of musical instruments though the latter is much less complex and its steps occur in reverse order. At the first step the dance movements are classified into main and secondary movements (major and minor limbs), and at the second they are divided according to part of the body involved. The instruments, on the other hand, are divided at the first step into their specific classes (i.e., according to whether they are solid, covered, hollow, or stretched) and at the second step into the "major limb" and "minor limb" instruments.

Despite their different characters of division and the much greater complexity of the classification of dance movements than of instruments, both schemes were highly practical and systematic in their orientation and both were largely divorced from the religious speculation engaged in by other thinkers about the arts. In this respect the antique Indian classification of instruments differs from the mainstream Chinese and medieval European classifications of instruments and music, into which were integrated cosmological thought. Sections on dance and instrument classifications in the *Nātyaśāstra* are kept separate from discussions concerning ethical and philosophical issues related to the arts. The latter are introduced by accounts of the cosmic origins of the arts, as in the following (Sastri 1966, 27, translated by Ghosh):

> God Indra and other gods, who had been entrusted by the creator with various cosmic functions, told him that they desired the joys of the much needed spirit of creative play in the realms of vision and audition. Thereupon the creator created the art of dance as comprising the essence of all the scriptures and as embodying all the fine arts. Bharata says that Brahmā taught him *nātya* with the following objectives in view.
>
> Art is not merely a pastime (*vinoda*), but should illuminate the aims of life, should be a source of instruction and illumination, should soften the ills and griefs of life, should intensify the pleasures and joys of life, should exhibit the panorama of life, should teach what is auspicious for human life, should be a refuge from the storms and miseries of life existence, and should point the way to the highest life. (*Nātyaśāstra* I.75–86)

Such was the view of the unity of the arts, ethics, cosmic functions, and the scriptures in the *Nātyaśāstra*.

Let us digress for a moment to consider the comments by musicologists (including Galpin [1910] 1965, 27; Kunst 1969, 56; and Deva 1980, 128) on the similarity between the classification of instruments in the *Nātyaśāstra* and the classification developed by Hornbostel and Sachs in 1914, both of which comprise four categories. The similarities are actually rather remarkable, given the fact that the two schemes are separated from each other in time by two and a half millennia. Some musicologists, however, have mistakenly considered the two schemes to be identical. The main resemblance lies in the Hindu-Indian category of "solid" (*ghana*) instruments on the one hand and the Mahillon category of "autophones" on the other, which was borrowed and renamed "idiophones" by Hornbostel and Sachs. The opposition between solidity and elasticity that is used to distinguish the Hornbostel and Sachs idiophone category (1914, 14) also distinguishes the Hindu-Indian solid category. However, the Hindu-Indian "covered" category does not coincide in its meaning with the Hornbostel and Sachs "membranophone" category. The term *membranophone* clearly specifies the use of membranes while the covered category implies only that something covers an opening or hollow. Thus the Hindu-Indian category excludes the comb-and-paper, free kazoo type of membranophone included in the Hornbostel and Sachs category (Ellingson 1979, 547). Nor is the Hindu-Indian "stretched" category the same as the Hornbostel and Sachs "chordophone" category. The term *chordophone* designates instruments possessing strings, while the Hindu-Indian term *tata* (which derives from the word *tan,* meaning "to stretch" or "to tense"; see Deva 1980, 127) simply designates stretched parts. Although the stretched category does comprise stringed instruments, its literal meaning could also allow it to include stretched-skin instruments as in some versions of the Buddhist and Jain schemes discussed below. Like the Indian "hollow" category, Hornbostel and Sachs's fourth category, "aerophones," contains wind instruments. Their character of division in both cases is mode of sound activation.

Largely because of the great prestige of the *Nātyaśāstra,* the fourfold Hindu-Indian scheme has shown remarkable persistence, appearing in treatise after treatise until the present day. For example, the *Visnudharmottara-purāṇa* of the latter half of the first millennium CE made use of the scheme (Prajanananda 1979, 208). One of the best-known accounts of it appeared in the sixth chapter of the thirteenth-century work *Saṅgītaratnākara* by Saraṅga-deva. This and other treatises influenced so many authors, especially between the sixteenth and nineteenth centuries, that many twentieth-century writers have taken the scheme for granted as "India's classification scheme," mentioning or utilizing it without reference to any source. For example, Banerji (1976, 37) simply states that Indian instruments are divided into the four classes; and Kothari (1968) structures his discussion of "folk musical instruments" from various parts of India into the usual four categories.

An alternative classification in early India was the three-class scheme devised by Nārada in the first century CE. It divided instruments into *carma* (literally, "skin"), *tantrika* (literally, "one which has strings"), and *ghana* (solid) instruments. A four-class scheme by Kohala presented sometime before the sixth century CE divided instruments (as had the *Nātyaśāstra* scheme) into the *śuṣira, ghana, carma baddha* ("covered with a membrane"), and *tantri* ("string") categories (Deva 1980, 127).

A five-category Hindu scheme was developed by another writer called Nārada in his work *Saṅgītamakaranda* (*Sangitadhayaya,* section 1), written between the tenth and twelfth centuries CE (see Sambamoorthy 1967, 18).[15] Maintaining tradition, he accepted the *Nāṭyaśāstra*'s division of *saṅgīta* ("art") into vocal music (*gīta*), instrumental music (*vādita*), and dance (*nṛtya*). Distinguishing between spiritual and physical sound, he divided the latter into sounds produced on

1. instruments plucked with the fingernails (*nakha*, "fingernails"), such as the *vīṇā*[16]
2. wind instruments (*vayu*, "wind"), such as the reed flute (*vaṃśa*)
3. instruments with a (stretched) skin (*carma*), such as the drum *mṛdaṅga*
4. metal percussive instruments (*loha*), such as the *tāla*)
5. "human instruments" (*śarīra*), which included the voice and hand-clapping

This was the first Indian scheme to include a category of "human instruments." Its inclusion is somewhat surprising in view of the author's separate category of vocal music under *saṅgīta*, but that, of course, does not include the sound of hand-clapping, which is an extremely rare subcategory of instrument classifications.[17] Thus, *śarīra* is quite a different concept from *gīta*.

The first four categories of Nārada's scheme somewhat resemble the antique Hindu-Indian scheme, but the character of division differs. In Heyde's view, the parameters of the scheme lie outside the instrument conceived as a morphological object, which enabled Nārada to use a single character of division, that is, the place where the sound originates, including fingernails on skin, a wind column, a piece of stretched skin, a metal body, and the human throat or hands (Heyde 1977, 151). With ancient texts it is, of course, very difficult at times to know exactly which characters an author used; alternative analyses of these characters of division are therefore possible.

Another fairly widely accepted taxonomical principle of division is the musical function of instruments, which applies both to ensembles and to individual instruments. The distinction between solo and accompanimental instruments mentioned in the *Nāṭyaśāstra* has been alluded to. The treatise mentions three kinds of relationships between a solo vocalist and accompanying flute, string, and drum parts: (1) the accompanist doubling the vocalist's part, (2) the accompanist elaborating but essentially preserving the work's melodic or rhythmic aspects, with virtuoso playing on sustained vocal tones or pauses between sections, and (3) the accompanying string player alternating antiphonally with the voice while the drummer indulges in virtuoso playing (Ghosh 1961, 108–10, 118–20;

Powers 1980, 114). In another source, the thirteenth-century work *Saṅgītaratnākara* by Śaraṅga-deva, instruments were assigned to one of four categories according to their musical function: (1) *suṣkam* for instruments played solo, (2) *gītānugam* for instruments that accompany vocal music, (3) *nrittāngam* for instruments used to accompany dance, and (4) *dvayānugam* for instruments used to accompany both dance and vocal music (Sambamoorthy 1967, 17). This classification was also mentioned in Adiyārkkunallār's commentary (in the fifteenth century) on the *Śilappadikāram* (c. first or second century CE), which substituted *ubhayānugam* (literally, "one which has strings") for *dvayānugam*.

Subdivisions of an instrument type, such as the *vīṇā* genus, and descriptions and iconographic depictions of them serve to document organological changes as well as changes in the tone system over the centuries. The two main subcategories of *vīṇā* mentioned in the *Nātyaśāstra* (chap. 29) are the bow harp and ovoid lute, also found among the iconographical sources.[18] Some of the playing techniques described in the treatise refer to an open string instrument plucked with both hands. The early medieval treatise *Saṅgītaratnākara*

> "describes in some detail a very different playing technique for the one-string *eka-tantrī vīṇā*, a variety of stick zither" (vi: 65–87) . . . ; the technique is declared applicable to all instruments of the class. It is based on a separation of functions of the left and right hands of the player with special two-hand techniques as well. This early mediaeval shift represents not only an organological change but also a music-conceptual change toward the idea of a single system tonic. (Powers 1980, 78–79)

A stopped string instrument differs fundamentally from an open string instrument in that "the stopped pitches can easily be conceived as a function of the pitch of the open string, and ultimately as subordinate to it" (Powers 1980, 79). As in Leisiö's Finnish-Karelian classification, we have here a case of instrument classification schemes widely separated in time serving as clues for the reconstruction of the history of music and instruments in a culture.

Further research of the Muslim-Indian treatises is needed to establish whether or not the division of classical Indian music into the northern and southern styles influenced the classification of instruments. No distinction at all was made between styles in the two regions in the ancient period, which is considered to have drawn to a close by about the mid–thirteenth century. Hindustani and Carnatic divisions were mentioned in a treatise by Haripala entitled *Saṅgītasudhākara*, which was written between 1309 and 1313, but a clear distinction between the two style areas was made only from the beginning of the modern period (mid–sixteenth century), when the Moguls gained control in the north and new instruments such as the horns, trumpets, and drums of the royal Muslim *naubat* (wind and drum) ensembles were being introduced. The South Indian style began to be called Carnatic only after North Indian scholars came under the influence of Persian ideas and historical writing style (Powers, 1980, 77). Nevertheless, the many new treatises written during this period belonging either to the Hindustani or to the Carnatic traditions were still greatly influenced by the old Sanskrit doctrines. In fact, the earliest known Persian work on Indian music, the *Ghunyat-ul-Munya* (fourteenth century?), borrowed, though not blindly, from the *Saṅgītaratnākara* as well as from the Persian music treatise tradition (Sarmadee 1978, 1).

The old Hindu classification of instruments does not, however, appear to have been replaced in the treatises by any new formal scheme. The *vīṇā* (or *bīṇ*) remained the instrument of status and theoretical reference in Mogul court circles. Various instruments rose and fell in hierarchical status throughout the Mogul and the British colonial periods. In the sixteenth and seventeenth centuries certain instruments and associated musical styles of the Mogul courts achieved prominence and prestige throughout northern India because the Moguls were the dominant power and they were the chief patrons of the arts. As McNeil's researches indicate, the *bīṇ, seniya rabāb* (plucked stringed instruments which performed the genre *dhrupad*) were at the summit of the musical hierarchy when the Mogul court was at its political height in the seventeenth century. In the nineteenth century mobility within the hierarchy brought instruments such as the *sitar, tānpūrā* (lutes), and *tablā* into prominence, when the *khyāl* genre displaced *dhrupad* as the dominant musical genre. McNeil's proposal to group Hindustani instruments according to diachronic patterns of patronage during the Mogul court period and the colonial period represents a new and fruitful methodological departure in the classification of instruments (McNeil diss. in progress).

THE TAMIL CLASSIFICATIONS

The Tamil epic *Śilappadikāram* (written in the first or the second century CE) included mention of various kinds of flutes distinguished according to the materials of which they were made; for example, bamboo, sandalwood, bronze, and ebony. The oldest extant Tamil classification of instruments as a whole, however, is found in the literature of the Sangam and post-Sangam periods (c. second to sixth centuries CE). This scheme used the oldest Dravidian term for "instrument": *karuvi,* which also meant "tool." Five categories of instruments were recognized: (1) *torkaruvi* or *tolekaruvi* (*tole* means "leather," Deva 1977, 6), comprising drums; (2) *tulaikkaruvi* (*tulai* means "hole" or "hollow"), comprising hollow or wind instruments; (3) *narampukkaruvi* (*narampu* means "animal gut"), comprising gut-stringed instruments; (4) *mītattrukaruvi,* consisting of the human vocal instrument; and (5) *kancakkaruvi* (*kancam* means "metal"), consisting of metal instruments, such as cymbals (Krishna Murthy 1985, 6, 9). The first two categories resemble the antique Hindu scheme but the other three differ. The third and fifth categories are distinguished by the main sound-producing material of the instrument. Except for its order of categories, this scheme resembles Nārada's five-category classification of the tenth to twelfth centuries, which also includes a category for the human vocal instrument.

According to Raman (1979, 85), another Tamil scheme grouped instruments into the "stringed," "hollow," and "leather" categories, a classification based on an instrument's morphological and material attributes. Another divided instruments into the solo and accompanying varieties, a basic division that is customarily made, as we have noticed, not only in Tamil but in most other traditions of Indian classical music also. Most Tamil musical forms eventually merged into what came to be known as Carnatic music. According to present knowledge, no distinctive Tamil classification of instruments has appeared in recent centuries.

THE BUDDHIST CLASSIFICATIONS

Most of our knowledge of ancient Indian musical instruments derives from early Buddhist sculpture and painting (see illustrations in Marcel-Dubois 1941 and Krishna Murthy 1985). From the development of Buddhism in approximately the sixth century BCE, Indian Buddhist culture used musical instruments for three main purposes: religious devotions, palace entertainment, and marking military or royal occasions (e.g., sending troops off to battle, announcing victories, and making royal proclamations) (Shakuntala 1968). The dominant Buddhist classification of instruments was developed in the devotional context of the ancient temple ritual (Seneviratna 1979, 49).[19]

The ancient Buddhist classification of instruments is called *pañcatūryanāda*, "sounds of the five classes of instruments," or "fivefold musical sounds." The Buddhist scheme divided instruments into the *ātata, vitata, ātatavitata, ghana,* and *śuṣira* categories, which is the hierarchical order used in its presentation in the *Pāli Vaṃsatthappakasini* commentary on the chronicle *Mahāvaṃsa,* written in the sixth century BCE (Malalasekara 1935, 518). This classification was used in ancient India until the decline of Buddhism but remains the dominant classification of instruments in Srilanka today.[20]

Srilanka first adopted Buddhism in the third century BCE but its early adoption of Theravada doctrines curtailed the performance of devotional music because of the belief that the sensual pleasure of music led the common people to evil. Sinhalese treatises, however, refer to music, and they bear many similarities to Indian treatises. For example, the ancient Sinhalese treatise *Saṅgītasastra* divides music according to ancient Sanskrit tradition into dancing (*nacca, nṛtya*), singing (*gīta*), and instrumental music (*vādita*) (Atwood 1980, 33). According to Amaradeva, historical records indicate that in ancient Srilanka there were seventy-five instruments that were divided into the same five categories of the Buddhist scheme, *pañcatūryanāda* (Amaradeva 1971, 74). The last two categories (*ghana* and *śuṣira*) are the same as the solid and hollow instrumental categories in the antique Hindu scheme. Unfortunately, however, the sources are contradictory as to the meaning of the other three categories. In some sources, *ātata* means a single-headed drum of the *mṛdaṅga* type, and *vitata* means a double-headed drum; in others *ātata* means a drum played with one hand, and *vitata* means a drum played with a stick (Seneviratna 1979, 50–51). According to Sivaramamurti (n.d; 144), *ātatavitata,* "which is a combination of *Ātata* and *Vitata,* must refer to some combination instrument like the *Tantipatahik* or stringed drum" (n.d: 144), a view supported by Seneviratna because it is based on "literary references to various kinds of *vīṇās* that were used in the past, though they are no more in the tradition" (Seneviratna 1979: 51).[21] Ellingson suggested that *ātata* refers to membranes "stretched onto" a resonator, *vitata* to strings "stretched against" or across the surface of a resonator, and *ātatavitata* to an instrument combining both principles of construction—an interpretation that at least yields a consistent classification system. However, the question demands further research (Ellingson 1979: 160).

THE JAIN CLASSIFICATIONS

Except for bells, Jain monks do not play instruments. One reason for this is that skins are not allowed in the temples. However, this prohibition does not mean that the Jain literature excludes mention of instruments. On the contrary, from the sixth century BCE some Jain texts have included lengthy lists of instruments intended to inform Jains about which instruments they should avoid.[22]

The main classification of instruments in the Jain texts divides instruments into four categories somewhat resembling those of the antique Hindu and Buddhist schemes. According to the canonical text *Jīvājīvābhigama* (c. first half of the fifth century), the categories of the scheme are labeled *tata,* comprising stretched strings; *vitata* or *anaddha,* including stretched skin instruments, or drums; *ghana,* consisting of solid instruments, or idiophones; and *śuṣira,* comprising hollow, or wind, instruments (Kapadia 1970, pt. 1, 45; Krishna Murthy 1985, 9). However, a different meaning for the first two categories is given in Malayagiri Sūri's commentary (c. 1150) on the canonical text *Rāyappaseṇaijja,* where the *pataha* (drum) is said to exemplify the *tata* category and the *vīṇā,* the *vitata.* This view was supported by several other writers (Kapadia 1970, pt. 1, 46). Siddhasena Gani's commentary (c. ninth century) on Umasva-ti's *Tattvārthādhigamasūtra* (c. third century), on the other hand, divides instruments into six categories: *tata* (e.g., the *mṛdaṅga* drum), *vitata* (e.g., the *vīṇā*), *ghana* (e.g., bronze vessel instruments), *śuṣira* (e.g., flutes), *saṅgharṣa* (i.e., a saw and wood), and *bhāsā* (i.e., the speaking voice), and this scheme was cited by several other writers (Kapadia, pt. 1, 46–47). Jinadāsa Gaṇi Mahattara, who wrote a work entitled *Nisīhacuṇṇi* (*Visehacuṇṇi*) in approximately the seventh century CE, implied that *vitata* meant a multistringed instrument (Kapadia, pt. 1, 49). Various Jain writers, then, have presented contradictory meanings of the two major categories of instruments, which makes it difficult to draw precise conclusions about the nature of the mainstream Jain classification. The reason for the confusion, as in the case of the Buddhist classification, appears to be the fact that both strings and skins are stretched (the literal meaning of *tata,* already noted, is "stretched").

Another Jain classification divides instruments into eighteen groups, not all of which, however, are independent of each other or easily translatable into English. The Sanskrit commentary by Malayagiri Sūri on the *Rāyappaseṇaijja* mentions Sanskrit equivalents of sixty-three names of instruments and subdivides them according to eighteen different modes of sound excitation. They include striking (e.g., cymbals), beating (drums), blowing (flutes), sounding (horns), touching (guitars), twanging (fiddles), tolling (bells), and others that "are left untranslated for want of exact equivalents in English" (Shastri 1973, 52).

The development of Jainism paralleled that of Hinduism; and the concepts of instruments in the two cultures resemble each other in many ways. Jain literary sources make reference to some of the Jain goddesses holding instruments, much as the Hindu sources refer to the famous celestial musician Visnu. Thus, Rohiṇī is said to have "a conch and Mahākālī a bell" (Kapadia 1970, 45). The two cultures also have a similar attitude to the healing power of instruments. The power of the sound of the *bherī* (drum) is referred to in a Jain legend recounted by Malayagiri Sūri in his commentary on the *Rāyappaseṇaijja*.

> This *bherī* was to be beaten every six months so that whoever heard its sound got cured from the disease he (or she) had. The person in charge of this *bherī* on being bribed by rich men went on selling its pieces and replaced them by ordinary ones. So it became useless and Kṛṣṇa got another from that very god by propitiating him by observing fast for three days. (Kapadia 1970, pt. 2, 36)

As this statement suggests, a classification of instruments based on their links with particular supernatural beings and healing powers may exist, or may once have existed, in Jain nontemple culture. However, the present state of knowledge does not allow a clear picture to be formed of the matter.

Recent Indian Schemes

Several classifications of instruments have been developed by Indian authors for scholarly or for museological purposes in recent decades. Like European authors such as Boethius, Pollux, and Porphyry, who began their schemes with an ancient structure, or like Chinese writers who began their scheme with the *pa yin*, contemporary Indian writers tend to begin their classifications with the *Nāṭyaśāstra* scheme, thus preserving their ties with tradition and promoting a sense of Indian identity in their writing. Some of them deal with a limited instrumentarium, for example, the folk instruments of India, while others try to cover the whole instrumentarium of India. In the lower steps of division, however, they tend to be influenced by Western scholars such as Galpin or Hornbostel and Sachs, whose divisions are based primarily on acoustic and morphological considerations and, to a degree, on performance technique.

A scheme presented by Kothari (1968, 12–13) classifies about three hundred kinds of folk (i.e, nonclassical) musical instruments found all over India. First he divides his collection in traditional fashion into *ghan vādya* (idiophones), *avanaddha vādya* (covered instruments), *sushir vādya* (hollow instruments), and *tat vādya* (stretched instruments). He reorders the categories of the antique Indian scheme and adds his own subdivisions based on the mode of sound excitation. He acknowledges a debt to Galpin, Sachs, and Bessaraboff. Idiophones are divided into the "struck" and the "plucked," where the former are subdivided into the "clashed," "struck," and "shaken" and the latter into those "plucked with the fingers" and those "plucked with a ratchet." The drums are divided into the "struck," "plucked," and "friction-activated." The struck drums are then further subdivided according to their shape into the hourglass-, rim-, pitcher-, bowl-, and cylindrical-shaped. The winds, however, are subdivided according to the structure of their mouthpieces into the "lip," "flue," and "reed-voiced" instruments, and then further subdivided into two kinds of lip, three kinds of flue ("endblown," "vertical," and "transverse"), and three kinds of reed ("free," "single-beating," and "double-beating"). The strings are classified according to the mode of sound excitation into the "bowed" and the "plucked," where both types are subdivided into those with or without frets.

A recent classification by Mansukhani divides instruments into "melodic instruments" (*suara vad*), such as the *sitar* and *sarod,* and "rhythm instruments" (*tal vad*), such as the *tabla* and *mṛdaṅga* (1982, 49). He subdivides the four traditional Hindu categories according to performance technique. Thus the *tat vad* or *tantra vad* ("stretched" instruments) are grouped into the plucked and the bowed, where the former divide into those plucked with the fingers and those plucked with a plectrum. The *sushir vad* ("hollow" instruments) are subdivided into the "mouth-blown" (e.g., the flutes) and the "bellows-blown" (e.g., the harmonium). The *avanad vad* ("covered" instruments) have no subdivisions, but the *ghan vad* ("solid" instruments) are grouped into those that are "struck together" (e.g., cymbals, clappers), those that are "struck singly" (e.g., bells and gongs), and those that are "shaken" (rattles and earthen pots), where the shaken instruments are further subdivided according to whether they are made of wood, metal, or both materials (1982, 50–51).

The most comprehensive classification of Indian instruments, however, was conceived by Deva. It is based primarily on the mode of sound excitation (Deva 1980, 130). It is intended to include historical, current, tribal, folk, and concert instruments of India and to exclude all instruments used in foreign contexts, such as keyboards. Foreign instruments that have been adopted as Indian instruments, such as the harmonium, are included, however. The harmonium is classified not by its possession of a keyboard but on acoustic grounds, apparently because the author considers the former to be a non-Indian character of division. Deva explicitly aims at achieving a functional and operationally convenient scheme rather than a perfectly logical one, presenting ambiguous categories without apology (1980, 129). For example, he classifies the solid instruments according to their shape and consequent acoustic properties and groups the covered instruments according to their performing technique. He also recognizes the scheme's unavoidably ambiguous and borderline cases such as the *chonka* (a plucked drum), which he chooses to classify as a chordophone while admitting the feasibility of its being classed as a membranophone.

The scheme differs from Indian classifications in previous centuries in that it is intended for use by organologists and museologists (e.g., in the instrument collection in the Sangeet Natak Akademi in New Delhi). Because of its intended practical use, it applies the Dewey decimal system as follows: the number 780 designates music, 5 designates Asian music, 54 designates Indian music, and 0.543 designates Indian instruments. It then adds 1 for solid instruments, 2 for covered instruments, 3 for wind instruments, and 4 for strings. Thus a solid instrument (idiophone) is given the number 780.5431. The main categories are then further subdivided. For example, idiophones are subclassified into four groups at the next step: 1 for bells, 2 for pots, 3 for plates, and 4 for rods and rings. Bells are then subdivided into the struck (1), shaken, (2), and rubbed (3) varieties, and further subgrouped where relevant according to whether they produce indefinite pitch (1) or definite pitch (2). A shaken bell of definite pitch is therefore numbered 780.5431 122.

The combination of Indian and Western organological and taxonomical ideas in this scheme makes it an attractive one for contemporary Indian scholarship. It is one of the first modern schemes to be created for a particular nation's instrumentarium. Most twentieth-century schemes have aimed at the classification of all possible instruments, or they have limited themselves to particular ensembles, such as the Javanese gamelan. Although the multicharacter division of Deva's scheme results in its being difficult to draw in chart form, its author's preference for functionality over logic (where necessary) was a matter of deliberate choice in the face of difficult odds.

CONCLUSION

The main taxonomical traditions in India and Srilanka are the Hindu, Buddhist, and Jain, with Tamil classifications forming a subsection of the Hindu schemes. Indian Buddhist schemes survive in Srilanka today. Unlike mainstream Chinese and medieval European schemes, the Indian classifications are quite removed from the sphere of cosmology and religion and have a practical orientation. Traces of a classification linking instruments to particular Hindu supernatural beings are observable, however.

The antique Hindu scheme presented in the *Nātyaśāstra* divides instruments into four categories at the first step: stretched (strings), covered (drums), hollow (winds), and solid (idiophones). The principle of division is the physical characteristics of the sounding body. Division of categories at the second step is made by analogy with the major and minor limbs of the human body, which is a characteristically Indian way of classifying knowledge.

A five-category Hindu scheme of the early second millennium is notable in that it includes a category of "human" instruments (comprising the voice and hand-clapping) as well as plucked, wind, stretched, and metal percussive categories, being divided according to one interpretation on the single principle of the place of origin of sound. A different kind of practice-oriented Hindu scheme consists of four categories: solo instruments, instruments that accompany vocal music, instruments that accompany dance, and instruments that accompany dance and vocal music. As the solo-accompaniment dichotomy is basic to Indian classical music, it is therefore not surprising to find it influencing taxonomies such as this one and others in India.

The main Tamil classification somewhat resembles the above-mentioned five-category scheme. Its categories are leather, hollow, gut (stringed), human vocal, and metal instruments. Another scheme divides instruments into the stringed, hollow, and leather categories, while yet another divides instruments into those that play solo and those used for accompaniment.

The main Buddhist scheme, which developed in the context of ancient Indian temple ritual and survives in modern Sri Lanka today, divides instruments into five categories. Two of them resemble the *Nātyaśāstra*'s solid and hollow categories, while the other three are the subject of divided opinion in the treatises. This is largely due to the fact that these three categories (*ātata, vitata,* and *ātata vitata*) all have *tata* ("stretched") in their labels, which has been differently interpreted to mean stretched strings or stretched skins. Thus some writers include drums in the first category and strings in the second, or vice versa, and some interpret the other category as meaning instruments that combine stretched strings and stretched skins.

The four categories of the main Jain scheme somewhat resemble those of the antique Hindu and Buddhist schemes. As in the Buddhist schemes, the meanings of its *tata* categories are controversial. A fifth-century version of the Jain scheme lists stretched strings (*tata*), stretched skins (*vitata*), solid instruments, and hollow instruments, but several other sources interpret the first two categories as meaning stretched skins and stretched strings respectively. Another Jain scheme divides instruments into eighteen categories according to the mode of sound excitation.

Our knowledge of the classifications of instruments in India's many orally transmitting subcultures and the classifications belonging to Muslim India is minimal. The available evidence suggests that Muslim treatises on Indian music in the second millennium made use of the antique Hindu classification, but these sources need much more study.

Twentieth-century schemes have a different nature from those of previous centuries, having different aims in view—mostly organological or museological or both. Though often acknowledging a debt to Western organologists they have a distinctively Indian identity. This is partly achieved by the exclusive concentration on Indian instruments, whether a limited instrumentarium (e.g., the folk instruments only) or the whole instrumentarium is involved. It is also partly due to the fact that like the Chinese and the pre-nineteenth-century European scholars, they begin their schemes with a deferential high-level reference to an antique scheme of their heritage (in India's case, the *Nātyaśāstra* scheme). Their lower steps of division are usually based on mode of sound excitation, morphological features, or performing technique. The most comprehensive modern scheme to be devised (by Deva) classifies all Indian instruments in several steps according to characters based on morphology and performing technique, rejecting the possession of a keyboard (e.g., in the case of the Indian harmonium) as a Western character of division.

SIX

The Priority of Musical over Religious Characters in Grouping Tibetan Monastic Instruments

Music in ceremonies is an offering (*Mchod pa*) to please the ears of the deity: it is like inviting a guest to your home and offering him the best you have. . . . There should be as much music as possible; but, if no instruments are present, the offering is equally good, since we always offer instrumental music mentally. . . . Only the phenomenal bodies of the Buddhas can receive such offerings; and since they themselves have no need for them, the music is for our own benefit, to help us admire their qualities.

Organ Tshe brtan[1]

Like European and Chinese scholars until recent times, Tibetan Buddhist monks wrote hundreds of treatises referring to music and instruments over the centuries, and they are still writing them to this day. However, they have been more practical in their orientation than their European and Chinese counterparts and their writings actually often served as editions of the performance practice.[2]

Unlike the Chinese and the Europeans, Tibetan Buddhist writers did not develop a cosmological theory of music and instruments. Only writers adhering to the indigenous Tibetan Bon religion[3] wrote about cosmology in connection with instruments, including the cosmological significance of drums, which play an important role in their doctrine. Like their European counterparts, however, Tibetan Buddhist monks from the early diffusion period (c. seventh century CE) presented classifications of science, including music, in their treatises. For example, the eighteenth-century lama Klong rdol bla ma classified the Indo-Tibetan sciences into five major categories, of which communication/phonology was one, which he then subdivided into the "five minor sciences," including the performing arts. He subdivided the performing arts by the Indian analogy with limbs into five subcategories (the "five limbs"), of which one was music (*rol mo*), and this he further subdivided into "mental music" (including study, thought, meditation, etc.) and "auditory music" (speech, melody, etc.) (Ellingson 1979, 374).

Mental music consists of sounds—vocal and instrumental—that are projected by the mind during meditation on ritual occasions. Though not physically present, these sounds augment the subjects' perception of the monastic ritual music being played. They are conceived as religious offerings, as mentioned in the quotation at the head of this chapter. Thus, monks skilled in the art of meditation may mentally "hear" a variety of instruments in addition to those in the actually sounding monastic ensemble (*rol mo*)[4] and these may include Indian, Chinese, celestial, and exotic or imaginary instruments[5] as well as Tibetan stringed instruments, which, however, are never played in monastic ensembles.

Nevertheless, physically present stringed instruments are not entirely removed from the realm of the monastic ensemble. Though normally played only in secular contexts, they may be placed on the altar or carried in silent procession as offerings on monastic ritual occasions. Nonphysical, meditated string sound removes the need for close classification of the stringed instrument category, as there would be little point in classifying a sound experience that exists only in the enriched perception of initiated, meditating individuals. Besides, the Tibetan varieties of plucked, bowed, and beaten strings are very few in number, which makes it unnecessary, even in the context of their secular function, to distinguish between them in formal categories.

In its celestial aspect and its conceptual function of aiding religious contemplation and understanding, the concept of mental music somewhat resembles the medieval European notion of the music of the spheres. However, it differs radically from it in at least two respects. The music of the spheres is cosmologically conceived and consists of humanly inaudible sounds, while mental music is a noncosmological concept and is clearly perceived as real music in the mind; that is, its rhythms, instruments, and other concrete aspects can be described by its perceivers after it is experienced.

Tibetan religious thought derives largely from Indian Buddhism, expanding and developing in Tibet from the time of its first royal sponsorship there in the seventh century. Unlike Hinayana Buddhist doctrine (as practiced, for example, on the Southeast Asian mainland), which largely rejects the use of music in worship, Mahayana Buddhist thought in Tibet and elsewhere conceives of music as a prerequisite to significant religious experience on ritual occasions. Tibetan ideology is based on aesthetic quality first and religious understanding second. Thus the divisions of the standard Tibetan classification of monastic ensemble instruments are based primarily on musical, not religious, factors.

Even the literal meaning of the Tibetan word for "instruments"—*rol cha,* that is, "makers of musical parts"—indicates the priority of the musical over the religious significance of instruments in ritual ensembles. It is therefore not surprising that the beaten (*brdung ba*) instruments, which are musically the most important, appear first in the scheme. The cymbals in particular are essential instruments, as they outline the key aspects of musical structure, while the frame drums, which are also musically important, play a louder, simplified version of the cymbal part (Ellingson 1979: 584). The rung (*'khrol ba*) instruments, which include metal bells and drums with suspended strikers, take second place, even though musically they are the least important instruments in the ensemble, serving to enrich the timbre and provide a counterrhythmic element at times. Blown (*'bud pa*) instruments appear third, having the musically important function of performing the melodies; they include long and short trumpets made of metal or (rarely) thighbone, as well as double-reed instruments. The stringed instruments (*rgyud can*) are most commonly called "cause and agent" (*rgyu rkyen*) instruments,[6] and they appear last in the scheme because, as we have noted, they are the only category of instruments not physically played in monastic ensembles, though they may be projected by the mind as mental music on meditative ritual occasions.

The fourfold division of instruments in the standard Tibetan scheme first appeared in treatises dating from the twelfth century. It has mostly been presented in the order of beaten, rung, blown, and cause-and-agent instruments. An alternative order was given by the scholar and composer Tsong kha pa, who wrote in his *Lam Rim Chen mo* (Great stages on the path to perfection) of 1403 that a musical offering should consist of four classes of "Stringed instruments, and Blown instruments, and Beaten instruments, and Rung instruments" (Ellingson 1979, 362–63). While Indians classify instruments (and other entities) by analogy with limbs of the body, Tibetans usually classify instruments (and other things) by analogy with families (*rigs*) or abstract classes (*sde*). However, as previously mentioned, Klong rdol bla ma did use the limb analogy in his classification of the five minor Indo-Tibetan sciences.

Only the uppermost division of the scheme presented in figure 6.1 is homologous with the standard classification of instruments presented in Tibetan treatises. The other levels are based on Ellingson's synthesis of the

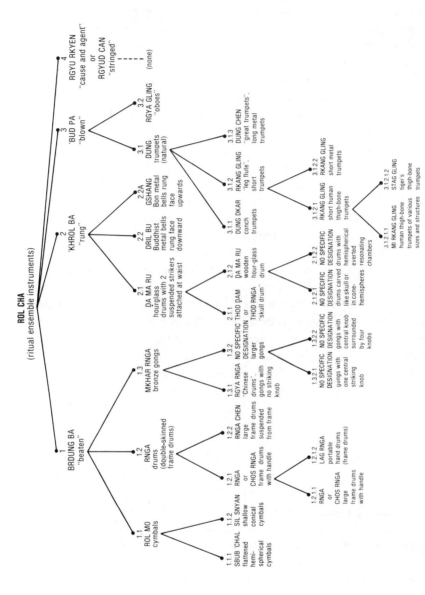

FIGURE 6.1 Classification of the main Tibetan monastic ensemble instruments (based on Ellingson 1979, 107, 552–75)

classification of instruments in treatises and word-of-mouth accounts by contemporary Tibetan musicians. There are five steps in the case of trumpets and four each with the beaten and rung instruments. The addition of the decimal numbers by Ellingson was intended to make the scheme more usable. Moreover such numeration is not unacceptable from a mainstream Tibetan viewpoint as it follows a centuries-old Tibetan practice of decimalizing subdivisions is treatises, where each new subdivision in a succession of subdivisions in indicated by a new series of numbers (Ellingson 1979: 551). The same system is used, of course, by Western taxonomists, as in the Dewey decimal system for library book cataloging and in the Hornbostel and Sachs classification of instruments.

The unusual category of rung (*'khrol ba*) instruments merits a note of explanation. These instruments are divided into three categories at the first step: drums and two kinds of bells rung in different ways. The hourglass-shaped drums (*ḍa ma ru*) have two strikers or clappers suspended at the waist; when the drums are oscillated, each striker produces alternate strokes on each of the two membranes. Thus they are distinguished by their ringing performance technique, called *'khrol ba*. One category of bells—Buddhist bells (*dril bu*)—are held with one hand by means of an attached handle and are shaken from side to side to allow the internal suspended striker to sound on the lower rim, where vibrations are strongest. Bells (*gshang*) played in Bon services, on the other hand, are rung face upward, being sounded near the rim by impact with the clapper, which is attached directly to the handle (Ellingson 1979, 558–62).

Many cultures distinguish, as the Tibetans do, between beaten, blown, and stringed instruments, but the Tibetans' category of rung instruments is apparently unique. Most other cultures incorporate bells (if relevant) under such headings as "percussion," "idiophones," "metal instruments," or "solid instruments," while the rare category of rung drums is classified like other drums under "percussion," "membranophones," "skin instruments," or "covered instruments." A separate major category of rung instruments is justified in the Tibetan context partly by virtue of their being the most important ritual instruments in monastic ensembles and partly, like the other categories, by their distinctive musical role, despite their being the least musically important of all the categories. Presumably they appear second in the hierarchy after the beaten instruments not only because of their ritual importance but also because they share the percussiveness of the musically important beaten instruments.

At the third and fourth steps of Ellingson's schematic presentation, the divisions are made according to a combination of morphological and material characters, for example, according to the shape of the cymbals and the material of the trumpets at the third step, and according to the size and number of bosses on gongs and the material (thighbone or metal) of trumpets at the fourth step. At the fifth step, trumpets are subdivided according to the primary material of which they are made: human thighbone or tiger thighbone. (Tigers are found in southeastern Tibet but tiger thighbone trumpets are extremely rare, and even human thighbone trumpets are seldom found.) Only at the fourth step, then, does the scheme not comply with strict logical division. Thus the "great trumpets" (*dung chen*) could be subdivided according to the materials of which they are made into three categories: copper, brass, or silver.[7]

The existence of alternative classifications of instruments reflects the high value placed in the culture on the challenging of received truths and the envisaging of alternatives in the process of perfecting wisdom by realizing the ultimate voidness of things, including logical thinking. One alternative classification is based on the Tantric Buddhist notion of the components of the human personality, an idea that derives from India after 500 CE. Tantric ideology adopted the symbolic model of the pacifying music of peaceful Buddhas as opposed to the wild music of fierce, protective Buddhas. Both peacefulness and tamed fierceness are regarded as good qualities. Monastic instruments may be divided into the peaceful and the fierce by analogy with components of human behavior. Thus, cymbals are classified into those used for fierce effects (the flattened, hemispherical cymbals, *sbub 'chal*) and those used for peaceful effects (the shallow, conical cymbals, *sil snyan*). Double-skinned frame drums are also divided into the fierce kind (those with handles, the *rnga*) and the peaceful kind (the large, suspended *rnga chen*). The rung instruments are all peaceful except for the hourglass skull drum of Indian Buddhist origin (the *thod dam*), as are also the conch trumpets and the oboes. Not all instruments have these extramusical associations, however. Gongs, which are relatively rarely used, are regarded as being neither peaceful nor fierce. This division of instruments is related to the four modes of musical performance (Ellingson 1979: 198), or to a particular orchestration or series of orchestrations used in a ritual. The four modes are the "pacifying" (i.e., the slowly and softly performed), "extending" (i.e., clearly performed, reverberating), "powerful" (i.e., performed in an emotionally gratifying, pleasant, passionate, and rhythmic way), and "fierce" (i.e., fast and overpowering), where the extending category refers to music that has the effect of extending good qualities (such as learning) attained by meditation, ritual music, and mental music. Therefore, written texts may on occasion refer to four kinds of drums used in four different parts or modes of a ritual.

Another way of grouping Tibetan instruments is based on the Bon belief in the cosmological importance of drums. Drums are so highly venerated in Bon ideology that they are sometimes regarded as the all-encompassing category for instruments of whatever kind. For example, the following excerpt from an anonymous Bon poem with Buddhist terminological influence subsumes various kinds of instruments—even stringed instruments—under the one general category of drums.

> I seek to beat the drums, great in wonders:
> The seven-jewelled drum of the wish-granting tree,
> The clay drum, the hourglass drum, and the great drum
> The splendid sandalwood many-stringed drum,
> The unthinkable killer-of-the-*Ma trang*-demon-drum,
> This great drum, the secret great pattern drum,
> The *Ru tra*-demon-killing drum of two symmetric skulls:
> Beaten, it is beaten in the highest heaven;
> The drum-sound sounds in the worldly realms.
> Fright, it frightens all sentient beings;
> Fear, the Eight Gods and Demons fear it
> Overcome, all demon-realms are overcome.[8]

To this poet, then, the category of drums includes a sandalwood instrument of many strings, by which he probably meant a struck zither, a plucked lute, or some mentally conceived, metal-stringed instrument.

Another broad classificatory idea in Tibetan Buddhist culture is the association of instruments with ethical effects. The conch trumpet (*dung dkar*) is regarded as producing the symbolic voice of the Buddha and is therefore attributed with having a high ethical effect. Only seen and heard instruments, however, are believed to have potential moral effects, and their precise effect depends on the intent and circumstances of their use and the attitude of the perceiver. This classificatory idea, then, remains a general one and cannot be translated into a hard and fast scheme.

CONCLUSION

The standard Tibetan Buddhist monastic classification of musical instruments, with its four major categories plus the lower steps of its division in the culture (as shown in fig. 6.1), is based on performance technique and morphological and material characters, is related to the broad classification of music as a component of scientific knowledge, and possesses powerful religious associations. The category of stringed instruments in the Tibetan Buddhist scheme is unusually broad because of its mainly secular connotations and the fact that there are so few types of stringed instruments. Also highly unusual is the major category of rung instruments, which are the most ritually important but least musically significant of all the categories.

How was it that Mahayana beliefs were able to penetrate Tibetan classificatory thinking about instruments so much more pervasively than, say, Sunni beliefs in Arabic cultures? Part of the reason is that Tibetans allowed a syncretism of Indian-Buddhist and indigenous Bon beliefs and rituals to develop over the centuries. Whereas Islam rejected native Arab religious beliefs and musical practices from its birth in the seventh century and became *more* rather than less austere over time in its attitude to the use of instruments in mainstream Sunni worship (see chapter 9), Mahayana Buddhism in Tibet not only tolerated but promoted the efficacious use of instruments in monastic ritual while incorporating some Bon elements into its fabric. From the seventh century, when Buddhist scriptures were translated into Tibetan, the monastic scribal tradition appears to have been successfully integrated into mainstream musical practice and religious thought, one reflection of which is the standard classification of instruments propagated from the twelfth century.

The standard Tibetan Buddhist scheme showed great stability over the centuries because it was based on monastic musical practice and was closely related to core ideological notions such as auditory and mental music. It was persistently documented in treatises. Since Tibetan Buddhism "is aesthetically a musical religion" (Tambiah 1970, 124) in which "completely pure musical performances . . . are more beneficial than a hundred years of meditation and a hundred years of mantra recitations by others" (Kun dga' bsod nams [1624] 1969, 96), its scholars have been able readily to absorb musical instruments into their speculations about the meaning of existence. Followers of Sunni Islam, in contrast, maintained a strong disapproval of the use of instruments in worship, and except in the case of Sufi thought excluded them from their religious speculations. In this respect the Tibetan scheme is a positive example of the potency of instrument classifications as cultural symbols, while the Sunni Arab schemes are notable either for their exclusion of the religious symbolism of instruments or for the negative religious associations of instruments as a consequence of their desire to purify Islam of the sensual gratification afforded by instrumental music.

The symbolic propensity of Tibetan classificatory thinking is also reflected in the fact that many variant classifications of instruments, of which only a few are mentioned above, have been allowed to coexist over the centuries, largely as a result of the conviction that one should envisage alternatives in the process of making manifest the ultimate emptiness of things.

The Case of Java: Classifications in Oral Tradition and the Recent Development of Literary Schemes

The sound of the gong, beaten heavily, rolls on, its ponderous beats like the ocean tide.

Ko Mo An (1897)[1]

The science of karawitan (art of producing sound) has been in existence for a long time. However, it has yet to gain the general understanding of most students . . . , because in former times it was only transmitted orally in the form of moral lectures and conversation.

Benedictus Yusuf Harjamulya
Sastrapustaka, unpublished manuscript,
1953–1978[2]

Although Java's literary tradition is many centuries old and her literary achievements—especially in the field of belletristic literature—are considerable and well documented (Pigeaud 1960), her musical practices, pedagogical tradition, and classifications of instruments have until recently had a primarily oral orientation. Only in recent decades have a number of Javanese musicians begun to write down their classificatory schemes for use in the conservatoria and music academies.

The first part of this chapter presents classifications of instruments and ensembles that are still transmitted mainly in oral form, though some have recently been written down for pedagogical purposes, while the second part discusses scholar-imposed classifications that have been devised and written down fairly recently by Javanese and foreign musicians, musicologists, or teachers. Until the mid–nineteenth century Javanese musical practice, scholarship, and pedagogy clearly belonged to oral tradition. However, there are many signs now that these practices are in a state of transition to a partly literary tradition (see Becker 1980); and this includes the classification of instruments and ensembles. Java is an interesting case for the study of instrument classification in that it allows us to view both orally transmitted schemes that developed over a considerable period of time and recently developed literary schemes and to examine a period of transition from culture-emerging to scholar-imposed schemes.

CLASSIFICATIONS TRANSMITTED ORALLY

The great gong of the Javanese gamelan is the most highly revered instrument in Java. Incense is burned in front of it before it is played, gong-smiths and their craft are attributed with magic power, and poets compare the sound of the gong with the rumbling of thunder or the ocean tide. Its main musical function in a gamelan work is to mark off the major structural periods.

The great gong, however, is but a small part of the realm of Javanese percussion instruments, for the great majority of instrumental types in Java are percussive. Probably Java has as many varieties of percussion instruments as any culture in the world. The fact that all Javanese instruments, even winds and strings, may be said to be *ditabuh* (literally, "beaten") indicates that the Javanese have traditionally regarded beaten instruments as the norm. Probably *ditabuh* broadened in its meaning over time for it is presently used to mean either "beaten" or "played" (i.e., beaten, plucked, pulled, bowed, or shaken), as indicated in the following orally transmitted model:

1. *ricikan dijagur/ditabuh:* "instruments beaten with a padded hammer," e.g., the suspended gongs
2. *ricikan dithuthuk/ditabuh:* "instruments knocked with a hard or a semihard hammer," e.g., the *saron* (keyed metallophones) and the *bonang* (gong-chimes)
3. *ricikan dikebuk/ditabuh:* "hand-beaten instruments," e.g., the *kendhang* (drum)
4. *ricikan dipethik/ditabuh:* "plucked instruments," e.g., zithers
5. *ricikan disendal/ditabuh:* "pulled instruments," e.g., jew's-harp with string mechanism
6. *ricikan dikosok/ditabuh:* "bowed instruments," e.g., the *rebab*
7. *ricikan disebul/ditabuh:* "blown instruments," e.g., the *suling* (flute)
8. *ricikan dikocok/ditabuh:* "shaken instruments," e.g., the *angklung* (bamboo idiophone)

This scheme is shown in figure 7.1. The four categories of beaten instruments are determined by the kinds of motion of the players' hands. This character of division also applies to the plucked and pulled instruments,

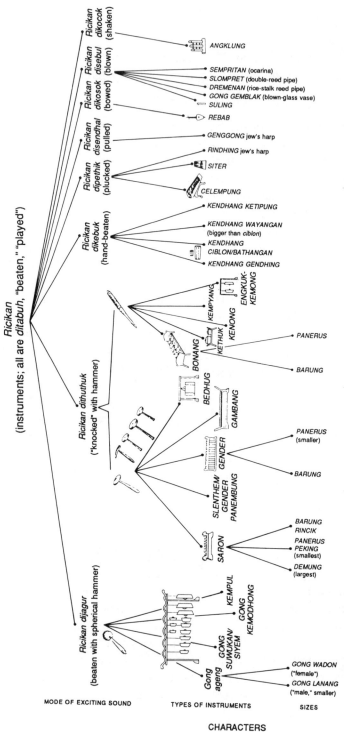

FIGURE 7.1 Classification of Javanese instruments according to mode of sound excitation (based on a verbal communication from Poedijono)

while the action of the player's mouth distinguishes the blown category and the motion of the bow distinguishes the bowed category. In fact there is but one overriding character of division—the motion of the players' actions in producing sounds, and this characterizes the scheme as being one of logical division. A second step of division of some instruments is made according to size (the "female" gong is larger than the "male") and tint (octave pitch).

Though this model of organization does not have the status of the dominant schemes of, say, China or India, never having been transmitted in written form, it has considerable explanatory power in context. It is a culture-emerging scheme that reflects Java's musical identity in several respects. It includes all Javanese musical instruments; it bestows prominence on the culture's preferred instruments—gongs, drums, and *rebab*—by giving them each a separate category; and it distinguishes no less than four percussive categories according to their mode of sound excitation. Some Javanese learn the model's categories during childhood. Poedijono, a gamelan musician who was trained at the Conservatory of Music in Surakarta (*Kokar*) but imbibed the terms of the scheme as a child in the 1940s in his hometown of Wonogiri in Central Java, recounted them to me in 1985.

Unlike in European and Sunni Arab culture, where percussion instruments were for many centuries regarded as inferior and all but ignored, the Javanese value beaten instruments highly and make remarkably close divisions of them. They distinguish instruments beaten with a softly padded cylindrical hammer, those struck with a hard wooden mallet or a fairly hard hammer (covered with a thin layer of felt or wound cord), hand-beaten instruments, and shaken idiophones. The fact that such fine distinctions are made in a culture that possesses a greater diversity of percussion instruments than most other cultures in the world is hardly surprising. Besides the suspended gongs, gong-chimes, xylophones, double- and single-headed drums, and frame drums that are found in many Southeast Asian cultures, Java has slab metallophones with hard beaters, beveled-key metallophones with soft beaters, and single boxed gongs. Moreover, these instruments may occur in more than one size or tint. Other percussion instruments include the clashing metal plates and wooden knockers used by puppeteers for sound effects and musical signaling in the shadow theater. There are also archaic or virtually obsolete instruments such as the boxed cymbals (*kecer*), pairs of banana-shaped metal concussion rods (*kemanak*), and metallic bells (*genta*). Rustic percussion instruments include rice-blocks (*lesung*), pairs of iron keys beaten simultaneously as a gong substitute (*gong kemodhong*), tilting bamboo water clatterers (*taluktak*), the split drums (*kenthongan*) used for signaling, and wooden bells (*klonthang*) hung around the necks of animals.[3]

Indeed, percussion is to the instrumental culture what the staple crop rice is to the food culture. Just as the Javanese have developed a rich vocabulary of terms for rice in its various types, its stages of growth, its harvested stage, its cooked form, and the many ways of preparing and serving it, so they have given names to the various types, sizes, and categories of percussion instruments, their specific performance practices, and the ensembles of which they are part. Long ago an aura of sacred mystery and ritual was attached to such special objects of the culture as rice and musical instruments (especially to gongs and drums but, actually, to all instruments). Taboos are operative against walking over instruments or sitting on bags of rice, because spirits are believed to reside in them. Indeed these spirits, when properly appeased, are thought to beautify the sounds of the instruments or to affect the quality of the rice they inhabit. Special rituals for the making, repairing, washing, and playing of gongs parallel the rituals for the planting, harvesting, and stamping of rice as well as other activities associated with cultivating, preparing and eating it. It is not exceptional to find multiple classifications of such important sets in a culture. In Java there are at least seven traditional ways of classifying musical instruments. Since these classifications are all orally transmitted, however, it is not known how old the schemes are nor how they may have changed over time.

Mode of sound excitation, then, is one way of classifying Javanese instruments. Another is according to the tone system to which they are tuned (see second step of classification in fig. 7.5). A number of melodic gamelan instruments occur in pairs, with one tuned to the pentatonic anhemitonic *slendro* tone system (tones 1, 2, 3, 5, 6) and the other to the heptatonic, hemitonic *pelog* (tones 1, 2, 3, 4, 5, 6, 7). The *gender* (metallophones) occur in threes, with one tuned in *slendro* and the other two in the two basic modal scales of *pelog* (tones 1, 2, 3, 5, 6 and 2, 3, 5, 6, 7 respectively). Instruments tuned to one of these systems are never, of course, played together in ensemble with instruments of the other tone system.

A third character of classification divides some gamelan instruments into "female" and "male" pairs or sets of pairs, where the female instruments are usually slightly larger and lower-pitched than their male counterparts. One reason given to explain why female instruments are larger is that the womb is larger than the penis. But as only a few instruments are thus divided, the scheme can only be regarded as a highly informal, incomplete one. The higher-pitched row of *bonang* kettles are called "male" and the lower pitched ones "female," and, likewise, the larger group is called the female and the smaller the male. The gender-based character of division is applied in more complete form in some other Indonesian cultures, such as in Mandailing and in Bali, where pairs of drums are also among the instruments designated as female and male (see Kartomi 1981; and McPhee 1966, 33, 37–38; respectively).[4]

A fourth classification commonly used by musicians divides the bronze gamelan instruments into those with slab keys and those with knobs or bosses; the former is called *wilahan* and the latter *pencon* (verbal communication from Sumarsam).

A fifth classification is based on the distinction between gamelan used to play loud-sounding pieces (which are termed *gendhing bebonangan* in Surakarta and *gendhing soran* in Yogyakarta) and those used to play soft-sounding pieces (*gendhing rebab* or *gendhing gender* in Surakarta and *gendhing lirih* in Yogyakarta) (verbal communication from Aline Scott Maxwell). The former comprises loud instruments played with hard or semihard hammers, including gong-chimes and metal-keyed instruments (the *bonang panerus, saron barung, saron demung, saron panerus,* and *slenthem*), plus gongs and drums, while the latter comprises soft instruments, including the *rebab,* flute, plucked strings, xylophones, multioctave metallophones (*gender panerus* and *gender barung*), and the human voice. When a soft-sounding piece is played, the hard-hammered instruments are either omitted altogether or played softly in the background.[5] This classification has recently been discussed in a short treatise by the Javanese musician Sindoesawarno, whose schematic presentation divides instruments of the gamelan into two categories according to whether they are arranged in the front or at the back of a performing area (Becker (ed.) 1984:398). As he explains, embellishing instruments of high status such as the *gender, rebab, kendhang, slenthem,* and *bonang* are placed at the front, partly so that their sounds can carry well, while instruments that do not embellish, such as the *saron* and the various gongs, are placed at the back.

Sixth, in Surakarta a similar, highly practical classification of gamelan instruments as well as instrumentalists is sometimes used in the main radio station (the local branch of Radio Republik Indonesia), though variants of it sometimes apply. It is based not only on the spatial arrangement of the instruments but also on the amount of payment received by the perform- ers. Players of instruments such as the *gender* and *rebab,* which are placed in the front (i.e., *ngajeng* [High Javanese] or *ngarep* [Low Javanese] of an arrangement of gamelan instruments, are paid more than players of *saron, gambang,* and other instruments placed in the middle (*tengah*), and they in turn are paid more than players of instruments such as the gongs that are placed at the back (*wingking* [High Javanese] or *buri* [Low Javanese]). According to the elderly Surakarta musician Maloyowidodo, the practice until the 1950s was for the gong player to sit at the back and double at times as a flute player. However, he was not paid any extra for playing the flute, which was regarded as an inessential instrument in the ensemble. In most rural areas, however, this classification of instruments and instru- mentalists is not known. Normally the leader (usually the drum player) is paid more than the other musicians, who receive the same amount each.[6]

BACK
Wingking (High Javanese), *Buri* (Low Javanese)

MIDDLE
Tengah

FRONT
Ngajeng (High Javanese), *Ngarep* (Low Javanese)

Seventh, as in Mandailing and Minangkabau and other parts of Southeast Asia, the Javanese put into practice a broad grouping of the whole instrumentarium according to the various strata and associated intellectual currents of their history. Orally transmitted classifications of instruments and instrumental ensembles are rooted in the history of thought in a culture. As epistemologies change or expand to absorb new elements, usually through foreign contact, so some of the concepts underlying the schemes devised for grouping instruments change or broaden to reflect the intellectual currents of the time. Over the past two millennia Central Java has absorbed Hindu-Buddhist, Muslim, Christian, European, and other foreign intellectual traditions into its own mystical world view, which is based on ancient Javanese religion (*agama Jawa*).

Distinctions made in Java between instruments associated with the various strata constitute a scheme of classification. It comprises (1) the instruments of the pre-Muslim, Tantric Javanese stratum (indigenous Javanese as well as Hindu and Buddhist components emanating from India in the first millennium), including the complete "standard" gamelan and the rural gamelan ensembles with their double and multiple reeds and archaic ensemble instruments; (2) the stratum resulting from Muslim contact from about the fourteenth century, which includes the *gambus* (pear-shaped lute) and various kinds of frame drums used to accompany devotional and Middle-Eastern-influence love songs; (3) the stratum deriving from the early period of European (initially Portuguese) contact from the end of the fifteenth century, which includes violins, (*biola*), cellos, ukeleles, and other European instruments used in *kroncong* and other harmonized Malay music; and (4) the stratum resulting from contact with international popular culture, which includes bongos and electric guitars.

With a few exceptions, the instruments of the gamelan and related ensembles are kept quite separate in their musical practice and social context from those of Muslim origin,[7] and they in turn are kept quite separate in their musical style and social context from instruments of Western origin or the international popular scene.[8] It is likely too that certain other foreign intellectual traditions (e.g., Chinese) left their mark at times in the past, but if so, evidence of their impact has apparently been lost.

Finally a bird's-eye view of Java's ensembles as a whole indicates that distinctions are made in oral culture between "complete" gamelan ensembles and "incomplete" ones, archaic and modern gamelan ensembles, and the large standard gamelan as opposed to smaller village gamelan, which vary on a regional basis. The various archaic gamelan are distinguished by their unique combinations of instruments and possession of obsolete instruments such as the bell-tree (*byong*) in the three-toned *gamelan kodhok ngorek*.[9] Regionally variable village gamelan combinations are frequently distinguishable from a standard gamelan (in which the *rebab* is the main melodic instrument) by their inclusion of a double-reed wind instrument (*selompret, slompret,* or *sompret*), which is given relatively low status,[10] in addition to their variable drum and gong components. Some also include the shaken bamboo *angklung* or other instruments not usually associated with gamelan. Instruments and sets of instruments are subclassified mainly on the basis of their size and, as has been mentioned, on whether instruments are placed at the back or the front of a performing area.

CLASSIFICATIONS TRANSMITTED IN LITERARY FORM

A number of Javanese musician-theorists have recently produced their own written classifications of instruments in their treatises on gamelan music, which are intended mainly for teaching in the music academies and special junior high schools for music. They are based partly on traditional Javanese taxonomical thought. These single-authored schemes differ from most of the orally transmitted ones in that they deal only with instruments of the complete gamelan, excluding the various rural instruments, because the performance and theory of rural ensembles and nongamelan instruments are not normally taught in the academies and schools. In all cases the schemes are mentioned only in passing as part of the authors' broader aims of explicating the theory and repertoire of Javanese musical and theatrical art. They illustrate how cultural and pedagogical background influences the way in which the objects and ensembles are classified.

One scheme, which was taught by the late Sindoesawarno in the Conservatory of Music (*Kokar*) in Surakarta beginning in the 1950s, is not related to an individual's theory of gamelan music, however. Like the main Chinese scheme (*pa yin*), the scheme is based on the materials of which instruments are made. Though a few Javanese musicians suspect it may be an old scheme, its age is unknown. One form in which it was taught in the 1950s is as follows:

1. *ricikan prunggu/wesi:* "bronze instruments" or "iron instruments," with bronze or iron sounding bodies, such as gongs
2. *ricikan kulit:* "leather instruments," with a sounding leather head or heads, such as single- or double-headed drums
3. *ricikan kayu:* "wooden instruments," with wooden sounding bodies, such as xylophones
4. *ricikan kawat/tali:* "wire or cord instruments," with one or more sounding wires or cords, such as zithers
5. *ricikan bambu pring:* "bamboo instruments," with bamboo sounding bodies or sound containers, such as flutes

Virtually all Javanese instruments fit into one or another of these categories.

Does this scheme, like the Chinese one, have any spiritual implications or links with nature? In traditional Javanese thought, all materials were sometimes attributed with spiritual significance. Metal, especially bronze, was and is regarded as being most potent, especially when forged into the form of the great gong of the gamelan, wherein the great spirit of the orchestra is believed normally to reside. In some gamelans, however, the main spirit is believed to reside in the bowed *rebab,* or even the metal-keyed *gender.* The magic power of metals, especially bronze, is linked to the power attributed to gong forgers and other blacksmiths. In a few rare gamelans, the main drum is regarded as being the most sacred instrument, being attributed with considerable spiritual and musical significance. Its leather material is associated with the respected art of making leather puppets, the shadows of which represent the shapes of the ancestors. The wooden category includes the xylophone (*gambang*), which, despite its great age (see the relief of a *gambang*-type instrument on the ninth-century Barabudur temple in Central Java), is not considered to be even near the top of the hierarchy of instruments. The material having the lowest status of all is bamboo, which grows prolifically in Java and is one of the cheapest materials to acquire. Bamboo flutes are optional instruments in the gamelan and have low status, as have other bamboo instruments such as the shaken idiophone (*angklung*) and bamboo-keyed *calung,* which are reserved for rustic ensembles only. Some very old *angklung* in Bungko, West Java, however, are highly venerated for their age.

There is a link, then, though a loose one, between the status of Javanese instruments and the materials of which they are made. However, unlike the Chinese, the Javanese do not make precise connections between materials and cosmology or the elements of nature, such as the winds or the directions. It is possible, then, that the five-category, tree-form presentation of figure 7.2 is a fairly recent scheme, devised for conservatory teaching purposes.

Most of the other schemes to be discussed below illustrate their respective author's particular intellectual bent and pedagogical purpose, though based partly on traditional Javanese categories. They are moderately influenced by the foreign literature on gamelan, to which they obliquely or directly refer on occasion, especially to Kunst 1949, who in his attempts to comprehend and explain gamelan music to other foreigners devised his own scheme of classification. Some of the Javanese writers make no mention of the Western literature at all but offer their own solutions to problems isolated by Western scholars. In these respects and in their focus on detailed musical matters, these treatises represent a

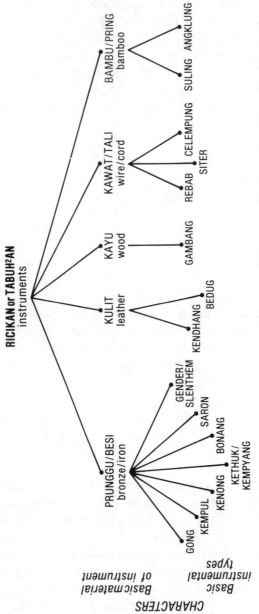

FIGURE 7.2 Classification of Javanese instruments according to their basic material (based on verbal communication from Poedijono)

departure from Java's literary and scholarly tradition in general as well as Java's orally transmitted tradition of instrument classification in particular.

Over the past millennium, a rich tradition of literary, historical, and didactic scholarship developed in Java, influenced first by Hindu and Buddhist thought and literature and then, from about the fifteenth century, by Muslim literary scholarship. Many thousands of literary works were produced in *kidung, babad,* and other literary forms and often in poetic meters that were intended to be sung or recited. These treatises contain frequent references to music and instruments, but only in passing; none of them discusses music in detail or at any length.[11]

In the latter half of the nineteenth century, the Javanese began to be exposed to the methods of Dutch scholarship. The colonial government felt the need to train public servants from among the sons of the regional Javanese administrative heads and offered them opportunities to obtain a Dutch education. They also encouraged court scribes to develop methods of music notation with which to write down the outlines of gamelan works for posterity, with the result that beautifully decorated books of notated gamelan pieces were prepared and deposited in court libraries. The Java Instituut even organized a contest, probably in the early years of the twentieth century, for the best treatise on Javanese music. It awarded an honorable mention to R. A. A. Tjakrahadikusuma, ex-regent (regional head) of Temanggung, for a manuscript containing a classification of gamelan instruments. The work was entitled "De regelen der gendhing" (Rules of gamelan works).[12] This treatise presented an analogy between gamelan instrument groupings and batik cloth designs, dividing the instruments into three categories: those that were analogous to a batik pattern outline (the *kalowongan*), those that were analogous to batik's "more or less neutral background" (the *plataran*), and those that were analogous to the ornamental fill-in (the [*h*]*isen-*[*h*]*isen*) (Kunst 1949, 248). Tjakrahadikusuma included in the first category not only the suspended and boxed gongs (*gong, kethuk,* and *kempul*) but also the *saron demung* (a keyed metallophone), thus combining two types of instruments that two later Western musicologists (Kunst and Hood) saw as belonging to separate categories.

It is interesting to compare this classification of gamelan instruments with the one developed a few years later by the leading musicologist of the Dutch East Indies, Jaap Kunst (Kunst 1949, 247). Kunst divided the instruments into five categories, which he grouped according to their musical functions in gamelan works.

1. Those that play the so-called *cantus firmus,* or "nuclear theme" (in Javanese, the *balunganing gendhing,* "skeletal framework of a piece," also *balungan*), especially the keyed metallophones *saron demung* and *sarong barung*
2. The interpunctuating or colotomic (*dhongdhing gendhing*) instruments, which mark the structural periods; namely, the gongs (*gong, kempul, kenong, kethuk,* and *kempyang*) (Kunst invented the word "colotomic" for this purpose)
3. Those that play a more or less independent countermelody (presumably Kunst meant instruments such as the *rebab* and *suling* here)
4. The paraphrasing (Javanese, *panerusan*) instruments, which he subdivided into those that keep fairly close to the nuclear theme and those that supply variations or ornamental filling (Javanese, [*h*]*isenan*) to the theme; namely, the *bonang panerus, gender,* and *gambang*)
5. The agogic instruments, which set and control changes of tempo; namely, the drums *kendhang* and *ketipung*

The five categories of instruments are not mutually exclusive; the gong-chimes, for example, may belong to the first category in some works and to the fourth category in others.

Although Kunst's classification has proved helpful to many Western listeners in their efforts to comprehend gamelan music, and it has been accepted in partly modified form by some other foreign scholars (e.g., Hood 1954, 9–12),[13] most of the prewar and postwar Javanese theorists mentioned below used quite different categories. Kunst did not claim that his scheme was elicited from Javanese informants. Although Kunst gave Javanese names to four of his categories: *balunganing gendhing, dhongdhing gendhing, panerusan,* and (*h*)*isenan,* not all of these terms are generally used by Javanese theorists, who in any case either do not adhere or only partly adhere to Kunst's concept of the musical functions of the instruments of the gamelan. Significantly, Kunst himself noted that Tjakrahadikusuma did "not feel any essential difference—quite a defensible view, too—between colotomy (*dhongdhing gendhing*) and the nuclear theme (*balunganing gendhing*)," as he included the colotomic instruments in the same category as the *saron demung,* which he termed a "nuclear theme instrument" (Kunst 1949, 248). Nor, it seems, do contemporary Javanese musicians normally accept Kunst's distinction between what he calls colotomic instruments and instruments that play the nuclear theme.

Of the Western gamelan theorists, it was Judith Becker who attempted most thoroughly to base her categories on Javanese terms and concepts.

On the basis of her readings of works of Javanese musician-theorists, Becker rejected Kunst's use of the term *nuclear theme,* claiming that it places undue emphasis on the melodic role of the *saron barung,* which dominates in some pieces but not in others. She also rejected the terms *colotomy* and *elaborating parts* (Kunst's categories 2 and 4) in favor of the view that all instruments play parts representing grades of subdivision of the gong period (*gongan*) (Becker 1980, 34). Although she did not present a formal classification scheme of her own, she implied that she accepted a functional grouping whereby instruments are ordered according to the manner in which they subdivide the gong period.

With the help of various translators, Becker has begun to publish in English a series of volumes containing the writings of Javanese musicians and music theorists. (Becker 1984). Given the dearth of published and translated writings by indigenous musicians and theorists in Java (as in most other non-Western cultures), this book is a valuable data base and needs to be emulated for other cultures. Yet even the works of indigenous writers have, of course, to be read critically.

The most influential of contemporary Javanese theorists is the late R. L. Martopangrawit, two of whose contributions written in the early 1970s have been translated into English (1984). Martopangrawit introduces himself as a practicing musician, and his writings were intended to serve as a guide to his students of gamelan at the Academy of Music (ASKI) in Surakarta (1984, 8, 126). Like Sindoesawarno, he divided the instruments of a complete gamelan into two basic sections according to his concept of their musical function: (1) instruments relating to *irama* (i.e., tone density in relation to tempo, or levels of rhythmic-melodic filling [*cengkok*] between pulses, occurring in groups of four) and (2) instruments relating to *lagu* (i.e., arrangement of tones, or melody).

In the first (*irama*-related) category, the main drum is said to serve as the "supervisor" of the instruments and to provide the filling-in between pulses. Together the gong and cymbals (if present) serve as the "upholders" of the *irama,* though the various gongs each have specific musical functions too. In the second (*lagu*-related) category, the bowed stringed instrument (*rebab*) serves as the supervisor of the melody or melodic levels, with the various keyed metallophones, the xylophone, the gong-chimes, the flute, and the plucked strings serving as the upholders of melody. At the third level of division of this asymmetrical scheme, Martopangrawit divides the drums into four types, according to size and shape. For a diagram summarizing this classification, see figure 7.3.

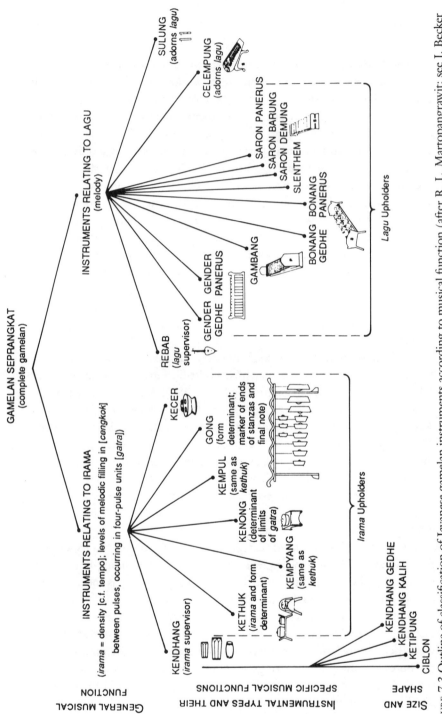

FIGURE 7.3 Outline of classification of Javanese gamelan instruments according to musical function (after R. L. Martopangrawit; see J. Becker 1984, 12–13; drawing designed by Kartomi)

Like Kunst's classification, this scheme of Martopangrawit's may serve as a useful aid for some listeners wishing to comprehend gamelan music. Martopangrawit's two categories contrast with Kunst's five; Kunst's categories 1, 3, and 4 are viewed as one category called *lagu,* and his categories 2 and 5 are seen as one category called *irama.* Both Martopangrawit and Kunst use the term *balungan* (*balunganing gendhing*) in their accounts of gamelan, though Martopangrawit sees more complexity in the concept than does Kunst (without, however, defining it) and gives a detailed discussion of the various types and roles of *balungan* (1984, especially 83–91). But he makes no mention of Kunst's other key concepts or terms, that is, *dhongdhing gendhing* used in the sense of colotomy, *panerusan* (he only mentions the *panerus*—higher-pitched, smaller-keyed—sizes of instruments—i.e., the higher-pitched *saron* and *bonang,* which are normally played at a higher degree of tone density than the *barung* sizes), and (*h*)*isen*-(*h*)*isen.*

It might be argued that Martopangrawit's scheme is not a purely traditional Javanese system but that it partly represents the individual view of its author, who was inspired by Sindoesawarno in his explanation of the rudiments of gamelan (verbal communication from Sumarsam). Martopangrawit's key terms—*lagu* and *irama*—are given specific and complex theoretical meanings that are not necessarily commonly used or understood as such by other musicians throughout the province of Central Java.

Moreover, Martopangrawit's choice of the *rebab* as one of the two leading gamelan instruments is based primarily on musical-functional reasoning. He felt the need to explain his reasons for choosing it: the *rebab* "has the authority to make decisions" and "determines the course of the melody" (1984, 15). It is true that the *rebab* is regarded as an anthropomorphic object in traditional thought. Its parts are named after the parts of the body, such as the head, ears, nostrils, neck, stomach, leg, and foot, as shown in figure 7.4. "The *rebab* is as a beautiful woman, an elder sister," wrote the poet Ko Mo An (verse 176, stanza 1; Kunst 1949, 229); indeed the *rebab* does play a relatively individualistic or personal melodic role in a gamelan work. However, in terms of spiritual and economic value as well as perceived beauty of tone and formal structural power, it is the gong that is traditionally regarded as being the supreme instrument of the gamelan,[14] with the lead drum (*kendhang*) also being accorded considerable spiritual and musical stature, controlling as it does such vital matters as structure, tempo, and the length of a performance. Martopangrawit chose the *rebab* and *kendhang* as the main instruments not because they are

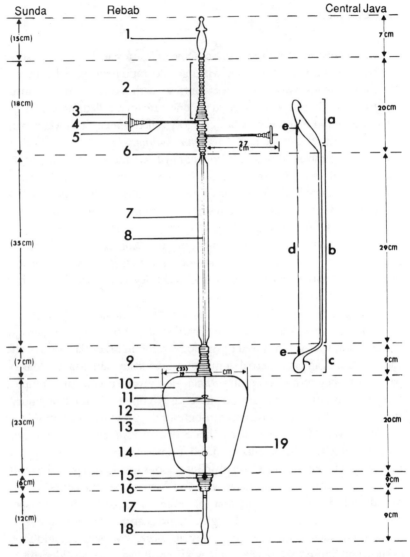

1   Menur, cahayan, or pucuk (halo)
2   Irah-irahan (head)
3   Kupingan (ears)
4   Kudping mlati (head of a
      jasmine flower)
5   Mangol or bapang (pegs)
6   Irung-irungan (nostrils)
7   Watangan (neck)
8   Kawat (strings)
9   Popor atas or umpak nginggil (collar)
10 Babad, usus-usus, or wangkis
      (stomach)

11 Srenten, inang, or tumpang sari
      (bridge or breast)
12 Batok (body)
13 Srawing
14 Seser
15 Cakil (nut)
16 Popor bawah or umpak ngisor or
      ngandap (collar)
17 Sukulan (leg)
18 Palemahan or sangga buwana (foot)
19 Nawa or lubang suara
      (sound holes)

a   Urang-urangan or buntuk telek   d   Yoga
b   Rangkung   e   Lombokan
c   Benda

FIGURE 7.4 Names of parts of the *rebab* (reproduced with permission from Falk
    1978, 59)

the only or most widely accepted high-status instruments but because their musical "supervising" roles fit into his concept or theory of gamelan. He did not explain if he inherited this theory; nor is it clear how he arrived at the particular ordering of instruments presented in figure 7.3, but possibly it was somewhat influenced by the degree of performing difficulty of these instruments as perceived in the academy in Surakarta.

Martopangrawit's scheme is important, then, not only because it is in part traditionally Javanese but also because it offers a well-informed, court-oriented, Surakarta musician's way of comprehending gamelan and classifying its instrumental parts in terms of their musical role.

Another scheme by a Javanese writer, Sulaiman Gitosaprodjo, is summarized in figure 7.5. Materials for his work (1984: 335–388) were compiled on the basis of lectures given by five teachers at the academy and the junior music high school in Surakarta, including Martopangrawit. Gitosaprodjo divides the instruments of the complete gamelan into twenty instrumental types, in no particular order except that he begins with the *rebab* and *kendhang* (after Martopangrawit) and ends with five optional instruments (three types of zither, xylophone, and flute). He divides the drums and gongs according to size and shape. All the instruments except the drums are divided according to the tone system used (*slendro, pelog bem,* or *pelog barang*) or tuning of individual gongs, recognizing that these tunings vary from gamelan to gamelan. Besides the instrumentation of the complete *gamelan ageng* ("great gamelan"), he presents a listing of the smaller, soft-sounding *gamelan klenengan* and the somewhat variable instrumentation of the even smaller and softer-sounding *gamelan gadhon* (1984: 343).

Of all the Javanese writers only Poerbapangrawit lends support to some of Kunst's categories, though he renamed some of them and added some of his own (1984, 20). His broad, sixfold classification is as follows:

1. The *balungan* (skeletal theme-playing) instruments, such as the *saron, demung,* and *slenthem*
2. The *rerenggan* (ornamentational) instruments, such as the *gender, gambang,* and *bonang*
3. The *wiletan* (variable formulaic melody) instruments (by which the *rebab* or male chorus [*gerong*] was presumably meant; see Poerbapangrawit 1984, 437, n. 1)
4. The *singgetan* (interpunctuating) instruments, including the gongs (*kempyang, kethuk, kempul, kenong,* and *gong*), which bind the ensemble together

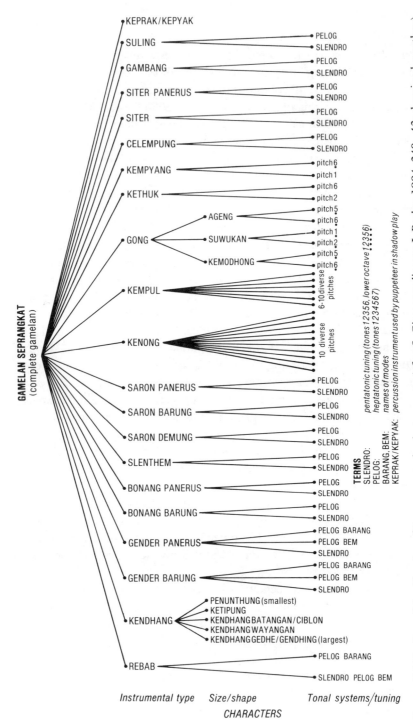

FIGURE 7.5 Outline of classification of Javanese gamelan instruments (after S. Gitosaprodjo; see J. Becker 1984, 340–43; drawing by author)

5. The *kembang* (literally "flowers") instruments, which include the more delicately embellishing flute and *pesindhen* (female vocalist)
6. The *jejeging wirama* (the tempo-regulating) instruments, such as the drums

Thus, Poerbapangrawit substituted a Javanese name for two of Kunst's categories (4 and 6 above), added another category (3) and distinguished two categories of embellishing instruments (2 and 5), compared with Kunst's one. The difference between the embellishing instrument categories is primarily that category (2) includes instruments that embellish mainly in metrical fashion while category (5) includes instruments that embellish in a relatively free-metered manner. Unlike most of his fellow Javanese theorists, Poerbapangrawit regards the female vocalist as an instrument. In this respect as well as in the fact that his scheme partly resembles Kunst's classification, Poerbapangrawit's scheme stands apart. His work preceded that of Martopangrawit.

The Javanese writer and gamelan musician Sumarsam received his musical education in Java and the United States. He presented his own theory of gamelan on which he based a classification of instruments. Sumarsam refuted Kunst's understanding of the concept of nuclear theme (*balungan*) and used it in the sense of "the melodic abstraction of a composition" (Sumarsam 1984, 112). "It seems that no instrument in the gamelan is solely responsible for the melodic motion in a gending. I believe that it is the individual musician's conception of melody, sung audibly or in their minds, that directs the melodic motion" (Sumarsam 1975, 7). To him the *saron* has no more important a role than the other instruments; its range is narrow; therefore, its player "can never completely succeed in following the inner melody. He therefore interprets a melody which flows in a smooth line within the melodic range of the *saron*" (1975, 11).

Sumarsam's classification of gamelan instruments is based on his perception of their musical roles in the gamelan (see fig. 7.6). He presents it in the form of a mandala. Its three intersecting parameters are arranged in concentric form: the instruments that carry the melody, or *lagu,* occupy the inner circle; the instruments that underline the structure of a work (the gongs) occupy the outer circle; and instruments that set up the timing of a work, control tempo, and signal a work's end occupy the open space surrounding the outer circle. The last two categories, time and structure, are not subdivided; they comprise the drums and the various gongs,

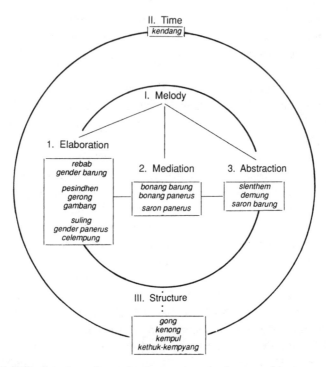

<small>FIGURE</small> 7.6 The function of gamelan instruments in the ensemble

respectively. "Instruments and vocalists that carry the melody in both single and more elaborate form," however, are subdivided into

1. Instruments with a relatively wide range that produce "elaborated melody," including free-metered instruments such as the flute (*suling*), bowed stringed instrument (*rebab*), and female voice (*pesindhen*) as well as instruments playing metrical parts such as the soft metallophones (*gender*), xylophone (*gambang*), and plucked strings (*celempung*)

2. The "melodically mediating" instruments, that is, those mediating between the first and third categories, including the gong-chimes (*bonang*) and loud metallophones (*saron panerus*)

3. The "abstracting" instruments, that is, those playing a "melodic abstraction" (*balungan*) of a composition within their one-octave range, such as the loud and soft metallophones (*saron barung, demung,* and *slenthem*) (Sumarsam 1984, 112)

   Like the classifications of instruments by the other Javanese musicians, this scheme reflects its author's personal theory about gamelan and inner melody. It is a remarkably thought-provoking and widely encompassing scheme that, although it is based partly on traditional concepts, is no less individualistic than the schemes of the other Javanese writers.

CONCLUSION

Though the Javanese have been engaged in literary activity for centuries, only recently has the knowledge of classifications of instruments been passed on in written form. Thus no ancient scheme has been passed down across the generations. However, the Javanese currently have several orally transmitted ways of classifying their instrumentarium as well as ways of classifying the gamelan ensemble in its various forms. They are generally single-step schemes based on the method of logical division.

Doubtless, there are various taxonomical ideas in the culture that can claim great age. The division of some groups of instruments into "female" and "male" pairs, where the female instrument is slightly larger than the male, is widespread in Southeast Asia and probably ancient. Vestiges of this classificatory idea are still to be found in Java, where pairs of gongs, gong-chimes, and drums are so distinguished. Four other principles of division, which are apparent in the traditional performance practice, are based on the practical demands of music making, namely, the tuning system, the size or tint of an instrument, loudness level, and spatial arrangement of the gamelan. We may observe another division based on musical practice: instruments used in a Muslim context are normally kept quite separate from those of the Tantric (pre-Muslim), the European-influenced, and other broad cultural strata resulting from the history of foreign contact in Java.

The high status bestowed on percussion instruments in Java contrasts strongly with the attitude toward them among the ancient Greeks, Arabs, and medieval and Renaissance Europeans, who regarded them as being inferior to strings and winds. This was partly on the grounds that their percussion instruments could not produce melody. In view of the fact that the Javanese have as rich a variety of percussion instruments as any other culture in the world, it is not surprising that some of these instruments, especially the great gong and the drum, are attributed with having a special spiritual potency. The mainstream Javanese concept of instruments is spiritually based.

The most distinctive of the orally transmitted Javanese taxonomies of instruments, however, is only indirectly related to the spiritual concept of instruments. Instead it is based on practical performing and timbral aspects. Its character of division—mode of sound excitation—governs classifications in many parts of the world, including the well-known three-category scheme used in Europe from Roman to modern times. However, this Javanese scheme is unusual cross-culturally in that it has four separate categories of beaten instruments distinguished by the motion of the players' hands (plus four other categories). There would be little point in dividing gamelan instruments into strings, winds, and percussion, or in applying the four Hornbostel and Sachs divisions, for the Javanese instrumentarium is exceedingly rich in types of percussion instruments, having only tiny categories of winds and strings. This scheme reflects the sensitivity of the Javanese ear to the timbres produced by the different kinds of objects used to excite sounds by striking on instruments.

The writing of treatises on music by Javanese authors was encouraged from the late nineteenth century by the colonial government and in recent decades by the national government. Thus contemporary Java offers the opportunity to observe not only old orally transmitted taxonomies but also the transition to scholar- or pedagogue-imposed schemes, schemes that are individual and unique but that nevertheless reflect traditional concepts and even, in some cases, precise foreign influences.

In the absence of a dominant ancient scheme, modern Javanese authors have been free to develop schemes based on the prevailing modern interest in performance practice and musical theory. Like most of the old schemes, the recently authored classifications are downward taxonomies, usually having two or three steps of division, though one is presented in the form of a mandala. None of the new schemes are totally divorced from traditional taxonomical ideas. The recent schemes differ from the old ones mainly in that they tend to be closer and more detailed, and in this they reflect their aim of teaching specialist music students. They are presented in passing as part of the author's larger music theory. Each offers an individual musician's way of understanding gamelan from the dominant, functional-musical concept of instrument on which the taxonomies are based. Each scheme divides the gamelan into categories of instruments according to the author's perception and interpretation of their functional roles in the whole texture of gamelan sound.

The diversity of schemes espoused by contemporary Javanese musicians was not widely known until the recent compilation and publication of their works in translation. The similarities between some of them is due partly to the enormous influence of the musician and theorist Martopangrawit. Some writers, however, resist his influence. Their personal views are influenced by the increasing individualism of the performing artists and teachers in Java, the demand for more clinical accounts and textbooks in the modern educational system, and Western musicologists and scholars, especially Kunst, whose name and the musical problems he isolated are well known to Javanese musician-scholars.

Kunst's classification of gamelan instruments was influenced not only by Javanese terms and concepts but also by his own Western musical and intellectual background. His translation of the term *balungan* by the Western musical concept of *cantus firmus* was a case in point. Another was his invention of the term *colotomy*, or punctuation patterns, for the analogy he saw between gong periodization in gamelan music and the grammar of language, whereby colotomic instruments became a category of his classification of instruments. Of the Javanese authors from Tjakrahadikusuma in the nineteenth century to the present day, only Poerbapangrawit accepted Kunst's division between the *balungan* and colotomy categories. However, his agogic instrument category resembles the *irama* (tempo compared to melodic density) category used by most Javanese theorists. His independent countermelody and melodic paraphrasing instrument categories very slightly resemble some aspects of two of the three subcategories of Sumarsam's melody category: melodic elaboration and melodic mediation, but of course Sumarsam's two subdivisions can only be understood in conjunction with his third, namely, the melodic abstraction of a composition.

EIGHT

Greek Taxonomical Thought from Archaic to Hellenistic Times

> It is strange how the divine art seems to operate and to do something even through inanimate things.
>
> For that the soul is moved naturally by music through instruments, everyone knows.
>
> Aristides Quintilianus[1]

Fascinated by the science of sound, including the sound of plucked strings and even the blacksmith's hammer,[2] Greek writers on music in the Hellenic archaic period gave a good deal of attention to acoustic experiments, especially those made on a stretched string, which was regarded as the theoretical instrument par excellence. Their interest in tunings, intervals, and consonance and the parallels they drew between their scientific findings and cosmology had far-reaching consequences during the common era in the development of the Western scientific approach and acoustical and musical science.

The dominant European classification of instruments from medieval to modern times had its origin in ancient Greek thought, which preferred stringed instruments to winds and gave the lowest place in the hierarchy to percussion instruments. The medieval preference for animate (vocal) to inanimate (instrumental) music also originated in Hellenic and Hellenistic times,[3] as did the belief that all motion produced sound and that therefore the movements of heavenly bodies produced constant though humanly inaudible sound that was called "music of the spheres." This music was believed to influence human behavior and emotions through the impact of its sympathetic vibrations on the soul.

The Greeks, then, preferred the human vocal instrument to all others. Both Plato (428–348 BCE) and Aristotle (384–322 BCE) expressed this preference. Plato banned inanimate instruments from his ideal city-state of the Republic but Aristotle saw them as a legitimate "mode of imitation"[4] (see his *Poetics* 1.4–5; and also *Problems,* 19.27.919B (*Problems,* 27).[5] In his tract *De anima,* he distinguished between "animate instruments" (*organon psychon*), which denote the human voice, and "inanimate instruments" (*organon apsychon*), which denote regular instruments such as strings and winds. Here *organon* means "mechanical contrivance" while *psychon* means "soul." Aristoxenos (c. 354–300 BCE) made the same distinction in his *Harmonica.* As we shall see in the next chapter, the idea of the priority of the vocal instrument persisted into and beyond the European Middle Ages.

Once Hellenic writers had made the distinction between animate and inanimate instruments, however, they had created a paradox—that sounds produced by nonliving objects can actually move the human passions.[6] What is the connection between a dead instrument and human feelings or character? This question was posed by the Hellenistic writer Aristides Quintilianus in the quotation at the head of this chapter, a question that he tried to solve by a theory of musical aesthetics that in fact contained a classification of the instruments of his time. This question also characterized the aesthetic thinking of a number of Western writers long after Aristides.[7] Of course, such a problem would not arise at all in the thought of societies with a more anthropomorphic concept of instruments, such as in the West African cultures that accept instruments as surrogate participants in musical events.

Originally the Greeks had partly answered the question with their religious concept of *katharsis,* or purification. The Pythagorean principle of the cathartic power of music[8] had its main source in Hellenic religion, or, more specifically, in Orphic beliefs. The Pythagoreans[9] introduced the idea that "music more than anything else serves to purify the soul" (Tatarkiewicz 1970, 82) through its cathartic power, which had both religious and ethical overtones.[10] Much later, Aristides Quintilianus presented another more complex solution to this question, as we shall see below.

Actually, the Greeks were much more interested in classifying musical knowledge and investigating sound and its effects on humans than they were in classifying instruments, which they relegated in any case to second place after the vocal instrument. Aristoxenos, for example, classified his complex concept of the "knowledge of music" in a five-step scheme, beginning with a major division into the theory and the practice. (Aristoxenos 1968).[11] Plato and Aristotle were very interested in classification itself, but neither they nor any other Greek writer produced a concrete classification of instruments to rival the eightfold scheme of China or the fourfold scheme of India. Implied in brief discussions of instruments by various Greek authors, however, is a two-category division comprising strings and winds that remained in vogue until the first few centuries CE.

To understand the beginnings of Greek classificatory ideas, which at first were only implied in the writings of Homer and others, it is necessary to look first at the relevant hierarchies of ratings of instruments and their associations with particular gods. An idea of the instruments used in the various periods of ancient Greek history may be drawn together from surviving drawings, marble statues and other objects of visual art dating from prehistoric Cycladean times (2800–2000 BCE) to the historic Hellenic era (750–300 BCE), as well as from literary evidence from the eighth century before the common era.[12] According to the Aegean sources, the Greek instrumentarium was restricted to certain kinds of *lyra*, *kithara* (a more elaborate kind of lyre), harps, and *aulos*-type instruments, which had one or two pipes (fig. 8.1). However, percussion instruments such as frame drums (*tympana*), castanets (*krotala*), and cymbals (*kymbala*) were used in the "orgiastic cults of Cybele and Dionysius, from which the former two infiltrated into light entertainment" (Winnington-Ingram 1980, 663).[13]

The Greeks clearly preferred stringed instruments to winds, while percussion instruments, which were apparently perceived as having no real musical or ethical value, came lowest in the hierarchy. Vase paintings and other sources show that percussion instruments were played around the Mediterranean from ancient Hellenic times; and though their use was noted by various Greek writers (e.g., Athenaeus 14.636C–D), their significance was slight. The Hellenic *lyra* may originally have come from the north and the *cithara* from Asia Minor (Sachs 1924, 45), but if so, the Greeks came early on to regard the *lyra* as their national symbol par excellence, while the *kithara* was held in great honor at national games and contests (Michaelides 1978, 168). The *lyra* was highly respected for its association with the cult of Apollo, god of reason and the arts. As the *lyra* was commonly played by amateurs, Plato saw it as being suited to the role of the free citizen while the *kithara* and the *aulos,* which were usually played by professional musicians, were not (Winnington-Ingram 1980, 663; Thomas Mathiesen, personal communication).[14] Plato, gave serious attention in his writings only to the *kithara*- and *aulos*-type instruments and, as we have noted, banned them from his Republic for not being morally uplifting. Aristotle similarly referred to two types of instruments, mentioning that the playing of the *aulos* or *kithara* by a soloist required

FIGURE 8.1 A youth plays the *aulos* while a girl dances, accompanying herself with the rhythm of the *krotala*. Attic vase, early fifth century. (Reproduced by courtesy of the Trustees of the British Museum)

some kind of exhibitionism and virtuosity and therefore should be omitted from the educational curriculum, for virtuosity was a quality associated with vulgar, not free-born, men. The *aulos* in particular was seen as being distracting and exciting and therefore not morally beneficial. *Kithara*-type instruments were preferred to winds largely because they were associated with Apollo, while *aulos*-type instruments were associated more with the cult of the god of passion, Dionysius, than the god Apollo.

These associations were not always clear-cut. For example, although the strings were mostly associated with Apollo and the winds with Dionysius, the stringed instrument *barbitos* (fig. 8.2) was nearly always shown in scenes with Dionysius (Thomas Mathiesen, letter of September 1987). A legend recounted in Sendrey (1974, 287) attributes the inven-

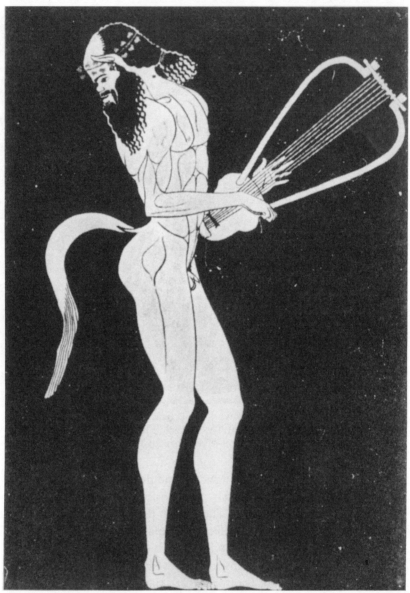

FIGURE 8.2 A satyr playing the *barbitos*. Having swept the plectrum across the strings, he damps some with the fingers of his left hand. Attic vase, late sixth or early fifth century. (Reproduced by kind permission of the Press Syndicate, University of Cambridge, publishers of Andrew Barker's *Greek Musical Writings*, vol. 1, *The Musicians and His Art*)

tion of the double *aulos* to Marsyas, a Phrygian demon. Athena, on seeing in her mirror how her beautiful face was disfigured by blowing the *aulos,* angrily threw away and cursed the pipes. The Phrygian musician Marsyas found and restored them and, becoming a master on the instrument, challenged Apollo to a musical contest with the Muses as judges. On their declaring Apollo (who played the lyre) the winner, Athena's curse took effect and the loser was subjected to the power of his victor, who flayed Marsyas alive. As Sendrey pointed out, "the saga . . . reflects the difference between two kinds of music–the playing of the sweet-stringed instruments and the orgiastic sound of the Phrygian *aulos*" (1974, 287). The art of the *aulos* was, nevertheless, held in high esteem. *Aulos*-type instruments played a very prominent part in Greek social life, being used in many ceremonies, processions, dramas, national games, banquets, and dance performances as well as to regulate the movements of rowers and the marching of soldiers (Michaelides 1978, 42–46). They were played solo or with the voice or a stringed instrument.

The oldest representations of musicians with instruments from the Aegean region are found on marble statues on graves from the southern Cyclades and the south–west Anatolian coast, an area belonging to the younger period of Cycladean culture (c. 2200–2000 BCE). (see Aign 1963, 29ff). Other sources reveal that the double *aulos* and a metal bugle called *sistrum* occurred on Crete in 2200 BCE; that bells, lyres, harps, and *aulos*-type instruments were played in the early Greek Minoan period (2000–1400 BCE); that harps, lyres, and *aulos*-type instruments were found in western Anatolia and the islands from c. 800 to c. 600 BCE, and that the early Greek Mykenian culture (1400–1100 BCE) had *aulos*-type instruments, harps, and the percussion instrument called *kymbala* (small cymbals) (see Aign 1963, 49, 54–55, 78, 106).[15] Several sources deal with the social role of musical instruments in Hellenic society. For example, Aign hypothesizes that music and instruments were cult-bound in the prehistoric era (2800–2000 BCE) and were slightly secularized from the early Minoan period on Crete, when music was still controlled by priests but was used to accompany ecstatic dances by female *lyra* players.

The most important early literary sources mentioning instruments are the *Iliad,* dated about 750 BCE, and the *Odyssey,* dated about 720 BCE. Mention is made of three wind instruments called *aulos, syrinx,* and *salpinx* and of two stringed instruments named *kitharis* (which later became known as the *kithara*) and *phorminx*. The *syrinx* was a set of Greek panpipes used by shepherds from the sixth century BCE[16] and the *salphynx* was a trumpet (Aign 1963, 292, 78).

The *aulos* and other wind instruments, however, are not often mentioned in the epics and the contexts of the references suggest that the term *aulos* meant "reeds" or "sound reeds." Only after the time of Homer did *aulos* come to mean *aulos*-type wind instruments, which suggests that they were not of Greek Mykenian origin (Aign 1963, 292ff.). Husmann believed that the *aulos* came to Greece from Syria through Asia Minor (1938, 36–37).

Homer's discussions of instruments implied a division into strings and winds, though this division was never stated. Indeed, general terms for "strings" and "winds" did not exist until the late Hellenistic period. In the absence of such terms most Greek writers, such as Aristotle, referred simply to "*kithara*-type instruments" (citharoetics) and "*aulos*-type instruments" (auletics) (Tatarkiewcicz 1970, 19).

Though Hellenic writers did not produce clear-cut classifications of instruments, some did point in their theoretical expositions on sound to the existence of various higher, louder, or more acute sounds and to the difference between continuous as opposed to discontinuous sounds, which could be demonstrated with the help of musical instruments. These concerns were also taken up by some Hellenistic and medieval writers, such as Archytas, Aristoxenos, Ptolemy, Nicomachus, and Porphyry (Hickmann 1971, 25).[17] Thus, Aristoxenos's *Harmonikon* mentioned Aristotle's animate and inanimate instruments, subdividing them into those producing continuous as opposed to discontinuous sounds. By continuous sounds he meant sounds of indefinite pitch that are unsuitable for interval and melody building, as in the case of the speaking voice. By discontinuous sounds he meant sounds of definite pitch that fulfill the requirements for music making, such as the singing voice (Hickmann 1971, 26). This dichotomous idea persisted well into the European Middle Ages and may partly explain the Greek preference for melodic stringed and wind instruments over nonmelodic percussion.

Though not really interested in classifying instruments, Aristotle was interested in the principles and methods of classifying per se; in fact, he "was a master of classification" (Tatarkiewcicz 1970, 141). He presented two different classificatory methods. In his earlier writings on logic he expounded the method of classifying by logical division, a method that had already been presented in the writings of Plato. However, in his later work on biology, Aristotle ridiculed the idea of classifying biological species in a logically based, downward hierarchy. Being interested in species rather than genera, he classified his specimens by an upward method based on detailed inspection of their characteristics. As Mayr (1982, 150) noted, however, Aristotle's followers throughout and even beyond the Middle Ages were misled by the use of biological examples in his writings on logical division and applied this method even in their biological classifications. Only in the eighteenth and nineteenth centuries did biologists shift to Aristotle's original idea of upward division for biological specimens. From the Greek classical period until relatively recent times, the study of both musical instruments and biological specimens was dominated by an essentialist concept of the instruments and the specimens in question were regarded as being essentially stable, unchanging entities. This concept had been expounded by Plato, was adhered to by the Thomists of the Middle Ages, and was influential in the West until modern times.

One assumption made by the Greeks that had far-reaching musical consequences was the idea that all regular motion necessarily produces sound, including the motion of the planets. Like the Chinese and the Babylonians, the Greeks associated the movements of the planets with music. Convinced of the harmonious nature of the universe, to which the Pythagoreans gave the name of *kosmos* ("order"), they thereby introduced an aesthetic feature into cosmology (Tatarkiewicz 1970, 81) and indulged in far-reaching speculations about the cosmic order. They thought that the universe produced a music of the spheres, a belief that persisted for millennia as a topic in European treatises on music.

Pythagoras explained the music of the spheres in terms of harmonic relationships among the planets as governed by their proportional speed of revolution and their fixed distance from the Earth. This postulation was the basis of the belief that the universe was ordered by numerical proportions that produce musical harmonies, a belief that resulted in detailed investigations by the Pythagoreans and a number of Hellenistic writers into the theory of tones, proportions, and tunings. Analogies made by Pythagoras between musical consonances were derived from the proportionate lengths of a stretched string, or monochord. The fact that Greek writers such as Pythagoras, Ptolemy, and Aristides Quintilianus found stretched strings indispensable in illustrating their theories of sound lent stringed instruments a prestige and superiority over other instruments, in addition to their being preferred for being an expression of Greek national character. Thus a distinction was made between theoretical and practical instruments, i.e., instruments used for theorizing about sound versus instruments used for practical music making, a division that was transmitted to Arabic and late medieval treatise writers. In other words, knowledge of music and instruments had both a theoretical and a practical aspect; this was believed to be so at least as early as the time of Aristoxenos, at the beginning of the Hellenistic age.

The harmony of the spheres formed part of the concept and classification of instruments presented by the most important theorist and historian of Greek music in late Hellenistic times: Aristides Quintilianus (second to fourth century CE), who was the author of *On Music in Three Books* (*Peri musikes* or *De musica libri tres*).[18] Aristides presented a classification of musical knowledge as well as of instruments.

In his first scheme (fig. 8.3) he divided his objects of inquiry into two categories: stringed and wind instruments, the character of division being their mode of sound production, which linked them to the cosmos and, by sympathetic response, to their ethical influence on the soul. Strings are analogous to the "plaited" lines of the orbits of the planets. As he put it, "the lines of the planetary orbits are plaited into a latticework of strands (or arteries), the surfaces of the orbits become membranes, and the aeroid breath of the earthly region is infused" (Aristides 1983, 37). Instruments, Aristides observed, are "similarly caused to sound: string instruments with strands, wind instruments with breath. Therefore, the soul will naturally experience sympathetic responses to instruments, and this is proven with an example of the sympathetic vibration of strings" (Aristides 1983, 37). Even the superiority of stringed instruments could be explained by his theory. By analogy with the strands of the heavenly orbits, the strings represented the higher regions while the winds represented the lower or inferior regions.[19]

Aristides could have included drums in his scheme by analogy with the membranes mentioned in the account quoted above, but in line with mainstream ancient Greek tradition he did not attribute favorable ethical qualities to them or other percussion instruments.

His second scheme (fig. 8.3) comprised three steps of symmetrical logical division. Remarkably, his chosen character of division was based on a theory of human character that provided another answer to the question as to how lifeless instruments can have an emotional effect on men and women. In this scheme he divided instruments into male, female, and medial types, where the character of division was the believed stimulus of musical instruments vis-à-vis his categories of human beings, that is men, effeminate men, masculine women, and women. The character stimulus

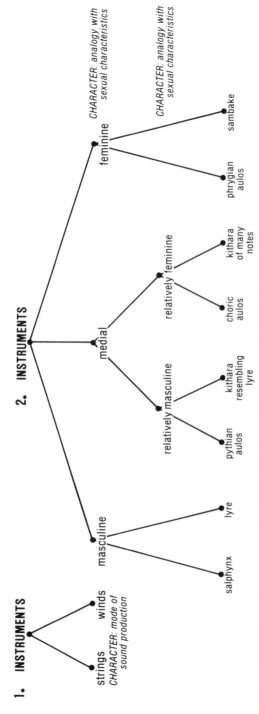

FIGURE 8.3 Schematic representations of classifications of instruments by Aristides Quintilianus

attributed to each instrument served to link it to the universal order. The "vehement" wind instrument called *salpinx* and the "deep," "rugged" lyre were said to be "analogous to the masculine part," while the "mournful," "threnodic" Phrygian *aulos* was seen as analogous to "femininity." The stringed *sambuke* (*samby ke, sambake*) was also regarded as being appealing to feminine listeners "because it is both ignoble and brings itself around to a condition of faintness through very high pitch because of the smallness of its strings" (Aristides 1983, 149–50).

Of the medial instruments, the Pythian *aulos* "participates more in masculinity because it is grave" (Aristides 1983, 149), as does also the *kithara* "of many notes." Though he did not mention all the instruments of his culture, Aristides observed that the nature of each can be inferred from his classification. After perusing it, the nature of other instruments "is no longer difficult to discern, since we have in general the characteristics by which we shall subjoin the particular instruments" (Aristides 1983, 150).

The view given by Aristides of the various kinds of male and female "character" as expressed by instruments was not just his subjective notion but was probably based on a widely held idea that reflected among other things the contemporary view of masculine superiority. A similar view about the sexual character of music itself had been attacked by Philodemus (c. 110–40/35 BCE), who claimed that the purported stimulus of music on which ethos theory was based was not general and that it only affected people of a certain type, principally women and effeminate men. He proposed that it be explained psychologically without reference to any particular power of music (Tatarkiewcicz 1970: 224).

The majority of Greek writers, however, believed that music and instruments had special power to move human listeners. Aristides explained this as follows: "The soul is a certain harmonia, and harmonia exists through numbers." Therefore, "because music is also so organised, the passions are moved through mimesis or sympathy" (Aristides 1983, 36).

Like Aristoxenos and many medieval writers after him, Aristides also presented a classification of the knowledge of music, dividing it into two large categories: the theoretical and the practical. By theory he meant "an act of contemplation" or "what might now be called precompositional theory," while by practice he meant "doing something," or what might now be called the theory of composition and performance (Palisca 1980, 741). Theoretical knowledge, he argued, had "natural causes" (including the arithmetic) and "technical rules" (the harmonic, rhythmic, and metric), while practical knowledge included the application of musical science (melic and rhythmic composition and poesy) and its instrumental, odic, and theatric expressions (Aristides 1983, 37). Instruments were seen as a necessary addition to the human voice because they enable us "to operate most effectively" (Aristides 1983, 149). Moreover, "just as the same voice and harmonia do not naturally happen to delight every hearer—but rather one is able to cheer some hearers and another others, so also it is the case with instruments: to whichever notes each person is likened by ethos these he loves and marvelled at in the suitable of the instruments" (Aristides 1983, 149).

As we have noted, the Greeks in the archaic and classical periods viewed instruments as comprising strings and winds. Aristides' formal classification also divided instruments into these two categories, while his presentation of the "character" of instruments divided them into four. However, this distinction, which was made at the second and third levels of division, was basically a grouping of sexually based human character rather than a division of instruments, despite the fact that it actually resulted in their fourfold classification.

A number of classifications of instruments were presented by middle to late Hellenistic writers, based in most cases on a larger inventory of instruments than used in Hellenic writings (Hickmann 1971, 30). Most of the early schemes had two major categories, but this was soon to change to three. The earliest sign of a shift from two-category to three-category classification is found in the theory of sound presented by Nicomachus in his work *Handbook of Harmonies* (*Enchiridion harmonikes*), written at the end of the first century CE. Mirroring the ancient Greek view that vocal music was superior to instrumental music, he mentioned that besides the human voice there were instruments fashioned after it and that they included strings, winds, and percussion instruments. As Hickmann points out, he was not thereby developing an independent three-category classification, but he foreshadowed its development (1971, 30).[20]

Some other Hellenistic writers, however, maintained the old divisions of strings and winds. An extremely interesting two-category scheme was presented in the second half of the second century CE by the Greek rhetorician Pollux in a chapter entitled "De musica" in his work *Omnastikon*. Pollux divided quite a large group of instruments into two categories entitled percussion and wind, where percussion included what were later regarded as two categories: strings and percussion (Hickmann

1971, 32). Like Aristides, Pollux relegated wind instruments to second place. His extensive description of the *aulos* (see H. Becker 1966, 20ff.) was divided first by function and then by morphological aspects. The scheme was illustrated by the largest list of instruments ever assembled in a Greek treatise, including Greek instruments of past and present epochs as well as instruments from neighboring cultures (Hickmann 1971, 32).[21]

As in West African cultures, the operative character of division in Pollux's logical, two-category scheme was the way the player excites sounds on the instruments. To strike an instrument and to bend or pluck a string with the hand were regarded as essentially similar actions on the part of the performer. Remarkably, this twofold classification of instruments into percussion (including strings) and wind instruments persisted in medieval and even post-medieval Europe.

The first full-blown three-category taxonomy of instruments known to us was presented by Porphyry (243 to the early fourth century CE). In his work *Ptolemai harmonica,* he divided instruments into the blown, stringed, and beaten varieties, not forgetting to mention the traditional category of "living voices." He based his classification of strings on a morphological attribute: the possession of strings. He grouped winds and percussion according to mode of sound production blowing and beating. Although Porphyry's three-category model is technically less logical than Pollux's two-category one, it became the dominant scheme in the ensuing one and a half millennia of Western history.

CONCLUSION

The Hellenic division of instruments into animate and inanimate was accompanied by an implied twofold classification of inanimate instruments into stringed and wind instruments. Ignoring percussion, the Hellenic Greeks preferred strings to winds because they saw the *kithara* as a national symbol, considered that strings had a superior moral effect on human beings when compared with winds, and found stretched strings to be an indispensable aid in conducting scientific experiments and theorizing about sound.

To the Greeks the human vocal instrument was superior to all inanimate instruments. Having divided instruments in this way however, they had then to try and explain how inanimate instruments can affect human emotions and character. The cult-bound concept of music and instruments held from the archaic period linked *kithara*-type instruments to Apollo, together with the morally superior quality of restraint, while *aulos*-type instruments were often linked to Dionysius and passionate expression. Moreover, as the sounds of stringed and wind instruments were considered to be analogous to the music of the spheres, these instruments were believed to influence the human soul through its sympathetic responses to them. However, it was the strings that were considered to be superior in this respect. These associations and analogies persisted in Greek culture for about a millennium and were eventually transmitted into medieval European thought as well.

Though most Greek writers from archaic times mentioned or discussed stringed and wind instruments, clear classifications of instruments are found only in the works of some writers in later Hellenistic times. These authors considered instruments to be essentially stable, unchanging entities, and when they classified them, they used the method of logical division in single-step form. Two schemes emerged: the two-category Pollux model, distinguishing percussion (including strings) and winds, and the three-category Porphyry model, including string, wind, and percussion categories. Only one scheme, that of Aristides, had three steps of symmetrical logical division. He used characters of division based on the appeal of the various instruments to the four proposed human sexual types. By dividing instruments according to a theory of human sexual character, Aristides suggested one more solution to the problem of how to explain the emotional effect of lifeless instruments on human beings.

National Identity and Other Themes of Classification in the Arab World

Each people has instruments reflecting its nature.

al-Kindī, ninth century CE[1]

According to an Arabic legend:

Hishām b. al-Kalbī mentioned that the first who made the *'ūd* and played on it was a man of the sons of Qābīl, some say Qabīn, the son of Ādam, called Lāmak. He had a long life; and as he had no children he married fifty wives and took two hundred concubines. Then two girls, one of whom was called Silā and the other Yamm, were born to him. Afterwards a boy was born to him ten years before he died, and he was extremely pleased. But the boy died when he was five years old, and Lāmak grieved sorely for him. So he took him and hung him on a tree and said: 'His form will not depart from my eyes until he falls in pieces, or I die'. Then his flesh began to fall from his bones till only the thigh remained, with the leg, foot and toes. So he took a piece of wood, split it, made it thin, and began to arrange one piece on another. Then he made a sound chest to represent the thigh, a neck to represent the leg, a peg-box the same size as the foot, and pegs (*malāwī*) like the toes; and to it (the instrument) he attached strings like the sinews. Then he began to play on it and weep and lament, until he became blind; and was the first who sang a lament. What he made was called an *'ūd* because it was made from a piece of wood (*'ūd*).[2]

As this legend indicates, traditional Arab belief holds that the *'ūd*—a short-necked lute that was considered to be the foremost of Arabic instruments—was invented by Lāmak (a son of Ādam), who used it to lament the death of his son.[3] Its attributed anthropomorphic qualities include a capacity for speech.[4] This story of the invention of the *'ūd* is part of a classification of some of the most important instruments in Arabic culture[5] based on their myths of origin. The classification also includes the *ṭanābīr* (long-necked lute), which was said to have been invented by Lot's people, who tried to appeal to an attractive beardless youth by playing the *ṭunbūr* (lyre) to him. *Mazāmīr* (wind instruments) were said to have been created by the children of Israel and to have been modeled on the throat of David. The *ma'āzif* (a stringed instrument) and drums, instruments of diversion (*malahī*), were said to have been invented by the daughters of Lāmak, while the invention of the *tubul* and *dufuf* (double-headed and frame drums) was attributed to Tubal, a member of the musical family of Lamech, father of Jubal, who is said (in Genesis 4) to have invented music itself.

This so-called little tradition of musical thought has "usually either been ignored or regarded as inferior by the elite and the intellectuals—that is to say, the pillars of the Great traditions" (Shiloah 1986, 110). A good deal of research needs to be made into these orally transmitted classifications. Much more is known about the long tradition of written classifications of instruments in Arab treatises. These treatises reveal that the early theorists of the Arabian empire were less interested in systematic studies of instruments than in considering them as a means of elucidating aspects of musical theory or reflecting national identity, as we shall see in what follows. Their main endeavors were devoted to such theoretical matters as the scales played on the instruments, theory of proportions, and theory of ethos. These scholars were strongly influenced by the Greek musical treatises, the most important of which, from Aristotle on, had been translated into Arabic from about the middle of the ninth century.

The prolific writings of the theorist al-Kindī, who died after 870, reflected the juxtaposition of Greek and Arab theory (Farmer 1966, 11). al-Kindī, who revered the works of the ancients (without mentioning particular authors' names) and adopted a similar theoretical stance, began to adapt and transform their ideas according to his own Arab background and purpose. He discussed the dimensions and construction of the *'ūd,* which he called the "instrument of philosophers" (Shiloah 1979a, 258). However, he did so primarily with larger theoretical matters in mind, including the theory of harmonic proportions, and these matters were linked to his interests in cosmology and numerology. In his *Kitāb al-muṣawwitāt al-watariyya min dhāt al-watar al-wāḥid ilā dhāt al-'asharat awtār* (Book of sounding stringed instruments of one to ten strings), he speculated on the correspondences of music, relating the four strings of the *'ūd* to the elliptic arcs, zodiac, position of the stars, seasons, days, ages, elements, winds, humors, colors, faculties of the soul, and character (Shiloah 1979a, 255). He linked instruments to the doctrine of ethos, seeing them as creators of harmony between the soul and the universe. He also linked instruments to the character of human groups, for "each people has instruments reflecting its nature" and "each instrument is said to express the specific beliefs and characteristics of the group to which it belongs" (Shiloah 1979a, 254). Thus, the character of Indians was said to be expressed by the one-stringed instrument, the nature of the Khorasanians by the two-stringed instrument, the character of the Byzantines by the three-stringed instrument, and the nature of three peoples—the Byzantines, the Greeks, and the Babylonians—by the four-stringed instrument (Shiloah 1979a, 254). At one level, al-Kindī's account gives recognition of a sociological observation that the national character of the peoples mentioned was partly defined in terms of the instrument mainly used by them, but on another level it draws together data about that sociological fact in the form of a one-step classification.

In similar fashion, the Iranian geographer Ibn Khurrādādhbih (d. 911) mentioned in his lexicographical discussion of instruments that the *ghandūrā* (lute) was the typical instrument of the Nabateans, that the *urghūn* (organ), *shilyānī* (probably harp or lyre), *lūrā* (lyre), and *ṣalandj* (probably a bagpipe) were typical of the Byzantines, and that the *kankala* (a one-stringed instrument) was typical of the Indians (Shiloah 1979a, 193–94). These national characterizations, like materials presented in other early Arabic treatises, may have been based on tradition rather than observation,[6] but their use as a character of division is a long-standing practice in Arab tradition. Associations of national character with chosen instruments persisted as one of the themes of Arab classification throughout the centuries.

al-Fārābī, who died in 950, was different. He restricted his discussion to Arab as opposed to foreign (particularly Greek) music; he once reproached al-Kindī for referring to Greek rhythms rather than to those known by Arabs (Shiloah 1979a, 101). However, the unique approach he took to the study of instruments was due not only to his Arab focus but to the fact that he himself was an accomplished musician who was able to bring his practical performing skills to bear on his scholarly work (Hickmann 1971, 67). His musical skills and talents as an *ʿūd* player were praised in several Arabic sources (Farmer [1929] 1973, 175), and his practical skills and knowledge are used in good stead in his writings on instruments. Though he borrowed openly from the Greeks, but not from any particular Greek writer, he based a great part of his investigations on the living music of his time, which used a large number of kinds of instruments.[7]

In his *Iḥṣa al-ʿulūm* (Classification of the sciences), which was known from the late Middle Ages in several Latin translations in medieval Europe (see discussion of Gundissalinus in chap. 10), al-Fārābī divided the art and science of music according to established practice into *musica speculativa* and *musica practica,* discussing instruments under both categories. His treatises show him to be a child of his time in many respects. His practical interests did not exclude his paying attention to traditional theoretical matters such as scales, tunings, fretting of strings, and the like. However, with the exception of one scheme, al-Fārābī directed his attention to instruments used in practical performance as opposed to those constructed for theoretical purposes or demonstration (d'Erlanger 1930, 304). Much more than the other Arab as well as early Greek and Latin writers, his schemes were based on a detailed knowledge of the morphological and acoustic qualities of instruments. To him the theory and the practice were inseparable, indeed complementary to each other. It was this realization, perhaps, that enabled him to establish the theory of instruments as part of the discipline of music theory (Hickmann 1971, 66–67).

His two-book treatise *Kitāb al-mūsīḳī al-kabīr* (The grand book on music) was one of the most systematic and comprehensive of Arab studies on music (Shiloah 1979a, 104). In it he presented a novel approach to organology, for it was based partly, as has been mentioned, on the standpoint of the practical musician. In the first book he described the *ʿūd,* which he followed with a discussion of (1) two types of *ṭunbūr* (long-necked lute), (2) flutes and reed winds, and (3) the bowed, stringed *rabāb,* making a further distinction between the categories of plucked, stopped strings, bowed strings, and open strings on the one hand and wind instruments on the other. Single- and double-reed instruments were grouped at this level into the one category.

al-Fārābī presented four classifications of instruments. In his introduction to his *Grand Book* he presented a fivefold classification of instruments (d'Erlanger 1930, I, 21–22).[8] In his scheme he included inanimate instruments and the human voice as well as, remarkably, dance.[9] That is, he divided instruments into the following categories: (1) the human voice, (2) the *rabāb* and wind instruments, (3) (plucked) stringed instruments, (4) percussion instruments such as tambourines and drums, and (5) dance. The character of division was duration (of tones or dance movements respectively). The most highly rated instrument was the human voice because it can produce sounds of long duration. In this respect al-Fārābī was reflecting "the belief in the entire primacy of vocal music in almost all the Near-Eastern musical traditions" (Shiloah 1979a, 405). The *rabāb* and the wind instruments, which resemble the human voice in that they can maintain a long-lasting sound, were of second rank, while plucked strings took third place, as they produce tones that die relatively quickly. Percussion instruments were given a low ranking on the grounds that they cannot produce long-lasting tones. Dance was rated last because its movements are regarded as being of short duration.

Another of his schemes distinguished between instruments well suited to produce "natural" and "consonant" tones and those less well suited. al-Fārābī defined his terms as follows: "If our ears receive an internal sound which is agreeable, it is consonant (*muttafiq*). If our ears are not pleased it is dissonant (*mutanāfir*)" (Farmer 1965, XVII). By "natural" and "consonant" he meant all tones and melodies played by inhabitants of the Arabian empire; and they were said to be best produced by the short- and long-necked lutes and *rabāb* (d'Erlanger 1930, 39ff.).

In another scheme, al-Fārābī classified selected instruments, though not always in clearly ordered groups, according to their usefulness in demonstrating aspects of music theory. He wrote that all instruments were created for practical purposes and none for theoretical purposes; however, some are more suitable than others for theoretical demonstrations (d'Erlanger 1930, 304). He regarded stringed instruments as being more suitable than wind instruments for the purpose (d'Erlanger 1930, 39ff.), and chose the construction of an instrument of the zither type for experimental verification of certain theoretical features (Shiloah 1979a, 105).

Finally, al-Fārābī presented a classification that was more complex and closer in form than the others. Like Porphyry's scheme, al-Fārābī's was based on the method of sound activation. But unlike Porphyry, he omitted percussion instruments and gave a two-category classification. This consisted of stringed and wind instruments, where the former were distinguished by the fact that they made sounds by setting their strings in motion and the latter by the fact that they were sounded by blowing. At the second step, the strings were subdivided according to performance technique into the bowed and the plucked, while wind instruments were divided into those with and without finger holes, as well as into those with one or two reeds. Classification at the lower steps was unsystematic, covering only a small selection of instruments. For example, instruments that produce one tone per string (such as harps and lyres) were classified separately from instruments that produce several tones per string (such as the lute and the *rabāb*). He chose the *rabāb* for classification according to whether they had one, two, or four (two pairs of) strings, not specifying this character of division for other kinds of instruments such as harps and lyres; and he subdivided the double-reed instruments into separated double and bound double reeds (Hickmann 1971, 64–66).

In his *Kitāb iḥṣā ʿal-īḳā ʿāt* (Book on the classification of rhythms), al-Fārābī briefly mentioned percussion and concussion instruments but did not discuss them (Shiloah 1979a, 101). Clearly he did not rate them highly. Despite the later preference of Muslims for frame drums, Arab writers have traditionally regarded percussion instruments as having low status, as particularly evidenced by treatises dating from the twelfth century. Beaten instruments were associated either with "black people," whose culture they identified with drumming and dancing, or with "folk" music, which they regarded as inferior to "art" music (Amnon Shiloah, verbal communication). Metal instrumental sounds were used in exorcism and putting demons and ghosts to flight from antiquity onward (Shiloah 1979b, 400).

Like the early Greek and Latin schemes, then, all of al-Fārābī's classifications except for one divided a specific instrumentarium into two categories, though different ones in each case. The other divided his broad concept of instruments, which included the human voice and dance, into five categories. al-Fārābī classified by logical division, but in very broad fashion, with only one or two symmetrically applied steps. In the last of his classifications, further subdivisions were formally or informally presented in the detailed descriptions of some groups of instrumental types. Double reeds were logically subdivided at the fourth step of his division of winds, and *rabābs* at the third step of his division of strings. But these divisions were not applied explicitly across the board. The first three classifications also differed from the last one in that they covered the whole instrumentarium of the Arabian empire as opposed to only the stringed and wind instruments in the fourth. Single-character division was the rule at each step; and the different characters which were applied clearly distinguished each scheme from the other.

In some respects, al-Fārābī's schemes did not differ radically from those of the Greek and Latin writers before him. The main differences between al-Fārābī's and their schemes are the much greater interest shown by al-Fārābī in the detailed practical study of performed instruments, the partly different instrumentaria, and the different concepts of instruments. An example of a conceptual difference is the character of division chosen for al-Fārābī's first classification, namely, the consonant and dissonant tones produced by instruments of the empire as opposed to unnatural and dissonant tones sounded by instruments from outside its borders, a character based on a local, culturally conditioned concept of instruments and music. Although some of his European counterparts established divisions on the basis of religious and ethical concerns, al-Fārābī did not make such distinctions. Yet his classifications of instruments into the theoretical and the practical is reminiscent of Aristotle, Ptolemy, and other Greek as well as Roman writers, while the variable governing the first step of the fourth scheme—method of sound activation—also governed schemes of Aristides, Pollux, Boethius, and Isidor. Morphological characters of division were not yet common; al-Fārābī used a morphological character to distinguish wind instruments only in the second step of the fourth scheme, rather like his predecessor Pollux, who subdivided winds at the third step according to a morphological character. al-Fārābī, like the European writers before him, gave supremacy to the human vocal instrument and to instruments producing sounds resembling it.

Many manuscripts by Arab, Turkish, Egyptian, and other scholars written in the region during the second millennium give attention to musical instruments, as documented in Shiloah's book of 1979. Some of these sources give measurements for and describe the parts of the instruments, regarding them with a typically classical theoretical detachment. Others offered selective lists of instruments for a particular purpose of the author, without necessarily paying attention to classificatory principles, though these are sometimes inherent in the presentations.

Ibn Sīnā, who was born of Persian parents and died in 1037, discussed instruments at length in his *Kītāb al-shifā'* (Book of healing [of the soul]). After discussing composition he included a section on instruments, which he subdivided into four stringed categories, two wind categories with three subcategories, and one idiophone category:

1. Fretted, plucked instruments, such as the *barbaṭ* (a kind of *ʿūd*) and the *ṭunbūr* (short and long-necked lutes)
2. Nonfretted (open), plucked strings, as exemplified by the *shahrūd* (board zither)
3. Lyres and harps, such as the *shilyāk* (lyre) and *ṣandji* (harp)
4. Bowed strings, such as the *rabāb*

5. Winds, including reed instruments (*mizmār*), *surnāy* (flute), and *mizmār al-djarab* (bagpipe)
6. Other wind instruments, such as the *urghanūn* (organ)
7. The stick-beaten instrument called *sanṭūr* (board zither)

This scheme emphasized the diversity of stringed instruments and their high rating, subdividing them in classical Arab fashion into the open and the stopped as well as the plucked and the bowed. The main character of division was the mode of sound excitation: categories 1, 2, and 3 are plucked, category 4 is bowed, category 5 is blown, category 6 is fingered, and category 7 is beaten.

In another work, *Kitāb al-nadjāt* (Book of the delivery), Ibn Sīnā borrowed one of al-Fārābī's two-category classifications noted above. He divided his data into (1) the category of instruments producing one note per string, for example, the *ṣandji* (harp); and (2) the category of instruments whose strings or pipes can be made to sound many notes (Shiloah 1979a, 213), such as the lutes (*barbaṭ, ṭunbūr,* and *shahrūd*) and wind instruments (*mazāmīr*). That is, he used performance technique as the character of division.

In the fourteenth century, an anonymous Iranian treatise *Kanz al-tuḥaf* (Treasury of rarities) described nine instruments in unusual detail, without, however, arranging them in the form of a classification. The author mentioned the material of which the instruments were made as well as discussing their proportions and construction.

More remarkable was the work of the minstrel-scholar Ibn Ghaybī, alias Abd al-Ḳādir (d. 1435), who classified a large body of instruments. In his treatise *Djāmi 'al-alḥān* (Compiler of melodies), which was written in Persian, he discussed the practical art of music as well as matters of music theory (Shiloah 1979a, 168). His classification of instruments included an idiophone category, but the only categories he illustrated were aerophones and chordophones. He listed as many as twenty-five varieties of stringed instruments as well as nine wind and three percussion instruments. He too subdivided stringed instruments into the open and the stopped and made a similar subdivision of winds. The character of division, then, was playing technique (the fingering of holes or strings) combined with morphological characters (the presence or absence of finger holes or frets). The interests of this scholar extended not only to the "folk" and "art" instruments of his country but also to some exotic instruments. In fact, he specifically stated that some of the instruments listed were Chinese, that one was Indian, and that one (the *urghanūn,* or organ, which he described) was European (Shiloah 1979a, 172; Wright 1980, 521).

Most of the writers of the Arab world, then, divided instruments into two categories distinguished by mode of sound excitation—strings and winds—though they sometimes suggested the existence of a third category—percussion, of which they usually avoided discussion. The Turkish encyclopedist Hadjī Khalīfa (d. 1657) presented a clear, threefold classification by mode of sound excitation (drums, winds [*mazāmīr*], and strings), giving examples of instruments in each category. This classification was presented in a discussion of the origin and construction of musical instruments, and it included such instruments as the *'ūd* and the *urganun.* He entitled his work *Kashf al-ẓunūn 'an asāmī al-kutub wa'-funūn* (Clarification of conjectures about the names of books and sciences) (Shiloah 1979a, 221).

Do the Arabs, like the Indians and Europeans and others, sometimes classify by analogy with trees and branches, limbs of the body, or other systems? Accounts of treatises discussed by Shiloah suggest that the tree branch analogy is quite important in the culture. For example, the Ottoman encyclopedist and biographer Tashköprüzāde (1495–1561) drew an analogy between knowledge on the one hand and trees and branches on the other. A classification of instruments was presented in his encyclopedia, *Miftāḥ al-sa'āda wamiṣbāḥ al-siyāda fi mawdū'āt al-'ulūm* (Key to happiness and lantern to mastership concerning the subjects of sciences), which was written in Arabic (Shiloah 1979a, 345). This classification of instruments was presented as part of a comprehensive, complex classification of the whole realm of music, art, and knowledge itself. He divided the fifteen arts and sciences into "seven big trees" (*daḥwa*) of knowledge, each of which was subdivided into several "branches." The ninth branch of the fourth tree dealt with the three (sub)branches of the science of music: (1) *musica instrumentalis,* (2) the science of dance (*raḳṣ*), and (3) the science of co-quetry, by which mime (*ghundj*) was probably meant. In his *musica instrumentalis* section he selected for mention the *'ūd, mazāmīr* in its limited, more recent sense of (reed winds), *kanun* (zither), and in particular the *urghanūn* (organ), an instrument that he had frequently seen and heard (Shiloah 1979a, 345). As usual, he omitted mention of percussion. Another example of the tree analogy (though not one applied to instruments) is the one presented by the early seventeenth-century writer al-Kādirī in his *Rāḥ al-djām fi shadjarat al-anghām* (Wine of the cup regarding the tree of melodies). In this work he discussed the eight branches of the four principal melodic modes and then presented the modes in the form of a tree (Shiloah 1979a, 239–40).

Like some of his forebears dating as far back as the ninth century, al-Kādirī also classified instruments according to national character. Certain stringed and wind instruments typically used by various nationalities when at war were said to include the *rabāb* used by the Arabs, the *kemandje* (fiddles) used by the Kurds, the *ifrandj* or *būk* (trumpets) used by the Europeans, and the *nāy* (flutes) used by the Turks (Shiloah 1979a, 240). As we have noted, classification according to national character remained a persistent theme in Arab classifications over the centuries. Not surprisingly in view of the low status of percussion instruments, no nation was typified by a percussion instrument, even in the case of instruments used in war.

Listings and implied classifications of instruments are also occasionally to be found in works of writers indulging in the religious controversy between Sufi inspirationists and mainstream Sunni Muslims. Some Sufi mystics find the use of certain instruments efficacious in rituals called *samā‘* (remembrance of God), which aim at achieving ecstatic union with God. Mainstream Muslim theologicans, on the other hand, believe it is heretical to use instruments in worship, seeing music and dance as diversions from the practice of meditating on religious matters. The Sufi authority and jurist Ibn Zaghdūn, who died in Cairo in 1477, wrote a defence of the use of certain instruments in *samā‘*, making a distinction between two types of Sufi singing: (1) singing accompanied by the *shabbāba* (flute and *duff* [frame drum]) and (2) singing accompanied by plucked strings (e.g., the *‘ūd* and the *ṭunbūr*) and wind instruments (*mazāmīr*) (Shiloah 1979a, 151). He mentioned three categories of instruments—strings, percussion, and winds—in two ensembles used by Sufi worshipers, though without classifying them as such.

One anti-Sufi writer who mentioned instruments and argued strongly against their religious use was Ibn Taymīyya (d. 1328), who rejected all *samā‘* rituals using instruments, denouncing the intoxicating effects of instruments as originating in satanic possession and allowing only the listening to and reading of the Koran for the purposes of *samā‘*.[10] He appears to have regarded clapping and other bodily noises in the same category as instruments, for he rejected whistling, hissing, and clapping as acts of idolatry, claiming that the Prophet had tolerated drumming and clapping only by women and only during special rejoicings (Shiloah 1979a, 221). His treatise was entitled *Fatwā fi'l-samā* (Legal decision on listening to music).

Certain drums were approved of by some Muslim writers, while others were banned, depending on their function. For example, drums used on approved pilgrimages were naturally not banned, while drums and all other instruments used for entertainment—and hence diversion from religious meditation—normally were. Large drums used by Persians in war were also, not surprisingly, banned by Arabs. Strings were also forbidden by strict theologians because they belonged to the mundane urban world and had no religious efficacy (Amnon Shiloah, personal communication).

An anti-Sufi writer who presented a classification of the instruments he condemned was the Egyptian-born al-Haythamī (d. Mecca 1567). He entitled this work *Kaff al-raʿāʿan muḥarramat al-lahw waʾl-samāʿ* (Restraint of rash young from forbidden distractions and listening to music). He urged rash youth to restrain itself from musical distractions and even boasted that "he destroyed instruments and brought musicians to punishment" (Shiloah 1979a, 129). An adherent of the Shāfiʿ school, he attached three categories of instruments: (1) *maʿāzif,* or certain kinds of stringed instruments (lyres); (2) *mazāmīr,* or wind instruments; and (3) *awtār* (strings) (Shiloah 1979a, 129). Of the large list of instruments which he attacked, he began with percussion, that is, the *duff* (frame drum), followed by the *kūba* (large cylindrical drum), the *ṣaffāḳatayn* or *ṣandj* (cymbals), the *ḳaḍīb* (wand), hand-clapping, and beating a copper plate. Then he attacked the winds: the *shabbāb* (flute), *zammarā, yarāʿ* (flute and clarinet-like instrument). Lastly, he attacked the strings, such as the *ṭunbūr, ʿūd, rabāb* (Shiloah 1979a, 129).

Nineteenth- and twentieth-century Arab writers have shown little interest in developing schemes for classifying instruments. The mid-nineteenth-century writer Mikhael Mashaka, for example, gave the matter little attention. Twentieth-century writers have not developed any new schemes to date; nor have they rejected the old schemes. They either defer to the old classifications or use the Hornbostel and Sachs system, where appropriate (Amnon Shiloah, personal communication).

CONCLUSION

At least one ancient taxonomy from oral tradition has survived; it distinguished instruments according to myths of their origin. Unlike the mainstream written tradition of classification, which gave low status to percussion instruments (if they were mentioned at all), this orally transmitted scheme did include percussion instruments on an equal basis with the winds and strings.

Early theorists of the Arabian empire such as al-Kindī listed and discussed instruments mainly according to (1) music-theoretical considerations such as theory of proportions and the dimensions and construction of instruments or (2) extramusical matters such as theory of ethos, cosmology and numerology, or the character of various human groups and nationalities. These works by early Arab scholars somewhat resembled those of their Greek forebears, whose works they knew in translation, though their scholarship soon took on a specifically Arab identity.

Early Arab writers frequently listed or described instruments rather than formally classifying them. Relatively complex schemes by analogy with trees and branches apparently developed not earlier than the middle of the second millennium. Some early writers produced single-step schemes that were very limited in scope and were intended primarily to express or exemplify a point of view, as with al-Kindī's attempt to explain national character by linking it to certain instruments. One early writer, al-Fārābī, presented a quite complex and broad-ranging classification as well as a number of simpler schemes. The instrumentarium he considered was limited to the Arab world and, typically for his culture, it excluded all percussion instruments.

al-Fārābī's performing skills and national Arab consciousness influenced his tree diagram classifications of instruments and theoretical approach. He grouped instruments according to four different schemes. The characters of division were whether an instrument can produce sounds of long or short duration, whether or not it can produce tones and melodies natural and pleasing to the Arab ear, whether or not it is useful in demonstrating music theory, and (in a classification of strings and winds only) according to its mode of sound excitation. In all these schemes, strings (notably the *ʿūd* but also all lutes, zithers, and bowed strings) were given the highest status, then winds, and finally percussion (if they were mentioned at all). Basic subdivisions were made between bowed and plucked strings and between open and stopped strings, with some attention being paid to the morphology of wind instruments, such as the number of finger holes and the presence or absence of and number of reeds. In one scheme, even the type of reed was taken into account. Three of the schemes were quite broad, whereas the fourth scheme was close without being highly systematic or symmetrical at the lower steps.

Later Arab writers borrowed several of al-Fārābī's characters of division for their classifications but did not always use them at the same step. In some schemes, writers subdivided strings according to whether they are plucked, bowed, or beaten. Flutes and reed winds were usually included in the same subcategory. Organs were frequently allocated a category of their own. al-Fārābī's five-category classification of instruments also gave attention to the all-important human voice as well as to dance.

In general, chordophones were by far the most highly rated instruments in the Arab world over the past millennium. Not only were they discussed in the greatest amount of detail but they were enumerated in by far the greatest number of examples (e.g., Ibn Ghaybī listed twenty-five varieties).

To what extent did Islam influence the study and classification of instruments? In most respects it had little influence, because mainstream theology and worship did not concern themselves with instruments. Indeed, most Sunni leaders have tended to disapprove of the use of instruments in worship, a factor that clearly mitigated against developing the habit of theorizing about instruments. Only Sufi writers defended the use of instruments in *samā'* rituals. However, not only Sufi writers but also anti-Sufi protagonists necessarily implied classifications of instruments in their theological discussions about whether or not it was lawful to play instruments in *samā'*-style worship. In this respect they resemble the Jains of India, who prohibit most musical instruments in their services but in so doing list and give implied classifications of them.

TEN

European Classifications from Medieval Times to the Eighteenth Century

> Musical instruments may be described as the ingenious work of able and
> earnest artisans who devised them after much diligent thought and work,
> fashioned them out of good materials and designed them in the true
> proportions of art, such that they produce a beautiful accord of sound
> . . .; their purpose is . . . the magnification of God and the fitting and
> proper entertainment of men.
>
> Michael Praetorius (1619)[1]

Europe in the Middle Ages was remarkable among the cultures of the
world for its wealth of treatises dealing with musical knowledge. Much of
their content was derived from the Greek or the Arabic world, or both. As
in China, treatises were at first heavily oriented toward the past and
divorced from practical music making. Only tiny portions of the medieval
musical treatises dealt with musical instruments and their classifications.
Like the Greeks, medieval Europeans were much more interested in
classifying knowledge about music than classifying instruments. When
they did, they mostly classified in the form of a key or tree diagram, but
frequently not in strict logical division.

This chapter cannot refer to more than a small selection of the many
relevant literary sources. It aims to demonstrate the broad continuities and
shifts in the form and content of classifications and concepts of instruments over twelve hundred years, giving more detailed attention to a few
outstanding sixteenth- and seventeenth- century schemes. It is in four
parts. The first deals with terminology, the second with dominant concepts
and classifications of instruments in the Middle Ages, the third with an
alchemic Byzantine scheme, and the fourth with the postmedieval shift to
a humanistic, empirical concept of instruments. As we shall see, the tree
diagram used by Boethius was standard throughout the Middle Ages and
the Renaissance. Except for a few authors mentioned below, virtually all
writers used it. In fact, however, instruments were only a small part of the
currently espoused concept of music, which was seen as having relevance

to knowledge in general and therefore to the discussion of religious and contemplative matters. The church fathers dismissed many musical instruments as having pagan associations. Music itself was significant, but musical instruments were actually peripheral to major religious and contemplative issues.

Presumably a number of orally transmitted taxonomies like the Finnish-Karelian one discussed in chapter 18 were current throughout medieval and postmedieval Europe but traces of them are scanty. This chapter refers to only one scheme with a "folk" character—an anonymous, literarily transmitted, ninth-century Byzantine scheme with an alchemic purpose.

TERMINOLOGIES OF THE DOMINANT CLASSIFICATIONS FROM MEDIEVAL TIMES TO THE EIGHTEENTH CENTURY

The most persistent European classification of instruments was the three-category scheme borrowed from Hellenistic times. It was used in three different hierarchical sequences. Porphyry had first presented it in the order of winds, strings, and percussion, but the Late Roman theoretician A. M. S. Boethius (c. 470–c. 524) used it in the order of strings, winds, and percussion,[2] and his younger contemporary M. A. Cassiodorus (477–520) in the sequence of percussion, strings, and winds.[3]

Porphyry's model took the same order of categories as that used in the 150th Psalm,[4] which made it attractive to some later Christian writers, including Cassiodorus. (He used it, however, only in his Psalms commentary and in the context of the music of the spheres, writing that the instruments and voices of the music of the spheres were not "audible by the carnal ear but incline to the purest musical contemplation.")[5] The Spanish theoretician and Archbishop of Segovia—Domenicus Gundissalinus also used this model in his work of 1150,[6] as did Filippo Bonanni (1722, 45, 88, 111).

Among the authors who followed the Boethian order of categories were Regino of Prüm (see n. 15), Aurelianus of Reome,[7] Johannes de Muris (see n. 16), Sebastian Virdung (1970, 28), Gioseffo Zarlino (1966, 216), Marin Mersenne, Sebastian de Brossard (see n. 17), and Johann Eisel (see n. 19) in the ninth, thirteenth, fourteenth, fifteenth, sixteenth, seventeenth, and eighteenth centuries.

There is no ostensible reason why Cassiodorus placed percussion instruments first in his main classification of instruments, though it has been suggested that he was influenced by the legend of Pythagoras and his interest in the percussive sounds of the blacksmith's hammer.[8] The

English theoretician Roger Bacon used the same order in his scheme in the thirteenth century (see no. 14).

Late Roman writers devoted little space to discussion of their characters of division or other details of their classifications of instruments. However, Boethius clearly mentioned that stringed instruments produce sounds by tension, winds by blowing ("as in those instruments activated by moisture," by which he meant the breath), and percussion by striking ("as in instruments which are struck on certain bronze concavities") (see quotation from Boethius in n. 2). The first category was determined by the morphological attribute of the possession of stretched strings and the other two by mode of sound excitation, that is, blowing and beating. The meaning of these characters was in fact built into the labels Boethius gave to his categories. Thus his *intensione ut nervis* label derives from the Latin *tendere,* meaning "stretch" and *nervus* meaning "nerve" or "string"; his *inflatilia* label comes from *flare,* meaning "blow"; and his *percussionalia* title derives from *percutere,* meaning "strike." The fact that the scheme applies two different characters at the same (and only) step means that it is not, of course, in the form of strict logical division.

Another broad Hellenistic scheme that has shown surprising persistence is the two-category classification first presented by Pollux. As we have noted, it comprises winds and percussion, where percussion includes both plucked ("beaten") strings and percussion instruments in the modern sense, as both are "sounded with the fingers" (Isidore of Seville 1980, 14).[9] Its single character of division is the instrument's mode of sound excitation.[10] Isidore of Seville, Hugh of St. Victor,[11] Magister Lambertus,[12] and Michael Praetorius (1980, 6–7) used the scheme in the sixth to seventh, twelfth, thirteenth, and seventeenth centuries respectively. Despite its superior logical status, however, it proved to be much less popular in medieval and postmedieval Europe than the three-category scheme, thus testifying to the strength of Boethian influence on European musical thought for well over a thousand years (and in some respects to this day).[13]

Some remarkable continuities but also some shifts may be observed in the terms applied to categories of instruments over the centuries. Boethius's label *intensione ut nervis* ("tension of strings") for the stringed category was *tensibilia* for Cassiodorus, *tensilia* for Roger Bacon,[14] *tensible* for Regino of Prüm,[15] *chordalia* (from L. *chorda,* "string") for Johannes de Muris,[16] *intensione ut nervis* for Ugolino of Orvieto (1959, 17), *enchorda* or *entata* for Sebastian de Brossard,[17] *chordata* for Majer,[18] *fidicinia* for Eisel,[19] and *chordophone* for Mahillon and Hornbostel and Sachs. Boethius's *spiritu ut tibiis* ("breath in tube") for wind instruments was *inflatilia* (from L. *flare*, "blow") for Cassiodorus, *inflativa* for Bacon, *inflatile* for Regino of Prüm, *foraminalia* for Johannes de Muris (see n. 16), *spiritu ut tibiis* for Ugolino, *pneumatica* (from Gk. *pneuma*, "wind") for Majer and Eisel, and *aerophone* (from L. *aerem*, "air") for Mahillon and Hornbostel and Sachs. Boethius's term *percussione* (from L. *percutere*, "strike") was Cassiodorus's and Bacon's *percussionalia*, Regino of Prüm's *percussionabile*, Ugolino's *percussionibus*, Majer's and Eisel's *pulsatilia* (from L. *pulsare*, "vibrate"), Mahillon's *autophones*, Hornbostel and Sachs's *idiophones* (from Gk. *idios*, "own," and *phone*, "voice"; i.e., self-sounders), and Mahillon's and Hornbostel and Sachs's *membranophones* (from L. *membrana*, "parchment").

CONCEPTS AND CLASSIFICATIONS OF INSTRUMENTS IN THE MIDDLE AGES

Some early writers adhered to a spiritual concept of music that required that they not classify musical instruments at all. To theologians Clement of Alexandria (who died c. 215) and St. Augustine (354–430), all sounding instruments shared the same extramusical function of praising God and doing good; in this sense they were all one. Sounding instruments included the human voice, called "the instrument of God," by Clement of Alexandria,[20] while for Augustine they also included nonmusical instruments or tools. To both writers the human voice was the complete instrument; all other instruments were united and subsumed into the human being (van Deusen 1987, 4, 10, 35). For example, St. Augustine referred to two instruments by name (the *psaltarium* and the *kithara*), commenting that they were an indivisible unit within the overwhelming idea that "Christ's body is integer" ("duo organ video, corpus autem Christi unum video" [*Enarrationes in Psalmos* 56:16 (CCL 2, 705f.); see van Deusen 1987, 14]).[21]

In the Late Roman period the effects of music and therefore of instruments were believed to depend on the goodness of God (Pietzsch 1929, 49–50). As Isidore of Seville put it, "Music stirs the emotions; it rouses and transforms our feelings. . . . Scripture says that David delivered Saul from an unclean spirit with the art of melody" (Isidore of Seville 1980, 414). The notion was current that the whole world was music. "If we habitually live in agreement with the good we always show that we are allied with music. But when we engage in evil, we do not have this music within us. This world was formed by music and is governed by it" (Cassiodorus 1980, 3–4). Hugh of St. Victor also commented on musical ethics in a treatise written in the 1120s: "Music is characteristic of the soul partly in its virtues, like justice, piety and temperance; and partly in its powers, like reason, wrath and concupiscence" (Hugh of St. Victor 1961, 69).

Medieval writers were less interested in classifying musical instruments than they were in classifying music or musical knowledge itself. Music was linked to cosmological beliefs and was seen as an edifying object of spiritual reflections. Music was taught in universities as a discipline that allowed students to see in practice how the rational basis of the universe operates. Instruments were grouped under the classification of musical knowledge and they were regarded as valuable both as sound-producing objects in their own right and as objects of religious contemplation.

The concept of the moral affects of music took a more precise form in the writings of Cassiodorus, who was able to reconcile the idea of the unity of Creation with a broad classification of music and instruments. Why, he asked, are instruments so often mentioned in the Psalms? For two reasons, he wrote. One was a musical reason: that instruments are functional, sounding objects in their own right. The other was a Christian theory of music's emotional and moral effects that held that instruments are also nonfunctional objects of reflection, signifying invisible realities. Thus the *psalterium* makes known the incarnation of God and "signifies divine love leading to conversion (while the) cithara signifies movement (passion)." The paradox in this view, which is somewhat reminiscent of Aristides' paradox of inanimate instruments affecting people's morals and emotions, is that the musical instrument, despite its visible body, is "particularly adapted to making the invisible known" (van Deusen 1987, 14, 17). The moral effects of instruments, then, lie in their spiritual significance.

The grandest exposition of the contemplative spirituality of music—including that made by inanimate instruments—was by Boethius. His broad classification of instruments was subordinate to his classification of music itself. Based on his knowledge of a number of treatises of antiquity, he wrote a compendium in Latin of selections of Greek music theory, including references to the music of the spheres, which he included in his famous three-category classification of music (Boethius 1867: I,viii: 189). The first category, *musica mundana,* included musical sounds made by the movements of the spheres, the elements, and the changes of the seasons, sounds that are inaudible because they are constant and unbroken. The second was *musica humana,* which was music audible to human beings. The third was *musica quae in quibusdam constituta est instrumentalis,* or the realm of music theory that presents mathematical relations between tones through musical instruments (Hickmann 1971, 35–37), a gift of God to man, who is thereby brought into harmony with the universe (Pietzsch 1929, 40).

Boethius's treatise was not intended to be read by musicians but by the religious community of theoreticians and clerics in training, who were mainly interested in celestial abstractions, theology, and philosophy. Thus his classification of music—instrumental and vocal—was totally divorced from practical music making. Among the writers who transmitted this theoretical Boethian classification to successive generations were Cassiodorus, Isidore of Seville, Roger Bacon, Johannes de Muris, and Bartholomaeus Ramos de Pareja.

In time the meaning of Boethius's three-category classification of music was modified. By the twelfth century, for example, Johannes Cottonius used the third category, which he called *musica instrumentalis,* in the sense of "ability to produce tones" (Pietzsch 1929, 7). To Hugh of St. Victor, the three categories simply meant "that belonging to the universe, that belonging to man, and that which is instrumental" (Hugh of St. Victor 1961, 69). Around 1280, Johannes de Grocheo referred to the use of the categories by traditional theoreticians as follows: "By musica mundana they designate that harmony caused from the motion of heavenly bodies, by humana that balance of association existing in the human body because of the best mixture of elements within it. But by instrumentalis they mean that music which is of the sounds of instruments, be they natural or artificial" (Grocheo 1967, 10).

Ugolino of Orvieto (c. 1380–1149) also distinguished between the three categories of music, adding a class called *musica caelestis,* which he saw as the origin of all the categories of music as well as its supreme manifestation. He considered that celestial music led to recognition of the immeasurable goodness, power, and wisdom of God and that it was also the source of the immense sweetness and loveliness of *musica mundana,* which was linked to the movements of the heavenly bodies and the elements.[22]

The preference for the vocal instrument, which had prevailed since the time of Plato, took on Christian overtones and continued to serve as a principle of classification of medieval treatises. Aristotle's distinction between animate and inanimate instruments was perpetuated by many later writers. For example, Cassiodorus used it in his Psalms commentary, pointing out that the voice produces speech as well as song, while inanimate instruments only make sounds that are idiomatic to them.

Regino of Prüm (Regino of Prüm [1784] 1931, 237), Gundissalinus (work c. 1300), Johannes de Muris (work c. 1300), and Bartholomaeus Ramos de Pareja (1440–1491) were among those who made the distinction under the labels of *vox* and *sonus* or *instrumenta naturalis* and *instrumenta artificialis*. Regino of Prüm claimed that *musica naturalis* existed in the movements of the heavenly bodies and the human voice while *musica artificialis* was bound to the sounds of certain instruments, namely, strings, winds, and percussion. He stressed the "God-given," self-sounding quality of natural music and the humanly achieved aspect of artificial music (Regino of Prüm [1784] 1931, 236). As de Muris expressed it, the voice is the most excellent of instruments because it simultaneously produces tones and words (Pietzsch 1929, 100). Even as late as the sixteenth century, Zarlino divided instruments into the natural and the artificial (Zarlino [1588] 1966, 216).

The hierarchy of inanimate instruments underwent two major shifts. Late Roman writers somewhat preferred winds to strings, despite the Greek preference for strings. Also unlike the Greeks, they did not ignore percussion instruments in their classifications. As we have noted, Cassiodorus even presented the percussion category first in his main classification of instruments. However, he implied the superiority of winds on the grounds that they "imitate the sound of the human voice" (Cassiodorus 1980, 4–5).

A clearer indication of the shift to winds is to be found in the work of Isidore of Seville. Like Cassiodorus, he wrote that wind instruments "imitate the sound of the human voice" (Isidore of Seville 1980, 16). Exhorted by the 150th Psalm to praise God with the sounds of the trumpets and other instruments, he placed the wind category first in his two-category classification of instruments. He distinguished three divisions of music: "the singing of the voice," wind instruments, and beaten instruments (including strings); but like Cassiodorus, he gave the winds the most extensive treatment and listed a larger number of their types and names than for the other categories (Isidore of Seville 1980, 14).[23]

Despite the occasional reference to the fact that winds are the instruments most like the human voice as they use the human breath to make sounds, a gradual shift away from winds and back again to strings occurred between the eighth and sixteenth centuries. Not least because the Bible (and especially the Psalms) contains frequent mention of stringed instruments played in the praise of God, writers such as Hrabanus Maurus

(776–856) and Aurelianus of Reome (ninth century) showed a preference for strings by including longer lists of examples or detailed descriptions of them (Hickmann 1971, 90).

The attitude to percussion throughout the medieval period was ambivalent, though less so in early than later times. To place percussion first in a scheme, as Cassiodorus did, was rare. In some schemes percussion instruments did not even rate a mention, and if included, they normally came last. Like Aristides, Ramos de Pareja excluded percussion altogether in the chapter on instruments in his *Musica practica* of 1482; he mentioned only strings and winds (*sonus*) and the human voice (*vox*). Percussion instruments had likewise been excluded from the list of instruments given in Daniel, Chapter 3, which included only strings and winds. A number of Hellenistic and medieval writers referred in their treatises to the famous story about Pythagoras discovering the fundamentals of music "from the sound of hammers and of taut strings when plucked" (Isidore of Seville 1980, 13), but they did not develop this idea and the general interest in percussion remained slight.

There were two other Greek ideas that affected (though in changed form) the second level of some medieval classifications of instruments. One was Aristoxenós's key-form division between continuous and discontinuous sounds, where the former meant vocal or instrumental sounds of definite pitch suitable for melody building and the latter sounds of indefinite pitch as in speech. This character of division was combined with the key-form *vox-sonus* distinction in a work in 1100 by Johannes of Affligem. He subdivided instruments at the first step of his key into the so-called *naturalia,* or continuous, indefinite-pitched category, and the *artificialia,* or discontinuous, definite-pitched category. At the second step he gave laughter as an expression of a natural "instrument" producing indefinite-pitched sound, a toy drum and a bird-catching pipe as examples of artificial instruments of indefinite pitch, vocal music as the example of a natural, definite-pitched instrument, and stringed instruments as examples of artificial, definite-pitched instruments (Hickmann 1971, 69). The resulting key-form scheme was speculative in nature but quite logical in form, with its four mutually exclusive categories. Similarly, Aegidius of Zamora subdivided his "living" and "dead" categories of instruments into those of definite and indefinite pitch, where the former included only strings and the latter only percussion (Aegidius of Zamora [1784] 1931, 378).

The other Greek idea was the dichotomy between musical theory and practice, which had been discussed by such writers as Aristoxenos and

Aristides. Their notion of *theoretikon* included what is now known as precompositional theory; *praktikon,* however, was also theoretical, for it covered what is now called the theory of composition and performance (Palisca 1980, 241). This theory-practice concept was altered during its transmission to Europe, where it arrived in a new, partly performance-oriented form in the latter part of the twelfth century, through the translations of al-Fārābī's works. As we have noted, al-Fārābī had divided music into the *speculativa,* contemplative, research-oriented musical inquiry, and the *practica,* practical music making. Under the latter category he included the performance of "acute, grave and medial sounds" and under the former the principles of the creation of music, its materials, its methods of research, neumes, theory of proportions, the kinds of rhythms that most tones have, and aspects of rhythm, melody, and meter (Pietzsch 1929, 79–80). Domenicus Gundissalinus—also used the distinction, having led a group of scholars in the translation and transmission of al-Fārābī's thought to late medieval Europe.

Considerable evidence exists that in the Middle Ages not only instruments but also the musicians who played them were ordered hierarchically, and a deep social gulf separated educated and noneducated musicians. Wind players were more highly regarded than string players, and at weddings and the like the former usually received double the payment of the latter, which created class distinctions among musicians. Similarly, bards and singers of heroic song were regarded as being on a higher social level than minstrels. A division of instruments into a superior and an inferior category was widespread: "instruments high and low," "altas et baxas," "hauts de bas," "strumenti sottili e grossi." Distinctions were also made between loud and soft instruments and between their associations with heaven and earth, angel and devil, good and bad, eternal and time-bound. By the end of the Middle Ages, the concepts and classifications of instruments were clearly linked to corresponding music and dance forms and to the social levels of musicians' professions, for example, "hauts et bas ménetriers" and "jouglerie seigneuriale" and "jouglerie foraine et populaire." Such distinctions, including the sexual associations of male and female, were widely made until the early seventeenth century. For example, in the folk theater of Luzern and in bridal processions in Frankfurt, the male partner was associated with drums, trumpets, and pipes and the female with harps, viols, and lutes. Such class and sex distinctions, though different in detail, are also found in other cultures, such as India and Java (see chaps. 5 and 7).[24]

AN ALCHEMIC BYZANTINE CLASSIFICATION

The stated aim of a tree-form classification that made no reference to Christian belief at all was to show the similarities between the elements of alchemy and music (Hickmann 1971, 20, 58–59). This threefold classification, which was presented in an anonymous, ninth-century Byzantine treatise, is clearly based in part on Greek precedent and retains a "pagan" quality and context. When compared with contemporary mainstream European schemes, it is unusually close in form. At the highest step it distinguishes between percussion, "aulos instruments," and "cithara instruments." At the second step the strings are subdivided according to their number of strings, the winds are grouped according to the materials of which they are made, and the percussion instruments are classified by the same character but with a special taxon reserved for cymbals. The list of strings given comprises instruments with strings ranging from three to thirty-three in number, while the winds are divided into two categories: one for the most important instrument, which is made of copper, and the other for noncopper instruments.[25] The percussion instruments are divided into three classes: one for cymbals, one for copper or glass instruments, and the other for instruments made of a composite of several metals. At the third step instruments are classified according to their mode of performance; for example, cymbals are divided into those played with the hands and those played with the feet.

This fairly symmetrical, three-category classification has three steps, and except at the second step, it applies a single character per category per step after the method of logical division. Its characters of division are mode of sound excitation (including the tensing of strings, the blowing of air into tubes, and the striking of an instrument); morphological aspects; and materials of construction. Presumably it is the last character that is most significant from an alchemic point of view.

THE POSTMEDIEVAL SHIFT TO A HUMANISTIC, EMPIRICAL CONCEPT OF INSTRUMENTS

Approximately by the time of the Renaissance, a more humanistic concept of instruments was developing in Europe that included the notion that instruments serve to entertain human beings as well as to glorify God, a view which is expressed in the quotation at the head of this chapter. The shift coincided with a growing interest in contemporary instruments and music making. It resulted partly from the spread of knowledge of works by al-Fārābī, whose division of music into the *speculativa* and the *practica* had brought issues of practical music making into classificatory thought. Jerome of Moravia, who was one writer influenced by al-Fārābī, wrote a new kind of treatise in 1292 that surveyed the contemporary state of music theory (Palisca 1980, 749).

Another reason for the shift was the fact that the Boethian concept of music was beginning to be questioned. Boethius's threefold classification of music was criticized by Johannes of Grocheo:

> Those who make this kind of division either invent their opinion . . . or they are ignorant of nature and logic . . . they say universally that music is a science concerning numbered sound. Nevertheless, celestial bodies in movement do not make a sound, although our ancestors believed this. . . . Not also is sound properly to be found in the human constitution. Who has heard a constitution sounding? The third type which is called *musica instrumentalis* is distributed in three parts, that is, in the diatonic, chromatic and enharmonic, according to which they say the three concords of the monochord come. They call that diatonic which proceeds by tone, tone and semitone . . . chromatic which proceeds by diesis, diesis and three semitones. And they say the planets use such a song. They also call that enharmonic which proceeds by diesis, diesis and ditone. They say this is the sweetest, since angels use it. We do not understand this division, since they distinguish here only *musica instrumentalis,* leaving out the other categories. Nor is it pertinent for a musician to treat of the song of angels, unless he has been at the same time a theologian and a prophet; no one can have any experience of such song except by divine inspiration. When they say the planets sing, they seem to be ignorant of what is a sound. (Grocheo 1967, 10)

With this critique by Grocheo, who was one of the few really independent thinkers on music of his time, the classification of instruments began to be emancipated from the speculative classification of musical knowledge under which it had been subsumed for so long. The way was beginning to open for the classification of instruments in their own right and in their many attributes. Instruments were conceived of not only as complex objects intimately related to contemporary music theory and music making but also as agents of entertainment and secular pleasure.

Until the time of Grocheo it was the practice to make mention only of ancient and theoretical instruments in treatises. In 1267, however, Bacon referred in his *Opus tertium* to a contemporary instrument—the *fidula* (a cithara-type instrument)—in a short list that otherwise included only ancient instruments (Brewer 1859). Aegidius of Zamora (work c. 1260) and

Johannes de Muris (work c. 1300) also mentioned the names of contemporary as well as ancient instruments (Hickmann 1971, 72, 73, 80).

Key-form classifications based on the social or extramusical function of instruments began to be produced from this time. A forerunner of this trend was Odo's division of music in the ninth century into *vulgaris* and the *ecclesiastica*, where the character of division was the use of music in church as opposed to its popular or secular function. The *fistula* (reed pipe), cithara, and *fidula* were given as examples of the secular category (Odo [1784] 1931, 118). In about 1260, Aegidius of Zamora divided instruments into those discovered in earlier times, by which he meant the winds and strings mentioned in the third chapter of Daniel, as opposed to the instruments of his own time (Aegidius of Zamora [1784] 1931, 388–93).[26]

The most interesting classification by social function, however, was presented by the Parisian Grocheo in the thirteenth century. Grocheo was interested in the practical music-making scene of his environment and, as we have noted, questioned the Boethian classification of music. He also queried Pollux's classification of instruments (without naming Pollux), presenting it in his treatise only in order to reject it on the logical grounds that all instrumental sounds—not just those created by percussion instruments—are actually caused by the action of striking, whereupon he proceeded to present his own scheme (Grocheo 1967, 11).[27] Firstly, however, he discussed some of the problems inherent in the nature of classification itself, pointing out that it is "not easy to divide music correctly, since . . . the dividing factors ought to exhaust the full nature of the whole that is divided" (Grocheo 1967, 11). He therefore decided to classify music according to local use, or "how the men in Paris use it" (Grocheo 1967, 11). He distinguished between secular music, composed music, and the music used in church, or, as he put it, the "civil or simple music, which they call vulgar music, . . . the composed or regular music by rule, which they call measured music, (and) . . . that which is made for these two and to which these two are best adapted. This is called ecclesiastic and is designed for praising the Creator" (Grocheo 1967, 11). He then briefly discussed instruments in reference to the musical forms played on them, without excluding reference on occasion to their social content. For example, he referred to "the drum and trumpet in war games and tournaments" (Grocheo 1967, 18).

Grocheo was the first of a number of writers to take contemporary music making into account in their classifications of instruments. His questioning of traditional ideas marked the beginning of a more secular, empirical attitude to musical scholarship. Just as Ma Tuan-Lin had found it helpful to subdivide the *pa yin* scheme and classify instruments according to contemporary social usage, so Grocheo rejected Pollux's classification of instruments by performance technique and reclassified instruments according to social function. Both scholars initially paid formal deference to tradition but were concerned to change the theoretical nature of traditional scholarship in order somehow to match the reality of contemporary musical life.

Iconographic sources suggest that two models for classifying sounds made by voices and instruments were influential in the fourteenth century (H. M. Brown 1984, 40). One was the Pollux-influenced classification of musical sounds—and, by extension, instruments—of St. Augustine. This scheme comprised three classes: sounds produced by (1) wind instruments, (2) the human voice, and (3) percussion and stringed instruments, which produced "organic," "harmonic," and "rhythmic" sounds respectively. The other influential model was Boethius's division of musical instruments into sounds produced by the tension of strings, winds, and percussion. This scheme was presented in graphic form in a fourteenth-century Neapolitan drawing of Lady Music and Jubal, who were surrounded by plucked and bowed strings, winds, and percussion instruments.[28] It

> helps to remind us that Lady Music and Jubal with the Augustinian divisions of their art into organic, harmonic, and rhythmic types was not the only image of music prevalent in fourteenth-century Italy. Indeed the Neapolitan illustration hearkens back to a much older and different tradition of portraying music derived directly from Boethius: sounds produced by the tension of strings, winds and percussion. . . . This division is made manifest by the composition of the picture, the string players spread across the top, the percussion players arranged in a V beside and below the central figure, with the wind players in an interlocked, inverted V with Lady Music at its apex. The Neapolitan Boethius is a trecento adaptation of an old theme: a picture that reinterprets earlier medieval imagery for the contemporary world. It is a complex image consisting of the Boethian categories modified by Biblical and late classical imagery (King David and the personification of music derived from Martianus Capella) that at the same time offers a conspectus of contemporary practice, a representative rather than an exhaustive sample of the trecento instrumentarium, doubtless to help the noble students who first read their Boethius from this elegant manuscript to interpret this ancient authority in terms they could understand and indeed in terms of the instruments they themselves saw around them in the real world. (Brown 1984: 40)

Although both bowed and plucked strings were in widespread use in the fourteenth century (and presumably for at least two or three centuries before that), there is no evidence to date that they were separately subclassified in the instrument taxonomies of the time. Nor were keyboard instruments, which were beginning to interest authors greatly, given a separate category; they were included at first under the heading of stringed instruments.

Fifteenth-century writers on instruments, including Ramos de Pareja (work 1482), mirrored the empirical mood of the time and exhibited the new interest in keyboard instruments. Ramos paid his dues to tradition by first dividing instruments in the key form into the *vox* and *sonus* categories and then subdividing the latter into strings and winds, omitting percussion entirely. Demonstrating the preference of his time for stringed instruments, Ramos gave detailed descriptions of lutes and monochords and subclassified the stringed instruments according to the length and thickness of their strings. His descriptions of wind instruments also included reference to morphological qualities, including the number and placement of finger holes on an instrument. Ramos de Pareja took a special, pioneering interest in the mechanics and construction of the various keyboard instruments that were becoming popular, the description of which also engrossed other writers, such as Paulus Paulirinus. Their works were the forerunner of a stream of independent treatises that included discussion of the construction and mechanics of keyboards (Hickmann 1971, 83). They viewed keyboards as part of the strings category.

The preference of the time for stringed instruments was also apparent in the works of Johannes de Muris and Philipp de Vitry in the fourteenth century. Both gave large lists of examples or detailed descriptions of them. In the Bible, especially in the Psalms, the cithara and the *psalterium* are most frequently mentioned as instruments with which to praise God.[29] Grocheo, however, gave a musical reason for the preference: "stringed instruments hold the major place, (instruments) whose types are the psalter, the cithara, the lyre, the Saracen guitar, and the vielle. In these there is a subtler and better difference of sound because of the shortening and lengthening of strings" (Grocheo 1967, 19). Presumably he was referring here to the more subtle intonation engendered by the playing technique of the stringed instruments.

Ramos de Pareja's instrumental preferences were demonstrated by the special attention he gave to the clavichord and the stringed instruments without keyboards (Hickmann 1971, 103). Dividing *sonus* into strings and winds, he subdivided the strings according to their acoustical length and thickness. Besides various keyboard instruments he described lutes and the monochord, emphasizing tunings and proportions; and his accounts of wind instruments included the number and placement of finger holes.

Of the sixteenth and seventeenth-century writers, Sebastian Virdung (born c. 1465), Gioseffo Zarlino (1570–1590), Michael Praetorius (work 1619), and Marin Mersenne (work 1636) were among the most innovative instrument taxonomists. Their relatively complex investigations into instruments and chosen characters of division clearly reflected the music-theoretical thought of the time.

They held strings and keyboards, including organs, in high regard, grouping keyboards under the stringed category. Virdung mentioned the organ first in his list of instruments mentioned in the Bible ('the Book') (Virdung 1931, 6). Praetorius gave it a high rating, as did some later writers, including de Brossard (1703). However, they showed very little interest in percussion. Virdung openly admitted to the view that various kinds of small drums were "instruments invented by the devil" as they lacked any goodness (*holtseligkeit*); their sound afforded him great disquiet (*vil onruwe*), being noisy and tending to drown out the sound of the music being played. He also disliked percussion sounds because they did not fit into his sound ideal of sweet melody. However, he made an exception with the *tympanum*, which must "be quite another thing" as it had been used in church services (Virdung 1931, 23) (fig. 10.1).[30] His contemporary Ramos de Pareja, as we noted, left percussion out of his classification altogether. Praetorius held to the doctrinaire and ill-informed view that certain Muslim percussion (and wind) instruments were evil:

> Mohammed, in the interest of extending his tyrannical reign, his devilish cult, and coarse inhuman barbarism, forbad throughout his land the

FIGURE 10.1 Drawing of drums "invented by the Devil" and *Tympana*, which "had been used in church services" (reproduced from Virdung 1931, 23)

practise of the liberal arts, conducive to friendliness, and everything else which might lead to happiness, such as wine and the playing of stringed instruments. In their place he prescribed an infernal gong, a drum and rattling, cackling kinds of shawms. The Turks still value these instruments highly and use them for weddings and joyful feasts, and also in war. (Praetorius 1980, e–f)

Despite their innovativeness, these sixteenth- and seventeenth-century writers did not reject all traditional classificatory practices in their schemes. All four writers began their classifications with reference to a Greek or Roman model. Virdung and Mersenne divided instruments according to the Boethian model into strings, winds, and percussion. Zarlino, having divided instruments into natural and artificial categories according to Aristotelian tradition, then proceeded to subdivide them into winds, strings, and percussion along the lines of the Porphyry model. Praetorius classified instruments à la Pollux into percussion and winds.

The characters chosen for application at the lower steps, however, were closely related to contemporary performing and theoretical concerns, especially the ability of instruments to produce fixed or relatively fixed pitches by mechanical means. Virdung applied two categories at the second step. His four subcategories of strings comprised keyboards (e.g., the *virginal* and *clavichordium*), fretted keyboards (e.g., the lutes and the *grosz Geigen,* or gambas), the multiple-sound producing instruments (e.g., the harps and the *psalterium*), and fretted fingerboards (e.g., the *Trumscheit* and *clein Geigen;* see fig. 10.2), where the character of division was morphological or, more precisely, the mechanics controlling change of pitch (Virdung 1931, 7–11). Only three of the thirteen stringed instruments that he mentioned and illustrated were bowed instruments (the *Trumscheit, clein Geigen,* and *grosz Geigen,* but he did not formally subdivide the strings into the plucked and the bowed. The mechanics controlling change of pitch also served as the character dividing the wind instruments. Winds were classified according to whether they had finger holes (as in the case of the recorders), sacks rather than finger holes (e.g., bagpipes), or bellows instead of finger holes (e.g., organs). The first category was then subdivided by the number of finger holes. As was not unusual in his time, he discussed percussion instruments rather unsystematically, defining them rather vaguely as *aller instrument die vo den metalle oder ander clingende materien werden gemacht* and grouping them, as we have seen, according to whether they were invented by the devil or were used in church services.

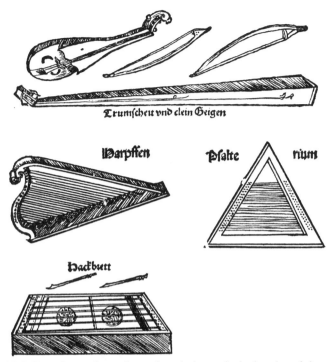

FIGURE 10.2 Drawings of two-bowed and three-plucked stringed instruments (reproduced from Virdung 1931, 10, 11)

Zarlino's main classification was a four-step table (fig. 10.3) that divided its categories at the second and (partly) third steps in key form (Zarlino [1588] 1966, 217). After replicating the Porphyry model he subdivided the winds and the strings morphologically, classifying the percussion by the materials of the instruments. He divided the winds into composite-reed instruments (as exemplified by the organ) and single reeds, which he grouped like Virdung according to whether they had finger holes or not. Single-reed winds with finger holes were exemplified by the *piffaro* (small shawms) and the *flauto* (flute), while single-reed winds without finger holes were divided into one-piece instruments, such as trumpets, and multiple-piece instruments, such as trombones. His classification of strings was more complex. Firstly they were subdivided into those with or without keys, whereupon the keyed instruments were subdivided into the *istromenti mobili* (those that had some moving parts) and *istromenti stabili* (with tuning pegs fixed to the neck of the instrument) (Zarlino [1588] 1966, 216). The *istromenti mobili* were divided into instruments with keys

TAVOLA DE GLI ISTRVMENTI ARTEFICIALI, I QVALI IN. MOLTE MANIERE PERCOSSI, FANNO DIVERSI SVONI.

Come.

Dall'Aria spinta dal Vento, ò dal Fiato in una parte, ò diuerfe dell'Iftrumento, che fi troua effer di due forti.

Dalle Chorde dell'Iftrumento moffe dal Sonatore, che percuotono l'Aria che fi troua effer di due maniere.

Da cofa di legno, ò di ferro, che in effi percuota, & fono di due forti.

O' compofto di molti Corpi.

O' femplice & d'un folo Corpo, che è di due forti.

O' con Tafti.

O' fenza Tafti.

O' femplice.

O' compofto, & è di due forti.

& fi fuona premendo i Tafti có ambe le mani, come l'Organo.

Con fori. & fi fuona con ambe le mani, hora aprendoli hora ferrandoli; com'è il Piffaro, il Flauto & fimili.

O' fenza fori, & di due forti.

O' di due pezzi.

O' d'un pezzo.

Che fi fuona col fiato folo, con l'arteficio del Labro, longando, & hora accorciando l'iftrumento; com'è la Trombetta militare ò campeftre, & altri fimili.

Mobili di due forti.

Stabili di tre forti.

O' che fi fuona con la ruota, che fi uolge có una mano, & con l'altra fi premono le chorde fopra i Tafti, come l'Arpichordo il Grauecembalo & altri fimili.

O' che fi fuona fopra i Tafti con ambe due le mani, & con l'altra fi prono li Tafti fopra una fola chorda; com'è il Violone & altri fimili.

O' che fi fuonano có l'archetto, fregando le chorde có la penna, premendo le chorde con le dita fopra'l manico dell'Iftrumento, come fopra i Tafti del manico dell'Iftrumento, com'è il Violone il Violino, & altri fimili.

O' che fi fuona mouendo le chorde có una mano, & con l'altra premédole fopra i Tafti nel manico dell'Iftrumento, com'è il Liuto, la Viola, & altri fimili.

O' che fi fuona có l'Archetto fregando le chorde, & fi premono fopra i Tafti nel manico dell'Iftrumento, come la Lira, il Violino, & altri fimili.

Che fi fuona có l'Archetto fregando le chorde, & fi premono fopra i Tafti nel manico dell'Iftrumento, come la Cetera & famiglia fua.

Che fi fuona col martello, com'è la Campana ò altri fimili.

O' che fi fuona con ambedue le mani, com'è l'Arpa, il Salterio & altri fimili.

Di legno concauo & cuoio.

O' di legno cócauo & chorde, & di due maniere.

Di metallo.

O' d'inftefti ni.

Che fi percuote con due mazette con ambedue le mani, com'è il Tamburo, & fimili li altri.

Che fi percuote có uerga di metallo, con'è il Dolcimelo, & altri con cofi fatti.

Che fuona percotédolo con una bachetta, & fi fuona inhfieme con un Flauto lungo col Altro baffo, & fimili.

FIGURE 10.3 A classification in Zarlino's *Sopplimenti musicali* (1966, 217)

played by one hand and a wheel rotated by the other (the *sinfonia,* or hurdy-gurdy, was named as the example[31]) and instruments on which the player needed to use both hands to play the keys, as in the case of the *arpichordo* (harp or spinet). Significantly, in view of the fact that writers before Zarlino tended not to group stringed instruments by performance technique, the *istromenti stabili* were subdivided into the bowed instruments (e.g., the *violone,* or gamba), the plectrum-plucked instruments (e.g., the *cetera,* a kind of guitar), and the fingernail-plucked instruments (e.g., lute and *viola,* or *gitarra battente*). In the second main category of strings, which had no keys, he grouped the *lira* (fiddle) and *violino* (viol) into one category and the harp and *psalterium* into another.

Zarlino gave an unusually complex classification of percussion instruments for his time. They were divided into the simple and the composite and then further subdivided according to the materials from which they were made. The simple instruments were made of metal, as exemplified by the *campana* (bells struck with a hammer). He divided the composite instruments into those made of wood and leather (i.e., drums), those beaten with wooden sticks held in both the player's hands, and those made of wood and metal. Instruments in the last category had wooden bodies strung with metal strings. These were divided into two classes. The first of these was exemplified by the *dolcimello,* which was beaten with two metal sticks. The example given for the second category was the *altobasso,* the strings of which were beaten with small sticks by the performer, who also played a flute held in the other hand (Zarlino 1588, 216–18).

Zarlino presented two different classifications of instruments, the second of which entirely dispensed with the traditional threefold and twofold models. It was based on morphological variables combined with performing techniques as they related to tuning, that is, to what extent a player needs to use performing techniques to produce a complete scale of whole and half notes. At the first step he divided instruments into the ones with variable pitches (*istromenti mobili*), such as trombones, and the ones with fixed pitches (*istromenti stabili*) (Zarlino 1588, 218). The fixed-pitch instruments (i.e., those with keys or finger holes) were subdivided at the second step into (1) those whose pitch cannot be changed by playing technique (e.g., the organ, harp, and harpsichord) and (2) those whose pitch and volume can easily be modified by blowing or fingering. The latter category, which was termed *istromenti stabili ma si bene mobili,* was therefore subdivided at the third step into *istromenti stabili ma alterabili* (stable instruments with changeable tunings), such as the viola and lute, and *istromenti stabili ma non senze instabilita* (stable instruments with fixed tuning but not without instability) (Zarlino [1588] 1966, 219).

Tuning was also the main character of division in a classification of Praetorius. As has been mentioned, Praetorius adopted the Pollux model, dividing instruments into categories called *inflatile* (wind) and *percussa* (percussion, including strings) according to the so-called qualitative character of the mode of sound activation. Elsewhere, however, he tabled instruments under the headings of strings and winds (Praetorius 1980, 10) according to three "quantitative" characters: (1) how long the instrument can hold a tone and whether its tuning is fixed or not, a character that he called *respectu longitudinis;* (2) whether it can be made to produce all the tones and voices of a piece or only some or only one voice at a time, which he called *respectu latitudinis;* and (3) whether it can play notes beyond its natural range or not, which he called *respectu profunditatis vel elevationis et depressionis* (Praetorius 1980, 6–7).

Praetorius also grouped instruments by analogy with other segregates under the labels of "families," "sorts," and "accords," naming the "viol family" and the "keyboard family" according to the performance practice of the time. This practice persists in Western countries to this day: the *wind family, the string family,* and so on are still commonly used terms. Praetorius defined *accords* as "entire set(s) of . . . instruments, ranging successively from the deepest and largest instrument to the highest and smallest." An accord of recorders consisted of eight sorts (alto, tenor, basset, and so on), and a complete accord of recorders consisted of twenty-one instruments (Praetorius 1980, 6–7, 12, 13). These classifications somewhat resemble the analogy with families in some Tibetan classifications of instruments, as opposed to the analogies with limbs of the body in India or trees and branches in Arab culture.

The Jesuit mathematician Marin Mersenne divided stringed instruments according to morphological attributes that influenced the tuning system or length of strings. Mersenne was an accomplished acoustician and was well informed about the performance practice of his time. He divided stringed instruments into two categories according to whether they had necks or not, where the former were subdivided into those with and without frets and the latter into those with and without keys. His scheme was not, however, systematically developed. Mersenne was much more interested in the currently developing physics of sound and lower-step grouping of instruments than in large downward classifications, and he included very little on classification in his writings. He preferred to write about nontaxonomically organized details such as an instrument's acoustic qualities, construction methods, materials, and current French performance practice, giving attention to such matters as the length and thickness of spinet strings, hand positions for lute playing, and ornamentation style. Indeed, his interest in precise, detailed descriptions of instruments and consequent lack of interest in large-scale downward division may be seen as a forerunner of the upward classificatory thinking in organology that gained acceptance in the second half of the twentieth century.

Of the four schemes discussed above, Zarlino's was the most innovative in form and content. His chosen characters reflected the interest of his time in an instrument's performing modes, tuning techniques, morphology, and mechanical aspects. His division of strings into those with or without keyboards was mirrored in classifications by his successors right into the twentieth century. Like Virdung and Praetorius, distinctions between instruments with fixed and changeable pitch were important to him.

Zarlino was also the first writer (to my knowledge) to make a clear-cut division of stringed instruments without keyboards into the bowed and the plucked varieties, where the latter consisted of the plectrum-plucked and the fingernail-plucked instruments. There is considerable literary and iconographical evidence that bowed strings had been played in Europe from the early eleventh century. However, it was not usual before Zarlino's time to make distinctions between bowed and plucked strings. This may have been due to the fact that time was needed to build up a tradition of distinguishing between stringed instruments on the basis of playing technique. It may also have been because stringed instruments had until about the thirteenth century been built with a dual purpose; that is, they could be either bowed or plucked, and therefore no taxonomical distinction needed to be made between them. It must also have been because performing techniques were not acceptable as characters of division until after the middle of the twelfth century, when al-Fārābī's works began to be read in Latin.

All four writers, however, were remarkable for their systematic adaptation of current musical trends to traditional classificatory practice. All four wrote in the vernacular rather than the traditional Latin. Indeed, only with a modern vocabulary could they begin to discuss aspects of the contemporary musical scene. All four dealt with a much larger instrumentarium than earlier writers. Their classifications gave prominence to the development of mechanically complex instruments and were related to the current interest in tunings, intervals, and scales. All conceived of instruments as performed objects. Their attempts to describe and draw instruments coincided with the publication of performance manuals for individual instruments from the early seventeenth century.

Of the four writers, Praetorius had the most colorful prose style. He had a knack for formulating concise expressions of the concept of instrument of his day. Nowhere has the Renaissance concept of instrument been so precisely stated as by Praetorius in the passage quoted at the head of this chapter.

In the sixteenth and seventeenth centuries the concept of instrument was expanding to include non-European instruments. Praetorius, for one, claimed to include in his work "all Ancient and Modern Musical Instruments, foreign, barbarian, rustic and unfamiliar as well as indigenous, artistic, agreeable and familiar" (1980, viii). In this respect he resembled the astonishingly forward looking scholar al-Fārābī, who aimed to cover all instruments of the Arabian empire in his account. Virdung also conceived of a large instrumentarium, which included "vernacular and popular instruments," and Mersenne likewise included Turkish, Indian, and other exotic instruments in his discussions. In sixteenth- and seventeenth-century Europe, an awareness of the variety of instruments throughout the world was growing as the great expeditions and voyages of discovery were taking place.

Interest in non-European instruments expanded somewhat in the eighteenth century. Filippo Bonanni included quite a number of drawings of African (e.g., from the Congo), Persian, Indian, Chinese, and Capri ("heathen") instruments in his book of 1722, and Benjamin de la Borde did likewise in his work of 1780. Father Amiot published his account of China's *pa yin* scheme in 1780. Being less technically minded than their forebears in the previous two centuries, they tended to present their world of instruments in terms of sociohistorical characters of division. Thus Bonanni divided his wind, stringed, and percussion instruments into those of the past and the present, deriving eleven categories that were distinguished by geography, social function (e.g., use at feasts, funerals, in the military, or in church services), and so on (1722, 45–176). Similarly, la Borde subdivided instruments into those of the church, of the Negroes, of Abyssinians, of Chinese, of Arabs, of Turks, of Greeks, and of the Bible (Hickmann 1971, 347). These classifications were similar in principle to the scheme of Grocheo, though it is unlikely that their authors were aware of the precedent.

In general, eighteenth-century classifications show little advance on the acoustic and mechanical knowledge applied in classifications of instruments in the previous two centuries.[32] Given this state of affairs, it is perhaps not surprising that in 1713 the music journalist Johann Matthieson complained about the lack of systematic knowledge among musicians and composers about the construction of musical instruments (including their mechanics, materials and potential for improvement) as well as the best instrument makers and performers (Matthieson 1713, 457ff.). As Hickmann points out, Matthieson's point was made in the context of the newly developing bourgeois musical culture, with its many lay musicians (Hickmann 1971, 342).

Eighteenth-century writers generally classed keyboard instruments under percussion rather than strings, unlike their immediate predecessors. Remarkably, this appears to have been due to the persistence of Pollux's classification, which, as we know, included strings and other "beaten" instruments in the percussion category. Thus Majer included keyboards, plucked strings, and tympani under his percussion heading ([1732] 1934, 44). de Brossard's percussion category also included the harpsichord and the spinet (1703, 117). And Barnickel included the harpsichord in his percussion category (1737, 81, 197).

Eighteenth-century authors still paid formal obeisance to tradition by beginning their classifications with ancient models and terms, though sometimes they used labels in the vernacular. For example, Bonanni's three categories, with the vernacular names of *sonori per il fiato, sonori per la tensione,* and *sonori per la percussione,* were based on the Porphyry model (Bonanni 1722, 45, 88, 111).

Stringed instruments were mostly subgrouped by eighteenth-century writers into the bowed and the plucked. Eisel (1738, 24) discussed strings in the order of the bowed and the plucked, without making a formal division between the categories. de Brossard subgrouped instruments in his *enchorda* category into the plucked, the bowed, and the mechanically sounded categories, but he also somewhat redundantly allowed keyboards, hammered bells, and plucked strings to be included in his percussion category, which he named *krusta* or *pulsatilia* (1703, 117).[33] Unusually, Majer even reserved a major category for bowed strings alone (allocating the plucked strings to the percussion, as mentioned above); his three categories were winds (*pneumatica*), percussion (*pulsatilia*), and bowed strings (*chordata*) ([1732] 1934, 29, 44, 75).

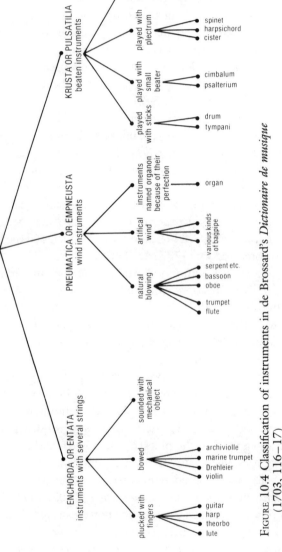

FIGURE 10.4 Classification of instruments in de Brossard's *Dictionaire de musique* (1703, 116–17)

Bowed strings and keyboards were the preferred instruments in the eighteenth century, though the ancient idea that winds are superior because they most resemble the human voice kept recurring also—for example, in Ugolino's thesaurus of 1767 (Hickmann 1971, 346–47). The organ was so highly regarded that one writer bestowed on it a category all its own because of its perfection and referred to it as "the instrument" (*organon*) (see de Brossard's third wind category in fig. 10.4).

Interest in percussion instruments was growing. Both de Brossard and Barnickel (see Barnickel 1737, 81, 197) gave considerable attention to percussion instruments. Eisel, however, included only three instruments in his percussion category. Barnickel divided his *pulsatilia* category into instruments beaten with special pieces of wood (e.g., the drum) and instruments with knockers (e.g., bells), the latter grouping resembling the "rung" category of Tibetan monastic instruments. Winds were subdivided according to broad morphological attributes. For example, instruments sounded "through the breath" were divided into those with special mouthpieces (e.g., trombones and flutes) and those with reeds (such as the *Schallmeyer*), thereby using a morphological character that became important in nineteenth- and twentieth-century classifications.

Conclusion

Greek and Roman ideas, terminologies, and tree-form schemes persisted in European classifications of instruments for at least twelve hundred years, though from the thirteenth and especially the sixteenth centuries they assumed an increasingly formal significance only. From early Roman times, certain Greek notions were merged with Christian ideas. An example is the Greek idea of the superiority of the human vocal instrument, which persisted because of the syncretic idea that it was "God's instrument." Related to this was the dichotomy of continuous versus discontinuous sound, which also assumed a speculative Christian character. The Greek theory of ethos adopted a Christian orientation (only after the Renaissance did it become a more general theory of effects by association). Music and instruments became objects of Christian as well as academic contemplation. And the idea of the harmony of the spheres expanded into a three-category, spiritually oriented classification of musical knowledge that included instruments.

The dominant concept of instruments in the Middle Ages was primarily religious, speculative, and theoretical, being far removed from practical music making. Treatises referred only to antique and biblical instruments, making no mention of contemporary ones. Approximately from the time of the Renaissance, however, the dominant concept of instrument became more humanistically inclined, focusing on the instrument as a contemporary performing tool within particular social or regional contexts and used for the entertainment of people as well as the glory of God. This conceptual shift coincided with the translation of al-Fārābī's works into Latin and the exposure in Europe to his practice-oriented interpretation of the Greek idea of theoretical and practical instruments.

Though early Christian theologians sometimes emphasized the unity of creation and did not classify the instruments to which they referred at all, most later medieval writers grouped instruments as part of their classification of musical sound on the basis of the spiritual, cosmological concept of music presented by Boethius. The chosen characters were aspects of morphology or mode of sound excitation. Beginning with the Renaissance, however, principles of classification had expanded to include aspects of mechanics, tuning, and performance practice as well as broad historical factors (ancient and modern) and social function. The most innovative classificatory schemes were produced by Grocheo in the thirteenth century and by Virdung, Zarlino, and Praetorius in the sixteenth and seventeenth centuries. Eighteenth-century schemes largely consolidated earlier achievements.

The predominant structure of classification schemes from Late Roman to quite modern times was the three-category Boethian model (strings, winds, and percussion), though the Porphyry scheme (winds, strings, and percussion) and the Cassiodorus scheme (percussion, strings, and winds) also showed some persistence, as did the two-category Pollux model (percussion [including strings] and winds). The vocal instrument continued to reign supreme until modern times, but the reputation of inanimate instruments, especially strings and winds, grew steadily. A shift in preference from strings to winds among Late Roman writers was reversed in approximately the ninth century. Some writers and painters expressed in their works a reverence for the organ, which was not only one of the oldest instruments but also the subject of intensive scientific investigation (especially regarding its pipes) in the Middle Ages and the only instrument allowed to be used in church (see H. M. Brown 1984, 41).[34]

The delineation of categories of bowed and plucked stringed instruments developed gradually. Writers since the early part of the second millennium had mentioned both bowed and plucked or dual-purpose strings in their writings; but the evidence suggests that a clear classificatory distinction was not made between them until the sixteenth century. Keyboard instruments shifted from the stringed to the percussion category. From the fifteenth century keyboards were classed under strings, but eighteenth-century writers tended to group them under percussion.

The number of instruments mentioned in medieval treatises was normally quite small and was restricted to ancient instruments. From the thirteenth century, however, contemporary as well as ancient instruments began to rate a mention, while from the sixteenth century not only newly invented but also non-European instruments began to be taken into account. The voyages of discovery, the growing ease of communications, and the accumulation of collections of instruments from around the world in eighteenth-century Europe combined to prepare the way for the development of a complex, global concept of instruments having many attributes, including the morphological, ergological, acoustic, performing, social, and historical.

The Expanding Concept of Instruments in the West during the Nineteenth and Twentieth Centuries

We might as well divide Americans into Californians, bankers, and Catholics as divide instruments [into strings, winds, and percussion.]
Curt Sachs, *The History of Musical Instruments*

From the time of the expeditions and great voyages of discovery, and especially from the early eighteenth century, large collections of instruments were beginning to be amassed. Travelers to the corners of the globe were bringing home specimens of instruments, many of which were eventually displayed in the museums being built throughout Europe. Interest in exotic and ancient instruments grew apace, as exemplified by the work of Villoteau (1759–1839) on Egyptian instruments.

By the nineteenth century, museum instrument collections had been established in Germany, Belgium, Sweden, Holland, Czechoslovakia, the United States, and elsewhere. The explosion in the number of specimens collected, which were generally poorly documented, engendered a new interest in taxonomical problems, foremost among which were the diagnosis of specimens of instruments and the creation of systems of information storage and retrieval in museum situations. In practice, the diagnoses and naming of specimens by museologists were often wrong. As Hornbostel and Sachs complained about museum catalogues that they had encountered, "the same instrument may be indiscriminately called a lute, guitar, mandoline or banjo" (1914, 5). The need was felt in parts of Europe from the latter part of the nineteenth century for a relatively accurate, detailed, and preferably logical tree- or key-form classification scheme to cover and identify all instruments the world over, if only for purposes of museum displays and catalogues. Previous classifications had been designed for limited—not worldwide—instrumentaria and were based on concepts of instruments or had theoretical or practical purposes that were no longer seen as appropriate for contemporary needs.

MAHILLON

The first classification of musical instruments suitable for worldwide use was inspired by museological use. A remarkable scheme was developed by the organologist and acoustician Mahillon (1893), whose achievements have been somewhat unfairly overshadowed by the later adaptation of his scheme by Hornbostel and Sachs in 1914. Mahillon was the curator of the large and growing collection of instruments held in the *Musée Instrumental du Conservatoire Royale de Musique* in Brussels, which included his own collection. Like all previous European schemes, Mahillon's used the method of downward logical division.

Mahillon published his classification with an introductory essay explaining the system. The scheme applied a single character of division at three of its four steps. It was fairly logical therefore and also had quite a symmetrical structure (see fig. 11.1). At the first step the instruments were divided into four "classes," governed by the nature of the vibrating, sound-producing body. The first class was called "autophones" (self-sounders), in which sound is maintained not by any kind of applied tension but by the elasticity of the instrument's body. The second class was named "membranophones," in which the sound waves are excited by tightly stretched membranes. The third class comprised "chordophones," or instruments that produce sound by the excitation of stretched strings. And the fourth was called "aerophones," or instruments containing a column of air that is set in vibration by wind or breath in a column or across a reed.

Mahillon named his second step of division "branches," using a similar analogy to the Indian one. Here the character of division was the mode of sound activation. At his third level of division, which he named "sections," two different characters operated. Some aerophones and all the membranophones were grouped according to whether they produced sounds of determinate or indeterminate pitch, whereas all the other instruments were governed by the precise form of the sound activator; in some cases this was a plectrum, in others a keyboard, and so on. At the fourth step, which Mahillon called "subsections," the character of division was a morphological detail, such as "slides" or "pistons," which governed timbre or pitch.

The concept of instrument that this ingenious scheme exemplified was a secular, ahistorical one. Unlike some more modern schemes it took little account of an instrument's performing techniques, the social background

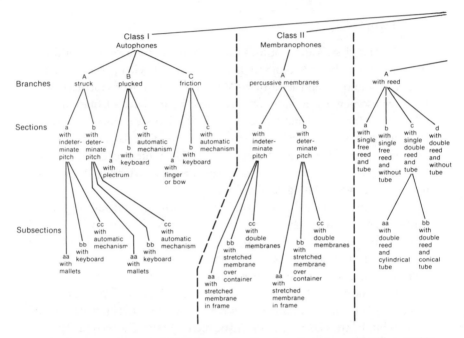

Figure 11.1 Structure of Mahillon's classification (based on Mahillon 1893, 503–5)

of the performer and the instrument, change in the instrument, or the musical styles that typified it. Nor was the ergology of instruments considered, for to Mahillon the object of classification was the finished instrument, not its mode of construction. Mahillon saw instruments primarily as musically functioning, acoustical, and morphological objects that occur in multifarious forms. As an instrument curator, he was aware of the similarities and the diversity of instruments and their nomenclatures throughout the world, but his concept of instruments was based on the experience primarily of European instruments. This was reflected in his classification, which in Hornbostel and Sachs's view (1914, 7) gave undue prominence to specifically European subdivisions of instruments, such as of keyboards and mechanical instruments.

The strengths of Mahillon's scheme included its wide coverage of instruments, its potential for logical exhaustiveness, and its careful attention to detail. As Hornbostel and Sachs commented (1961: 6–7), the scheme could absorb "almost the whole range of ancient and modern,

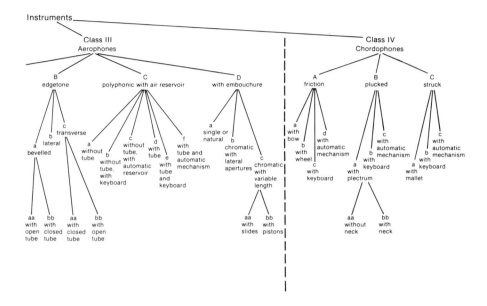

European and non-European instruments . . . not only does it meet the demands of logic, but also it provides those who use it with a tool which is simple and proof against subjective preferences. Moreover, it is not so far removed from previously-used divisions as to offend well-established custom." It gave much greater attention to percussion instruments than did previous European schemes, dividing them into the self-sounders and instruments sounded by stretched membranes. Except for this extra division, it resembled the well-established tripartite scheme of percussion, strings, and winds.

Galpin's First Scheme

The burgeoning of knowledge about instruments continued unabated in the late nineteenth and early twentieth centuries, with "a flood of historical monographs on all important instruments" (Winternitz in Sachs [1913] 1964). The monographs included Eichborn on trumpets in 1881, Hipkins on the pianoforte and older keyboard instruments in 1896, and Kinkeldey on the sixteenth-century organ in 1910. The only classification schemes to be presented, however, were two by Galpin, one of which was drawn up in 1900 (Galpin [1910] 1965) for the International Music Exhibition held in London's Crystal Palace, and the incomparably more intricate and influential scheme of Hornbostel and Sachs.

Rejecting the traditional tripartite division of instruments as "incomplete" and the subdivision of winds into wood and brass as "superficial," Galpin adopted Mahillon's four classes for his scheme, reordering and renaming them (A) "sonorous substances," (B) "vibrating membranes," (C) "wind instruments," and (D) "stringed instruments" (Galpin 1910, 231–34). He made up to seven subdivisions, naming them "classes," "divisions," "groups," "sections," "subsections," "branches," and "families," and designating them by small capitals, roman numerals, roman capitals letters, lowercase roman numerals, lowercase italic letters, and asterisks respectively (fig. 11.2). Like Mahillon, whose work he knew, he chose the nature of the vibrating material as the character of division at the highest step. At the second step, however, the operating character was whether there was a keyboard or not, as opposed to an automatic mechanism. This highly weighted character was a more appropriate choice for the European instrumentarium than for the rest of the world in view of the fact that Europeans evaluate keyboard and other mechanical instruments more highly than others. It also gave the scheme a somewhat unbalanced structure and a quality of being divorced from the music practice, as only two of the four main categories contained any examples of keyboards. As Galpin admitted (1910, 233), the keyboard taxon in the category of

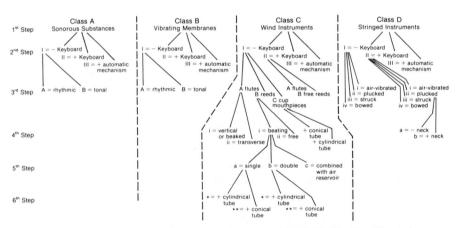

FIGURE 11.2 Structure of Galpin's classification ([1910] 1965). Families (where applicable) are placed together in successive order (treble, alto, tenor, bass, etc.)

sonorous substances was "not yet in use"; that is, no concrete example could be found for it. Moreover, the automatic-mechanism taxa were not further subdivided at all. At the third step, nonkeyboard instruments in the first two main categories were divided into the "rhythmic and tonal" by use of a character reminiscent of the medieval distinction between instruments with nonfixed and fixed pitch; and thereafter the first two main categories ceased to be subdivided. Winds without keyboards were subdivided morphologically according to whether they were flutes, had reeds, or had cup mouthpieces; while winds with keyboards were subdivided according to whether they were flutes with beating and retreating reeds or were free reeds. Winds with automatic mechanisms were not subdivided. The strings were subdivided according to whether they were air-vibrated, plucked, struck, or bowed.

This first classification scheme of Galpin was fairly logical in structure, applying strict logical division in the first two steps and more than one character per step thereafter. It was not very symmetrical, with only two steps of division in the first two categories, five for some of the wind category, and three for some of the stringed category. But its practicality was demonstrated by its use in the London Exhibition in 1900 as well as in instrument catalogues of two museums. It accompanied Galpin's discussions (e.g., in his book of 1910) about the morphological, historical, and other aspects of instruments, thus contributing to the trend toward their more comprehensive study. Galpin's scheme was very different from Hornbostel and Sachs's scheme of 1914. Not being an ethnologist, he included only Western instruments in his considerations.

HORNBOSTEL AND SACHS

The increasing explosion of organological knowledge on both systematic and historical fronts urgently required synthesis. This need was partly fulfilled in Berlin by Curt Sachs in collaboration with Erich von Hornbostel, who drew together the collective organological knowledge of the time, relying heavily on the achievements of Mahillon. Unlike his predecessors, Sachs had presented a mass of ethnological as well as linguistic information about instruments in his *Reallexikon der Musikinstrumente* (1913) as well as in some influential monographs (e.g., Sachs [1929] 1965, 1940). He rejected the traditional tripartite scheme, which he quoted in its Boethian form (Sachs 1940, 454), claiming that it does not suffice for scientific purposes as it is "illogical, and is by no means comprehensive" and it lacks a "consistent principle of division. . . . The usual division of the orchestra into stinged, wind and percussion instruments is based on three different principles instead of one: the sonorous material acted upon, in 'strings'; the activating force, in 'wind'; and the action itself, in 'percussion.' "

Recognizing the achievements of Mahillon's (relatively) "logical as well as universal classification" (Sachs 1940, 454), Hornbostel and Sachs drew up an even more intricate classification scheme based on Mahillon's.[1] Their classification was intended to serve both as a conceptual framework for cross-cultural comparative purposes in their own writings and to remedy the still somewhat chaotic state of instrument collections in museums. It aimed to allow for the disconcerting variety of instruments, something that the "rough classification of our modern orchestra" does not allow (Sachs 1940, 454). "Friction instruments, the glass harmonica for instance, or instruments with plucked tongues, like the jew's-harp and the musical box, are neither stringed, wind nor percussion instruments; and if the endless world of historic, folk and exotic instruments are included—and no scientific history can exclude them—the disconcerting category, 'Varia,' grows disproportionately" (Sachs 1940, 454).

By adapting, enlarging, and adding numerical categories to Mahillon's scheme, Hornbostel and Sachs developed for museum collections of instruments an information storage and retrieval system which superficially resembles that developed for libraries by the American librarian Melvil Dewey (1851–1931). The Dewey Decimal System of Classification was "a hierarchical system for dividing and organizing knowledge in a library based on the decimal principle. In it, knowledge is divided into groups, with each group assigned 100 numbers; e.g. religion is in the 2000s. . . . Within each class, the principle sub-series are subdivided by 10. In practice, the notation always consists of at least three digits, although its theoretical expression could be extremely long. The notation lends itself to memory through the constant repetition of a standard pattern" (Parker 1979, 508). However, it is not advisable to think of the Hornbostel and Sachs scheme as being comparable to Dewey's classification system for library books; the similarity is only apparent initially. The Hornbostel and Sachs scheme uses a varying set of criteria to distinguish its various subcategories under the four main taxa, while the Dewey system applies a single author and subject across the board.

Hornbostel and Sachs gave a clear account of the rationale behind their scheme. It is therefore possible to note the differences between their total concept of instruments as reflected in their own writings about instruments and the limited concept of instruments that they adopted for classificatory purposes, and also why they chose to reject some of the tenets of logic and symmetry in the structure of their scheme. Hornbostel and Sachs's total concept of instruments was a broad one, including not only the instrument's ergological, acoustic, morphological, musical-stylistic, linguistic, and other aspects but also its historical and social parameters. They described instruments as being "alive and dynamic," as growing and changing "without reference to any conceptual scheme" such as theirs (Hornbostel and Sachs [1914] 1961, 4). But like all other macrotaxono-mists, they found that for purposes of classification they had to adopt a restricted concept of instruments, because unlike the instruments to be classified, "systems are static and depend upon sharply drawn demarcations and categories" (Hornbostel and Sachs 1961, 4). They clearly realized the contradictions between systems and reality. Their scheme as they envis-aged it had to be able to order all existing and conceivable instruments in a manner independent of space and time (for "all nations and all times" [1961], 5); that is, they wanted it to be logically exhaustive, in theory at least. Thus, it had to limit its characters to the nature of the sounding body and some aspects of the playing method of each instrument. As with Mahillon, the concept behind their classification was a static, ahistorical view of the instrument as a musically functioning and morphological object. The scheme had some historical implications, in that its subdivisions are able to serve as a basis of "the observation of cultural history" (Hornbostel and Sachs, 1961, 10). But it was devised first and foremost for systematic and practical museological purposes, not to show historical change.

In the Hornbostel and Sachs scheme, the first step and character of division were the same as Mahillon's but they renamed the first of his four categories "idiophones." Idiophones were defined as instruments sounded by "the substance of the instrument itself, owing to its solidity and elasticity . . . without requiring stretched membranes or strings"; mem-branophones as instruments "excited by tightly stretched membranes"; chordophones as instruments "with one or more strings stretched between fixed points"; and aerophones as instruments in which "the air itself is the vibrator in the primary sense" (1914, 14, 17, 20, 24). Thus all four categories were divided according to the one general character: "the physical characteristics of sound production" (1914, 8). The structure of their classification of idiophones may be sketched as in figure 11.3. They described their method by using the example of an idiophone:

> Say, for example, that it is a bell chime (*Glockenspiel*) which is to be coded and placed in the system. In the context of the system we are dealing with an idiophone, the class to which the initial code-figure is allotted. Since

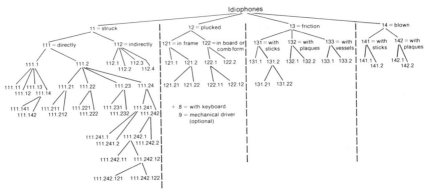

FIGURE 11.3 Structure of Hornbostel and Sachs's classification of idiophones

the instrument is struck it belongs to the first sub-class, and so another 1 is added (struck idiophones—II). Further addition of relevant code-figures produces the ranking 111 since it is struck directly; and then, as a struck-upon [percussion] idiophone, it earns a fourth figure, in this case 1 (1112 = percussion idiophones). Further specification leads to 11124 (percussion vessels), 111242 (bells), 1112422 (sets of bells), 11124222 (sets of hanging bells), and 111242222 (ditto with internal strikers)— obviously everyone must decide for himself how far to go in a given case. Instead of the unmanageable number now arrived at, we write 111.242.222. The first cluster shows that we are dealing with an idiophone that is struck directly, while the second and third together imply that we are dealing with bells. 1914 (1961, 11)

As heirs to a long tradition of downward classification Hornbostel and Sachs had a high regard for the method of logical division.[2] However, they were forced to conclude that reality as they conceived it was too complex to allow single-character division to operate beyond the first step in their classification. They let the principle of division be "dictated by the nature of the groups concerned, so that ranks of a given position within a group may not always correspond between one group and another" (1961, 9). Thus, their second step of division of idiophones and membranophones was made according to the mode of sound activation, while that of the chordophones was made on a morphological basis and that of the aero-phones on a morphological and acoustic principle.[3] At the third step, the operative characters were mode of sound activation (e.g., the struck idio-phones were subdivided into those struck directly and those struck indi-rectly) on the one hand and morphological aspects (e.g., whether plucked idiophones are fixed in a frame or occur in board or comb form) on the other. Further morphological and performance-practice-determined characters governed the lower steps.

Hornbostel and Sachs decided against using a symmetrical structure, refraining from "providing a subdivision containing no known existing representative, save in cases where a composite type may be assumed to have had a precursor in a simpler type now extinct." Moreover, "where the wealth of forms is exceptionally vast, as with rattles, only the more general aspects of their classification can be outlined in the scheme, and these will certainly require further elaboration" (1961, 10). Thus, idiophones had three to five steps of division in the case of the struck variety, three to four in the case of the plucked ones, and two each in the friction and blown varieties, as is shown in figure 11.3. They rejected schematic symmetry, conscious as they were of the changeability and varying degrees of complexity of different kinds of instruments; moreover, they wished to leave room for additions and further development of their scheme as and when new data came to light.

Except perhaps for the traditional tripartite scheme, Hornbostel and Sachs's scheme has had the most use and the greatest effect of any classification of instruments during this century. But as has been noted, use of the scheme has mostly been limited to its upper one to three steps of division. Moreover, its adoption in museums has been nowhere near as widespread as that of Dewey's scheme in libraries. Its limitations have been pointed out by a number of writers, though it could be argued that some of the criticisms are based on somewhat unrealistic demands. Sakurai (1981, 824) criticized its "somewhat ethnocentric" nomenclature on the grounds that terms such as zithers, harps, lyres, or lutes derive mainly from "European cultures or those circumferential to Europe." He was also concerned about its "lack of uniform standard for establishing lower order categories" (1981, 824). Grame was one who compared it with Dewey's scheme, which indicates only tenuous relationships between adjacent books on a library shelf, namely, that they are on the same or nearly the same subjects and that their authors' names are in close alphabetical order. Thus, he wrote that the

> instruments that Sachs and von Hornbostel have placed numerically close to one another in their system—even instruments that possess identical numbers—have only a physical and acoustical relationship. Their close juxtaposition does not allow us to deduce that their functions are similar, that they are constructed of identical material, that they are similarly decorated, or that they are historically related to each other. (1963, 138)

Grame noted "an alarming tendency on the part of some to use the system as a basis for scholarly investigation" (1963, 138). However, in the decades after Hornbostel and Sachs's scheme was developed, a shift of interest occurred away from limited-character, downward classification to the intensive study of individual instruments. Such scholars as Izikowitz, who made a detailed study of South American Indian instruments (1935), and Ling, who researched the many-sided complexities of the keyed fiddle (1967), made little or no use of the Hornbostel and Sachs scheme or any other scheme devised for the purpose of classifying large instrumentaria. There was a realization that one cannot have one's cake and eat it too; a scheme that allows for the quick diagnosis of instruments and easy information storage and retrieval does not lend itself to the accurate, detailed study of individual instruments and their ordering or grouping for study purposes.

Several writers have complained about the crudity of the high-level divisions and consequent borderline cases that arise in the Hornbostel and Sachs' scheme. For example, Ledang (1972, 102) queried the classification of the jew's harp as an idiophone, and Yamaguchi (1969, 190–91) questioned the classification of reed instruments as aerophones. But this kind of complaint can also, of course, be leveled against other schemes possessing a high degree of generality. The problem was recognized by Hornbostel and Sachs themselves when they noted that the practice of subdividing, say, violins on the basis of playing action was "a dubious procedure; a violin remains a violin whether one bows it with a bow, plays it *pizzicato* with the finger, or strikes it *col legno*" ([1914] 1961, 7–8). A borderline case such as the ancient Celtic *crwth*, which was "plucked in earliest times, but which came to be bowed in the High Middle Ages" (Hornbostle and Sachs [1914 [1961]: 8) can only be resolved by allocating it more than one place in the classification. While this solution may not be very elegant, it is a necessary one for only a limited number of specimens. It is true that ambiguous or borderline cases cannot be dealt with in a perfectly satisfactory way in Hornbostel and Sachs's system, but such cases must logically occur in all downward classifications whether they be Western "scientific" or homegrown schemes. Far from invalidating the system, their occurrence is a logical consequence of a scheme's conceptual basis, which must impose some boundaries or other.

In 1940 Sachs added to the scheme a fifth category, which he called "electrophones" (Sachs 1940, 447–49, 467), dividing them into three subcategories.[4] The first subcategory comprised instruments with an electronic action instead of the common mechanical or pneumatic action, as in the electric organ. The second category, which he named "electro-mechanical" instruments, produced sounds in the usual mechanical ways (e.g., by hammers striking piano strings or a bow acting on a violin) but transformed them into electric vibrations by amplification through an electrical device.[5] An example of an electro-mechanical instrument was the Neo-Bechstein piano of 1931, in which eighteen microphones were included, allowing for the production of a much longer tone, for greater dynamic change, and for a great variety of timbres, despite its being smaller than an ordinary piano. As Sachs noted, none of the electrome-chanical instruments actually became important in musical life. The third category of instruments, which he termed "radioelectric," were based on oscillating electric circuits. Some of them had a gliding scale and were playable either with or without a manual (1940, 447–49).

The electrophone category, which was also proposed or used by Galpin, Hood, and others, has become accepted in its broad outlines, though it has been somewhat loosely used. Logically it should include only the first and third of Sachs's three subcategories. As the basic character of division of the Hornbostel and Sachs scheme was the "physical characteristics of sound production," only instruments that actually produce sound by electrical means should in fact be included, not instruments that produce sounds in traditional ways and then alter or amplify their sounds through an electrical device.[6] The electric guitar, for example, is not technically an electrophone as its vibrations are mechani-cally produced and then electronically converted into instrumental sound by means of a variety of added equipment. Electro-mechanical instruments such as the electric violin or harpsichord are not electrophones either, as they produce sounds by conventional means (such as by reeds or strings) and then modify or amplify them electronically. For example, the vibra-phone played in jazz and some orchestral Western music produces a vibrato effect through modifying its mechanically produced sounds by the rotation of electrically operated fans placed at the top of its resonating tubes.

Instruments using electronic action (e.g., the electric organ) as well as radioelectric instruments (e.g., synthesizers) are characterized by their electric source of sound. The electric organ produces sound by signals created by oscillations of electronic circuits, unlike a traditional organ, which creates sound by forcing air through pipes. The ancestors of synthesizers such as the theremin and the ondes martenot, which hail from the 1920s, as well as modern synthesizers, which date from the 1940s, are true electrophones. The "synthetic" music they produce can generate but also modify and shape electrically produced sounds. In a Moog synthesizer, for example, oscillators produce electric impulses, creating sounds that may then be mixed (i.e., two or more sounds may be combined). They may also be filtered to emphasize or suppress groups of harmonics, amplified to vary dynamic level, and controlled by a device such as a keyboard. Pieces of digital signal-processing equipment are also classifiable as electrophones because they produce their own sound; they also process it, "giving the composer and musician a level of freedom and precision of control never before obtainable" (Moorer 1977, 1108).

Recent articles by Moorer (1977) and Risset and Wessel (1982) clarify the distinction between instruments that produce sounds electronically as opposed to those that simply process natural sounds. Moorer's article surveys the analytical use of natural sounds for musical synthesis, in particular discussing the role of special-purpose hardware in digital musical synthesis. It distinguishes three kinds of synthesis of musical sound: (1) synthesis in which the composer writes a computer program that produces the samples of the waveforms of the sounds he wishes to produce; (2) "analysis-based synthesis," in which existing natural tones are digitized and analyzed, creating the data to drive the synthesis; and (3) *musique concrete*, where natural sounds are digitized and processed by the computer in various ways without analyzing and resynthesizing them. Risset and Wessel's article also discusses how a computer electrophone can produce "cross-synthesis," which is the production of a sound that compounds certain aspects of one sound with another, and also how a computer can best produce, for example, brasslike sounds (1982, 30–32, 36) as well as other simulated instrumental sounds.

SCHAEFFNER

In 1932 Andre Schaeffner, the instrument curator at the Musée de l'Homme, developed a new classification method (revised in 1936) that returned to the division of two major categories and to the strict application of logical principle. The scheme was suited to instruments of all cultures and was based on the ideas of Mahillon. However, Schaeffner rejected Mahillon's and Hornbostel and Sachs's category of autophones/idiophones, which, as defined by Montandon (1919, 47), meant instruments "in which the vibration is caused by the body, and not by a membrane, a string or, primarily, the air" (see Kunst 1974, 59–60). The idiophone category, Schaeffner wrote, is not sufficiently differentiated and therefore cannot avoid the faulty classification of instruments such as the African *sanza*, whose plucked tongues—not the body or soundboard— vibrate, thus making them linguaphones rather than idiophones,[7] or East Asian and African xylophones, whose keys, not the body or box, vibrate. More importantly, the presence of the idiophone category destroyed the only basis for the Hornbostel and Sachs classification's claim to logical structure, namely, single-character division at the highest step. Kunst (1974, 61) wrote that he did not mind waiving this objection to Hornbostel and Sachs's scheme "purely from considerations of expedience." However, Schaeffner could not accept the differentiation of this category, nor its logical inadequacy. Schaeffner also argued that the physical structure of an instrument, not its playing method, should be the main criterion for its classification. He constructed a key, making a basic distinction between wind instruments and all others and dividing the latter into those that are operated by tension and those that are not. Thus, at the highest level his downward classification divided the world instrumentarium into two categories: (I) instruments with solid, vibrating bodies and (II) instruments containing vibrating air. The solid bodies were then subdivided into (A) those that are not susceptible to tension (i.e., nontensile instruments, such as the xylophone), (B) those that are flexible (i.e., with plucked tongues, such as the *sanza*), and (C) those that are susceptible to tension (i.e., tensile instruments, such as strings). The second category, which comprises instruments containing vibrating air, was subdivided into (A) those with ambient air, such as sirens, accordions, and harmoniums; (B) those containing free cavities, such as earthen drums; and (C) those containing an air column, for example, (a) various kinds of flutes, (b) trumpets and horns, and (c) clarinets and oboes, and so on. Nontensile solid bodies (IA) were subdivided at the third step according to the material of which they were made (wood, bamboo, metal, etc.) and then, at the fourth step, according to morphological characters, i.e., tensile solids (IC) (strings, for example), were subdivided into the single and the composite. At the fifth step, morphological characters again dominate; thus solid bodies such as xylophones [IAIb)] and boomerangs [IAIb)3] were placed close together, as were *angklung* and *calung* (shaken [IAIIa)2] and beaten [IAIIa)3] Sundanese bamboo instruments, respectively), castanets and cymbals, and gongs and bronze drums.

Schaeffner's system meets the demands of logic in virtually all respects. Not only is it logically exhaustive, potentially covering all real and conceivable instruments, but its two major categories are mutually exclusive, and it applies single-character division at all its five steps (although its lowest step is a little more hazy than the others). It is not a symmetrically developed scheme, as its second category has only two steps in the case of instruments containing free cavities, three steps in the case of instruments with ambient air, and four steps in the case of instruments with air columns), as opposed to five in the first category.

Unlike the Hornbostel and Sachs classification, Schaeffner's scheme has not been translated into English and has had little impact outside France. Its comparative novelty or, in other words, its lack of continuity with past classifications, the greater prestige of Hornbostel and Sachs as scholars, and the greater exposure of Hornbostel and Sachs's classification mediated against the widespread acceptance of Schaeffner's scheme, despite its elegantly logical quality.

GALPIN'S SECOND SCHEME

In 1937 Galpin devised and published a second classification scheme. As in his first, he based this scheme on Mahillon's four highest categories, which he renamed "autophonic instruments or self-vibrators," "membranophonic instruments or skin-vibrators," "chordophonic instruments or string-vibrators," and "aerophonic instruments or wind-vibrators." To accommodate recent developments in electronics, he added a fifth category comprising "electrophonic instruments or electric vibrators," in which "sound-waves are formed by oscillations set up in electric valves" (1937, 29–30). He reversed the order of the last two categories in his first system to match those of Mahillon and Hornbostel and Sachs, retaining a similar scheme of numerical and letter designation.

His concept of instruments, as reflected in this classification, was governed by acoustic and morphological aspects. He was the first to include a category of electrophonic instruments. At the first three steps, the respective characters of division were the nature of the vibrating body, the mode of sound activation, and whether a sound was directly or indirectly activated. Thus, electrophones were divided at the second step into three taxa according to whether the sound was formed by oscillations set up in electric valves by electromagnetism or by electrostatic means. For example, the Hammond organ exemplified the electromagnetic, indirectly activated electrophone with a keyboard. Single-character division was abandoned at the fourth (and last) step, which was governed either by the mode of sound activation or by a morphological character.

This fairly logical scheme of Galpin's was also relatively symmetrical, although (except in the case of the directly plucked, neckless strings) the third and fifth categories had one less step of subdivision than the other three and considerably fewer taxa. Its relegation of the keyboard variable to the fourth step gave it a less Eurocentric flavor than the earlier scheme, where the keyboard variable was applied at the second step. In the new scheme keyboards were omitted altogether in the membranophonic category but were combined with other categories at the fourth step. It still had a slightly Eurocentric quality, however, in its emphasis on automatic mechanisms and electrophones. It may also be criticized for its imprecisions and incomplete characters of division. For example, the bagpipe classification—IV.ii.B.a.—omits the arguably crucial consideration of the instrument's confinement of air, defining it only as an indirect reed-voice aerophone with finger holes, where the meaning of *indirect* is not clearly specified. It has its borderline cases; for example, the designation of the carillon—I.i.B.a.—implies by its last letter that it has a keyboard, thus excluding automatic carillons. This classification problem can only be overcome by giving the carillon two classification numbers, which is comparable to giving a double classification for jew's harps in the Hornbostel and Sachs scheme. Though the practicability of Galpin's scheme has been demonstrated by its use in the Vleeshuis Museum in Antwerp, the system has not in any sense become a rival of the Hornbostel and Sachs scheme. Reasons for this include its less-intricate subdivisions, its slightly greater Eurocentric quality, its imprecisions, its lack of a clearly explained rationale, and the greater musicological stature of Hornbostel and Sachs.

NORLIND AND IZIKOWITZ

Galpin's concept of instrument was quite limited compared with the vision of Tobias Norlind, a contemporary Swedish writer, who did not, however, develop his own method of classification. In an article on musical instrument systematics published in 1932, Norlind suggested that besides such matters as morphology, tone quality, and scales, characters governing performance practice, aspects of nomenclature, geographical distribution, and cultural history should be taken into account. This article was part of the beginning of a shift away from a largely morphological concept of instrument, associated as it was with downward classification by logical division, to a more dynamic, expansive view of the instrument as part of musical and sociohistorical behavior, for which methods of multivariable upward grouping would eventually be developed. Norlind's dissatisfaction with the limited concept of instruments that lay behind classifications of instruments until his time prepared the way for a broader view and classification to match. It is comparable to the disquiet felt by a student of medicine who cannot understand or cure the ills of a patient by considering factors of anatomy alone and consequently feels the need to consider the patient's total physiology, psychology, environment, and history before diagnosing the problem and prescribing a cure. Norlind's concept resembled, yet went beyond, the one to which Sachs theoretically adhered but was not able to apply in its full complexity in his and Hornbostel's famous classification scheme of 1914.

An even broader concept of instruments was held by Karl Izikowitz (1935). Although he adhered rigidly to a general classification of instruments according to acoustic principles, he recommended that ethnographic work include comprehensive research into special classes of artifacts, such as instruments.

> Artefact, regarded as a cultural element, is always at bottom the outward form of a complex of ideas in the minds of the human beings by whom it is made and used. It arises through certain wants, desires and ideas, i.e. it fills certain purposes or functions, and its form also depends on the technical ideas and the skill of its maker. All scientific investigations of material objects should be made with a view to increasing our knowledge either of a technique, which in its turn is influenced by the environment and the natural materials at hand, or of the functions of the artefact or of both. . . . The complex of functions associated with a material object may include not only the direct uses to which it is put in social life, but also religious, ritualistic, and other conceptions. These latter conceptions may also influence the technique and form of the artefact. . . . A sound instrument with which supernatural conceptions about a good harvest are associated may have spread together with the technical ideas regarding the materials of agriculture itself. From this viewpoint, studies of material objects form a natural starting point for investigations of cultural influences and dissemination. (Izikowitz 1935, 2)

Musical instruments are especially adapted to a study of this kind, since they are almost always associated with ceremonies and other complexes of ideas in social life.

DRÄGER

It remained for the German scholar Hans Heinz Dräger to take the first step toward developing an upward method of classification based on the detailed inspection and delineation of an instrument's characteristics. He found single- and limited-character division to be inadequate for his concept of instrument. Indeed he felt that a large number of distinctive characteristics (*Kennzeichnen*)—not one or a few characters—needed to be considered simultaneously if the instrument was to be viewed and classified in its true complexity. Though he commenced inquiry at the specific level, he did not take the next step, as Oskár Elschek did in 1969 (1969a, 1969b), and classify similar types of instruments by upward grouping. He simply added his clusters of variables, or "facets" as Michael Ramey termed them, to the entries of the Hornbostel and Sachs scheme. He had planned to apply several clusters of facets to each of their entries under idiophones, membranophones, chordophones, and aerophones, adding a fifth *Elektrophone* class (Dräger 1947, 43–46). The clusters included technomorphic facets, acoustic facets, facets determining an instrument's ability to produce single or multiple voices, and facets relating to musical movement, tone, duration, loudness, dynamic range, range of register, and timbre. Clusters also included anthropomorphic facets, or facets derived from the relation between the performer and the instrument (see Dräger 1947, 12–22). However, the size of his project (unaided by a computer) prohibited Dräger from developing it fully; he fulfilled only the morphological part of the classification. It remained for Ramey, over two decades later, to develop Dräger's approach by use of a computer. The fourteen variables Dräger listed in his classification (1947, 15–17, 23–46) were

   I. The functional relationship between the activation and vibration of sound

  II. How many sounding bodies are excited by the one activator (1 = one, 2 = two, 3 = many)

 III. The relationship between the activator and the sounding body (1 = free, 2 = not free, where 2 is subdivided into 1 = with fastened activating devices and 2 = without the same)

 IV. The shape of the vibrating body, including

    (a) the shape itself,

    (b) the origin of the shape (e.g., whether it is made of unaltered natural material, is an imitation of a natural model, is cult-determined, is made with a concrete purpose, or is a product of fantasy),

    (c) where relevant, the surface (e.g., whether it is polished, rough, has grooves, or is notched), and

    (d) the form of vibration

V. How many sounding bodies are being played, including

(a) the number of sounding bodies per player,

(b) the total number of sounding bodies, and

(c) the number of players

VI. How the sounding bodies are assembled (subdivided according to the particular case)

VII. Whether there is a single system or scale-producig parts

VIII. The vibrating material

IX. How the vibration is transferred, including its

(a) form,

(b) surface,

(c) mode of hastening and

(d) form of vibration

X. The presence of resonators, including cases where sound is produced by

(1) sounding bodies plus a resonator and

(2) a resonator alone

XI. The number of activators

(a) per sounding body and sound impulse and

(b) altogether

XII. The assembly of the activator (subdivided as in VI)

XIII. The form of the activator (subdivided as in VI)

XIV. The material of the activator. For example, morphological information about Hornbostel and Sachs's taxon of a bedded trough xylophone (1112.21.44) may be classified in shorthand form under idiophone as

(1) the sounding body and activator have separate functions,

(2) one,

(3) free activator,

(4) bar,

(5) many (a variable number),

(6) lying in a row,

(7) scale-producing parts,

(8) wood,

(9) not applicable,

(10) trough,

(11) two,

(12) hand-held,

(13) mallet, and

(14) wood.

The morphological questions Dräger asked were more precise and numerous than those asked by previous taxonomists, and they were broad-ranging, including even cult-determined and other sociological facets. The structure of the set of questions asked was chainlike, where each question was related to a property of a previous one, with up to two steps of logical division. Thus, the method served as a means of storing and retrieving information as well as identifying specimens and facilitating the multifaceted comparison of instruments in their variable forms. It introduced the concept of graded parameters, for example, of dynamics. Dräger's contribution, then, was to offer a method of lateral expansion of a previously existing classification that was based on a more comprehensive treatment of the morphological facets of instruments than could be incorporated in earlier schemes.

In another publication (1957), Dräger also clarified the task and limitations of downward taxonomy, or *Systematik* (systematics), which he distinguished from the cultural-historical, sociological, and physiological studies of instruments.

> A (systematic) description should progress from the functionally important parts to the accessory ones, where the former are characters determined by the physical qualities of the instrument's primary vibrating material, its shape and assemblage, the playing techniques used, the material of its primary vibrating material, and finally its sound activator. An ideal systematics would bring these elements into relation with each other in such a way that if the same series of questions were to be applied to each instrument, each would correspondingly be placed next to its most closely related instrument. But because this relationship can be determined by the most varied factors, this aim is not achievable.[8] (1957, 1290) (my translation)

This influential formulation by Dräger of the task of systematics served to clear the way for the development of a microtaxonomical, or faceted, approach to classification. Dräger's work on classification theory and method was a major contribution to the more comprehensive study of individual instruments, as well as to the clarification of the quite different tenets of systematics.

Reinhard

The nature of a classification scheme, as we have noted, is determined by its purpose. In 1960 the German musicologist Kurt Reinhard proposed a scheme that had the limited aim of classifying instruments according to characters deemed important in style research. He recommended that the "well thought out," "complete" scheme of Hornbostel and Sachs be retained for the morphological classification of instruments (1960, 160). However, for the study of musical style and the history of performance practice, he argued, it is important to know how an instrument is used in music making: whether, say, it is used to make single- or multiple-voiced music. For example, some South American panpipes play in chords, certain fiddles and xylophones play two tones simultaneously, and the "oriental flute" plays only one tone at a time.

Strictly applying the method of logical division, Reinhard divided the instruments of the world into two categories at the highest step according to whether they are used for single- or multiple-voiced music making (see fig. 11.4). He then subdivided these two categories into three subcategories according to pitch changeability. Single-character division was applied at the third step, where each of the six subcategories at the second step were subdivided according to whether their tones die away quickly or not (i.e. are continuous).

	Group of Instruments	With tones that die away	With continuous tones
	not changeable	drum gong musical bow	musical bow pipe trumpet/horn
Instruments used for single-voiced music making	freely changeable	percussion pot rod zither	singing saw siren
	changeable by fixed intervals	jew's harp bar zither	various wind instruments
Instruments used for multi-voiced music making	not changeable	dulcimer harp piano	panpipe glass harmonica organ
	freely changeable	lute	stringed intrument
	changeable by fixed intervals	guitar zither	double oboe bagpipe

FIGURE 11.4 Structure of Reinhard's classification (based on a translation of an outline of part of Reinhard's table, 1960, 162)

In addition, Reinhard proposed that instruments be grouped according to whether they produce dynamically variable tones or not, a factor that separates whole epochs from each other (e.g., the baroque from the classical), as illustrated by the transition from the terraced dynamics of the harpischord to crescendo playing on the piano (Reinhard 1960, 161). Instruments should also be graded, he wrote, in their degree of absolute loudness (which varies greatly from instrument to instrument) and in their timbral spectra, which—due to advances in electroacoustic research—can be analyzed fairly exactly and graded correspondingly. Other factors Reinhard saw as important were whether or not instruments are tunable (a factor that reflects on the player's degree of musicality), the degree of sound resonance, whether single- or multiple-voiced music is played on multiple-voiced instruments, whether changeable and nonchangeable tones are produced on the same instrument, and whether single-tone instruments produce multiple-voiced music by their use in orchestras.

Reinhard's scheme introduced many new characters and was based on a yet broader concept of instrument than that of previous schemes, a concept that emphasized the historical-stylistic aspects of the field. As well as using the time-worn method of logical division, he introduced the concept of gradings of such parameters as timbre and dynamics, a methodological aspect that had been introduced by Dräger and was later developed by Hood and others. Without actually proposing a hard and fast method of faceted grouping, he was tending toward an informal faceted approach.

MONTAGU AND BURTON

In 1971 the English scholars Montagu and Burton expressed their dissatisfaction with Hornbostel and Sachs's scheme by devising and publishing another new classification. They believed that there should be more steps of division, that Hornbostel and Sachs's long numerical designations were difficult to remember, and that it was difficult to insert some new—expecially combination or hybridized—instruments into their scheme. Characters of division in the new classification were largely morphological, though geographic and ethnic details, instrument maker, and whether an instrument was patented or not were included in the lower steps. They chose a nominal, rather than a numerical, method of designating classes, borrowing names for their system of divisions from the biologist Linnaeus (1707–1778). Theirs was still conceptually an enumerative scheme, not a faceted one.

In a numerical system, they argued, only nine indicators are available, all indicators must be repeated every time, and no elision is possible, while in a nominal system the infinite possibilities of human ingenuity in the invention of single-word names are at one's disposal. Using the method of logical division in asymmetrical fashion, they divided the so-called kingdoms of instruments (comprising all noise-makers) into the subkingdoms (aerophones, chordophones, membranophones, and idiophones), the superphyla (e.g., struck idiophones), the phyla (e.g., concussion and percussion idiophones), the subphyla, the classes, the subclasses, the orders, the suborders, the superfamilies, the families, the genera, the species, and the subspecies. These steps are subjectable to infinite lateral expansion, and any new specimen can easily be inserted. Moreover, hybrid instruments are easy to indicate and the detailed names can easily be remembered (Montagu and Burton 1971, 51).

Despite these advantages, the scheme has not been as well received as it perhaps deserves.[9] The application of borrowed eighteenth-century biological terms to inanimate instruments has possibly weighed against the scheme. Hornbostel and Sachs argued (1914: 9) against Mahillon's use of similar terms (e.g., *class* and *subclass*)[10] by reason of the fact that ranks at the same step do not always correspond between groups; moreover, the number of possible steps is unmanageably large.

HOOD

Like Galpin, Mantle Hood used five categories in his classifications (1971), naming but not subdividing the last category, which he termed "electronophones" (Hood 1971, 144). Hood's contribution—like Dräger's— was not to develop a new scheme of classification but to offer a method of lateral expansion of the lowest levels of the Hornbostel and Sachs scheme. He classified the extra parameters at the lowest levels by means of so-called hardness scales, which denoted maximum and minimum ranges of loudness, pitch, timbre (partial structure), and density (pulse per minute) of sound. As we have noted, Dräger and Reinhard (1960) also independently introduced the concept of grading timbre and dynamics. Hood's main contribution to methodology was to develop, partly by use of his hardness scales, an elaborate graphic coding system of "organograms" for each of the terminal entries of the Hornbostel and Sachs scheme.

Hood held to a comprehensive concept of instruments that included physical aspects, techniques of performance, musical function, decoration, and sociocultural considerations. The physical parameters, for example, included the instrument's external and internal shape, while techniques of performance included precise information about the means of excitation and the relationship between performer and instrument. Musical function included such matters as loudness and pitch, while decoration included decorative techniques, finishes and motifs—matters which can carry some weight in the gathering of data about culture contact. Sociocultural parameters include the value of the instrument, its use in magic or other rituals, the social status of the performer, and the visual finish and decoration of the instrument.

Figure 11.5 is an organogram of the *atumpan*, the pair of master drums of the Ashanti and other Akan peoples of Ghana. As Hood explains, this organogram indicates that the atumpan

> has the external and internal shape of a bowl opening into a cylinder made of (5) wood, has a single head fastened by a H(oop) R(ing) and is played with two crooked sticks, is used in pairs (the pair is called atumpan), is tuned by W(etting) the heads and by means of tuning pegs, . . . , supporting V lacing, to a R(elative) pitch of H(igh) and L(ow). The drums are held in a slanting position by a stand. The pair has the following Hardness Scale ratings: loudness, 8; pitch, 3; quality, 4; density, 7–9; technique, 4; finish, 1; motif, 4. They are associated with a G(roup) of H(igh) social status that values them at 10, they S(ymbolize) the soul of ancestor drummers and a tree, are honored with L(ibations), have magic P(ower), and R(itual) is involved in their manufacture and when they are played. S(ociety) values tham at 10, the P(layer) values them at 10, the M(aker) of the drums is accorded a special S(tatus), their M(onetary) value is 8, they are indispensible in the life C(ycle) of man. (1971, 155–56)

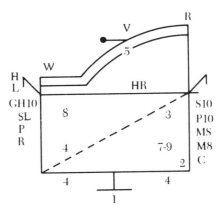

FIGURE 11.5 An organogram

Hood's organograms, which are inspired by the symbolic dance language of Labanotation, have been criticized for being complex and difficult to remember. Yet the same complaints have been made about the Hornbostel and Sachs system; and they may also be made of any graphic or other classification based on a comprehensive view of instruments. In fact, organograms give a remarkably neat, compact, and easily comprehended account of an instrument at first glance. Once their technique is learnt and practiced, they are not in principle difficult to construct; they may be time-consuming to prepare because they demand the gathering of a great deal of precise information that is not necessarily easy to come by. Neither Hornbostel and Sachs's scheme nor Hood's are easy to memorize, except in their broad outlines, but arguably the usefulness of neither scheme depends on their being mnemonic to the last detail, which is not their primary purpose.

In terms of logical structure, Hood's system resembles that of Hornbostel and Sachs, for each organogram is given opposite a numerical Hornbostel and Sachs entry. The extra facts about each instrument in Hood's graphic system "offer no particular problem for incorporation within a system of instrumental classification" (Hood 1971, 138), for they are seen as a supplement to, not a substitute for, the Hornbostel and Sachs scheme. Hood's major contribution to instrument classification was to expand its horizon of variables and offer an elegant methodology with which to classify more parameters of this already extremely large and ever-growing body of knowledge. In these respects his work forms part of the overall shift over the past few decades toward a much more comprehensive concept of instruments.

RAMEY

As has been mentioned, the practical completion of Dräger's faceted classification scheme awaited the development of the computer. In fact, as Ramey notes,

> the means of making Dräger's system feasible was achieved in the same decade [the nineteen-forties] as the successful completion of the proto-type modern digital computer. [But] today [for the first time] we are able to implement computer dependent multivariate information storage and retrieval systems. It is thus possible not only to implement a faceted classification of the scope that Dräger envisioned, but also . . . to extend the boundaries of such a classification to encompass any criteria which the researcher might find useful. (1974, 27)

Handling his data by computer, Ramey developed a scheme that, like Hood's, was based on that of Hornbostel and Sachs, to whose terminal entries he added a greatly enlarged number of characters organized as an extended key. His morphological criteria resembled those of Dräger, but he added to them data developed by Hood and himself about secondary sources of vibration, decoration of the instrument, the individual sound-producing units of instruments comprising more than one unit, and anthropological data (including data about performance behavior) obtained by examining the source culture of the instrument. He identified thirty-nine morphological, fifteen acoustic, and twenty-one anthropological characters. The three groups of data were each subdivided into five or six taxa, which were then further subdivided in two steps; for example, the anthropological data were classified as follows (Ramey 1974, 67):

III. Anthropological data
  A. Performance practice
      1. Playing position
          a. Angle
          b. Height
      2. Use of performer's body
      3. Tuning process
          a. type
          b. tuner
      4. Solo and ensemble usage
  B. Sociocultural information
      1. Extra-aesthetic function
      2. Sex
          a. Instrument
          b. Performer
      3. Value
          a. Musical
          b. Social
          c. Monetary
      4. Qualifications of performer
      5. Social status
          a. Performer
          b. Maker
      6. Tool technology of maker
  C. Identification of source culture
  D. Date of origin
  E. Name

Ramey borrowed Hood's concept of hardness scales, listing a large number of facets in scales of increasing magnitude, including material of vibration (in order of increasing hardness), tuning process, musical value, social value, monetary value, density range, range in octaves, musical versatility, ensemble size, and technology. The translation of Hornbostel and Sachs's entries into the language of Ramey's faceted systems resulted in a logical expression made up of variables, logical operators (and, or), parentheses (which may be nested), and six relational operators (equal to, less than, or equal to, etc.) (1974, 148). Despite some minor problems,[11] the scheme succeeded in organizing and interrelating a large body of knowledge about instruments and grafting this knowledge onto the classification scheme of Hornbostel and Sachs.

MALM

A little earlier than Ramey, the U.S. scholar W. P. Malm began a similar project called Musinst, which used the IBM 360 Assembly system to program data about instruments. Like Dräger, Hood, and Ramey, Malm did not develop a new classification of instruments but devised a method of using the upper levels of Hornbostel and Sachs's scheme for classifying a large body of information about the world instrumentarium, which was divided into idiophone, membranophone, chordophone, aerophone, and electrophone categories. He prepared checklists of data entries (exemplified in Malm 1974, 120–22), which he presented alongside corresponding numerical designations (0–3000). These presented data about a collected instrument's name, appearance, history, and maker (0–250), "construction materials" (260–450), "classification into the five categories" (460–500), "pitch-producing units" (510–610), "sounds per pitch-producing unit" (620–720), "activation" (730–840), and "further description" of morphological and tuning data, instrumental types, performance practice, cultural functions, and so on (580–3000). The first section of data included whether or not a "hologram" was available, by which Malm meant a dynamic, three-dimensional view of the instrument in its various possible elevations. His aim was to build up a computer bank of information about instruments, beginning with the University of Michigan's Stearns Collection. Though his classification of data was less complex and detailed than Ramey's, it left provision for the refinement or expansion of the scheme by computer. The advantage of Malm's scheme, in comparison to Ramey's, was that it could easily be handled by the nonexpert, who may obtain "a practical skeleton of information which can be described relatively quickly," and can help "in guiding one through the complicated body of organological information" (Malm 1974, 120). However, advances in computer technology have since made this experiment obsolete.

HEYDE

The German musicologist Herbert Heyde also contributed to the shift away from limited-character classification. He was more interested in categories of relationships between instruments (Heyde 1975, 121–27) than in the classification of instruments themselves.[12] Unlike the systematicians, he adopted a historical or genetic approach in his so-called natural system of classification that was based on a comprehensive concept of the instrument as it is played, including its structural, functional, and mensural aspects. In a work published in 1929, Sachs had also shown strong interest in the evolution of instruments, without, however, including it as a parameter of classification. Heyde attempted to correlate the total number of elements of an instrument with its historical development, presenting the information in the form of the "branches of a tree" (Heyde 1975, 10). The resulting tables (1975, 121–27) may be unconvincing to some (not least because of the lack of hard evidence). However, the practicability of Heyde's method has been tested by museum use.[13]

Like Dräger, Heyde made a sharp distinction between anthropomorphic and technomorphic characteristics, or, as he defined them, factors related to the player's body on the one hand and mechanical and electronic characteristics on the other. He organized this information, or "system," by means of flowcharts, which were sometimes very complex, as in the case of the glass harmonica and the automatic organ (1975, 66, 68). Perhaps the simplest is the one for the bull-roarer (1975, 73).

In the chart for the bull-roarer (fig. 11.6), the white sections indicate the generalized technomorphic elements and the shaded sections represent the anthropomorphic ones. The player's central nervous system (n) relates

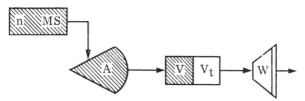

FIGURE 11.6 Heyde's (1975) system of a bull-roarer

to the control and direction of energy (MS), which affects the loudness, pitch, and timbre of the sound; the energy activates the sound (A), which relates to the player's arm and hand gripping the string (V), the string itself (V_t), and the rotating slat of the instrument (W), which transforms the energy into audible form.[14]

For comparative purposes, Heyde distinguished between four classes of abstraction of information, of which the most general class (the "system" class) enables comparisons to be made according to a few broad, abstracted functional properties. In the next class (the "formal" class), more precise anthropomorphic and technomorphic characters differentiate the system. In the third class (the "categorial" class), specific technomorphic aspects of the concrete instrument are considered and only their mensural aspects are abstracted. The fourth class (the "dimensional" class) gives precise measurements of the instrument. Thus, information about any and all instruments can be ordered into grades ranging from the most particular to the most general (1975, 10–15).

In the categorial class, Heyde used the method of logical division. For example, he divided beaten strings into three subcategories at the first step according to the mode of sound activation: instruments struck (1) manually, (2) with a tangential mechanism, and (3) with a hammer (1975, 129–30). At the second step, the manually struck instruments were subdivided according to whether they possess adjusting mechanisms (such as mutes or timbre adjusters) as well as a cluster of what Heyde views as their most important characters. Further steps were governed by morphological characters such as the number of strings and the shapes of boards. Finally, in the dimensional class of information, he gave precise measurements of particular specimens.

Hartmann

Hildegard Hartmann's scheme (1978), which uses only children's instruments, returns to Hornbostel and Sachs's four categories (which she names A, B, C, and D), giving them new subdivisions dictated by the instrumentarium at hand. Subgroupings are made according to instrumental type (e.g., "zoomorphic clapper," "earth xylophone"), material (e.g., glass, metal rings, tree bark), geographic area of use, and use by children (e.g., "boys' war play" or "New Year masquerade"). An example of an entry is:

Classification	Instrument	Material	Area	Use
AaI1.1	One-hand clapper	Maize stalk, wood	Switzerland	Boys' war toy

In the classification AaI1.1, A = idiophone, a = beaten, I = a clapper or "hit-back idiophone," 1 = with rods, and .1 = with one hand.

LUND

C. Lund's scheme (1980) divides a collection of music-archeological specimens into three categories: those intended to produce sounds, those that produce sound and also have a nonmusical function, and those that have a mainly nonmusical function. The remaining specimens have no known function.

SAKURAI

Tetsuo Sakurai of the National Museum of Ethnology in Kyoto published a classification method in 1980, with a revision in 1981 (see a reconstruction of these two schemes in figs. 11.7 and 11.8). He found the main Hornbostel and Sachs categories inadequate and some of the classifications inaccurate. He cited the case of reed instruments, which are not really aerophones, as their primary resonators are not vibrating air but vibrating reeds (Yamaguchi 1969, 190–91). Similarly, he wrote, jew's harps are not idiophones, because they produce sound by means of vibrating air, which presumably makes them aerophones (Ledang 1972, 102). Moreover, electrophones should not be regarded as one single group, because they actually have heterogeneous primary resonators (Sakurai 1980, 40). More serious, he argued, is the lack of a uniform standard for establishing lower-order divisions. It is also somewhat ethnocentric, as much of the terminology (e.g., zithers, lutes, and harps) is "derived mainly from European cultures or those circumferential to Europe" (Sakurai 1981, 824).

Like Hornbostel and Sachs, however, Sakurai used a decimal numbering system in his own schemes. The schemes are based on a two-dimensional concept of instrument, namely, instruments conceived as part of "material culture" and instruments conceived as part of "mental culture." Since instruments are tools or objects and all have the common characteristic of producing sound, special emphasis is given to the material

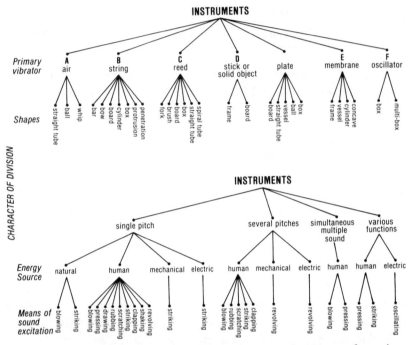

FIGURE 11.7 Reconstruction of Sakurai's classifications of 1980: *top,* from viewpoint of material culture; *bottom,* from viewpoint of mental culture

aspects, that is, the kind, shape, and number of primary vibrators. A vibrator is a mechanism "between the energy source and air vibration . . . which transforms . . . energy . . . into alternating vibration" (Sakurai 1981, 825). The so-called mental aspect includes both pitch function and the duration and strength of sounds produced. In his earlier classification (fig. 11.7), the mental aspect also included the action of the sound-producing player (e.g., blowing or pressing) or machine (striking).

His more recent scheme (fig. 11.8) is based on a combination of three classificatory schemes, the first two of which are based on the instrument's material aspects and the second on the instrument's mental aspects. Thus a xylophone (12) which is a "plane plate" instrument (12.31) with multiple damping sound (31), is classified as 12.31.31. Oboes and clarinets, which are reed instruments with a single vibrator (31), a straight tube (21), and plural sustaining sound (22), are classified as 31.21.22. Bagpipes, which are reed instruments with plural vibrators (32) of the round body projection type (62) and with multiple sustaining sound (32), are classified as 32.62.32.

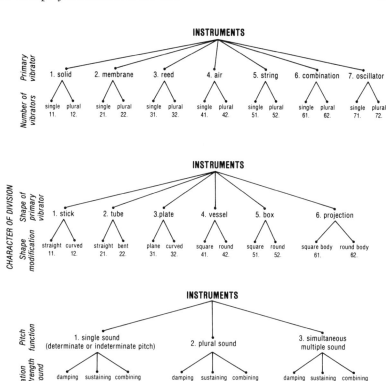

FIGURE 11.8 A reconstruction of Sakurai's classifications of 1981: *top*, primary classification of instrument as material object (material culture); *middle*, secondary classification of instrument as material object; *bottom*, classification of instrument as sound producer (mental culture)

As Sakurai points out (1981, 828), "with the assistance of computers this classification system may emerge as a new and powerful tool for the cross-cultural and comparative study of musical instruments." It is indeed an ingenious scheme and largely avoids ethnocentricity and problems of border-line cases and is easy to apply. It is weak, however, at the lower steps of classification, being able to accommodate only a limited amount of detail. Moreover, it is based on a concept of instruments that is limited almost solely to morphology and sound qualities (pitch function, duration and strength of sound). Because of the shift in this century away from such a limited concept of instrument, it appears somewhat dated. This is not to deny its usefulness, however, if combined with typological study based on a concept of instruments that does justice to their wider significance and breadth of meaning.

LYSLOFF AND MATSON

In 1985, René Lysloff and Jim Matson published an account of their graphic classification method. The scheme is based on thirty-seven variables grouped according to various characteristics of the sounding body, the substructure (supports, attachments), the resonator, the sympathetic vibrator, the sound initiator, the player-instrument relationship, performance context, sound context, and tuning.

Instruments are grouped according to observable shared characteristics, based on a data analysis technique called "multi-dimensional scalogram analysis." According to this method, each instrument is graphically represented as a point in space and located within a configuration of points in such a way as to reflect the shared characteristics (Lysloff and Matson 1985, 213). Figure 11.9, for example, gives a three-dimensional configuration of instruments according to six variables; if instruments share a large number of characteristics, they are placed near each other in the

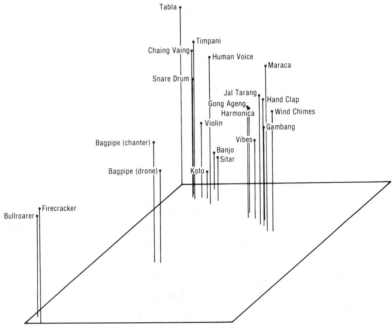

FIGURE 11.9 Six variables of the nature of the sounding body with twenty-two instrument types (based on Lysloff and Matson 1985)

scalogram. Other scalograms group instruments according to other variables, for example, into groups of tensile, nontensile, and "fluid" instruments or into groups differentiated according to characteristic shape or material of the sounding body or the tuning or the number of sounding bodies, and so on (1985, 227–32). As the authors point out, this method is universally applicable, easy to perceive and remember, and avoids a prescribed order of application. However, it is claiming too much to say that it represents "a new *approach* [their italics] to the intellectual problem of classification" on the grounds that their concept of instruments goes beyond that of a mere artifact and includes the "dynamic interaction between instruments and human behavior" (1985, 234, 213). Their graphic method is indeed new. But as we have noted the movement of scholarly thought toward a very broad concept of instrument began at least as long ago as the early nineteenth century and it included a number of parameters of which Lysloff and Matson have not taken account. Their method may, as they explain, be open-ended, but as it stands it does not—and without substantial modification cannot—include such complex factors as cultural history and nomenclatures of instruments. The authors' rejection of taxonomic hierarchies on the grounds that they discourage comparative study between instruments is only a partly convincing argument; Hornbostel and Sachs's scheme, for example, does succeed in forming a basis for comparing instruments and, like Lysloff and Matson's is adaptable, expandable, and easy to use. Moreover, Lysloff and Matson's variables are not new but were used by others. For example, Sakurai also makes important use of primary resonators and secondary vibrators in his scheme (Sakurai 1981, 826).

MITANI

Yoko Mitani classified Far Eastern long zithers according to morphology and performance technique, dividing at the first step into zithers with no bridges or frets, those with movable bridges, and those with movable bridges and fixed frets. At the next step the subcategories are subdivided according to whether instruments are played with the fingers or with artificial nails, bowed with a resined stick, or plucked/played with a bamboo rod (1980). Classifications like Mitani's, which have a specific purpose, have their own inner coherence and limitations and are not, of course, comparable to large-scale schemes that aim at expressing a comprehensive concept of instrument.

CLASSIFICATIONS FOR USE IN MUSEUMS

A few other schemes have been developed recently for museological or specifically scholarly puposes, most of which are based on, improve on, or in some way resemble the Hornbostel and Sachs scheme. In the museums the practical problems bemoaned by specialist and nonspecialist curators from the nineteenth century remain essentially the same, though they have eased somewhat in the late twentieth century.

The specialist-curator Dieter Krickeberg used the Hornbostel and Sachs system for his classification of specimens held in the Music Instrument Museum in Berlin, but he found its subdivisons insufficient for his purposes. He therefore devised and subsequently published some substantial additions to it, conceived of for use in his card index (Krickeberg 1975). He added scores of subdivisions with decimal numberings to cover characteristics of instruments from the field of European "art" music that are missing in the original scheme. For example, he added subdivisions to cover the shape of trumpet reeds, including the purely conical, the mostly conical, and the mostly cylindrical.

An article by C. Marcel-Dubois (1983–84), on the other hand, dealt sympathetically with the typological and classificatory problems encountered by nonspecialist museum curators. The article discussed and presented a decimalized classificatory scheme suitable for computer use and based on morphological criteria. It excluded "chronological, geographical or ethnic categories" as well as function because of the severe lack of documentation with which instrument curators are still frequently faced. The main practical problems encountered by nonspecialist curators, Marcel-Dubois wrote, are how to know whether an instrument is a complete specimen or not and whether there is something unusual about it—for example, as a result of experiments in its construction, of its being a reconstruction of a historic instrument, of its having developed as the result of the requirements of a new style, of its representing developments in the evolution of a new musical style, of its being the product of someone's overwrought imagination, or of its having been altered or being the remains of an instrument damaged by time. On gaining answers to these questions, Marcel-Dubois argues, instruments can safely be classified by nonspecialists on morphological grounds using his scheme. The problem with the scheme is that it requires the gathering of considerable chronological, geographical, and ethnic information to answer the questions specified.

CONCLUSION

A new approach to the ancient science of the classification of musical instruments emerged in the works of a number of organologists in the latter part of the nineteenth century. Inspired mainly by museological needs, Mahillon developed a systematic, open-ended scheme for classification of the world of instruments. This scheme appealed to the well-known musicologists Hornbostel and Sachs, who subjected it to further developments and refinements. Their revised scheme was destined to be used, albeit often in modified or reduced form, by generations of future musicologists and museologists.

The concept of instrument adhered to among organologists over the period continued to broaden extensively to cover not only the full range of instruments throughout the world, past and present, but also their many parameters of significance, meaning, and function. Early twentieth-century scholars such as Sachs, Izikowitz, and Norlind wrote of the need to conceive of instruments in their many facets.

Realizing that established classification schemes lagged behind the broadening concept of instrument, scholars in the middle to latter part of the century, such as Dräger, Hood, and Ramey, developed schemes based on the detailed inspection and delineation of an instrument's many characteristics. Dräger, for example, found that single- or limited-character division was inadequate for his purposes, and he therefore took simultaneous account of a large number of facets of an instrument, trying to incorporate into his scheme his concept of the instrument in all its complexity. He included clusters of morphological, technomorphic, sociological, anthropomorphic, and performance practice characteristics as well as the facets determining the sounds that an instrument produces (tone, duration, timbre, etc.). Dräger's formulation of the tasks of systematics as well as the more comprehensive study of individual instruments cleared the way for the development of a microtaxonomical approach to classification by upward grouping.

Upward Classification of Instruments: The Method of the Future?

While most of the twentieth-century organologists discussed earlier gave consideration—in theory at least—to the classification of all possible instruments, a substantial group of scholars focused specifically on the field of European "folk music instruments."[1] The study of these instruments was neglected before the late 1940s, partly because of the traditional attitude that instrumental music was dependent on or a supplement to vocal music and also because of the difficulty of recording sounds made on these instruments with the primitive recording equipment available (Stockmann 1972, 11–12). Presumably it was also due to the fact that European musicologists were conditioned to find the study of concert hall music a more worthy exercise than research into folk traditions and therefore concentrated their energies on the former.

In 1962 the Study Group on Folk Music Instruments was founded by Ernst Emsheimer and Erich Stockmann, and since then, this group of scholars has met periodically at conferences held under the auspices of the International Folk Music Council, now known as the International Council for Traditional Music. The group's key methodologists, Oskár Elschek and Erich Stockmann, were the first organologists to develop a fully conscious theory and method of upward classification by inspection.

The intensive field collection and study of European folk music instruments began after World War II. Many of the instruments were found to have disappeared and others to have survived only as relics, while some were recovered in the nick of time, photographed, and recorded on tape (Stockmann 1972, 11–12). The group's publications were both documentary and evaluative and were based not only on museum collections of archeological instruments and instruments collected in the field but also on literary and iconographical sources. They investigated many facets of the instruments, including their acoustics,[2] their playing techniques,[3] their use in ensembles,[4] their sound documentation,[5] their musical style, the ergology of instruments,[6] their performers, the socio-historical and anthropological aspects,[7] and player-instrument-music relationships.[8] Over a hundred scholars published in sources associated with the group, including the *Handbuch der europäischen Volksmusikinstrumente* series (1967–1986, Emsheimer and Stockmann, eds.) and the multivolume series *Studia Instrumentorum Musicae Popularis (SIMP)* (1969–1985, Stockmann, series ed.), the latter of which mostly contains papers delivered at study group meetings. Some published monographs (e.g., Ling on the keyed fiddle, 1967) and articles in musicological journals.[9]

The contribution of this group of organologists is of considerable significance yet it is not widely known and even less widely understood. This is partly because some of the key methodological articles are discourses in German.[10] It is also partly because their ideas and methodologies are still being developed and partly because full-blown accounts of their conceptual frameworks have not yet been published. More importantly, perhaps, it is also because of the rather insecure conceptual or terminological foundations and unclear orientations of the discipline of organology itself, which offers few guidelines by which to recognize and assess the significance of new—and old—contributions.

For although organology is one of the oldest disciplines in musicology, with a considerable body of literature on various aspects of individual instruments and instrumentaria, a tradition of well-argued critical comment on its classification theory and associated conceptual framework has not yet been built up. As we have noted, in the hundred years or so since Mahillon published the first classification scheme suitable for virtually all instruments, over twenty other worthy schemes have been devised. Yet most of them have attracted few, if any, practical followers and, with a few exceptions, little published follow-up comparative assessment. Only the Hornbostel and Sachs scheme has become well known. Yet while it is frequently praised and defended in the literature, its tools are rarely applied in classifications beyond its first or its upper one to three steps of division.

Perhaps the main reason why organological classification theory and method have lagged so far behind parallel developments in some other disciplines is that organologists have worked largely in isolation, both from each other and from theorists in other disciplines. The Study Group on Folk Music Instruments was the first group to make a partial break with this habit, at least to the extent that some of its members discovered themselves facing new corporate problems. For example, the editors of the *Handbuch* series had to find a suitable instrument classification system for their series. Although they were unable, of course, to find a perfect solution and they decided to rely mainly on the Hornbostel and Sachs scheme, they did stimulate thought about instrument classification method. In 1969 the Czechoslovakian organologist Oskár Elschek collaborated with Stockmann and published a joint paper on a new upward method of classification called "typology research." Typology had been the main theme of the study group's conference held in Brno, Czechoslovakia, in 1967. Elschek also published an article (1969a) and a book (1969b) giving the details of the typological method that he had developed and applied to a collection of aerophones.[11]

Like most other classifications of instruments, Elschek's method has not been used by others, but the significance of his work lies less in the methodological details, which need considerable further development, than in its theoretical direction and rationale. His method somewhat resembled, yet went further than, the method of faceted grouping developed by Ramey. Elschek was influenced by the typological classification of folk music that he had worked out with his wife, Elscheková.[12]

Despite the fact that they were working in the relative isolation of eastern Europe, Elschek and Stockmann's typological approach to classification actually represented the vanguard of organological classification theory. Through the study group they were in touch with the major currents of activity in the field. Their work represented the first attempts at typological instrument classification and the earliest clear-cut signs of a methodological shift from downward to upward classification. As we have noted, most organologists from the time of Sachs (1929) and Izikowitz (1935) appear to have been dissatisfied with the limited concept of instruments operating behind the Hornbostel and Sachs macrotaxonomy. They demanded a more comprehensive concept, and preferably one that could consider as many aspects of the instrument as possible. Like Mersenne, who was more interested in the detailed knowledge of each instrument than in their macrotaxonomy, Sachs, Izikowitz, Dräger, Hood, Reinhard, Ramey, Malm, Heyde, and others were all beginning to think microtaxonomically. Although they were still locked into the downward mode of classificatory thinking of past millennia, some of them were thinking in an upward direction also.

The development of typology research was accompanied by, indeed was dependent upon, the clarification by Elschek and Stockmann of the difference between downward systematics and upward grouping by inspection (Elschek and Stockmann 1969). The two authors noted Dräger's clear exposition (see chap. 11) of the nature of systematics and proceeded on that basis to outline the typological method. As they pointed out, the statement that an aerophone has a cylindrical bore is a systematic statement, limited as it is to a broad morphological feature. The ergological question, however, as to whether the cylindrical bore is bored out, burnt out, or consists of two halves joined together is not a systematic but a typological question (El-schek and Stockmann 1969, 16). The one belongs to the medium-level, downward classification of aerophones and the other to the low-level, historically and environmentally variable upward grouping of flutes into variants and types.

As we have noted, both these methods were known as long ago as the time of Aristotle. Throughout the history of organology, however, upward classification by inspection has been either totally neglected or confused with downward systematics (Elschek and Stockmann 1969, 14). The essential difference between the two methods, as they explained, was that systematics operates on only a few characters as applied to a whole instrumentarium, while typology research is based on as holistic a view as possible of the complex individual instrument in its environment. System-atics, they wrote, both helped and hindered the development of typology. It helped in that it offered clues for the discovery of the many character-istics of instruments and in that it provided a relatively firm basis for ordering instruments upon which typological investigations could be oriented. On the other hand, it hindered its development because the categories of systematics were sometimes given typological meaning, thus obscuring the differences between the methods.

Elschek's and Stockmann's contribution to classification theory and method is not yet widely accepted or even understood. Picken, for example, argued that it was unnecessary to devise a new scheme such as theirs when Hornbostel and Sachs's scheme could be adjusted to remedy any apparent inadequacies.[13] Despite Picken's view to the contrary (1975, 558–70), Hornbostel and Sachs's scheme was indeed essentially static or ahistorical, as Elschek and Stockmann argued, designed as its authors admitted it was to cover all possible instruments independently of time and place.[14] As has now become clear, simply to expand Hornbostel and Sachs's method or empirically to adjust it is not to solve all problems, as the two methods have essentially different purposes. As Elschek and Stockmann showed, typological (microtaxonomical) method aims at the precise, ordered study of the minute detail and low- to medium-level classification of groups or variants of instruments, while systematics aims at information storage and retrieval of the high- to low-level classification of specimens making up whole instrumentaria, the drawing of broad comparisons, and the reaching of abstract conclusions. The two methods are complementary and both clearly need further development and refinement.

In fact the division between Elschek's and Picken's positions are more apparent than real. Neither is content with presenting only the morphological and acoustic properties of the instruments they discuss. Both investigate many facets of the instrument and describe examples of variable specimens of it. The main difference is that Elschek orders his data typologically while Picken begins his account of an instrument with a Hornbostel and Sachs designation and then presents the ergological, performing, and sociological data in an essentially descriptive, additive fashion, as, for example, in his entry on the Turkish folk whistle called *duduk* (1975, 363–69). Picken thinks in a downward direction, while Elschek thinks upward (and, as we shall see, downward) and believes that a typological arrangement of the facets of an instrument has great explanatory power.

Elschek's method to date has been limited primarily to the detailed treatment of morphological, technological, acoustic, and ergological data on instruments, together with historical and sound documentation. The analyses of the measurable facets are presented in graphic sketches, or logograms, like those used in electrical engineering and in dance notation (Elschek 1969b, 13). Instrument sketches are more complex than dance sketches (as, e.g., in the case of Labanotation, devised in 1928), which consider only one changeless instrument, the human body, as opposed to the many varied, changeable forms of instruments (Elschek 1969b, 13). Elschek's sketches, which have so far been limited to the study of aerophones, are "in fact only a transformation of our knowledge" about them (Elschek 1969b, 14). They are seen as facilitating further intensive research into the instruments, which in turn may necessitate the revision of the sketches several times over.

Elschek's sketches of different specimens are then compared and the process of upward grouping begins. Not all instruments, of course, are closely comparable; only those with essentially the same or similar "essential" (ergological, technical, and acoustic) characteristics belong together. With instruments that are comparable, two kinds of variability are distinguished: quantitative and qualitative. If two handmade specimens of bark duct flutes vary from each other in relatively unimportant respects (in ways that do not affect the sound produced), then their differences are classed as quantitative, and the two instruments are grouped as "instruments with identical characteristics." For example, the lengths of tubes of the same kind of flute rarely happen to be exactly the same, nor are the sizes of the finger holes and the distance between holes the same; yet they are classed as identical. Other quantitative differences between non-factory-made instruments are based on their degree of crafts-manship, technical perfection, monetary value, and detail of decoration.

If, however, two instruments vary in ways that affect aspects of the sound they produce, such as timbre, register, pitch range, tone duration, dynamics, monophonic or multiphonic capacity or practice, or simply one or a few of these characters, then the differences between them are classed as qualitative, and they are said to be two variants within a type. The choice, number, and weightings of characters said to determine a variant vary according to the nature of the instruments being researched and their resulting analyses. The presence or absence of any stable character whatever that determines the sound produced can, in principle, distin-guish one variant from another. It can be a universal or a particular character; for example, the number of reeds that an aerophone has is a particular character, but the bag in bagpipes is a universal character (Elschek/Stockmann 1969:21).

A collection of variants is called a type; it is a model or center point with variable realizations. To constitute a type, two or more instruments must have several points of similarity, not just one or two. To the investigator of individual instruments, the type has a unifying function of grouping qualitatively different but essentially similar instruments to-gether. From the viewpoint of abstract categories of classification, on the other hand, it has a differentiating function, distinguishing identical instruments from the qualitatively different ones (Elschek and Stockmann 1969, 22).

A type is not, as Elschek and Stockmann emphasize, a stark, un-changeable model; it is subject to constant change. It develops at a particular point in time, lives for a limited period, and can be transformed into other types by innovation. Unlike systematics, which devises a theoretical, universal, logically based, hierarchically built up and therefore static and ahistorical classification system, typology is first and foremost empirical-historical research (Elschek and Stockmann 1969, 18–22). It is freely applicable and must continually be adjusted according to the nature of the actual instruments being researched. Both typological and system-atic investigations may finally be presented in a hierarchy of steps— moving from the group of identical instruments to the variant, from the variant to the type, and then from the type to the group of types. Thus, the structure of typological investigations by faceted grouping is that of logical division in reverse, the essential differences being that faceted grouping begins with the empirical investigation of individual specimens and bases its lower steps of division on the simultaneous consideration of many facets, not just one or a few as in logical division.

The graphic method developed by Elschek for typological research may be exemplified by some variable realizations of European willow-bark flutes.[15] The sketches are intended to be easily drawn and their cluster of features instantly recognizable to facilitate the quick comparison of the relatively stable and the variable ergological features of different instruments. They show an instrument's dimensions, its material(s) of construction, its technological qualities, and, where relevant, its decorations; for example, the symbols on the left of the sketch of a duct flute shown in figure 12.1 indicate lathe-turned decorations.

The following summary of the most important of these characters and their corresponding graphics will facilitate the reading of examples of a complete sketch and synoptic chart below (figs. 12.7 and 12.8). In figure 12.2, a = a straight rim-blown flute, b = an obliquely cut rim-blown flute, c and d = a notched flute (with different notched shapes), e = an obliquely cut rim-blown flute (a split-duct flute), f = a duct flute, g = a duct flute with a lengthened duct, h = an obliquely cut duct flute, i = an obliquely rounded-out duct flute, j = a closed duct flute, and k = a transverse flute. The cross with a dot at the top (k) depicts a cylindrical duct flute, where the vertical line depicts the tube, the dot depicts the duct, and the horizontal line depicts the labial or the lateral orifice. The cross with the dot at the top and the two converging vertical lines on the side (g) depicts a duct flute with a conical bore.

Illustrations 12.3–12.6 show Elschek's symbols for shapes of cutout labials, shapes of ducts, finger holes, and technology of flute tubing. One

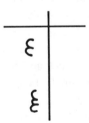

FIGURE 12.1 Sketch of a duct flute (based on Elschek 1969b, 30)

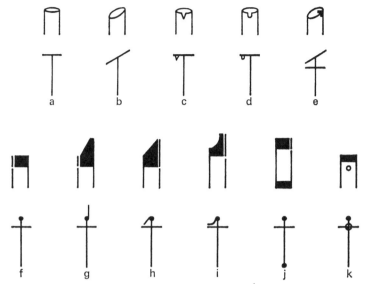

FIGURE 12.2 Elschek's graphic signs for kinds of mouthpieces (based on Elschek 1969b, table 2)

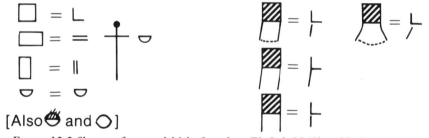

FIGURE 12.3 Shapes of cutout labials (based on Elschek 1969b, table 3)

of Elschek's simpler sketches is shown in figure 12.7. It depicts an obliquely cut duct flute with a thin, bored-out tube and four finger holes, where the vertical numbers list the flute's total length, its acoustic length (from the rim to the end of the tube), and the tube's outer and inner diameters. A comparison of this with sketches of other similar flutes yields the synoptic chart in figure 12.8.

These willow-bark flutes are divided into three variants. Their tubes, made of a species of willow tree bark, vary between 65 and 355 mm in length. The shape of the upper end of each flute is either flat like a plate,

FIGURE 12.4 Shapes of ducts (based on Elschek 1969b, table 3)

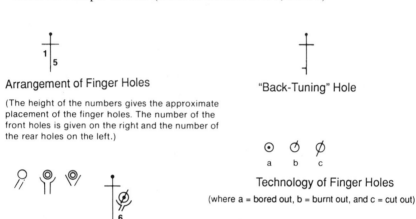

Arrangement of Finger Holes

(The height of the numbers gives the approximate placement of the finger holes. The number of the front holes is given on the right and the number of the rear holes on the left.)

"Back-Tuning" Hole

Technology of Finger Holes

(where a = bored out, b = burnt out, and c = cut out)

Kinds of Finger Holes

FIGURE 12.5 Finger holes (based on Elschek 1969b, table 4)

(where a = the material of which the flute is made (e.g., metal) forms the tube, b = of bark, c = bored out, d = burnt out, e = split, and f = split and wrapped around the bark)

FIGURE 12.6 Technology of flute tubing (based on Elschek 1969a, table 5, SIMP vol. I)

obliquely cut, obliquely rounded out, or with a lengthened duct. These instruments are mostly fundamental-tone flutes without finger holes, except for the variant A2b. The flutes that are partly stopped at one end are also occasionally used as overtone flutes (without finger holes). The flutes that are stopped at both ends may have a lengthened duct at the lower end, which is used partly as a pitch regulator. Thus, the willow-bark flutes are divided into types A (open), B (closed), and C (with a duct at the lower end that can be regulated). The groups of variant instruments further differentiate themselves by their possession of straight or obliquely cut

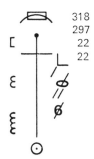

FIGURE 12.7 Sketch of a flute based on Elschek's (1969b) graphic method

ducts as well as by the shape of the cutout labial and of the duct itself (Elschek 1969a, 31–32).

Elschek intended his typological method to be clearly distinguishable from the Hornbostel and Sachs method yet also complementary to it.[16] To him the final step of the typological method was to compare the synoptic charts with the lower steps of the Hornbostel and Sachs macrotaxonomy to see how the types and groups of types delineated fit into its finer subdivisions, or whether its operational characters or structure need correcting. For example, the detailed study by Becker (1966, 1972) of the acoustics of reed instruments exposed a fault in Mahillon's and Hornbostel and Sachs's schemes, which differentiated clarinets and oboes according to the form of the mouthpiece (i.e., whether it had concussion or percussion lamellae). Becker was able to show that the manner of excitation of sound in the two kinds of instruments is not reliant on this factor and that it actually depends on whether their tubes are cylindrical or conical in shape.

The sociohistorical, archeological, iconographical, anthropological, and music-stylistic aspects of instruments (such as the role of instrumental ensembles), and the music communication system (player-instrument-music) are less precisely measurable than the ergological, technical, and acoustic ones.[17] Therefore, Elschek recommends that these taxonomical data (sources and argument about them) be presented in written form. Examples of such studies of historical, sociological, and music-stylistic aspects of groups of instruments are Ling's study of the music instrument players in Sweden's industrial society (1981, 53–57), Hickmann's article on the performer in animal form (1981, 58–64), and Kvifte's study of variability in Harding fiddle music (1981, 102–7). Other studies using verbal description and/or sketches include those presented by Macák,

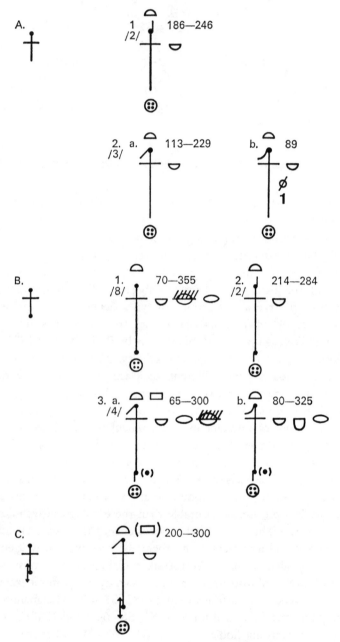

FIGURE 12.8 Synoptic chart of willow-bark flutes (based on Elschek 1969b)

Markl, and van der Meer on bagpipes; Moek and Sevåg on flutes; Emsheimer on wooden trumpets; and Habenicht on a type of bagpipe (all in *SIMP,* 1969 and 1974).

Elschek's partial development of a typological method and Elschek and Stockmann's theoretical account of its aims and significance are a logical development of the trend toward the multifaceted inspection of instruments and the desire to take the detail and the variability of instruments into account in the processes of classification. Perhaps Elschek's approach or something similar is or should be the way of the future. Possibly there will be a general shift toward upward grouping, as occurred in biology beginning in the seventeenth century, or the microtaxonomical approach will be used as a supplement to the macrotaxonomical one. Only time will tell whether or not a significant number of organologists will adopt an upward method of grouping. At the very least, however, Elschek and Stockmann with other members of the Study Group on Folk Music Instruments have begun to stimulate awareness among some scholars of the theoretical problems involved in the classification of instruments and to foster the beginnings of a critical dialogue about those problems.

PART THREE

Classification in Societies Oriented toward Oral Transmission

Most of the classifications of instruments and ensembles in the orally oriented cultures discussed in Part III serve first and foremost to facilitate practical music making by groups of performers rather than to express the intellectual concepts of individual scholars bent on illustrating a particular musical or extramusical theory, as in many of the written schemes discussed in Part II.

This does not, however, mean that these orally transmitted schemes are bereft of social, religious, visual artistic, and other extramusical concepts. On the contrary, the key schemes in these societies tend to be extremely rich in their connotations and are in some cases considered to be of great conceptual importance within the parent culture. In fact they may embody the very ideas that distinguish their particular kind of society from others. On the whole, the key schemes in orally transmitting societies have broader and more complex cultural implications than most of the ones in written traditions, while the latter, especially in recent times, may consist of many more substeps and subdivisions and consider many more facets of a much larger corpus of instruments in a more complex, complete, and systematic way. The preferred Mandailing classification of ensembles is based on concepts that are related to cosmological thought, kinship groupings, components of the family, social organization, and even village or town planning. Instrumental groupings made within some of the other societies discussed in the following chapters may be linked to a set of origin myths, as in the case of the Dan, or on the basis of which may sometimes be incompletely known sets of origin myths, as in some orally transmitted Kpelle, Javanese, and Indian schemes (or remnants of schemes). The classifications singled out as key schemes in a society tend to be related to basic cultural concepts.

Some regions have a great diversity of schemes, though the diversity may lie only in the detail. For example, in Minangkabau, an area of poor but recently developing communications, every village or group of villages has its own scheme devised for purposes of practical music making (e.g., to facilitate interlocking techniques played by the "lead" and the "follower" instruments), yet the principles on which these different regional schemes are based are very similar.

As we shall see, instruments considered to be most sacred or important in the hierarchy of instruments tend to be classified more closely than those of minor significance. They tend to be classified by multifaceted paradigms as opposed to single-character logical division. 'Are'are bamboo instruments, for example, which are assigned the greatest amount of magical significance, are classified paradigmatically according to mode of sound excitation as well as their ability or inability to perform melodies containing equiheptaphonic seconds. In each case the chosen facets of division are important musical or extramusical concepts in the culture. Similar multifaceted divisions for important instruments are made by the T'boli, the Mandailing, the Dan, and the Finns.

Besides the symbolic, myth-associated, and practical music-making characters, schemes discussed in Part III are based on such characters as mode of sound excitation, morphology, materials of which instruments are made, and timbres produced by them. Mode of sound excitation is a character found in all the cultures discussed. Yet the content of categories delineated by this character varies considerably across the cultures.

Structures of classification in the following chapters consist of tree-form taxonomies and paradigms only. The Mandailing, Minangkabau, and 'Are'are are among many orally oriented cultures whose members like to draw genealogical trees, though few of them draw classifications of instruments unless asked to do so by an observer. In my field experience, members of Minangkabau, Mandailing, Javanese, and a number of other Southeast Asian societies take considerable aesthetic pleasure in drawing tree diagrams, whether presenting genealogies or taxonomies of instruments. Similarly, multifaceted classifications are not uncommon, and the paradigms produced are highly varied in form.

As has been pointed out, the main difference between the study of orally transmitted taxonomies and schemes transmitted in writing is the method of compiling data about them. Study of the oral schemes depends largely on field research, while investigations into the literary classifications concentrate on other written sources in libraries and elsewhere. However, many more data about the content and form of the oral schemes need to be gathered, along with information about the relevant religions, beliefs, ritual practices, social structure, and musical practice, before the broad picture can be pieced together.

Unlike in societies with a long literary history, it is rarely possible in orally transmitting cultures to isolate evidence of historical change. Hence their study is largely synchronic. In some cases, however, diachronic factors can be pieced together if the multiple meanings of certain lexemes can be isolated and the loose ends or contradictions in a scheme are interpreted in the light of possible change. Some schemes in which synchronic and diachronic factors have been operating independently of each other may suggest to the researcher a course of historical change, which may lead to the making of convincing historical reconstructions or hypotheses. Two cases of this—in the Finnish and Minangkabau cultures—are discussed in the following chapters.

Parallels between Social Structure and Ensemble Classification in Mandailing

The Mandailing people, who live in the mountainous southwest of the province of North Sumatra, are one of six groups known by the common name of Batak. The music, dialect, and other cultural expressions of these groups are essentially similar, but they differ in detail.

LESSER CLASSIFICATIONS

Mandailing and other Batak languages contain terms that allow divisions to be made between instruments according to the mode of sound excitation.[1] The resulting four classes include the beaten instruments (*alat pukul* or *alat palu*), the blown instruments (*alat tiup*), the bowed instruments (*alat gesek*),[2] and the plucked instruments (*alat petik*).[3] It is indeed interesting to group the large inventory of Mandailing and other Batak instruments under these four headings and to conclude that three-quarters of them are beaten instruments, over a third are blown instruments, and that the bowed and plucked instruments are statistically not important, as Simon did in 1985. But naturally the Batak themselves never list and group their instrumentarium in this way. In fact, the operating character of division in this classification—mode of sound excitation—is one of only secondary importance in the culture.

Timbral and morphological considerations are likewise not of major significance within the Mandailing concept of instruments. Terminological distinctions are not made between such details as single and double reeds or percussion and concussion lamellae. "The Batak call both single-reed and double-reed types *sarunei*. The single-reed instruments are distinguished only by such attributes as 'small' (*sarunei na met-met*) or 'bamboo' (*sarunei buluh*), . . . (despite) the fact that each of the . . . sub-groups of the Batak has its own special type of *sarunei*" (Simon 1985, 115–16).

Another taxonomy emerging from the culture is based on the broad, somewhat evolutionary idea of sociohistorical or religiohistorical strata. Such strata are not conceived of as precise historical periods but as broad cultural movements, usually marked by culture contact over long periods and persisting even after the initial ideas on which they were based have in part been discarded. (On the concept of strata see Kunst 1949 [1934]: I, 2 and Kartomi 1980: 111–33.) The oldest stratum in Mandailing is based on *pele begu* (animist) thought but is also influenced by Tantric Hindu and Buddhist culture. (A combination of Hindu and Buddhist influences in Indonesia was operative between the early centuries of our era and about the fifteenth century, though it occurred in the later centuries in Mandailing.) These two streams of thought merged so thoroughly in Mandailing that they are regarded now to all intents and purposes as constituting one stratum; thus cultural expressions containing elements of both are usually described by the one word—*asli* ("authentic"). The second, Islamic-influenced stratum dates from the early nineteenth century in Mandailing (and from about the fourteenth century in Aceh and elsewhere in the region). It has its own independent cultural forms, including music played on instruments from foreign Muslim sources. The third stratum, which is marked by European influences and dates from about the sixteenth century in Indonesia but from the early nineteenth century in Mandailing, was associated with Christianity and later with Western secularism and popular culture. Vestiges of these strata and other substrata are still seen as coexisting and overlapping with each other, and all musical instruments used in Mandailing can clearly be linked to one or another of them (see Kartomi 1985, 5–22).

To all intents and purposes, then, the Mandailing have a taxonomy that clearly distinguishes instruments of the *pele begu* stratum from both the Muslim-influenced and the Western-influenced strata. Instruments used in the Muslim performing arts are not normally grouped together or played with *asli* Mandailing instruments. Nor are Western popular or church instruments confused with the other strata. This culture-emerging or natural classification, however, is not regarded by the leaders and practitioners of the culture as being of major conceptual importance either.

The Primary Mandailing Taxonomy of Ensembles

The primary taxonomy in Mandailing is of ensembles, not individual instruments. It is much richer in its connotations and is based on a much more complex cognitive structure than the two schemes mentioned above. It was presented to me in its entirety on several separate occasions by a group of elders and always with an electric sense of aesthetic delight in the elegance of the scheme, whether they presented it in its simple graphic form or in the full complexity of its epistemological connotations.

This scheme reflects the tenets of the old *pele begu* religious beliefs and philosophical ideas about the nature of existence and social organization.[4] In this intensely communal society, the clan and the village are much more significant entities than the individual, the concept of which hardly exists, and one's first duty is to the community, not to oneself. The social hierarchy is led by the *raja* (headman, chief of the dominant clan and village) or his descendant (the title is no longer allowed to be used) and the elders; and it is they who decide on strategies to ensure the common good and, together with the host, who is usually one of them, preside at ceremonies. On the occasion of funerals, weddings, and other important occasions, the whole community is asked to cooperate in preparing a ritual feast, at which orchestral music and ceremonial dancing are performed in order to attract the ancestral and other spirits to come and bless the gathering by their presence. Each social category has a specific ritual role to play. Likewise the various ensembles have clearly defined ritual roles.

The Mandailing do not normally see the need to classify individual instruments. Instruments are simply not conceived of as individual entities except in a mundane, nonritual context, which is not important. Nonritual instruments such as the paddy shawm or split drum, which are played to scare away the birds in a rice field, for example, are not included in discussions by the elders about music and cosmology.[5] Instruments attain maximal potency when played in a group; and in principle, the larger the group, the more powerful it is. Thus the Mandailing prefer to classify ensembles, not instruments. They also try to ensure that their ensembles are "complete," for an incomplete ensemble or entity loses considerably in its effectiveness, magic power, and beauty.

In musical and symbolic terms, by far the most important component of all three Mandailing ensembles is the set of drums they contain (fig. 13.1). In the least important of the ensembles—the *gondang* (or *gondang dua,* or *gondang sidua-dua*), which was traditionally reserved for basic mystical rites and the funerals and weddings of commoners—the drum component comprises a pair of double-headed drums (*gondang*) played in a soft, subtle manner, with one player on each drum. In the ensemble of medium potency—the *gordang lima* ("five-drum ensemble"), which was traditionally played outside the shaman's home in shaman-led ceremonies for the purposes of healing, clairvoyance, and the like—five single-headed drums (*gordang*) graded from large to small and grouped in two "male"-"female" pairs plus one "child" drum are beaten by three players. Only in this ensemble is a specially potent buzzing instrument (either a piece of shredded bamboo or

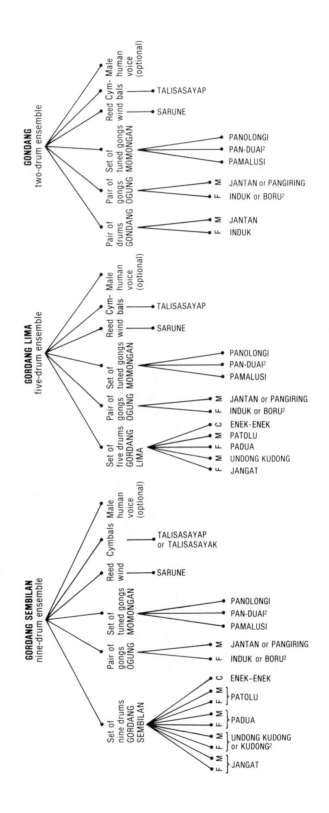

FIGURE 13.1 Classification of three Mandailing ritual ensembles

a broken gong) attached to one of the drums, making a magically evocative, whirring sound, rather like a bull-roarer's. In the largest ensemble—the *gordang sembilan* ("nine-drum ensemble"), which is ritually the most "complete" of the three orchestras—nine single-headed drums graded in size and grouped in four pairs plus a single drum are beaten by four players. The instruments are normally attached to a lower outside part of the wall-less pavilion (*sopo godang*) that serves as a ritual house (fig. 13.2). Its triangular-shaped gable design, which contains a number of diametric and concentric dualistic symbols (fig. 13.3), is conceived of as symbolizing the cosmos.

In fact, the major distinguishing element between the three main ensembles is their drum component. All the ensembles otherwise contain identical instruments: including a pair of suspended gongs (*ogung*); a set of two, three, or more small hand-held gongs (*momongan, mongmongan*); a single small gong (*doal*); a pair of cymbals (*talisasayap*); and a reed wind instrument (*sarune*); plus an optional male voice (which, however, is not considered to be an instrument). Each ensemble, then, is divided at the first step into three subsets (including the drum set, the pair of gongs, and the hand-held gongs) and three single instruments (a small gong, cymbals, reed winds), where the single instruments have lower status than the sets within the ensemble and virtually none outside it.

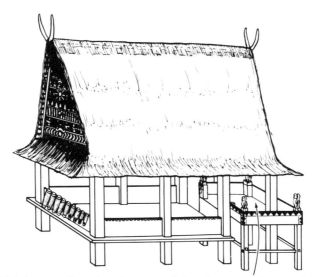

FIGURE 13.2 A *sopo godang* showing a set of nine drums (*gordang sembilan*) and a raised platform for the *raja*

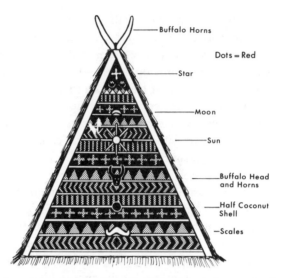

Figure 13.3 A traditional Mandailing (Lubis) gable design on the front and back gables of a *sopo godang*

Only the three subsets, of course, can be subdivided at the second step, where two principles of division intersect paradigmatically. The scheme presented in figure 13.1 is satisfactory except at the second step, which is more adequately depicted in the paradigms in figure 13.4. The two intersecting parameters of division are the binary (female/male) and ternary (female/male/child) distinctions on the one hand and the order of musical entry, or musical function, on the other.

The four pairs of drums in the *gordang sembilan* are completed by the presence of a single drum called *enek-enek,* meaning "small" or "child." The two largest drums form a female/male (*induk/jantan*) pair called *jangat* ("to do something with pleasure," or "cow skin").[6] The next largest pair is called *undong kudong*[7] ("beginning to sound"), and its player is the first to make a musical entry in a piece. The middle pair is termed *padua,* meaning "second entry," and the next smallest is called "*patolu,* meaning "third entry." While the principles of sexual division and order of entry intersect in the case of the drums, another two principles operate in the case of the pair of gongs, the slightly larger of which is called *induk, indung,* or *boru-boru* ("female"), and the other *jantan* ("male") or *pangiring* ("accompanying").[8] Here the first gong is distinguished not only by its "femaleness" and larger size but also by the fact that it plays the leading musical role of the pair, while the second ("male") gong plays a secondary

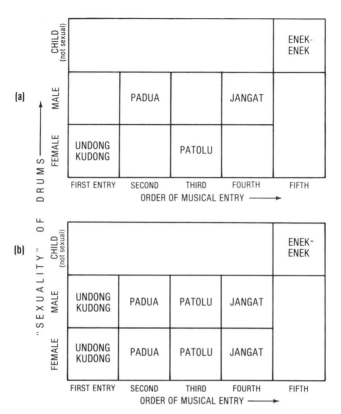

FIGURE 13.4 Paradigm of features of drum sets in Mandailing: *top,* five-drum ensemble; *bottom,* nine-drum ensemble

role. The set of hand-held tuned gongs, which is less important and less magically potent, breaks by simple logical division at the second step into three categories distinguished according to musical function. The first to enter among the small gongs is the one called *pamalusi* ("beater"), the second is the *panduai-duai* ("the second one"), and the third is the *panolongi* ("the helper") or *paniga* ("the third one").

The drum component of the *gordang lima* and *gondang* ensembles is classified similarly to that of the *gordang sembilan.* Thus, in the *gordang* ensemble, the larger of the pair of drums is called *induk* or *indung* and the smaller *jantan,* and the female drum is normally the first to make a musical entry.

The binary female/male and ternary female/male/child distinctions shown in the paradigms in figure 13.4 are symbolic of Mandailing cosmological thought and social organization, which are similarly imbued with binary and ternary principles of classification. But dualism is itself twofold (Lévi-Strauss 1963, 133); it is structurally either diametric or concentric. Moreover, concentric dualism actually has a ternary nature, since the outer circle contrasts with the open space encircling it.[9] This dual organization is "in many instances (and perhaps in all) actually an inextricable mixture of the three types. . . . triadism and dualism are inseparable, since dualism is never conceived of as such, but only as a 'borderline' form of the triadic type" (Lévi-Strauss 1963: 151).

However, the sexual dualism of the drums in the nine-drum ensembles assumes a triadic form in that a nonsexual, "child" category is added (see second paradigm in fig. 13.4). A similar ambiguity in Mandailing visual art is the dualistic concept of blackness (symbolizing femaleness) and whiteness (symbolizing maleness) as exemplified in the gable design of the ritual houses; this is inherently a triadic concept since the color red, symbolizing courage, is also used. Another example of diametric dualism with triadic implications is the asymmetric Mandailing marriage system, which is based on the dichotomy of the "bride givers" (or kinship superiors) and the "bride takers" (or kinship inferiors), as in many other parts of Southeast Asia (van der Kroef 1954, 847–62). However, on ritual occasions, these divisions are matched by a third—the ceremonial host and retinue. The host organizes and basically pays for the ceremony, while the bride takers do most of the hard work, and the bride givers bestow their magically powerful presence on the gathering.

In Mandailing, the pre-Muslim philosophy holds that there is an eternal tension in life between sets of dualistic principles that are at once opposite and complementary. The most basic dualistic principle is the female/male dichotomy, which pertains not only to people but also to animals and inanimate objects such as gongs, drums, and the *linga-yoni* stones in the graveyards and elsewhere, which rumble in warning at times of danger and protect the village, and the four two-faced, protective wooden figures with ambiguous sexual or bisexual features placed on a platform in a ritual house. The sexual personification of these art objects and musical instruments ensures their magic power and consequently their respected treatment by the community, as they are believed to house spirits who beautify their appearance and sound them by their presence.

In Mandailing religious thought, then, a bisexual unit is regarded as being more complete and powerful than a single-sex unit, and groups of bisexual units as being more powerful than a single bisexual unit. But the highest degree of potency and completeness is attained when an entity comprises an odd number of components, which represent a combination of the dualisms and their product. As has been noted, the four pairs of female/male drums in the nine-drum ensemble are made fully complete by the presence of the smallest drum, *enek-enek,* which represents the child, the product of the female/male dualisms. Like a family or a village, a musical ensemble is philosophically complete only if it contains several "couples" plus a product that is the common property of both sexes. Thus only the nine-drum ensemble is supremely powerful, which is the reason why its use is traditionally reserved for royal ceremonies. The pairs of female/male drums and gongs and the lesser instruments of the three ensembles may also be understood as symbolizing communal unity, while the single solo wind instrument and optional singing voice symbolize individualism, forming yet another diametric dualism (Kartomi 1973, 13).

The completeness of the nine-drum ensemble may also be linked to the clan (*marga*) system and the folk history of a settlement. In the village of Pakantan, for instance, the nine drums of the *gordang sembilan* are seen as representing the original nine clans that settled there over the centuries. Music played on this ritual ensemble is regarded as being more beautiful and mystically satisfying than that of other ensembles because it is philosophically, musically, and—by analogy—socially more "complete." As the elders in Pakantan explain, each single drum of the ensembles represents a particular clan or subclan. Each time a drum was added to an ensemble in the past it meant that a new clan had settled in and accepted the jurisdiction of the *raja.* Thus the five-drum ensemble represented a relatively early stage in the settlement of the village, the seven-drum ensemble (which is now almost obsolete) a later stage, and the nine-drum ensemble the final stage of clan settlement. Five of the drums represent the Nasution, Lintang, Hasibuan, Kotalanca, and Hutagambir clans. Three of the drums represent the dominant Lubis clan with its three subclans. And one drum represents their common leader, the *raja,* who is required to be a member of the first clan believed to have settled in the village, that is, the Lubis clan.

The classification of the nine-drum ensemble is linked, then, to the clan system as well as to the idea of sexual dualism and sexual-dualism-plus-product. The ensembles symbolize the social structure, with its specific numerical symbolism. In addition, the instruments are assigned personal characteristics. Each drum, gong, and member of a tuned gong set in the *gordang lima* and *gondang* ensembles has its own name, as do the pairs into which the drums are grouped in the *gordang sembilan* ensemble.

A similar example of the personification of instruments is the practice in the neighboring Pakpak Batak area of bestowing proper names on respected individual instruments. In the village of Sukaramai, for example, the ritual *genderang* ensemble (which is similar to the *gordang*) has a set of nine graded drums, of which the largest—the "mother" drum (*indungna*)— is called by the respected onomatopoeic name of Raja Gumaruguh, where *raja* means "royal chieftain" and *gumaruguh* is a verbal imitation of the "sound of rolling stones like that heard in a landslide" (Simon 1985, 136).

CONCLUSION

Mandailing schemes are either taxonomies or paradigms. The Mandailing vocabulary allows the classification of all instruments according to the way the player makes sounds on them. However, the four "beaten," "blown," "plucked," and "bowed" divisions are not the primary classification in the culture. And although taxonomical classification according to sociohistorical strata is inherent in Mandailing musical practice, this is not of major importance either.

The primary classification of instruments in Mandailing is based on religious and philosophical ideas about the nature of existence and social organization. It is a taxonomy with a paradigmatic grouping of the drums at the second level. Instrumental ensembles, like the ritual house gable designs, symbolize the structure of the family, the clan system, the social unit of the village, and the philosophical unity of the cosmos. At the first step the ensembles divide into the various drums, gongs, and small gongs as well as the less important individual instruments, which have taxonomic importance only when they are part of an ensemble. Only the sets of instruments are classified at the second step, being grouped paradigmatically by the principle of sexual dualism or sexual-dualism-plus-product on the one hand and musical function on the other.

Instruments played in ensemble in the correct ritual setting not only parallel the social hierarchy but also invite the presence of the spirits of nature and the ancestors to inhabit them and beautify their sound, thus contributing to the social cohesion of the community. The concept of instruments and their consequent classification are based on deep-seated spiritual beliefs. In both their form and content, Mandailing classifications of instrumental ensembles reflect the structure and social beliefs and practices of the Mandailing culture.

Taxonomical Models of the Instrumentarium and Regional Ensembles in Minangkabau

Mahindang manampeh bareh bapiliah atak ciek-ciek (Winnow the rice on the bamboo tray, pick out the whole grains one by one).
A Minangkabau saying

Like the Mandailing, the Minangkabau people of West Sumatra are virtually all Muslim, yet they still preserve some of the tenets and artistic expressions of their pre-Muslim beliefs.[1] Musicians make a clear, practical distinction between musical instruments (*bunyi-bunyian,* "objects that sound") used in the Muslim art forms and those used in agricultural, tiger-capturing, and other rituals belonging to the pre-Muslim stratum of culture. Instruments "of Arabic origin" (*asal Arab*) are therefore clearly distinguished in the practical music-making scene from the "authentic Minangkabau" (*Minangkabau asli*) stratum of culture. Similarly, instruments "of Western origin" (*asal Barat*) are normally kept quite separate from both the Muslim and the pre-Muslim instruments. With very few exceptions, instruments used in the social or musical context of one stratum are never played in the context of either of the other two. But legend has it that the instrument called *indang* is a link between the two, as suggested by the context of the saying at the head of this chapter.[2]

A three-category taxonomy of instruments based on sociohistorical strata exists, then, in Minangkabau musical practice, thought, and language, although musicians do not normally present or discuss this classification. The system was elicited in the field and is presented graphically in figure 14.1. Subcategories based on another character are added in the illustration at the second step; this character is the mode of sound excitation. To classify instruments according to sociohistorical strata as well as mode of sound excitation is common in many Indonesian cultures, including the Mandailing and the Javanese, though the details of the characters and of the specimens included are culture-specific.

The division of instruments into categories according to sociohistorical or religiohistorical strata (or the historical processes of culture contact

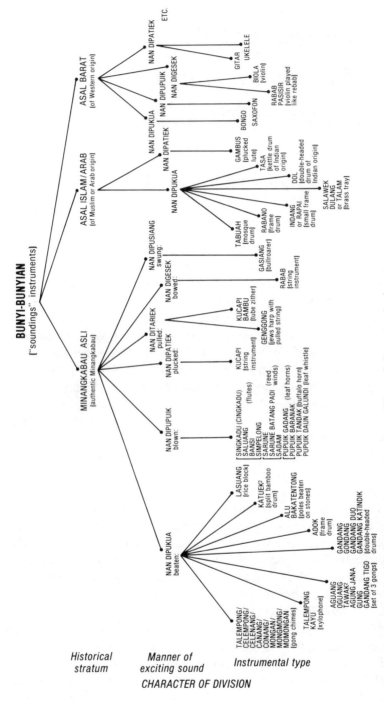

FIGURE 14.1 Classification of instruments based on Minangkabau terminology

and synthesis) is related to the concept of what instruments mean and how they are valued in Minangkabau culture. The most beautiful, sacred, and highly rated instruments are the gong-chimes and drums (and, rarely, in very few villages, also the gongs),[3] which belong to the *asli* stratum. These combine to form the basis of the main ritual ensembles, called *talempong*, with different names being given to the instruments in different areas. Flutes such as the *saluang* and the *simpelong* are also highly rated for their sonic beauty and mystical power, especially in the context of love magic. Shamans in some areas are asked to paint a white lime cross on *asli* instruments at special ceremonies in order to enhance their magic power and beauty of sound (according to my field information). In fact, as in some other Indonesian cultures, the sacredness of all traditional instruments is reflected in the belief that a traveler who comes within earshot of instrumental sound is immediately and irresistibly drawn toward its source. In fact, musical sounds are perceived as being at their most beautiful and potent when heard from afar.

The high evaluation of the *asli* ensembles in Minangkabau is tied up with the matrilineal social system and female ownership of land and other valuable property such as bronze or brass instruments. In some areas, such as the Sijunjung region and the hinterland of the town of Pariaman, it is the women who play these instruments. Female instrumental performance is rare in Indonesian societies, and in Minangkabau it is apparently linked to their ownership of the instruments. In the patrilineal societies of Java, Bali, and other parts of Indonesia, normally only men play the instruments of the bronze ensembles, while the women join the men in singing and dancing.

The Muslim instruments (mainly frame drums), on the other hand, are not attributed with a magic aura, though sometimes they are spoken of as having a special power to affect players and listeners. In a land where virtually everyone is a Muslim, the sounds of these instruments induce feelings of religious devotion and may even assist a Sufi-oriented worshiper in the attempt to achieve unity with God. Some instruments, such as the *gambus* (a lute of probably Middle Eastern origin) and frame drums, are used to accompany Arabic-style secular love songs and exchanges of witty or advice-offering quatrains (*pantun*). The large two-headed *dol* and single-headed, earthenware *tasa* drums, which were probably transplanted from Muslim India in the eighteenth century, accompany dirges and mock battles in the Sh'ia rites called *tabut* (see Kartomi 1986, 141–62) and entertain at weddings, drumming competitions, and the like. As in

Muslim countries elsewhere, the most highly regarded Muslim instruments are drums, especially frame drums.

Western musical instruments are different from instruments of the other two strata in that they are regarded as secular symbols of modernity. To some they symbolize economic and social progressiveness, to others moral depravity. They belong to social contexts in which popular Malay music and popular band music are enjoyed.

As has been noted, the Minangkabau language has a lexical field denoting ways of exciting sound that serves as a taxonomy of Minangkabau instruments. Musicians distinguish the following categories:

> *bunyi-bunyian nan dipukua,* "beaten instruments"
> *bunyi-bunyian nan dipupuik,* "blown instruments"
> *bunyi-bunyian nan dipatiek,* "plucked instruments"
> *bunyi-bunyian nan ditariek,* "pulled instruments"
> *bunyi-bunyian nan digesek,* "bowed instruments"
> *bunyi-bunyian nan dipusiang,* "swung instruments"

The first category includes gong-chimes, gongs, xylophones, drums, percussion poles, bamboo split drums, and rice-blocks; the second includes flutes, trumpets, and reed winds of various kinds; the third includes plucked strings, including bamboo-stringed zithers; the fourth, jew's harps; the fifth, bowed strings; and the sixth, bull-roarers. A glance at the classification presented in figure 14.1 shows that the greatest variety of instruments occurs in the percussion category, followed by the wind instrument category, with the least variety occurring in the plucked, pulled, bowed, and swung instrument categories.

Apart from this lexical field and the sociohistorical strata concept, both of which are sources of instrument grouping, the Minangkabau do not have a comprehensive system of classification of their corpus of instruments. But this is hardly surprising, for theirs is a large region and it is a performer's rather than a scholar's musical culture. Because they have never gathered or played their instruments all at once, they have not felt the need to classify them as a whole. Only recently were some instruments collected from parts of the province and displayed according to regional distribution in a museum. No single Minangkabau musician has been in a position to obtain an overall view of the diversity of instruments and ensembles throughout the region, which until recently has not had an effective communication network. A local musician is normally able to supply taxonomical information about the ensembles in her or his own village—and often with great pride and aesthetic delight—but not for all the instruments and ensembles of the provincial mainland of Minangkabau.

The point bears emphasizing that the classification of the whole instrumental corpus as presented in figure 14.1—though it is based on indigenous terms and characters—would not normally be drawn up by Minangkabau musicians themselves, and it is of course but one of several possible schemes. As a summary of the instrumentarium, it is certainly of greater potential use to students or scholars than to insider musicians. Moreover, its generalizations skim over the diverse details of actual music making in the various types of village instrumental ensembles. It is within the classification of the ensembles typifying a village or group of villages that the real uniqueness and practical usefulness of Minangkabau taxonomical activity by insider musicians lies.

West Sumatra is remarkable for its high degree of regional musical diversity, as exemplified by the ritual ensembles, which are variously called *talempong, celempong,* and *canang.* As has been mentioned, the Minangkabau people have no practical need to classify their total corpus of instruments, nor any easy way to collect the data even if they wished to do so. However, they do divide their ensembles into their component parts, by logical division, according to musical function. Indeed they have a performing need to classify their gong-chime ensembles, for example, into those played by musicians carrying the instruments in procession as opposed to those played by seated performers. They also need to subclassify their ensembles according to their performers' musical functions in producing a continuous stream of melody by means of interlocking parts, as a result of which each musician has a clearly designated musical role to play. The practical requirements of group musicianship are clearly spelled out—albeit with different terminologies—in different villages, and these terminologies may actually be regarded as a set of taxa that can be grouped together into taxonomies of ensembles as in figure 14.2.

All ritual ensembles contain drums, most have gong-chimes, a few contain gongs, and some have double- or multiple-reed wind instruments. They vary from village to village or between groups of villages in their number and type of instrumental components, the names, sizes, and shapes of the instruments, and the terminology used for their performers' musical functions. Thus, it is not possible to present a single classification

X	=	player

TERMS

			paningkah, tingkahan	=	player of irregular rhythms, interjector
talempong, celempong canang	=	ensemble, gong-chime	pambaoan	=	player of repetitive patterns
duduak	=	seated	anak	=	child (lit.)
baarak	=	processional	pamain loram	=	player of repetitive rhythms
pacik	=	(hand) held	tongah tangah,		
gandang dabuih	=	double-headed drum	pangahan	=	middle; middle player
rabano	=	frame drum	tagok	=	strong
mongan, aguang, ogung (Payakumbuh)	=	suspended gong	pancingan	=	provoker
			pamalun	=	melody maker
betino	=	female	sarune	=	double reed wind
jantan	=	male	sarune batang padi	=	multiple reed wind
			dol	=	big double-headed drum

1. Celempong Ensembles in Talang Maur Village (Limapuluh Kota)

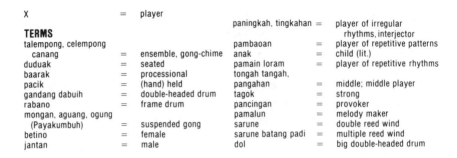

2. Celempong Ensembles in Sisawah Village (Sawahlunto—Sijunjung)

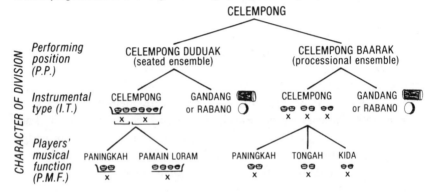

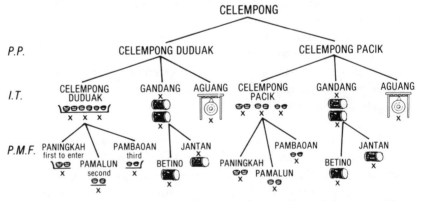

FIGURE 14.2 Orally transmitted classifications of some Minangkabau ensembles

3. Talempong Ensembles in Nan Duobale and Dalimo Villages (Sawahlunto—Sijunjung)

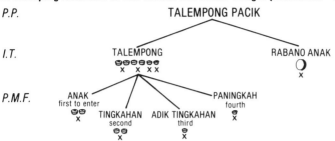

P.P.   TALEMPONG PACIK

I.T.   TALEMPONG   RABANO ANAK

P.M.F.   ANAK (first to enter)   PANINGKAH (fourth)   TINGKAHAN (second)   ADIK TINGKAHAN (third)

4. Talempong Ensembles in Salayu Village (Solok)

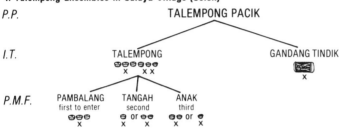

P.P.   TALEMPONG PACIK

I.T.   TALEMPONG   GANDANG TINDIK

P.M.F.   PAMBALANG (first to enter)   TANGAH (second)   ANAK (third)

5. Talempong Ensembles in Unggan Village (Sawahlunto—Sijunjung)

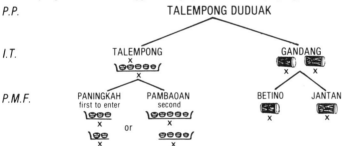

P.P.   TALEMPONG DUDUAK

I.T.   TALEMPONG   GANDANG

P.M.F.   PANINGKAH (first to enter)   PAMBAOAN (second)   or   BETINO   JANTAN

6. Canang and Gondang Ensembles in Kampuang Dalam Village (Sawahlunto—Sijunjung)

P.P.   CANANG PACIK   GONDANG

I.T.   CANANG PACIK   DABUIH   MONGAN   GONDANG

P.M.F.   PAMAIN TAGO[2] (first to enter)   PANGAHAN (second)   PANINGKAH (third)   PANCINGAN (fourth)   BETINO (first to enter)   JANTAN (second)   BETINO, PAMBAOAN   JANTAN, PANINGKAH (same size)

7. Canang Ensembles in Tanjung Ampalu Village (Sawahlunto—Sijunjung)

P.P. CANANG PACIK

I.T. CANANG PACIK   GANDANG   OGUANG

P.M.F. PANINGKAH first to enter   PAMALUN second   PAMBAOAN third   BETINO   JANTAN   BETINO   JANTAN

8. Talempong Ensembles in Sikaladi Village (Pariangan)

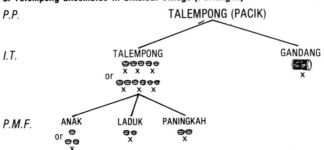

P.P. TALEMPONG (PACIK)

I.T. TALEMPONG or   GANDANG

P.M.F. ANAK or   LADUK   PANINGKAH

9. Talempong Ensembles in Painan Timur Village (Pasisir Selatan)

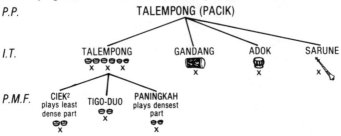

P.P. TALEMPONG (PACIK)

I.T. TALEMPONG   GANDANG   ADOK   SARUNE

P.M.F. CIEK^2 plays least dense part   TIGO-DUO   PANINGKAH plays densest part

10. Talempong Ensemble in Salido Village (Pasisir Selatan)

P.P. TALEMPONG (PACIK)

I.T. TALEMPONG   GANDANG   SARUNE BATANG PADI or KATOPONG

P.M.F. CIEK^2 TIGO-DUO   PANINGKAH

11. Talempong Ensemble in Pandang Kunik Village (Pariaman)

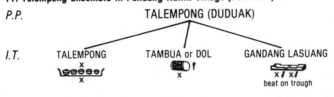

P.P. TALEMPONG (DUDUAK)

I.T. TALEMPONG   TAMBUA or DOL   GANDANG LASUANG

beat on trough

scheme for all of West Sumatra's ritual ensembles. At this stage of its musical history, a different scheme has to be drawn up for virtually every village or group of musically related villages.

The division made by Minangkabau musicians between processional and seated ensembles results not only from their different performance styles but also from the different items included in the two repertoires. Though some pieces are reserved for performance on the one kind of ensemble only, other pieces may be played on both. Some items are intended for one or two musicians playing on a gong-chime that consists of five gongs suspended on cords tied into a frame, as opposed to, say, an ensemble with three players performing interlocking parts on pairs of hand-held gongs. Each ensemble has a different style of playing.

If figure 14.2 suggests that the other character of division—the player's musical functions—is a rather complex matter, this may be because of the lexemes and other terminological diversity found in the musical practices of the various villages. The purpose of each classification is to specify which player enters first, second, third, or fourth (where relevant) and also who "leads" and who "follows." In the village called Kampuang Dalam, for example, the so-called male drum (which produces a "moist" sound) leads while the slightly smaller female drum (which produces a "bright" sound) follows. In other villages the female drum, which is sometimes slightly larger than the male, leads the drumming. A major distinction is made between interlocking gong-chime or drum players according to whether they play irregular or repetitive rhythms; the former is called *paningkah* (lit. "interjector") and the latter is called *pambaon* ("one who brings"). Some terms refer to the kind of rhythm played; for example, *ciek-ciek* ("one-one") in Salido village refers to the playing of one note on each beat, and *tigo-duo* ("three-two") designates the playing of three- and two-note rhythmic patterns.

As Leisiö noted (1977, 50), folk classifications serve as data for historical research into instruments; indeed they may reveal "a historical though not a temporal evolution." The first of the instrument classification schemes presented in this chapter (fig. 14.1) contains elements inviting historical hypothesis and research, and this also applies to similar orally transmitted classifications in Mandailing and Java. The stratum of instruments of so-called Arabic origin were transplanted from Arabia, Persia, or Muslim India. One of these instruments (listed in the second [Muslim] category of fig. 14.1), the *rabano* (frame drum), dates back at least as far as the beginning of conversion to Islam in Minangkabau, which probably took place in the seventeenth century. It may, of course, date back to a much earlier period than that, for Arabic and other traders who visited Sumatra's west coast from the first millennium CE may have introduced "Arabic" instruments or names of instruments to Sumatra from that time. The name of this frame drum, which was adapted from the Arabic *rabana,* also appears in the first ensemble presented in figure 14.2. This is an example of the occasional practice of substituting an instrument from the Muslim stratum into an ensemble of another stratum, in this case the "authentic" Minangkabau stratum. This substitution probably dates from the early nineteenth century when the inhabitants of virtually the whole Minangkabau region had been converted to Islam. At this time the Muslim performing arts practiced in the religious boys' schools (*surau*) developed and spread, together with the local manufacture of frame drums. Although the schemes do not offer exact dates for the developments referred to, they do present data amenable to historical interpretation and contain evidence of change wrought in periods of intense contact with outside cultures.

F I F T E E N

Groupings Governed by Key Cultural Concepts of the T'boli

Just as there is no general term for *music* or *tradition*, there is no term for *instruments* in the language of the T'boli people, who live in the uplands near the southern coast of Mindanao (southern Philippines).[1] Nor is a concrete classification of instruments—whether oral or written—to be found in the culture. Models of orderings of instruments as well as of instrumental ensembles are observable in the musical practice, however. Their taxonomies and paradigms are based on characters of division that are key concepts in the culture.

One of these concepts is the dichotomy of the individual and the group, a dichotomy that is basic to T'boli ideas of social structure. In various spheres, such as commerce and art, the individual assumes considerable importance, indeed considerably greater importance than in insular Southeast Asian cultures such as Java, Mandailing, and Minang-kabau. A basic distinction is made between instruments played solo and instruments played in ensemble (or instruments of the individual mode and instruments of the group mode, to use Mora's terms), as shown in the classification of thirteen solo instruments in figure 15.1 and thirteen ensembles in figure 15.2. To comprehend the lower steps of both schemes, however, it is necessary to investigate two more basic T'boli concepts.

One is the idea of gentleness versus strength, a dichotomy pervading T'boli thought about cosmology, the social characters of men and women, and artistic styles. Instruments are ascribed qualities related to the different social roles of men, who are "strong," and women, who are "gentle." The division between the gentle *(lemnoy)* and the strong *(megel)* approximates the division of human character in some other Southeast Asian cultures.[2]

Some T'boli instruments and ensembles produce a *lemnoy* sound and style, and others produce a *megel* one. This dichotomy is at the base of dualistic groupings both of the solo instruments shown at step one of figure 15.1 and of the three ensemble types in step two of figure 15.2. The lowest step of classification of one *megel*-sounding instrument with two

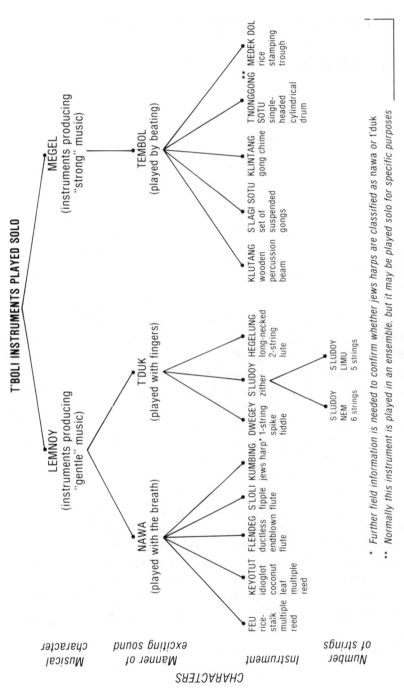

T'BOLI INSTRUMENTS PLAYED SOLO

FIGURE 15.1 Classification of T'boli instruments played solo (based on field information from Manolete Mora)

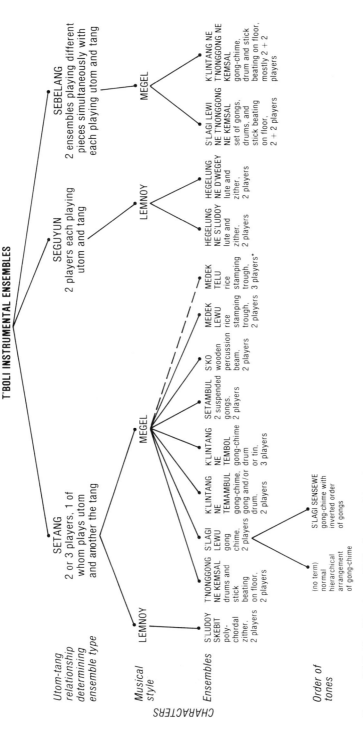

FIGURE 15.2 Classification of T'boli ensembles (based on field information from Manolete Mora)

players—the gong-chime *(s'lagi lewu)*—is based on the arrangement of the gongs according to their pitch (as shown in fig. 15.2).

Solo instruments that produce gentle music are all winds and strings, and solo instruments producing strong music are all percussion instruments. *Lemnoy* and *megel* instruments are never played together. Step two of figure 15.1 shows instruments divided according to the mode of sound excitation. Instruments producing gentle music divide into those played with the breath *(nawa)* and those played with the fingers *(t'duk)*, that is, the blown and the plucked. All instruments producing strong music, on the other hand, belong to the one category; they are all "played by beating" *(tembol)*. The three categories are then grouped into the individual instrumental types, one of which (the zither) is further subdivided at the fourth step according to the number of strings it possesses. In fact, because three characters of division are operating simultaneously here, figures 15.1 and 15.2 are more aptly presented in a paradigmatic diagram, as we have noted (see fig. 2.4).

The other important taxonomical concept basic to T'boli thought about artistic design in general is the idea of the figure, or main design *(utom)*, and the ground *(tang)*, or underlying, repetitive support. This dichotomy is at the base of traditional T'boli weaving design, which is based on a main figure and a repetitive background. It is also important in ensemble music, which is defined for present purposes as music played on one or more instruments by more than one performer. In some cases figure and ground are played by different performers on the same instrument or ensemble, while in others the figure and the ground are played on different instruments or ensembles. In other words, the T'boli distinguish between instruments that are able to play the ground and those that are not. The former are subdivided into two categories according to whether they are "played by beating," as in the case of the gongs,[3] or "played with fingers," as with lutes and zithers. The instruments that play only the ground are played either "with the breath," as in the case of flutes and reed pipes; "with the fingers," as in the case of fiddles; or "by beating," as in the case of drums or wooden percussion beams.

Figure-ground relationships are the crucial high-level character of division of ensembles (see fig. 15.2).[4] Each of the three types of ensembles have a different kind of figure-ground relationship. Thus, in ensembles called *setang*, one performer plays both *utom* and *tang*. Ensembles called *sebelang* are actually two ensembles performing different pieces simultaneously, where each ensemble plays both *utom* and *tang*. The *setang* ensemble may be subdivided according to musical style into the "gentle" and "strong" types, but the two kinds of *seguyun* ensemble are both gentle, and the two kinds of *sebelang* ensemble are both strong. The most diverse of the subcategories is the *setang* ensemble playing in *megel* style, which subdivides at the third level into seven or eight types of ensembles, each with its own name. That is, most ensembles are of the strong music producing variety, with one player performing the figure and another the ground, and a third performer (if present) having the option of one or the other. Only one ensemble (a two-player, gong-chime ensemble) is subdivided at the third level, and this is done according to the order of tonal placement of its gong-chime components.

Mora has isolated a number of religious associations of instruments. Knowledge about instruments, like knowledge about weaving designs, the cure of the sick, the musical composition, is believed to come directly from personal spirit guides in dreams. An instrument may be associated with a particular spiritual being; for example, the wooden percussion beam *(klutang)* is believed to belong to the ancestress Boi Henwu (and is, therefore, played by women). An instrument may also, however, have a specific ritual meaning; thus the percussion beam marks the entry of a soul into the house of *kayung* (heaven), where it may find a mate and come finally to rest. In another case, the *seguyun* ensemble, which consists of the two-stringed lute *(hegelung)* and the polychordal zither *(s'ludoy)*, symbolizes the complementarity of male and female respectively. A classification of instruments and ensembles by religious associations may be pieced together if and when enough data are compiled.

CONCLUSION

A basic musical division is made in T'boli culture between solo instruments and ensembles. Other characters of division are based on two tenets of the T'boli world view: the complementary opposites of gentle versus strong and figure versus ground. The former concept also governs the highest level of classification of solo instruments. The gentle-versus-strong dichotomy, with its cosmological implications, applies not only to music and instruments but also to human character, as is also the case in Java and some other Southeast Asian cultures. The figure-versus-ground concept governs the formal structure of music and instrumental performance as well as that of visual arts, in which sense it has resonances in

Java's *gamelan* and *batik* arts. Three taxonomical ideas—the two dichoto-
mies of gentle versus strong and solo versus ensemble as well as the
threefold division made according to mode of sound production—can be
illustrated in paradigmatic form. Lower steps of division of the schemes
are delineated according to mode of sound excitation and morphological
attributes, namely, the number of strings or the arrangement of gong-
chime pitches.

The Personification of Instruments in Some West African Classifications

> "I throw my hands into the beads"
> (instrumental interlude)
> "Its sound has risen
> My *konín* thank you, thank you."
> > A Kpelle song text sung by a player to
> > his instrument[1]

Unlike the Hellenic and Hellenistic views that musical instruments are inanimate objects, West African peoples such as the Dan in the Ivory Coast and neighboring Liberia (where they are known as the Gio) and the Kpelle of Liberia adhere to a human-centered concept of instruments, which governs the way they group these objects into taxonomical or paradigmatic classifications. It is the action of the player on the instrument, the myth of an instrument's creation or invention, or an element of social organization that is used as the basis of groupings. Personifications even govern the groupings of tunings of strings or parts of instruments.

Schemes based on nonhuman attributes such as the materials of which instruments are made exist, but their importance in the culture has not yet been fully researched. Schemes using the material of which an instrument is made are also found in China, Java, Byzantium, and some other cultures. The Dan also divide instruments into those playing a solo as opposed to an accompanying role; such schemes are also found in India, for example.

The typically West African way of classifying instruments, however, rests on the West African inclination to personify instruments. Not only the Dan or Gio but also some other West African peoples such as the Kpelle, Hausa, Akan, and Dogon conceive of instruments essentially as extensions of the human beings who play them. Their human-centered concept of instruments links them inextricably to their players or owners. It may safely be said that human-centered schemes uniquely identify West African cultures.

The Dan's concept of the unity of instruments and their owners, inventors, and makers, whether human or nonhuman, is intricately expressed in a series of myths about the origin of instruments (see Zemp 1971, 142–45). To the Dan or Gio, human beings are not the exclusive owners of the instruments that they play, nor consequently of music itself. On the contrary, most instruments are believed to have originally been owned by nonhuman beings such as spirits, masks, sorcerers, or animals, and can be specifically classified as such. Myth tells us how a hunter constructed the first specimen known to humans of a certain rattle–cattle bell according to instructions given in a dream by its first nonhuman owner, a pig. By means of a ruse, a villager removed a certain type of wooden drum from a woman's mask, which was its original owner. A spider gave the guardian of a sacred house the first specimen known to humans of a wooden drum, after acquiring it from its original owner, a cockroach; and on making a copy of it the guardian became its first human owner. Other instruments were first acquired by a farmer, a warrior, twins, a blacksmith, and a woman with a small girl (fig. 16.1).

The way in which an instrument was initially transmitted to the domain of human beings is also classifiable according to whether it arrived as a gift, by exchange, by contract, or by removal (see fig. 16.2). For example, legend has it that a type of drum from an orchestra consisting mainly of horns was acquired by its original human owner—a hunter—in exchange for some meat, and that a harp-lute was obtained by a hunter from a spirit on contract of life or death. The removal of an instrument to the domain of human beings can also occur by means of a ruse, by force, or by invitation of the original owner. For example, a hunter is said to have once borrowed a musical bow from a dwarf spirit and then to have made a copy of it.

These myths serve as the basis of a remarkable paradigmatic classification of instruments by four intersecting parameters (see fig. 16.3).[2] These are (1) an instrument's first nonhuman owner, (2) mode of transmission to a human owner, (3) the making of the instrument by man, and (4) its first human owner. Relationships between the four columns in figure 16.1 are shown in the trapezoidal shapes drawn in figure 16.3. The purpose here is not to present a complete classification; only two of the large number of instruments and their associated myths are shown by the drawing of the trapezia. For example, in the case of the sanza (myth 18), the linked boxes show us that this instrument's first human owner was the hunter of a sorcerer, who obtained it from its first nonhuman owner (a sorcerer) by exchange and made its first human-made sample by copying it.

Mythes	Premier propriétaire non humain	Transmission	Fabrication par l'homme	Premier propriétaire humain
	1	2	3	4
M₁. Tambour-de-bois	génie	don	—	(premier ?) cultivateur
M₂. Tambour-de-bois	pyã̀a³dὲa (génie)	contrat (vie/mort)	—	orphelin
M₃. Tambour-de-bois	masques (puis femmes)	enlèvement (par ruse)	—	villageois (hommes)
M₄. Tambour-de-bois	cafard	don (de l'araignée)	copie	gardien de la «maison sacrée»
M₅. Xylophone	—	—	invention (d'après le tambour-de-bois)	petit garçon
M₆. Hochet-sonnaille	génie	échange (non respecté)	copie	femme avec fillette
M₇. Hochet-sonnaille	porc-épic	enlèvement (par force)	selon instructions données en reve par le 1ᵉʳ propriétaire	chasseur
M₈. Hochet-sonnaille	porc-épic	enlèvement (par force)	invention	villageois
M₉. Hochet-sonnaille	—	—	selon instructions du 1ᵉʳ propriétaire	petit garçon, père
M₁₀. Hochet-sonnaille	génie	—	selon instructions du 1ᵉʳ propriétaire	villageois
M₁₁. Grelots	génie nain	enlèvement	selon instructions données en rêve par le 1ᵉʳ propriétaire	chasseur
M₁₂. Grelots	génie	—	selon instructions du 1ᵉʳ propriétaire	forgeron

FIGURE 16.1 Myths of origin of Dan musical instruments reproduced from Hugo Zemp (1971)

M₁₃. Cloche	Dieu	don	invention	jumeaux primordiaux
M₁₄. Cloche	—	—	copie	guerrier, forgeron
M₁₅. Cloche	masque malinké	invitation du propriétaire avec son instrument		hommes malinké
M₁₆. Sanza *kpɛ³la⁵*	—	—	invention	homme malheureux
M₁₇. Sanza *kpɛ³la⁵*	—	—	selon instructions de Dieu	homme malheureux
M₁₈. Sanza *kɔɔ̃la⁵*	sorcière	échange (contre vie sauve)	copie	chasseur-de-sorciers
M₁₉. Tambour (*baa⁴*)	chimpanzé	enlèvement (par force)	—	chasseur
M₂₀. Tambour (*baa⁴*)	chimpanzé	enlèvement (par force)	copie	chasseur
M₂₁. Tambour (*baa⁴*)	chimpanzé	—	copie (de mémoire)	chasseur
M₂₂. Tambour (*baa⁴*)	—	—	invention	vieux
M₂₃. Tambour (*baa⁴*)	génie	enlèvement (par ruse)	—	vieux avec plaie
M₂₄. Tambour (*baa⁴*)	génie	enlèvement (par force)	copie	chasseur
M₃₂. Tambour (*baa⁴*) de l'orchestre de trompes	Dieu	don	—	chef
M₃₃. Tambour (*baa⁴*) de l'orchestre de trompes	génie	don	copie	chef
M₃₄. Tambour (*baa⁴*) de l'orchestre de trompes	génie	échange (contre viande)	—	chasseur

Mythes	Premier propriétaire non humain	Transmission	Fabrication par l'homme	Premier propriétaire humain
M_{25}. Tambour (*lɨkpá*)	oiseau *gbōī*	—	invention (d'après comportement de *gbōī*)	guerriers
M_{26}. Arc-en-terre	—	—	invention	homme malheureux
M_{27}. Arc-en-terre	—	—	invention	chasseur
M_{28}. Arc musical	génie nain	enlèvement	copie	chasseur
M_{29}. Harpe-luth	*pɲā̃³¹dɛ³* (génie)	enlèvement (par force)	copie	chasseur
M_{30}. Harpe-luth	*pɲā̃³¹dɛ³* (génie)	contrat (vie/mort)	—	chasseur
M_{31}. Harpe-luth	*pɲā̃³¹dɛ³* (génie)	enlèvement (par ruse)	génie nain enseigne en rêve	chasseur
M_{32}. Trompe	Dieu	don	—	chef
M_{33}. Trompe	génie	don	copie	chef
M_{34}. Trompe	Dieu	don	—	guerrier

1. Instruments ayant appartenu à un être non humain et arrivés dans les mains des hommes par:

a) *Don*	de Dieu	M_{13}, M_{32}, M_{34} (trompe)
	du génie	M_1, M_{33}
	de l'araignée	M_4
b) *Échange*	avec un génie	M_6, M_{32}, M_{34} (tambour)
	avec une sorcière	M_{18}
c) *Contrat*	avec un génie	M_2, M_{30}
d) *Enlèvement*	aux animaux	M_7, M_8, M_{19}, M_{20}
	aux génies	M_{11}, M_{23}, M_{24}, M_{28}, M_{29}, M_{31}
	aux masques	M_{15}
	(puis aux femmes)	M_3

2. Instruments ayant été fabriqués directement par l'homme à la suite de:

a) *Enseignement*	de Dieu	M_{17}
	du génie	M_{10}, M_{12}
	(indirect)	
	d'un animal	M_{21}
b) *Invention*	d'un enfant	M_5, M_9
	d'un malheureux	M_{16}, M_{26}
	d'un guerrier	M_{14}, M_{25}
	d'un chasseur	M_{27}
	d'un vieux	M_{22}

FIGURE 16.2 Myths of origin of Dan musical instruments reproduced from Hugo Zemp (1971)

Some instruments, however, are believed to have been invented by human beings. For example, the xylophone was invented according to one legend by a small boy, a rattle–cattle bell was invented according to another legend by a small boy and his father, and a type of plucked idiophone—a lamellaphone with thin vibrating tongues—was invented, it is said, by a villain. All instruments, whether invented by human beings or not, are of course continually being made by humans. In some cases knowledge about how to make instruments was originally given to man by their first nonhuman owners. In other cases people learned how to make them on instructions from God or made copies from memory.

Myths attributing the origin of instruments to human contact with animals are also found among the Kpelle (Stone 1982, 95–96). For example, the goblet drum *fêli* (fig. 16.4) was first made after a hunter in the forest saw some chimpanzees beating their breasts, thus giving him the

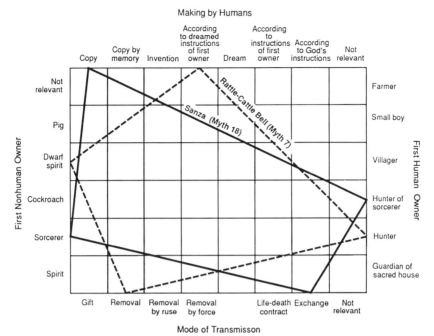

FIGURE 16.3 Four-parameter paradigmatic classifications by origin myth of the *Sanza* and the rattle-cattle bell. The four parameters of the paradigm are: (1) the first nonhuman owner of the instrument, (2) the mode of transmission, (3) the making by humans, and (4) the first human owner (based on Zemp 1971, 142–43)

idea of a drum. The chimpanzees showed him how to make a drum from a hollow log, and he brought this knowledge back with him to the town community. The idea of the horn called *túru*, on the other hand, originally came from the sounds of the *túu-túu* birds. Long ago a group of women fishing in the creek heard the voices of the birds and brought the chief to listen to them and to ponder how they could preserve their sounds. They decided to imitate their voices by means of a horn. The origins of these instruments were derived from *meni-polo* ("old matters"), which can be called origin myths (Stone, personal communication).[3]

The Dan, like their neighbors the Kpelle, have a concept that instruments are not simply material objects or acoustic phenomena but are actually extensions of the persons performing on them (Zemp 1971, 81; Stone 1982, 87). The idea that an instrument viewed as important in the culture is in fact a surrogate participant in musical events is expressed in the naming of its parts; the bestowing on it of a personal name; the

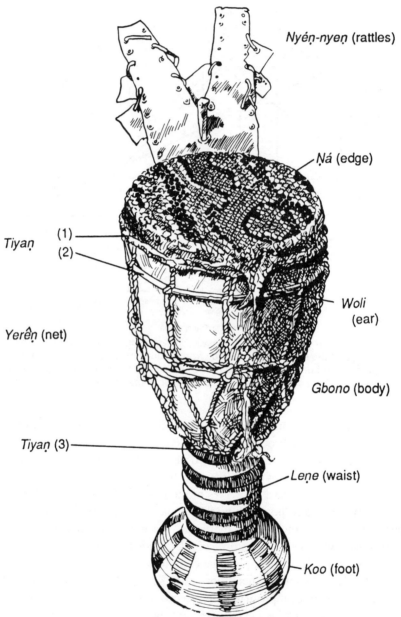

Nyéṇ-nyeṇ (rattles)

Ṇá (edge)

Tiyaṇ (1)
(2)

Woli
(ear)

Yerêṇ (net)

Gbono (body)

Tiyaṇ (3)

Leṇe (waist)

Koo (foot)

FIGURE 16.4 Names of parts of the fĕli—A Kpelle goblet drum (reproduced from Stone 1982, 95)

practice of addressing and listening to it in musical performance; and the assignation of the generations (i.e., mother, child, grandchild, etc.) or sexes to the tuning of strings on an instrument such as a *gbegbetêle* or multiple bow-lute (Stone 1982, 91–94).

The first case may be exemplified by the names assigned to the parts of a goblet drum called *fêli* (see fig. 16.4), which include "ear," "body," "waist," and "foot."[4] (Culturally unimportant instruments, however, do not have these personifying designations.) Instances of personification in Kpelle society cited by Stone include (1) the assignation of the personal name Nàa-kàa-nûu (meaning "person who looks on") to the goblet drum and the woman's name Goma to the triangular frame zither (*konîn*); (2) the quotation at the head of this chapter of a communication sung by a multiple bow-lute player to his instrument, his listening to the instrument's solo response, and finally his sung expression of thanks; and (3) the designation by two sanza (*gbèlee*) players of the tongues of their instruments by names such as "mother," "child," and "agreeing person." The pervasive personification of instruments in Kpelle society is further exemplified by the fact that the tuning of instruments designates a succession of generations. Thus the tuned strings of the multiple bow-lute are designated "mother's child," "grandchild," "sibling" (in the case of string three), "child" (string four), "child" (string five), and "end" string. Some instruments, such as aerophones, may also be associated with the voice of a certain spirit, as a result of which the playing of, say, the transverse horn (*túru*) is "forbidden in a town during the time the secret society is in session. Futhermore, players who have tutelaries believe that the tutelary's power resides in the instrument and flows to them as they play. Such a player is the only one allowed to touch a particular instrument" (Stone 1982, 95).

Both the Dan and the Kpelle use generations of performers to designate the tunings of strings, while other West African groups such as the Akan of Ghana and the Dogon of Mali attribute the tunings to the two sexes (Zemp 1971, 84). The application of personal names to instruments and the attribution of sexes and generations of parts of some instruments create low-level divisions in the classification of only a few instruments in a scheme, as only important instruments are given such names.

Stone shows that, in the case of the Kpelle, instruments are divided into two groups—the struck (*yále*) (including both beaten and plucked) and the blown (*fěe*)—that is, the character of division is the action of the performer in sounding the instrument (fig. 16.5).[5] As Stone points out,

FÊE--Blown	*YÁLE*--Struck
Boo--flute (rare)	A. *Gbèlee*--sanza
	Kóʋkoma--two- or three-
Túru--transverse horn	pronged sanza, box
	resonator
Kô-turu--war horn	
	B. *Konîʋ*--triangular frame-
Kwíi-turu--Western horn	zither
(trumpet)	*Gbegbetêle*--multiple bow-
	lute
	Gbẽe-kẽe--single string
	bow-lute
	Kɔ̀ʋ-kpàla--musical bow
	Kerâʋ-noʋ-koniʋ--harp-lute
	C. *Fêli*--goblet drum
	Bala--three *fêli* tied to-
	gether
	Gbʋ̂ʋ-gbʋ̀ʋ--two-headed drum
	Danîʋ--hourglass drum
	Gbólo--paired, footed drums
	D. *Kóno*--slit wooden or bamboo
	idiophone
	Kéleʋ--large slit idiophone
	Kpene-kee--double-slit idi-
	ophone
	Kone--iron idiophone
	E. *Kêe*--gourd rattle
	Kpe-kêe--container rattle
	Wéleʋ--leg bells
	Nyéʋ-nyéʋ--metal rattles
	Zóʋ-so--leg rattles
	Táníʋ--single bell
	Zoso-kee--basket rattle

FIGURE 16.5 Kpelle classification of instruments reproduced from Ruth Stone (1982)

however, this twofold taxonomy does not mean that the Kpelle "cannot distinguish between the striking action used to play a drum and the plucking action used to play a chordophone" (1982, 87). As in antique European classifications given by such writers as Pollux and Isidore of Seville, the stringed instruments are included in the percussion category. The word *yále*, which literally means "bend" or "break," denotes "the bending of the string or skin by the performer" (Stone 1982, 87). That is, the Kpelle "focus on the way the human produces the sound rather than on physical materials or the way sound vibrations are initiated in them" (Stone 1982, 87–88). The characters of subdivision in Stone's scheme (fig. 16.5) are (1) the possession of lamellae in category A, (2) the possession of single or multiple strings in category B, (3) the possession of membranes in category C, (4) whether an instrument is a hollow wooden, iron, or bottle container in category D, and (4) whether it has rattles with seeds inside or has beads inside or outside in category E. The five characters are all based on morphological qualities of instruments that govern their sound production.[6]

Because the Kpelle consider the sound of an instrument to be its most important characteristic, Kpelle instruments producing a similar timbre but belonging to quite different categories may assume the same name, a practice that affects the lower levels of division. Thus both a slit-log idiophone and a footed membranophone are named *kélen*. As an expression of the same attitude, the Kpelle often substitute a utensil in everyday use for a percussion instrument, such as when they strike an empty beer bottle with the blunt edge of a penknife instead of beating a regular struck idiophone called *kone* (Stone 1982, 88).[7]

Like most other cultures, the Kpelle have more than one way of viewing and classifying instruments. In subdividing the *yále* category, the Kpelle may also group their instruments according to the material of their construction. As the stringed instruments are all basically made of the same material, they form one category. Likewise, drums are grouped together, rattles form another category, and wooden struck idiophones yet another. A third practice, as Stone notes (1982, 88), is the selection of the musical function of instruments in ensemble performance as the character of division. Thus, instruments that play solo parts may be grouped together, including the sanza (*gbèlee*), triangular frame zither (*konîn*), goblet drum (*fĕli*), and horn (*túru*). Instruments that play accompanying parts are similarly grouped together.

Some instruments are grouped and named after an analogy between mother and child, where "mother" denotes instruments with "a large voice" and "child" denotes instruments with "a small voice." Another category consists of instruments of middle size or pitch. For example, a group of three hand-held slit drums (*kóno-na*) are subclassified into the "mother" *kóno* (called *kóno-lee*), the "middle-sized" *kóno* (named *kóno-sáma*), and the "child" *kóno* (called *kóno-lon*). In Stone's view, this organization of instruments in an ensemble embodies the basic Kpelle social grouping, which consists of mothers, people of middling size, and children.

Another expression of a human-centered conception of instruments is the practice found among the Hausa people of classifying players of instruments. Thus, the Hausa divide players into five categories: "drummers," "blowers," "singers," "acclaimers," and "talkers" (Ames and King 1971, 61). The last three categories comprise humans playing the "human instruments" (i.e., the human body). Only the first two are human beings playing on external instrumental objects.

Like the Kpelle and some early European writers, the Hausa and other West African peoples are content with one large category—beating—to comprise both the beating and the plucking kinds of sound activation. Thus the Hausa subdivide their "drummer" category into drummers who beat drums and drummers who "beat" (pluck) chordophones (Ames and King 1971, 61). It is the action of the player upon the instrument that is important in this culture, not the acoustics of sound production. And as plucking chordophones and beating drums are seen as constituting essentially the same kind of activity on the part of the player, resulting in the depression of a string in the first case and of a membrane in the second, it is sufficient to use the one verb to denote both, despite the obvious difference in timbres produced. Blowing an instrument, on the other hand, is seen as an essentially different kind of activity from beating, and therefore deserves its own high-level category.

Conclusion

The Dan classifications by origin myth are paradigmatic in form, based on links between the main parts of those myths. The Kpelle and Hausa classifications, on the other hand, are broad taxonomies governed by such parameters as the action of the player in sounding an instrument, the similarity of timbre of instruments, the material of which an instrument is made, whether an instrument assumes a solo or an accompanying role, and the relative size or pitch of an instrument. Not only individual instruments but also ensembles and performances are classified. The Kpelle classification of ensembles has two categories governed by the musical function of instruments in ensemble. The Hausa taxonomy of musical performers has five categories distinguished by the performers' physical actions when making sounds, with some categories distinguished by single-character division at the second level into two or three classes.

A number of West African societies adhere to a concept of instruments that includes their relationship to their players. This view is quite opposed to the tendency encountered throughout Western history to classify instruments according to a primarily acoustic and morphological concept of instrument. The propensity to personify instruments explains why several West African cultures think of stringed and percussion instruments as belonging to the one "beaten" category.

Whether the combination of the concept of the unity of instrument and performer, the classification by origin myths, and the personification of instruments and their parts is unique in the world's cultures is a matter awaiting the collection of cross-cultural data. We know, for example, that the assigning of sex, generations, and other human qualities to certain instruments and their parts is also found among a number of cultures in India and Southeast Asia (including the Malay, Batak, Sundanese, Javanese, T'boli, and various other Philippine and Indonesian as well as Thai cultures). The idea of instruments being invented, owned, or played by divine spirits, animals, and shamans as well as by human beings, who may acquire them from these sources is, however, exclusively West African.

Cognitive Categories, Paradigms, and Taxonomies among the 'Are'are

> Sacred instruments exist in all of the four types of panpipe ensembles. These are ancient instruments for which a special magical ritual was performed by the instrument maker, giving them permanent power. They are subject to certain taboos. . . . The magic makes the sound of the panpipe ensemble attract many people, causes the musicians to be appreciated . . . , ensures that they will obtain shell money for their performance (shell money has sacred character), and prevents sickness or death from striking them . . . the musicians may be possessed by ancestor spirits.
>
> Hugo Zemp, *Ethnomusicology 22*

To the ten thousand or so 'Are'are people of Malaita in the Solomon Islands, bamboo panpipes played in ensembles are the supreme musical instrument. They occur in a greater diversity of forms and ensemble combinations than other instruments and are attributed with having a greater measure of magic power. Panpipes are to the 'Are'are what gongs are to the Javanese, drums to the Thai, flutes to the Finns, and stringed instruments to the Arabs. 'Are'are instruments made of bamboo also include transverse flutes, the mouth zither, and tubes stamped on the ground. The main classifications of instruments inherent in the culture are reserved for the bamboo instruments, which are the most important and varied category. They are classified in four ways.

One way is according to the mode of exciting sound, that is, whether the instruments are blown or beaten. Eight kinds of bamboo instruments are blown and two are beaten.

Another classification is made according to whether instruments are played solo or in ensemble. Bamboo instruments played solo are referred to as "one-man bamboo." There are four such categories of solo instruments. However, one instrument—the stamping tubes—may be played either by a single performer producing three polyphonic parts or by a group of three performers playing each part separately. Solo panpipes and other one-man instruments are considered to be less efficacious than the various types of bamboo instruments played in ensembles. Similarly, the slit drum ensemble is much more highly valued than a single slit drum.[1] The panpipe ensemble called *'au tahana* possesses the highest prestige of all ensembles. According to legend this ensemble has the greatest age and the largest repertoire. It is also the most difficult to play and is capable of producing a complete equiheptaphonic scale, which is an important scale in 'Are'are musical thought.[2] As mentioned in the quotation at the head of this chapter, it is believed that the magic of panpipe ensembles attracts people and that the instruments are capable of bestowing many beneficial effects.

A third way of classifying bamboo instruments is according to whether they possess "big magic" or "small magic." The most magically potent of solo instruments—the obliquely held bundle panpipe (*'au ware*)—is made and preserved only by men in their "sacred house" (though young women also play them for love magic in the communal houses); when played in ensemble they are considered to possess big magic. On the other hand, the mouth zither (*'au pasiawa*) and the single bundle panpipe are considered to possess small magic and are played by women in their so-called menstruation house, especially on occasions of love magic ceremonies (Zemp 1978, 49). Some instruments possess minimal sacred significance, however. At the bottom of the magic hierarchy are the stamping tubes (*kiro*), transverse flutes (*'au porare*), and vertical bundle panpipes (*'au waa*), which are played by both men and women mainly for entertainment or for signaling and calling.

The capability of an instrument to produce a melody is the fourth character of division of both blown and beaten instruments. Instruments capable of producing melodies are more highly regarded than rhythmic percussion instruments, though both panpipe and slit drum ensembles are most highly valued. This preference is contained in the modern meaning of the lexeme *'au,* which "designates all music with melodic elements" (Zemp 1978, 62).

Some of these characters of division may in fact be combined into a single scheme by logical division, as Zemp has shown (fig. 17.1). Here the bamboo instruments are grouped by logical division in a tree diagram according to the mode of sound production: whether they are beaten or blown on the one hand and whether they are played solo or in group performance on the other. As Zemp notes, tree diagrams are not foreign to 'Are'are thinking since they traditionally draw genealogical trees in the sand (1978, 46). However, Zemp eventually saw that it was necessary to

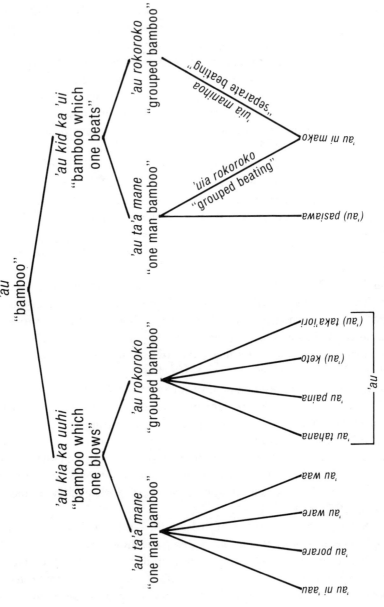

FIGURE 17.1 Classification of bamboo instruments (based on Zemp 1978, 42)

revise his opinion that tree diagrams were the best form in which to express 'Are'are relationships between instruments, for he came to realize that a third character of division needed to be taken into account, namely, whether an instrument used equiheptaphonic seconds in its melodic expression or not. He recognized that their classificatory thinking in this case was not really based on the method of logical division but was a matter of "what American cognitive anthropologists call a paradigm, characterized by multiple features of intersection" (cf. Tyler 1969, 10). Figure 17.2 shows the three features intersecting in nonhierarchical fashion.

Like the T'boli paradigm (fig. 2.4) and the Dan paradigm (fig. 16.3), the 'Are'are paradigm is technically "imperfect"; it does not have a category of ensembles comprising beaten bamboo instruments that can produce equiheptaphonic seconds. That is, the ethnographic practice does not include all the logical possibilities of the model. This is a normal finding about paradigms in any culture (Kay 1966, 21).

In addition to this paradigm, a detailed classification of blown bamboo instruments by logical division is observable in the culture (see fig. 17.3). Its principle of division at the first step is whether an instrument has one or several tubes of bamboo. At the second step the instruments with several tubes are subdivided according to whether the tubes are arranged in bundles or in "wing" (raft) form. At the third step the bundled bamboo instruments with "tiny mouthpieces" are distinguished from

	'au ta'a mane "one-man bamboo"	*'au rokoroko* "grouped bamboo"		
rapi 'au "equiheptaphonic seconds"	*'au ni aau* (panpipes with irregular order of lengths) *'au waa* (vertically held bundle panpipes)	*'au tahana* *'au paina*	panpipes with irregular order of lengths	*uuhi* "blown"
rapi 'au mao "no equiheptaphonic seconds"	*'au ware* (obliquely held bundle panpipes *'au porare* (transverse flute)	*('au) keto* *('au) taka'iori*		
rapi 'au "equiheptaphonic seconds"	*'au ni mako* (stamping tubes on ground)			*'ui* "beaten"
rapi 'au mao "no equiheptaphonic seconds"	*('au) pasiawa* (musical bow)			

FIGURE 17.2 Paradigm of features of *'au* types (based on Zemp 1978, 43)

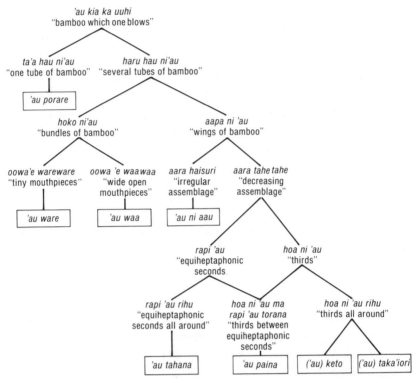

Figure 17.3 Classification of blown bamboo instruments (based on Zemp 1978, 46)

those with "wide open mouthpieces." Moreover the winged bamboo instruments having "irregular assemblage" of tubes are differentiated from those that have tubes arranged in decreasing heights. Instruments with "decreasing assemblage" that play equiheptaphonic seconds are distinguished from those that play thirds. The former divide into those that play "equiheptaphonic seconds all round" and those that play "thirds between the equiheptaphonic seconds." The latter divide into those that play "thirds between equiheptaphonic seconds" and those that play "thirds all round." Most of the characters in this scheme are morphological. The last two are musical-cum-morphological; that is, they are determined by the melodic intervals an instrument produces, and these are recognizable morphologically by the difference in length of two neighboring tubes (Zemp 1978, 44).

Besides thinking about instruments in the form of tree diagrams and paradigms, the 'Are'are have a remarkably complex way of thinking about

about two other cognitive categories: instrumental ensembles and musical forms. The three categories instruments, ensembles, and musical forms are linked by three lexemes, each of which includes *kiro,* a term which itself has five different meanings (see fig. 17.4). One of the three lexemes, *'au,* signifies "bamboo," and the *kiro,* which is subsumed under it has two meanings: an ensemble with large instruments or a number of small stamping tubes. The musical category *'oo,* on the other hand, designates a single nonbamboo instrument, the slit drum (the material of which is not specified), but it also can mean the sound made by the slit drum, and the term *kiro* which it incorporates means the beating of a slit drum ensemble (without shouting, as sometimes happens). The musical category *nuuha,* "song," groups all types of accompanied and unaccompanied song, and the category called *kiro,* which is included in the *nuuha* category, designates the large stamping tubes that accompany singing. But the primary designation of the lexeme *kiro* is the sound game played in the river, that is, the rhythms of water-play when children or adults are bathing in the river. In this popular game, one makes sounds of varying pitch and loudness by forming air pockets in the river water with the palms of the hands, thus causing the air in the hollows to explode and make a sound. Each player produces a variety of rhythms in interlocking fashion, producing what might be called "music" in this way.

Another classification of bamboo instruments observable in the culture is based on the mythical origin of the instruments. The data Zemp was able to collect on this aspect are less complete than the data he

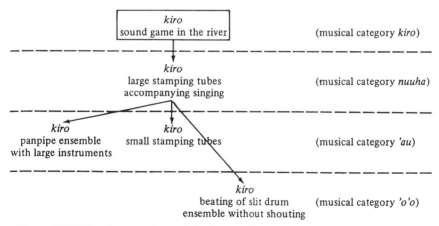

FIGURE 17.4 The five meanings of the lexeme *kiro* (Zemp 1978, 41)

compiled on the origin of the Dan instruments in West Africa, but they are sufficient to suggest the basis of a scheme that may once have been quite extensive. The transverse flute, for example, is said to have been invented by a gardener in order to imitate the cry of birds, which he wished to attract and kill because they were stealing from his garden. The first slit drum was carved after the cultural hero Teakeni taught men how to manufacture stone tools. The first slit drum ensemble was created for a feast in return for the price of a man (Zemp 1978, 54). The obliquely held bundle panpipe *'au ware,* it was claimed, originated from the transverse flute, while instruments of the panpipe ensemble *'au tahana* derived from the solo panpipe *'au ni aau.* The delicate sound of the *'au ware* gave a woman the idea of creating a mouth zither. The stamping tubes called *'au ni mako* are said to have been invented about five or six generations ago by a group of people producing lime from burning seashells and beating empty bamboo containers on stones (Zemp 1978, 51). According to one of Zemp's informants, it was claimed that these events all happened in mythical time thirty-four generations ago.

Together the myths cover all the main types of 'Are'are instruments and ensembles except the vertically held bundle panpipes. These, however, are among the least important of instruments, along with the transverse flute, the slit drum, the solo panpipe *'au ni aau,* and the stamping tubes, while the obliquely held bundle panpipe and the mouth zither are somewhat more highly valued.

CONCLUSION

Classification made according to whether instruments are played solo or in ensemble resembles one of the T'boli classifications discussed earlier. Like other communally oriented cultures in Java, Minangkabau, and Mandailing, the 'Are'are value ensembles more highly than single instruments. The most highly respected ensemble is the oldest, has the largest repertoire, and is the most difficult to play, and it can play melodies with the complete equiheptaphonic scale. Instruments capable of producing melodies are grouped separately from those producing nonmelodic percussive sounds only.

Another character of division of instruments is the mode of performance, whether they are blown or beaten. 'Are'are also value and classify their instruments according to the degree of magic they possess, a factor related to their power to attract listeners, prevent sickness or death from striking, and perform other magic effects.

Zemp's findings indicate that 'Are'are bamboo instruments may be thought about not only in terms of a tree diagram but also in terms of an imperfect paradigm with three intersecting parameters: whether an instrument can produce equiheptaphonic seconds or thirds, whether an instrument is blown or beaten, and whether an instrument is played solo or in ensemble. Blown bamboo instruments are subclassified morphologically according to the way in which their bamboo tubes are arranged and according to the nature of their mouthpieces.

Zemp's ultimate justification for studying folk classifications such as those of the 'Are'are is the insights gained into aspects of musical thinking in a culture, including thought about the concept of music itself (Zemp 1978, 37, 63). One of the stated aims of his study was to delineate the types of instruments, ensembles, and musical forms, but in so doing he found that all three categories intermesh with each other. In attempting to investigate the main 'Are'are concept of instrument and the organizing principles underlying the way they use and think about instruments, Zemp had to select and explain the key lexeme *kiro* and the important nomenclatures and functions of the instruments. Remarkably, as he found, the one label—*kiro*—has the multiple meanings of sound game played in the river, the large stamping tubes accompanying singing, the panpipe ensemble with large instruments, the small stamping tubes, and the beating of the slit drum ensemble without shouting. His taxonomical and etymological investigation served to clarify and explain a complex term.

EIGHTEEN

A Finnish-Karelian Taxonomy as a Historiographical Tool

"Horns are clarinets used by shepherds."

Around the twelfth century the people of western Finland began to employ some new agricultural practices and in so doing adopted musical instruments associated with a farmer's lifestyle. They began to play idioglot clarinets made from straw, rushes, reed and bark. Similarly, long before Christ, the Finns had learnt shepherding and to construct and play musical instruments associated with shepherds, as will be mentioned below.

The generic term for clarinets was *pilli* and the various types were distinguished from each other by name through various prefixes referring to their materials. Thus a clarinet made from straw was called a *soropilli* (see fig. 18.1) or *olkipilli*, while a rush or reed clarinet was called a *putkipilli* (see fig. 18.4).

The lexeme *pilli* is derived from Middle Low German *Spill(e)*, which is the same as Old English *spill*, meaning "a small cylinder upon which yarn is wound; a spool." The Old Finnish form of the word was *spilli*, meaning "spool" or "reed spool," and this term thus adopted the brand new meaning of "idioglot clarinet." Later, the consonant *s* was dropped from the word, for Finnish never has two consonants beginning a word. The term was also known in western Karelia (in eastern Finland) but was known in Karelia proper only in the twentieth century.[1]

Timo Leisiö's organological investigations into the Finnish-Karelian instrumentarium (Leisiö 1977, 1983, 1985b) yielded the information that instruments called *pilli* included not only clarinets but also flutes and free aerophones (see fig. 18.2). He was puzzled when various Finnish musicians told him that the term *pilli* also includes horns called *torvi*, a word

Figure 18.1 A straw clarinet called *soropilli*

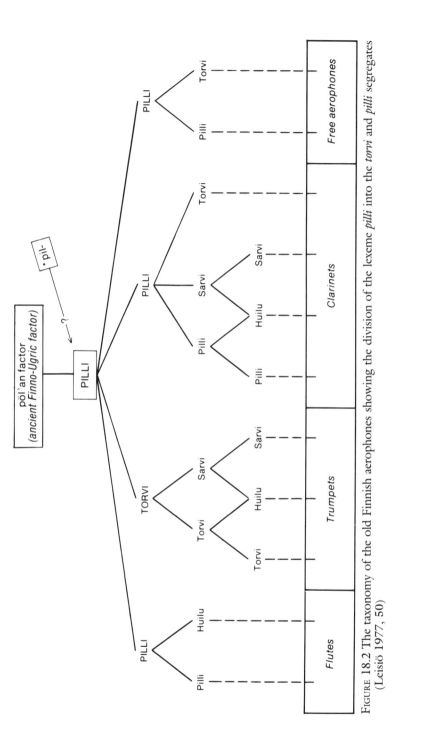

FIGURE 18.2 The taxonomy of the old Finnish aerophones showing the division of the lexeme *pilli* into the *torvi* and *pilli* segregates (Leisiö 1977, 50)

which is of proto-Baltic origin and means "a tube, horn, trumpet."[2] The lexeme *pilli* had expanded its meaning over the past eight hundred years to mean "all blown instruments."[3] The statement made at the head of this chapter that "horns (*torvi*) are clarinets (*pilli*) used by shepherds" is the basis of the hypothesis that the western Finnish idioglot clarinet is of German origin and was adopted by farmers in Finland due to extensive contact between Finns and Germans. As this example shows, research into taxonomical categories and instruments can inform etymological research and provide clues in the reconstruction of the history of instruments and culture contact.

The culture-emerging or "folk" instrument classification pieced together by Timo Leisiö in Finland-Karelia serves as an excellent example of the phenomenon noted in chapter 3 in which two determining factors—the synchronic and the diachronic—operate independently of each other in a classification. Contradictions between the synchronic and diachronic produce overlapping taxonomic categories and apparently self-contradictory labels or terms. Leisiö's method (1977) of isolating important musical concepts, cognitive procedures, and terminologies concerning instruments in order to construct instrument classification charts had the additional useful consequence in his case of suggesting a theory of the historical development of Finnish-Karelian musical culture over the past five millennia or so. It also proved to be the only way of making interpretative sense of the classification he had elicited.

As figure 18.3 shows, Finnish-Karelian culture now divides its instrumental resources into four categories at the first step: *kello* (comprising idiophones only), *kantele* (chordophones), *pilli* (aerophones), and *torvi* (aerophones).[4] The fact that there are two aerophone classes draws attention to the diversity and importance of aerophones in the culture, but it also presents an obvious problem in that there are two categories having the same character of division that are not mutually exclusive. For while the *pilli* taxon includes flutes and the *torvi* taxon includes trumpets, both also include clarinets and free aerophones. The scheme does not rest on straightforward logical division because the character of division—the mode of sound excitation—is not applied across the board. At the second step, *pilli* divides into *pilli* meaning "flute," "clarinet," or "free aerophone," and *huilu* meaning "flute" or "clarinet," while *torvi* divides into *torvi*, meaning "trumpet," "clarinet," or "free aerophone" and *sarvi* meaning "trumpet" or "clarinet."[5] The overlapping categories—flutes and clarinets in the case of *pilli* and *huilu* and trumpets and clarinets in the case of *torvi*

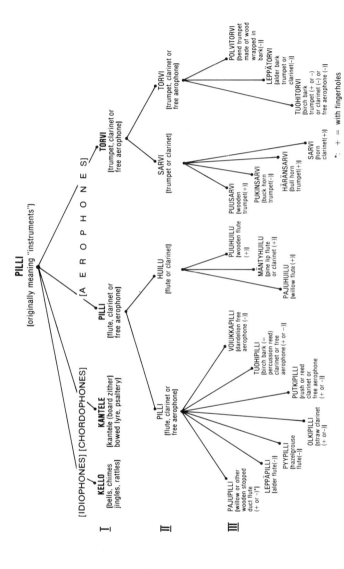

FIGURE 18.3 A reconstructed Finnish-Karelian instrument classification based on indigenous terms. Some instruments named by Leisiö, but for which insufficient information is available for the above classification, are omitted in this scheme. (Based on data from Leisiö 1977, 45–50)

and *sarvi*—are distinguishable in some cases by differences in instrument materials and construction. At the third step, each of the four categories in step two are divided on the basis of the materials of which the instruments are made. Thus, *pilli* meaning "flute," "clarinet," or "free aerophone" divides into segregates such as *pyypilli*, meaning "bark flutes," *olkipilli*, or *soropilli* meaning "straw clarinets," and *putkipilli* meaning "rush or reed clarinets" or "free aerophones." Characters of division at the first two steps are not clearly defined.

One of Leisiö's first approaches was to see whether sense could be made of the classification by inquiring into the presence or absence of finger holes in the case of the wind instruments. As figure 18.4 shows, instruments called *huilu* (i.e., flutes and clarinets) normally have finger-holes, whereas instruments called *pilli* (whether they be flutes, clarinets, or free aerophones) may have finger holes or they may not. Thus, Leisiö was forced to conclude that at this level "the organographical character" of the instruments is apparently "a matter of complete indifference" in the culture as far as classification is concerned (1977, 45).

The lexeme *torvi* resembles *pilli* in its multitude of meanings. At the highest level of division, *torvi* means any aerophone made of animal horn or bark, while at the next level it means certain kinds of trumpets, clarinets, or free aerophones. At the lowest level it forms part of the segregate name *tuohitorvi*, where *tuohi* means "(made of) birch bark."

As has been intimated, the four classificatory tables included in Leisiö's article (1977) are based on information gathered in the field as well as on a degree of historical hypothesizing on his part. His main initial aim was to determine the essential difference between the lexemes *pilli* and *torvi*. He found that not only the presence or absence of finger holes but also the shape of the instruments and the richness of the harmonics of the sounds produced were irrelevant to the question posed, for both the *pilli* and the *torvi* subcategories contain instruments with conical and nonconical shapes and instruments producing sounds with few or many harmonics.

The only way to solve the problem, Leisiö concluded, was to regard the inconsistencies in the scheme as elements of historical change. He gathered together all the historical and taxonomical information at his disposal and used it as a tool for historical and prehistorical reconstruction. Leisiö published his first hypothetical account of the history of Finnish-Karelian instruments over the past five thousand years in 1977. His theory included the proposal referred to above that at some time in the later centuries BCE the Baltic Finns learnt shepherding from the Balts and in so

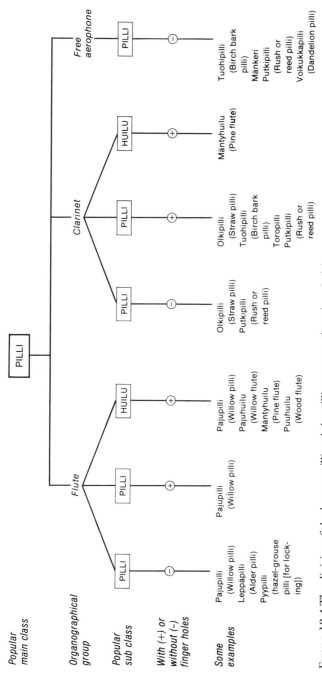

FIGURE 18.4 The division of the lexeme *pilli* and the *pilli* segregate (based on Leisiö 1977, 47)

doing adopted instruments associated with a shepherd's life-style. These instruments included chordophones called *kantele,* which included zithers, harps, and psalteries (fig. 18.5), and, more importantly, trumpets called *torvi.*

One of the results of the contact between the Finns and the Balts, as shown in figure 18.3, was the addition of the loud, large *torvi* instruments into the broad category of *pilli* meaning "instruments"; thus *torvi* were subsumed under *pilli.* The main meaning of *pilli* gradually narrowed, then, to include flutes, clarinets, and free aerophones. But when the Bible was translated into Finnish in about 1600, the German word *Pfeife* (pipe) was not translated by the word *pilli* but by the more modern and semantically precise word *huilu.* At the highest classificatory level, he concluded, *pilli* at that time meant soft, small, light aerophones while at the second level it shared its meaning of soft, small, and light with the flute or clarinet in the *huilu* category. At the third level, its types were differentiated according to the material of which they were made: wood, bark, rush, reed, or dandelion.

On obtaining much more data (especially about Karelian instruments), however, Leisiö revised his 1977 view in favor of his second hypothesis, which was as follows (Leisiö: personal communication, 1987). About five thousand years ago, the so-called Volga-Finnic people who lived between the River Volga and Finland, gained their livelihood as extractors of natural products. After about 2500 BCE they learned the principle of constructing trumpets (*torvi*) and fixed-plug flutes (fig. 18.6) from some Indo-Europeans who had invaded their land. The name they gave to the flutes is not known, but one of them may have been a word meaning "whistle." About 1000 BCE the Finns learned the principle of loose-plug flutes from the early Proto-Germans, and these flutes became known as *huilu* in Finnish (figs. 18.7 and 18.8). Possibly the Finnish term *sarvi* meant an animal horn and became part of the *torvi* segregate, which also included birch-bark horns. On learning the principle of the construction of the clarinet around the twelfth century they adopted a new term for it—*pilli,*—which in Finnish eventually came to mean any kind of blown

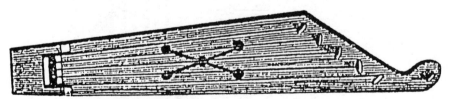

FIGURE 18.5 A Finnish-Karelian *kantele*

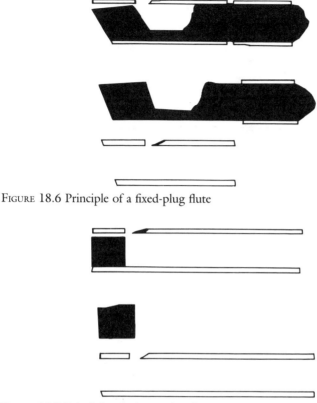

FIGURE 18.6 Principle of a fixed-plug flute

FIGURE 18.7 Principle of a loose-plug flute

instrument. A clarinet with a birch-bark horn used as a loudspeaker was naturally called *torvi,* but the very same instrument without a birch-bark cone was called *pilli.*

In the process of arriving at his second hypothesis, Leisiö made use of new evidence, including the fact that the Finnish word *pilli* could only be about eight hundred years old. He also found that the taxonomies of instruments that he had pieced together and published in 1977 were applicable to the instrumentaria of Finland and western Karelia but less so to that of Karelia proper, where the term *pilli* had developed very late. That Leisiö had to change his historical hypothesis is not surprising, for new data frequently alter a hypothesis. The need to modify his interpretation of the taxonomy did not lessen Leisiö's conviction—nor should it—that to reconstruct a classification of instruments and interpret it as a historio-

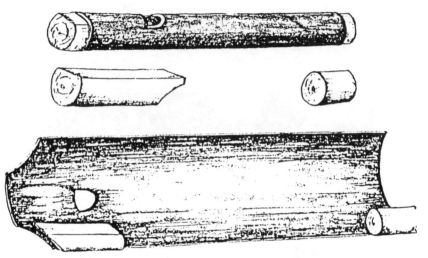

FIGURE 18.8 Two loose plugs made of bark

graphical document reinforced by other musical, folkloristic, archeological, linguistic, historical, and sociological data was an essentially useful research method. Indeed, given the practical difficulties involved in creating a historiography of instruments over the millennia, scholars clearly have to utilize methods like this, while seeking for as much corroborative evidence as possible to minimize false or incomplete interpretations.

It is, of course, probable that other classifications of instruments than the ones elicited by Leisiö coexist in Finnish culture, including one related to cosmographic Finno-Ugric religion. Traces of a classification of Finnish-Karelian instruments according to origin myth are evident in data presented in an article by Haavio (1952, 153) on the use of the *kantele* by the eternal sage, creator, and *kantele* musician Väinamöinen. A more complete account of Finnish instrument taxonomies awaits the further compilation of field data.

Epilogue: The Seamless Web

Concepts and classifications of instruments and ensembles are part of a seamless web of cultural knowledge. The process of classification is usually not just a one-dimensional activity resulting in the production of a tersely structured, systematic set of data. It is frequently a multilevel, creative way of thinking and organizing knowledge about instruments and ensembles in ways that are consistent with socially influenced or structured ideas or belief systems. Concepts and classifications are often so interrelated that they are practically indivisible, except on an analytical level.

Information gathered to date suggests that a culture or subculture normally has several coexisting ways of organizing information about musical instruments, ensembles, or both, some of which may be based on a number of intersecting facets and others on single- or multiple-character steps of division. Some schemes embody a culture's profoundest ideas. For instance, the most representative classification of instruments among the Mandailing people is intimately related to their social and kinship groupings as well as to their beliefs about nature, the ancestral spirits, and visual artistic organization. Schemes may intersect with classifications of specimens or aspects of other spheres within the culture, such as the classification of birds among the Kaluli in Papua Niugini. To classify instruments may serve not only as a functional aid for practical music making and as a useful way of meeting psychological needs in the mastery of fields of knowledge but also as an expression of a society's concepts, identity, and predilections. An example is the conscious association of ancient schemes with the expression of national identity, found not only in recent times in cultures of China, India, and Europe but also in the past, for example, in the Arabic world from the ninth until the seventeenth century and beyond.

Classifications of musical instruments based on an analogical concept of gender are also expressions of the social order. Sometimes this concept has a political or power aspect to it. Sometimes (as in medieval Europe) a classification is associated with the bride or groom at a wedding or with characters in a folk theater performance. At other times a scheme appears to be associated with the human anatomy. For example, the fact that pairs of instruments in many Southeast Asian cultures are termed male or female, with the larger member of the pair being called the female and the smaller the male, is possibly related to the anatomical size of the womb as opposed to the penis, having little apparent import beyond that. In Java and other patrilineal societies only men traditionally play instruments of the valuable bronze ensembles, while in parts of the matrilineal region of Minangkabau (e.g., in the Sijunjung region and the Pariaman hinterland), bronze ensembles are played by women rather than men, a practice related to the Minangkabau tradition whereby women own valuable property such as bronze instruments and land, while in Java and elsewhere it is normally the men who own them. The materialist argument that ownership leads to exclusive use of valuable objects or other benefits combines here with an argument based on the politics of gender. Similarly, Aristides Quintilianus's division of instruments in the Hellenistic period of Greek thought into the male, effeminate-masculine, masculine-feminine, and female instruments presumably reflects ideas of gender status and power in the culture at the time, namely, male superiority, female inferiority, and two stages in between. In Mandailing the division of ritual drums into female, male, and child reflects the culture's preoccupation with binary-ternary completeness of the family and broader social, artistic, and other units of existence. Interpretative gender analysis based on concepts and classifications of instruments, however, is difficult to make in most cultures, given the small amount of ethnographical or historical data available.

Classifications of instruments and ensembles and their operative taxonomical concepts of instruments are in a constant state of flux. Some schemes remain intact in their outlines for generations or millennia. Yet even in cultures adhering to an essentialist view—that is, that instruments are fixed entities—the schemes keep changing, for instance, in their hierarchical order of categories or in other small details, as the history of the dominant Chinese scheme indicates. More importantly, the purposes for which they are used change. A scheme developed primarily in the context of theatrical performance, as in ancient India, or as part of a cosmology, as in ancient China, may eventually lose all or most of its original connotations, be retained as a national symbol, have detailed subcategories added to it, and be re-presented as a scheme to be used for modern museological and scholarly purposes. Old schemes change and relatively novel ones are devised as the purposes of classification and concepts of instruments change. But as authors of new classifications need the legitimacy of tradition, if only to ensure that their schemes are quickly understood and are able to be widely adopted, entirely new schemes rarely, if ever, occur. Authors normally give their schemes some aspects of continuity with the past, such as commencing with categories accepted by tradition, and then present their new characters of division. When authors such as Deva, Hornbostel and Sachs, and Hood construct new classifications, they also tend to emphasize elements of continuity with past schemes in the explanations that accompany the publication of their work. Few people seem to want to claim total novelty when producing a new classification, for to do so may limit its application and use; nor could an author who wished to achieve total novelty manage to do so as she or he would automatically be influenced by or, indeed, react against previously known classifications.

Perhaps the most significant formal break with tradition in taxonomical organology to date was the method of "typology research" or upward classification by inspection presented by Elschek and Stockmann in 1969. This approach was presented with reference in its explanatory comments to earlier schemes, such as those of Dräger and Hornbostel and Sachs. Its multifaceted approach had been anticipated by Ramey and others, but so different was it from previous methods that it was soon attacked, though largely on the basis of a misunderstanding of its method and intent. Elschek and Stockmann in their article of 1969 had clearly emphasized the differences between typology and systematics or downward logical division. In self-defense Elschek later found it necessary to explain that he had had no intention of replacing systematics with typology. Depending on one's purpose, he pointed out, both methods could usefully be used in combination, as each had quite different aims in view.

Doubtless, human beings must continually alternate between upward, downward, and lateral thinking in their endeavors to attain any depth of understanding of a taxonomical problem, after passing through any number of false leads and digressions on the way. It is clear that even predominantly downward thinkers like Mahillon must have alternated between downward, upward, and lateral thinking while creating their classification schemes, just as Elschek admitted he did in constructing his primarily upward method. As biologists discovered long ago, the method of moving upward from a detailed knowledge of specimens to increasingly higher levels of generality is a corrective to the inaccuracies that tend to arise at the lower levels when engaging in primarily downward thinking. This has been shown in such cases as al-Fārābī's fourth scheme and the classification by Hornbostel and Sachs. Clearly if one holds to a concept of instruments that takes real cognizance of their physical, social, and musical complexity, classifying by multifaceted rather than single-character division is the more appropriate method. Conversely, classifications based on a very limited concept of instruments and taxonomical purpose are better expressed in the form of logical division, as in the cases of schemes developed by medieval European and Arabic and ancient Greek taxonomists, who restricted their operative taxonomical concept of instruments to the acoustic and the morphological aspects because their purpose was to elucidate tenets of music theory based on these data. Elschek and Stockmann argued convincingly that a clear distinction needs to be made between the systematic and typological approaches and that taxonomists can benefit by using a combination of both, depending on their classificatory purpose. From their point of view, single-character and multifaceted division are not rival but complementary methods.

In view of the preoccupation with the method of classification by logical division in most of the cultures I have studied, it can initially be surprising to learn that taxonomies and keys are not universally accepted as being the "natural" way of classifying. Some cultures have traditionally classified instruments and other items of culture or of the ecology by multifaceted intersection, that is, in the form of what have been called "paradigms." There is no evidence that members of orally transmitting cultures such as the 'Are'are or the T'boli prefer to group instruments in rigidly ordered taxonomies by single-character division, though this mode of thinking is not foreign to them. These peoples also group their instruments by two, three, or more simultaneously operating parameters. Each parameter can be isolated as a character of division in a separate scheme, but for observers to present them in this form does violence to the unity of their mode of cognition. We know that in many cultures several parameters are taken singly or simultaneously into account when constructing taxonomies of instruments. Possibly multifaceted division is much more widespread than we have previously suspected to be the case. Possibly, too, outsider-scholars' interpretations of these multifaceted schemes as consisting of several separate classifications by logical division result from their disinclination or inability to accept the culture's wholesale concept of instruments without breaking it down into manageable single-character division according to their own cognitive habits.

As I have attempted to show in the above case studies, the form of a classification is closely related to its aim and its taxonomically operative concept of instruments. If the aim of a classification is specifically museological, for example, it may consist of many detailed steps and subdivisions, but if the aim is to illustrate the basis of a cosmological point of view, say, the scheme may be much broader and may consist of only one step. However, the deviser or user of a classification of instruments will normally adhere to a much wider concept of instruments in everyday life than the concept applied in the classification in question, which is usually limited for practical reasons to a few facets or characters. The form of a scheme is also related to a culture's hierarchical preferences for certain instruments. Thus instruments that are highly valued in a culture are normally more intensively classified than the less-important instruments; for example, in some Javanese schemes gongs and drums, which are at the top of the hierarchy, are more closely subdivided than other instruments.

Structurally, the schemes discussed in this book vary widely in their number of steps, classes per step, characters or clusters of facets governing each step, and the degree of overall symmetry. In a scheme based on mode of sound excitation, the classifier's or culture's attitude to details of the way in which sounds are excited on an instrument partly or largely determines the number and content of categories of a scheme. For example, if members of a culture regard beaten and plucked instruments as having different modes of exciting sound vibrations, they will classify them into those two separate categories, while members of a culture that regards beating and plucking as similar performing actions will subsume them into one category. The classification by the Roman writer Boethius is an example of the former, and the scheme of the Hellenistic author Pollux and the dominant Dan and Kpelle schemes of West Africa are examples of the latter.

Many schemes discussed in this book take the form of logical division. However, it has become apparent that when strict logic comes into conflict with the functionality or simple systematic convenience of a scheme—that is, when ambiguous categories cannot easily be avoided—logic usually falls by the wayside. Some taxonomists, especially Europeans, defer to logic as an ideal and criticize others (e.g., Hornbostel and Sachs) for not always living up to its stringent demands. They themselves, however, usually encounter difficulties in matching the complexities of real instrumentaria with the categories they distinguish. As Tyler pointed out (1979, 33), certain cultures strive for the simple elegance of traditional formal systems and the mathematical pinnacle of certain knowledge; but if logic is used as the evaluative standard, the observer is put in the position of dismissing most inferences as deviant, faulty, or not up to standard. The rules of logical division are made to be broken where classification is concerned. Deva, who chose to use the dominant Hindu classification at the highest level of his modern scheme, made no apologies for the ambiguity of some of his categories. Indeed the logical inconsistencies in a scheme such as his should not necessarily be regarded in a negative light; in any case, there is normally no way of avoiding them. Sometimes, indeed, loose ends are useful in that they can be interpreted as being evidence of diachronic processes, as unwitting preservers of elements of change in terminologies or structures. They can be used in a positive way as tools of historical interpretation and reconstruction, as in the case of a Finnish and a Minangkabau scheme discussed earlier.

Schemes that fulfill the requirements of strict paradigmatic form or logical division and schematic symmetry are rare in any culture, whether or not it has a literary or an oral orientation. Sometimes this is because a scheme has developed spontaneously to illustrate a particular idea and therefore had no need to incorporate all the diversity of detail into a watertight, symmetrical scheme nor to account for possible loose ends. It may also be due to the fact that a scheme has expanded, contracted, or changed in some other way at certain moments in time and maintained some old components alongside the new, giving it a somewhat illogical or inconsistent appearance. Its nomenclatures and terminologies may have changed in meaning or have been attached to different instruments in the course of time. Ambiguous or contradictory titles of categories or other lexemes are sometimes comprehensible only when regarded as reflecting historical change, as in Leisiö's interpretation of the Finnish folk instrumentarium.

Inconsistencies in a scheme, whether apparent or real, and even if unaccountable, are partly to be attributed to the fact that the very imposition of boundaries creates problems, which applies as much to the fields of cartography, population groupings, and biological classification as it does to the grouping of instruments or other art objects. Borderline cases always arise when boundaries are imposed. By its very nature a given instrumentarium used in vital practice cannot be fitted into a perfectly logical classification scheme. The reason for this is the very expansiveness and the creativity of the human beings who conceive of, fashion, and continually change the form and meaning of instruments. Our human minds may need such schemes in order to assist us to comprehend a diverse body of objects or ideas and to aid memory. However, we must reconcile ourselves to the fact that perfectly logical schemes that deal adequately with all aspects of a body of data simply do not evolve in living cultures, since the primary aim is virtually never to comply with the requirements of strict logical division. Logic tends to be overridden by other competing purposes.

How different from each other are the forms of the classifications of instruments used in the various cultures of the world? Lévi-Strauss (1966), Geertz (1973), Douglas (1966), and Willis (1974) stressed the variation between cultures in their discussions concerning systems of classification of such entities as animals, plants, and colors, while Kay (1975), Berlin (1972), and Bulmer (1967, 1968, and 1970) reached the opposite finding: that different peoples often produce virtually identical classifications that vary only in their degrees of elaboration. A great many more data need to be gathered on the world's classifications of instruments before any well-based conclusions can be drawn concerning this question, though the preliminary findings of this study incline slightly toward the former view. As a whole, the basic structures of classifications considered in this book are very limited in number, and some characters of division recur in a number of cultures, yet the particular mixes of characters, steps, and categories in each scheme are highly variable, as are the concepts of instruments lying at the base of the schemes. With the compilation of much more cross-cultural data we may find that the norm lies somewhere between the two opposing views mentioned above.

There is no doubt, however, that classifications of instruments across the cultures resemble each other most closely if based on mode of sound excitation or other single, purely musical factors and differ most strongly from each other when based on broader social, religious, or other belief structures.

Some cultures discussed in this book resemble each other in their propensity to think of classifications of instruments with visual analogies in mind. Indians, Arabs, and Europeans are among those who sometimes think taxonomically by analogy with trees and branches, while Indians and Tibetans sometimes classify by analogy with limbs of the body. In the T'boli region, categories of instruments are seen as being analogous to the

figure and ground or ornamental filling of local cloth design, and a
Javanese writer (Tjakrahadikusuma) drew a similar analogy in the case of
gamelan instrumental categories and batik cloth design. Some Tibetan
treatises classify by means of a decimalized number system, as did
Hornbostel and Sachs, while a number of modern Western writers use
graphic or numerical systems instead of the usual word-based ones.
European tradition since the time of Praetorius or earlier also divided
certain groups of instruments (such as viols) into the analogical categories
of "families," "sorts," or "accords." Other traditions have used analogies
with genders, generations, and families.

Despite the common widespread use of certain characters and groups
of facets of division, a considerable diversity of characters may be seen in
the schemes considered in the present work. In some cultures instruments
are classified primarily on morphological and acoustic grounds, and in
others they are divided mainly according to functional symbols of cosmic
or spiritual ideas, sexuality, royal character and aplomb (as in the case of
the great gong in the Javanese gamelan), or as vessels housing various
spirits of nature or the ancestors (as in most of the Southeast Asian
cultures that I have encountered during field trips in Malaysia, Thailand,
Indonesia, and the Philippines). Instruments are commonly attributed
with specific social and musical functions, and since they may be artifacts
of considerable technical skill and visual artistic quality, they may possess
a corresponding set of visual symbols, as in the case of the gable design in
Mandailing.

At the highest level the divisions of an instrumentarium are frequently
made by large-scale historical, cosmological, philosophical, or religious
characters, including cultural strata (e.g., the distinctions made between
"authentic," "Muslim," and "Western" categories in some Indonesian
cultures) and indigenous schemes of dualistic ontological thought (e.g.,
the idea that instruments divide into those that play "gentle" music and
those that produce "strong" music, characters of division found among the
T'boli and the Javanese).

Other, rarer divisions are made according to whether instruments are
played solo or in groups, whether solo or accompanying parts are played
on them, according to performer-instrument relationships, mode of
performance, and tone systems, as well as loud versus soft instruments and
secular versus religious functions of instruments. In some cultures,
instruments may be grouped—though incompletely—according to their
respective origin myths, as in West Africa and India. The available evidence

indicates that classifications of instruments made according to their degree or kind of decorativeness or beauty are modern schemes that occasionally result from preparing displays of instruments in museums. Classifications based on this kind of character have not been encountered in any other context in this study.

As has been mentioned, classifications based on the mode of sound excitation are common and may resemble each other across the cultures. Considerable differences of detail are encountered, however. In the Malay Petalangan area of Riau, instruments are divided into the beaten, blown, plucked, pulled, and bowed, while in Minangkabua there is also a swung category and in monastic Tibet there is a unique rung or tolled category alongside its beaten, blown, and stringed ones. The T'boli divide instruments into those sounded by the breath, by the fingers, and by beating, which somewhat resembles the European wind, stringed, and percussion division, while the West Africans divide all instruments into the struck (i.e., plucked and beaten) and the blown, after the manner of Pollux and his followers. In the richly endowed percussive instrumental culture of Java, instruments are divided into those that are beaten with a padded spherical hammer, those beaten with a relatively hard wooden hammer, those beaten with the hands, and those that are shaken, as distinguished from various nonpercussive categories, which include the plucked, pulled, bowed, and blown groupings. Few cultures possess such a diversity of categories of percussion instruments as the Javanese. Other modes of sound excitation distinguished in various cultures include the rubbed, pressed, scratched, clapped, revolved, oscillated, swayed, and—since Galpin's presentation in 1937—electrically generated categories.

Morphological characters are also in widespread use. The resulting categories of instruments include the hollow, solid, stretched, covered, self-sounding (idiophonic), membranophonic, aerophonic, and chordophonic. Categories distinguished by the main material of which an instrument is made include metal, stone, silk, bamboo, gourd, clay, leather, and wood in China; bronze or iron, leather, wood, wire or cord, and bamboo in Java; and glass, copper, and noncopper in ninth-century Byzantium. Other characters of division include whether an instrument can hold a tone for long or not, whether it produces melodic or nonmelodic sound, and, especially since the sixteenth century in Europe, the mechanics of instruments. Yet others are an instrument's size, shape, and volume of sound produced (as in Finland), the number of reeds or strings (as in Arabic culture), the order of gongs in a gong-chime (as in

T'boli), and the tones or scales playable on an instrument or to which it is tuned (as with 'Are'are panpipes).

There are various ways of classifying ensembles. Sometimes they are grouped at the highest step according to characters based on the relevant performance practice. For example, a division is made in Minangkabau between ensembles with seated as opposed to processional players. Other performance-practice-related divisions are made according to whether an ensemble is archaic or not or whether it complies with the philosophical concept of being "complete" or not (as in Mandailing) or according to the regional variability of the kinds of ensembles found in a given culture area (such as the various categories of *talempong* ensemble in Minangkabau). They may also be grouped according to their social function. Among the 'Are'are people, ensembles with a signaling function are distinguished from (1) various grouped bamboo ensembles that mark specific ceremonial occasions and are associated with various taboos; (2) group stick beating (on the bow of a boat), which accompanies divination singing; and (3) bamboo stamping tubes, which are played mainly for entertainment and have no magic attributions at all. The role of certain groups of instruments in an ensemble may also be classified according to musical function, including the order of entry of instruments in ensemble playing. Thus, specific labels are given to gongs according to the order in which they make their musical entries in a *talempong* ensemble performance in Minangkabau. Another instance of musical functional grouping is the division of the Yogyakarta gamelan into two parts, which specifies that the louder instruments are placed at the back of an assigned performance area and the softer, intricately embellishing instruments in the front. In Surakarta, a functional, spatial grouping of the gamelan may even partly determine the levels of payment of the musicians. Similarly in the European Middle Ages a distinction was made between wind and string players. At weddings and the like the former mostly received double the payment of the latter, which created class distinctions between musicians. Class distinctions were also made between singers of heroic songs and minstrels. A deep social trough separated educated and noneducated musicians, and this was often linked to specific instruments.

Sometimes, as in the 'Are'are culture, a hierarchy is contained in a classification of instruments or ensembles. This can frequently be confirmed by an observer inquiring into the general concept of instruments in the culture. Among the 'Are'are, those panpipe ensembles played in the course of ceremonies related to the ancestor cult are the most highly rated,

followed by three other kinds of panpipe ensemble that have approximately equal hierarchical value. Other kinds of panpipes and the mouth
zither are associated with love magic and are classed highest among the
solo instruments. These are followed by instruments played mainly for
entertainment, such as the stamping tubes, the transverse flute, and the
vertical bundle panpipe as well as the panpipe called *'au ni auu*. A
hierarchical, court-oriented classification in Java, on the other hand, rates
gamelan instruments by analogy with the rankings of earthly power,
where, for example, the great gong is seen as having the stature of the king,
and the drum, the prime minister (verbal communication from the late
Yogyakarta court musician K. R. T. Madukusuma).

A point in common among a few cultures is the adherence to the idea
that certain uses of the human body, including the use of the throat for
singing and percussive body movements such as hand-clapping, are
analogous or homologous to the use of musical instruments—indeed, that
the human body is a musical instrument. In the Hellenic era a division was
made between animate and inanimate instruments; and preference was
expressed for the animate ones. People considered that inanimate instruments could express human emotion and they devised theories to explain
why. Early Christian Europeans regarded the human voice as God's
instrument and likewise preferred it to inanimate instruments. At the
beginning of the second millennium the Indian writer Nārada included the
singing voice and hand-clapping in one category of his fivefold categorization of instruments. The contemporary Javanese writer Sumarsam
included the female vocalist in his category of melodic elaborating
instruments, a category that otherwise contained bowed, beaten, and
blown instruments. And recently the American scholar Olson suggested
that a classification of instruments like the Hornbostel and Sachs scheme
should include a separate category called corpophones for "instruments,"
such as the singing voice, that comprise parts of the human body.

Members of a number of cultures discussed in this book regard
inanimate instruments as possessing human qualities, which they show
either by drawing analogies between instruments and parts of the human
body or by giving the instruments human names. Thus Indians classify and
name the parts of the *vīṇā* anthropomorphically, just as the Javanese
classify parts of the *rebab* and the Arabs parts of the *'ūd;* that is, they regard
them—by analogy—as having human parts. The Dan and the Kpelle also
name parts of instruments by analogy with the human body and regard
instruments as being performers or extensions of their human performer,

while the Hausa typically classify *players* of instruments as well as the instruments themselves. The personification of instruments in Mandailing results in the groupings of instruments by analogy with the traditional social classes and with the male, female, and child components of the family. Javanese classifications of ensembles personify and reflect the social hierarchy as well as the alleged social cohesion of the community. The practice of designating pairs or groups of instruments by the terms *male* and *female; male, female,* and *child; mother* and *child; mother, child,* and *grandchild;* and so on is found in several orally transmitting societies, though it is not yet known how widespread it is.

Both in Europe and in China the growth of a humanistic concept of instruments and an interest in the social and musical functions of instruments served to create effective changes in the classifications of instruments. Thus, the largely morphological-acoustic concept of instruments in ancient Greek and Roman musical theoretical writings expanded from the time of Grocheo in the thirteenth century to include a more humanistic concept in which instruments began to be classified according to their social function and geographical area, though the "scientific" concept of instruments as physical objects continued to be highly influential through to the twentieth century. In sixteenth-century China, Ma Tuan Lin similarly began to classify instruments according to their social function, finding the *pa yin* inadequate for his classification because he wished to include not only ancient but also contemporary instruments. He also wanted to use some new characters of division.

Some cultures or individuals in them choose to classify a large corpus of instruments, while others limit themselves to a small functional group. Some taxonomies are based on the whole instrumentarium of a culture, while others are based on a view of instruments as part of an even broader sphere, for example, the sphere of theoretical knowledge or of art or of music in general. Others are based on a specific ensemble. In some areas or periods classifications are restricted to local instruments only, though they may eventually be expanded to include exotic and historical instruments, as in the case of the eighteenth-century French writer Benjamin de la Borde mentioned earlier. Similarly, the fifteenth-century minstrel Ibn Ghaybī divided instruments into the folk, art, and exotic categories, listing the exotic categories as being Chinese, Indian, and European. In the sixteenth century, the German author Praetorius classified instruments into the foreign, barbarian, rustic, unfamiliar, and familiar, while in the eighteenth century the Italian writer Bonanni distinguished African,

Persian, Indian, Chinese, and Capri instruments. de la Borde grouped instruments into those of the past and those of the present. Deva, in contemporary India, included all Indian historical, current, tribal, folk, and concert instruments in his classification, excluding keyboards and other instruments used in a foreign context, such as pianos and other keyboards.

In seventeenth- and eighteenth-century Europe anonymous travelers brought back many instruments from overseas. An explosion of knowledge about instruments accompanied the collection of many specimens in museums, inducing a need for an even more global concept of instruments than Bonanni's and de la Borde's. In the twentieth century a view of instruments as multifaceted, highly variable, and changing entities began to develop. This was accompanied by a move away from a static, mainly morphological and acoustic concept to a dynamic, expansive view of instruments as elements of the musical and sociohistorical behavior of human beings, a view that led to the development of methods of classifying by multivariable grouping.

Some classifications are associated with a particular religious identity, as in the case of the three distinctive, though related, schemes that are still dominant in India's Hindu, Buddhist, and Jain traditions. However, these Indian schemes do not have a religious nature at all, being based instead on characters derived from performance practice. Likewise, Tibet's dominant classification of monastic instruments is based primarily on aesthetic or musical performing characters of division, and the religious aspects are relegated to second place.

Once a scheme is established, it may last a short while, fall into disuse and disappear, or its life may be guaranteed in traditional practice for centuries or millennia. Certain Greek and Roman ideas about categories of instrument taxonomy persisted in Europe for twelve hundred years, though from the thirteenth and especially the sixteenth century they were of increasingly formal significance only. Thus the Hellenistic scheme of Porphyry reappeared in the taxonomical writings on instruments by Praetorius in the seventeenth century. Even innovative sixteenth- and seventeenth-century taxonomists like Virdung and Zarlino began their classifications with deferential borrowings from ancient schemes. As we have noted, similar cases may be cited in the taxonomical history of other cultures, such as India and China.

The classifications of instruments referred to in this volume were devised in Arab, 'Are'are, Belgian, Byzantine, Chinese, Czechoslovakian,

Dutch, English, Finnish, French, German, Greek, Japanese, Javanese, Indian, Italian, Malay, Mandailing, Minangkabau, Srilankan, Swedish, T'boli, Tibetan, West African, white North American, and other cultures, in some cases covering long periods of history. Clearly the usefulness of this book's findings depends ultimately on many more cross-cultural studies being made, especially of orally transmitted schemes, for the validity of the conclusions drawn from these findings is limited by our ignorance of classifications devised over the millennia in the many other cultures and subcultures of the world. Yet only through a thorough knowledge of the place of each scheme in its own particular cultural web can it be understood in its own terms, let alone serve as a potential contribution to the theory of the concepts and classification of instruments across the world's cultures.

Notes

1. Though formal education in the United States, like many other countries, reflects only a small part of the real urban musical world in all its diversity, it leaves ideas associated with the classical musical tradition such as these in the minds of its pupils through to adulthood. These commonly accepted instrument classification schemes have limited applicability, of course, outside the classical tradition—for example, in the world of popular music, which has its own schemes. How do rock and roll players, for example, classify the guitars which normally predominate in their ensembles? Mostly by manufacturer, Mannheim found in his limited survey. The Nashville Music Instrument Museum's Roy Acuff Musical Collection at Opryland, for example, lays out its instruments (mostly strings) according to manufacturer groupings. On the other hand, folk music enthusiasts in the early 1960s tended to split electric from acoustic instruments (communication from James Mannheim).

2. As Lévi-Strauss shows so potently in *The Savage Mind*, human thinking in so-called primitive societies has frequently been shown to be highly intricate, precise, and detailed, as in some of the classifications of flora and fauna. People in many nonliterate or semiliterate societies can recognize, name, and discuss in detail the properties of a multitude of plants and animals in their environment, even those that are useless to them. For example, among the Hanunoo of the Philippines, almost all activities

> require an intimate familiarity with local plants and a precise knowledge of plant classification. Contrary to the assumption that subsistence level groups never use but a small segment of the local flora, ninety-three per cent of the total number of native plant types are recognised by the Hanunoo as culturally significant. (Conklin 1954, 249)

They may also have an astounding knowledge of the types of fauna:

> The Hanunoo classify all forms of the local avifauna into seventy-five categories . . . [they] distinguish about a dozen kinds of snakes . . . sixty odd types of fish . . . more than a dozen . . . types of fresh and salt water crustaceans . . . a similar number of types of arachnids and myriapods. . . . The thousands of insect forms present are grouped by the Hanunoo into a hundred and eight named categories, including thirteen for ants and termites. . . . Salt water molluscs . . . of more than sixty classes are recognised by the Hanunoo, while terrestrial and fresh water types number more than twenty-five. . . . Four distinct types of bloodsucking leeches are distinguished . . . altogether 461 animal types are recorded. (Conklin 1954, 67–70)

Lévi-Strauss found similar data in the writings of field-workers among various Filipino, African, Siberian, American Indian, and other groups spread around the globe and noted the amazement of a number of earlier scholars at the exhaustive observation and systematic cataloging and grouping of the facts of science in the realm of flora and fauna:

> This thirst for objective knowledge is one of the most neglected aspects of the thought of people we call 'primitive'. Even if it is rarely directed towards facts of the same level as those with which modern science is concerned, it implies comparable intellectual application and methods of observation. In both cases the universe is an object of thought at least as much as it is a means of satisfying needs. (Lévi-Strauss 1966, 3)

3. The Indian musicologist Deva, for example, presented the fourfold classification of instruments that appeared in the *Nāṭyaśāstra* at the upper level of his own modern, multilevel classification of Indian instruments (Deva 1980, 130). In so doing, he drew attention to the longevity of India's artistic and literary tradition, in a way that encourages nationalist pride.

4. As Kaplan pointed out:

> Even an artificial classification is not wholly arbitrary if it really serves its own limited purposes. A classification of books by size and weight is not 'as natural', we feel, as one based on their content. But the printer and the freight agent have claims as legitimate as the librarians. The point is that the former stand nearly alone in their interests; the librarian is joined by every reader, by everyone else who is concerned about his reading. Whether a concept is useful depends on the use we want to put it to; but there is always the additional question whether things so conceptualized will lend themselves to that use. (1964, 51)

CHAPTER TWO

1. Though the tenets and methods of cognitive anthropology have been called into question by various anthropologists, the work on classification theory by such scholars as Tyler and Conklin remains pertinent to the present study.

2. The biological taxonomist Mayr delimits the term *classification* to mean "the ordering of organisms into taxa on the basis of their similarity and relationship as determined by or inferred from their taxonomic characters" (Mayr 1982, 185).

3. The term *taxon* was first proposed in 1926 by Meyer-Abich, was taken up by the Dutch botanist Lam in the late 1940s, and was officially adopted by the International Botanical Congress in 1950, after which its use became common (Mayr 1982, 868).

4. In his study of Kaluli ornithology, Feld noted "the coexistence of two major taxonomic constructs, one based on the morphological criteria of shared beaks and feet, and the other based on sounds," which in Feld's view "indicates the extent to which Kaluli creatively organise their knowledge of birds in relation to ecological understanding and social needs" (1982, 218). Feld presented his field data in two separate tree diagrams. One of these divided birds into the terrestrial as opposed to the tree birds, partly on the basis of their beaks and feet, with various subdivisions into "families" and "small families." The other divided birds according to the various sounds that the Kaluli interpret them as producing. These two schemes could be combined into one paradigmatic diagram, which would more adequately than the dual schemes underline Feld's concluding point that cultural knowledge is the "creative ability to organize and think about . . . processes in ways consistent with socially structured beliefs about the world" (1982, 218).

CHAPTER THREE

1. Kunst exemplified this bias when congratulating Sachs, Hornbostel, and Mahillon for the part they played in developing "a most successful attempt to arrange in logical order all . . . instrumental forms" (1974, 55). Moreover, a taxonomist who is aware that instruments change form and meaning nevertheless adheres in practice—at least momentarily—to a static concept of instruments when applying a scheme such as Hornbostel and Sachs's or Mahillon's.

2. Such schemes sometimes contain data that show that borrowed instruments change in their new environment while retaining their old names or that the instruments remain the same but gain new labels. An example is the Hindu Indian plucked stringed instrument *kacchapī* or *kasyapi*, likenesses of which are carved on ancient temples both in India (Ajanta) and Java (Barabudhur). Variants of the original Sanskrit name Kacchapī vīṇā was eventually applied to three main types of stringed instruments throughout Southeast Asia: lutes, zithers, and tube zithers. Variants of the name that were attached to lutes include the *krajappi* of

Thailand, the *hasapi* in Toba (Sumatra), the *kulcapi* in Karo (Sumatra), the *kucapi* in Minangkabau, the Makassarese and Buginese *kacaping (kacapi)* in Sulawesi, the Ngayu Dayak *kasapi* in Borneo (Kalimantan and East Malaysia), and the Kayan, Kenyah, and Kelabit *sape* or *sampe* in northern Borneo. In West Java, the *kacapi* is a large zither with eighteen or so strings, tuning pegs, and movable bridges; the larger form is called *kacapi indung* (mother *kacapi*) and the smaller form is called *kacapi anak* (child *kacapi*). A tube zither is called *canang kacapi* in the Gayo and Apas areas of Aceh, Sumatra. Not all lutes, zithers, and tube zithers, however, are named after the *kacchapī;* the board zithers in the Javanese gamelan, for example, are called *cilempung* (large version) and *siter* (small version).

3. In the context of population thinking, the terms *type,* the *typical individual,* and *typology* were given different meanings from those used in the rest of typology research. Population thinking rejects the abstract notion of the typical or average individual: the individual is important, not the type (Mayr 1982, 263). Elschek and Stockmann (1969), on the other hand, use a different concept of *type,* defining it as an abstract model of essentially similar phenomena distinguished by a bundle of attributes.

CHAPTER FOUR

1. The *Shih ching* is an anonymous collection of ancient songs from the Chou period (ninth to fifth centuries BCE); for the translation see Legge 1966.

2. I am indebted to Zhang Wei Hau and Jerome Hu for kindly preparing the Chinese characters and translating parts of three contemporary sources published in Beijing. Wang Ying-fen translated parts of a contemporary source published in Taiwan. For the most part, Chinese words are romanized in this chapter according to the Wade-Giles system; but in the discussion of contemporary sources the Pinyin system (which is current in the People's Republic of China) is used.

3. In this chapter, the periodization of Chinese music history used is that presented by Yang Yin-Liu. It divides music history into three main periods: the ancient (from the Neolithic time to 246 BCE), the middle ancient (from 246 BCE to 907 CE), and the late historical (from 907 to 1911 CE) (Yang Yin-Liu 1952).

4. This belief is expressed, for example, in Yang Jia-luo (1975: I, 29) and in the *Cí-hài* (Committee of Editors 1980b: 235). The *pa yin* was also mentioned in a number of middle ancient sources, including the lost manuscript *Yo-fu tsa-lu* (Musical pieces with song or textual relationships—Various reports), which was written by the T'ang period theorist Tuan An-Chieh in approximately 900 CE (Gimm 1966, 57–58).

5. For example, in the year 18 BCE (during the reign of Emperor Cheng Ti) a great rock emitted a thunderous noise. The prognosis was that it was a disturbance of the element Metal due to the pugnaciousness of the rulers, whereupon the people simply said that soldiers would come (Needham and Robinson 1962, 130).

6. A further classification of sounds according to their pitch arose from the division of instruments, but this topic lies beyond the scope of this chapter (see Needham and Robinson 1962, 152–153).

7. It is not certain that such large-scale performances actually took place (see Kishibe 1980, 251–52).

8. Wang Ying Lin's chapter 109 was entitled "Wind and Percussion Instruments and So Forth," and his chapter 110 was headed "Stringed Instruments, Drums and Other Miscellaneous Instruments" (Pian 1967, 16).

9. This extract is from the *Lü-lü ching I,* a music encyclopedia compiled from various sources and dated 1596. It recapitulates much of the material in Chu Tsai-Yü's *Lü-hsüeh hsin-shuo* (The new account of the science of the pitch pipes), dated 1584 (Robinson 1980, 77).

CHAPTER FIVE

1. The *daṇḍa* (literally "stick") is the part of the *vīṇā* that connects the main resonator to the gourd. Vīṇā is the main indigenous term for chordophones in South Asia. The name and its derivatives have been used for almost three millennia.

2. Translation in Ananthapadmanabhan 1954, 5.

3. Some sources mention instruments but do not classify them. For example, the *Vēdas* simply refer to the names of various drums, idiophones, strings, and wind instruments (Sastri 1966, 22).

4. In 1970 approximately 83 percent of India's population was Hindu, 11 percent Muslim, 2 percent Sikh, 0.75 percent Buddhist, and less than 0.5 percent Jain (living mostly in Gujarat and Rajasthan). Sri Lanka had nine million Sinhalese Buddhists, two-and-a-half million Tamil Hindus, and almost a million Tamil-speaking Muslims.

5. Karaikudi S. Subramanian (1985, 15) wrote on the Hindu-Indian symbolism and numerology of the *vīṇā* as follows:

> The four main strings [of the *vīṇā*], the four main *biruḍais* [wooden pegs] and the dragon side and the four *langars* [metal wires], in themselves forming another trinity, could be interpreted as Man being essentially divine. . . . Thus *vīṇā* epitomises philosophy; due to his false knowledge Man forgets his primal divinity and goes astray; by following his *dharma* (duty), through self-discipline he conquers evil and attains salvation.

6. A miniature painting from the twelfth century CE depicting Sarasvati playing a *vīṇā* (the stick or tube zither type with a gourd resonator) is reproduced and discussed in Flora 1983, 209–14.

7. This legend about the original idea of the drum is presented in chapter 33 of the treatise *Nāṭyaśāstra:* "After observing the high, medium and low sounds produced on the lotus leaves as deep, sweet and pleasing, he (Svati) went back to his hermitage" (Ghosh 1961). See also Bhattacharya 1987, 89–90.

8. Parts of the human body are also linked to other taxonomies, for example, to the four Hindu castes. Thus, the head is associated with Brahmans and the feet with Sudras.

9. For a reference to a classification of the Indo-Tibetan sciences, see Ellingson 1979, 374. Indian Mahayana Buddhist *svarasvasti* chant melody is said to consist of the head, the body, and various limbs. The term *åṅga* is also used in the sense of musical beauty or quality. "In *svarasvasti*, the 'limbs' seem to be components of musical quality which are found throughout a piece: e.g. when employing the limbs of beauty . . ., the 'limbs' of the 'bones' (. . . apparently the skeletal structure of the melody) must not be lost" (Ellingson 1979, 184). In Hindu theory (*Nāṭyaśāstra*, chaps. 29 and 31 [Ghosh 1961]), however, the term *limbs* seems to refer to sequential subdivisions of the structure of a musical piece. As Brown explains (1965, 6–7): "A *tāla* is a metrical cycle of given length (*āvarta*), consisting of a certain number of durational units of equal size (*akṣara*) which are grouped into one or more subdivisional sections of variable size (*āṅga*). . . . The *āṅga*s into which the *āvarta*s of the most common South Indian *tāla*s are subdivided occur in lengths of 1, 2, 3, 4, 5, 7 and 9 *akṣara*s." "The *guṇas* (artistic mental qualities) and *alaṅkāras* suggested grace of expression) are the *åaṅga*s (limbs) of the suggested *rāsa*" (Sastri 1966: 11).

10. Sometimes, however, classifications are also made by analogy with trees and branches. In the sixth century BCE one of the schools of the four Vēdas was called *śākhā*, meaning "branch of a tree." "Two thousand years ago . . . *abhinaya* (i.e., 'bringing a situation near to the mind of the audience') was recognized as having four forms 'and that all these aspects are branches stemming from the trunk of *bhāva-rasa-dhvani*' (emotions-sentiments-

hidden meanings) which is fed by the root of *ānanda* (joy in creation and creativeness)" (Sastri 1966, 31–32).

11. Among the alternative versions of these labels are *tat vad* (stringed instruments), *sushir vad* (hollow instruments), *avanad vad* (leather or percussion instruments, and *ghan vad* (solid instruments) (Mansukhani 1982, 50). Bengali versions of the same terms are *tut* (strings), *bitut* (drums, with the term deriving from *vitata*), *ghun* (percussion instruments played "two at a time," such as cymbals and castanets, with the term deriving from *ghana*), and *sooghur* (winds) (Willard 1875, 93–94).

12. The parentheses in this quotation enclose Ghosh's explanatory additions; the brackets enclose my additions.

13. Bonnie Wade suggested this interpretation to me. Sounds produced by the *mṛdaãnga* are discussed in Brown 1965, chap. 4.

14. Shastri (1973) notes that not all of the 108 *karanas* are now taught or practiced by students of dance, but some have been incorporated in some southern Indian programs of *bharata nāṭya* (classical dance). For a description of the dance movements in the *Nāṭyassāstra* see Sastri 1966, 26–28, and Shastri 1973, 34–36.

15. The text of part of the first chapter (entitled "About Sound" of the *Saṅgītamakaranda* is presented in Heyde 1977, 150. The work has been translated by Telang for Baroda, 1920.

16. Bowed instruments were not mentioned in Nārada's scheme, presumably because they were not yet in common use in India. But because bowed sound is made by a bow on strings, bowed instruments could be incorporated logically into the scheme.

17. Hand-clapping is an important sound in some Javanese gamelan music, but the Javanese do not normally regard the sound as being produced on an instrument.

18. Marcel-Dubois isolated four evolutionary categories of a third type of *vīṇā*, i.e., stick or tube zither-type *vīṇās* in ancient India (1941, 72–80), a hypothesis that needs further modification and expansion in light of more recently investigated evidence of *vīṇās* in miniature paintings (Flora 1983, 209–16).

19. Instrumental music appears to have gained prominence in Indian Buddhist monasteries in the period of the expansion of Mahayana practices and beliefs, that is, during the first five centuries CE (Ellingson 1979: 186). A Chinese pilgrim in the fifth century described "keepers" of an Indian monastery who "beat great drums, blow conchs, and clash their copper cymbals" (Fa-hsien, n.d. E: 37).

20. Other Srilankan classifications of instruments may, of course, be uncovered by research on the pre-Buddhist animist culture and on the Tamil Muslim, and other minority groups in Srilanka. Presumably the Carnatic instruments introduced into Srilanka by Kandyan kings from South India in the sixteenth to nineteenth centuries (the Kandyan period) were subject to classification also.

21. The historical records indicate that there were eight kinds of *vīṇā*, with strings varying from three to twenty-one in number; twenty-six kinds of aerophones made of bamboo or wood; fifteen kinds of metal idiophones such as hand cymbals, metal bells, and tinkling anklets; and twenty-six kinds of drum (Amaradeva 1971, 74).

22. *The Science of Body Parts* is one such sixth-century text (communication from P. S. Jaini).

CHAPTER SIX

1. Words of a Tibetan Buddhist monk recorded by Terry Ellingson in Switzerland in 1970.

2. Basic materials for this chapter were mainly derived from Terry Ellingson's thesis (1979). Ellingson also kindly supplied extra materials by oral and written communications.

3. Bon is the religion that developed in Tibet before the acceptance of Buddhism:

> To practicing *bonpos*—and nowadays it has become comparatively easy to meet them if one knows where to look among the tens of thousands of Tibetans who have arrived as refugees in India and Nepal—BON simply means the true religion of Tibet. To the far greater number of other Tibetans, who are not *bonpos*, BON refers to false teachings and practices that were prevalent in Tibet before Buddhism finally succeeded in gaining a firm hold on the country. . . . By Western scholars BON is generally understood as referring to the pre-Buddhist beliefs and practices of the Tibetans (Snellgrove 1967: 1).

4. A standard *rol mo* ensemble consists of cymbals, frame drums with double skins, hand-bells, small hourglass drums with suspended strikers, conch trumpets, long metal trumpets, short trumpets of metal or (rarely) thighbone, double-reed winds, and optional gongs. Not all instruments are required for every performance, however; sometimes, for example, only cymbals and drums are used, while on other occasions the whole ensemble may be played.

5. For example, a monk may mentally produce music played on a lute three times larger than a normal one; such a lute could even be made and carried in a monastic procession, but it would not be played.

6. According to Ellingson (verbal communication), *rgyud can* is probably a corruption of *rgyu rkyen*, in which case "cause and agent" is the more correct label for the stringed category.

7. Classifications of musical instruments presented by the Western scholars Crossley-Holland (n.d.) and Kaufmann (1975: 17–18) divide Tibetan instruments into four categories according to whether they are used to play "melody," "calls," or "signals" or to serve as "time-beaters." In a primarily musical study Kaufmann also implies a grouping of Tibetan monastic music into a nonmusical or ritualistic class (i.e., instruments of no musical significance) and a class of instruments having considerable musical importance. Like the various contemporary classifications of Javanese gamelan instruments, the differences between the classifications of Tibetan instruments presented by Western scholars are due largely to their differing perceptions and analyses of the musical roles of the instruments. Ellingson criticizes Crossley-Holland's and Kaufmann's schemes on the grounds that they are not based on Tibetan musical concepts and practices, that they use incomplete symbolic data linking instruments and deities, and that they are incorrectly based on analogies with non-Tibetan styles with which they are more familiar (Ellingson 1979: 542–43). Ellingson has tried to base his scheme as closely as possible on Tibetan scholarly and musical practice, though of course he is also (though much more consciously) influenced by his own Western preconceptions and purposes.

8. This passage (dated 1042? CE) derives from a text entitled "Drum Lineage of the White, Black and Red Razor of Stag Lal Me 'Bar," which is claimed to have been discovered at an archeological site by Khu tsha Zla 'od (translated in an unpublished manuscript by Ellingson).

CHAPTER SEVEN

1. Translated in Kunst 1949, 142.
2. Translated in Becker (ed.) (1984: 307).
3. Many of these instruments are probably of great age; Javanese charters from the eleventh century mention the names of some of these percussion instruments (see Kunst 1968, 94–95).
4. In Malay areas and in West Java, the operative taxonomical principle is based not on the female/male analogy but on the analogy of mother and child. Pairs of Malay drums in

Riau, for example, are usually called *induk* ("mother") and *anak* ("child"), and the West Javanese *kacapi* (zither) is divided into the large *indung* ("mother") zither and the small *anak* ("child") zither (field information gathered by the author, H. Kartomi, and Ashley Turner).

5. For a discussion of the loud and soft ensembles in Yogyakarta, see Sutton 1982, 123ff and 154ff.

6. In the 1960s gamelan musicians of the Ramayana dance drama at Prambanan went on strike on the matter of their salary ratings, whereupon the minister of tourism, G. P. H. Djatikusumo, ruled that there would be only two levels of payment: the leaders and the others. The strike began after dancers were divided, for salary purposes, into lead dancers and others (Sumarsam, verbal communication).

7. A possible exception is the *rebab* (bowed fiddle), which is an important instrument in the Javanese gamelan. Falk argues that the *rebab* was introduced into Java only since the introduction of Islam (Falk 1978: 60). Also, frame drums of possible Middle Eastern origin are sometimes added to or substituted for double-headed drums in certain rural ensembles, such as in the *prajuritan* theater in the Kopeng area of Central Java (see Kartomi 1973: 196).

8. Violins, plucked strings, and other instruments of Western origin may be juxtaposed with instruments belonging to the Muslim stratum in certain mixed ensembles.

9. For listings and a description of instruments in the various archaic gamelan, see Kunst 1949, 257–74.

10. For descriptions of various small regional gamelan see Kartomi 1973, 163–208 and 1976, 85–130; the rural *gamelan reyog* in Ponorogo, East Java, for example, includes a *slompret, angklung*, drums, and gongs.

11. See Pigeaud 1970, 3:315–16, for locations of these Javanese treatises and details of their references to music, dance, and theater.

12. Kunst described the work but did not date it (Kunst 1949 [1934]: 248). I have been unable to consult the manuscript.

13. Hood's divisions of the instruments of the gamelan are (1) *balungan,* (2) interpunctuating, (3) *panerusan*, and (4) rhythm instruments.

14. I have heard the view of the supremacy of the gong and the drum expressed in many Javanese villages and some court circles. It is supported by the fact that venerable proper names are attributed to gongs, by the high respect traditionally afforded to gong-smiths, and by the reverential references to gongs in Javanese poetry, such as in the *Centhini* (a court poem written in the eighteenth and nineteenth centuries).

CHAPTER EIGHT

1. This quotation from the music theoretician Aristides Quintilianus (c. second to fourth century CE) can be found in Mathiesen 1983, 151, 155.

2. Pythagoras (sixth century BCE) is said to have passed by a forge and heard hammers ring out the intervals of the octave, fifth, and fourth. After inspection he formed the opinion that the different intervals were created by the weights of different hammers producing different notes, a physically impossible explanation but one that greatly influenced his music-theoretical thinking, including his acoustic experiments on the kanon, or octachord (a multistringed instrument referred to in Greek sources; Thomas Mathiesen, personal communication). From this experience the theory of proportions is said to have derived. Nicomachus, Boethius, Isidore of Seville, Guido d'Arezzo, and even some eighteenth-century writers referred to the Greek claim that Pythagoras had discovered the fundamentals of music "from the sound of hammers and of taut strings when plucked" (Isidore of Seville 1980, 13).

3. The Hellenic archaic period covers the sixth and early fifth centuries, the Hellenic classical period the late fifth to the end of the fourth, and the Hellenistic period the third century BCE to approximately the third century CE. Hellenic culture, which evolved when the

Greeks lived in relative isolation, spread to other countries from the beginning of the Hellenistic era (Tatarkiewcicz 1970, 11, 168).

4. In the archaic period, imitation *(mimesis)* meant "the expression of feelings and the manifestation of experiences through movement, sound and words" and probably originally signified "mimicry and the ritual dances of the [Dionysian cult] priests" (Tatarkiewcicz 1970, 16–17). The term also involved philosophical concepts of attraction, similarity, and otherness as well as *katharsis* and the like. Later it came to signify "the representation of reality through art" (Thomas Mathiesen, personal communication; see Else 1958 and Butcher [1911] 1951). In *Republic,* Plato divided the arts into three classes: "arts which utilise things, which produce them and which imitate them" (Tatarkiewcicz 1970, 121). In his classification of the arts, Aristotle stated that "the arts either *complement* Nature with what she is unable to do, or *imitate* her in what she has done" (Tatarkiewcicz 1970, 141), and he included music among the "imitative arts." Imitation he saw as the essential feature of these arts, not only in their means but also their aim (Tatarkiewcicz 1970, 142). See Aristotle's *Physica,* 199a, 15, trans. F. M. Cornford and P. H. Wickstead.

5. *Problems* are not generally considered to have been written by Aristotle, though attributed to him (Thomas Mathiesen, personal communication).

6. On the question of animate and inanimate instruments, see Mathiesen 1984, 264–79, who attempts to show how ethos was created by musicians. Also see Anderson 1966.

7. For example, Eduard Hanslick ([1854] 1957) and Leonard B. Meyer (1956 and 1957) took it upon themselves to explain how musical sound could influence human emotion.

8. The Greeks had no term for music in the sense in which it has been used in the West since the sixteenth century of our era. Their term *mousike*—which was an abbreviation of *mousike techne* ("the art of music")—referred to all activities of the muses, not just music making. It retained the ambiguity of the Greek term for *art,* which included both theory and practice (Tatarkiewcicz 1970, 218). The term *mousike,* when used as a substantive, refers to an epistemological, rather than a technical, quality (see Aristides 1983, 75, n.32).

9. The Pythagoreans were a group that originated in the Dorian colonies in Italy and were interested in moral and religious matters as well as scientific investigations (mainly mathematics). Their founder was Pythagoras, but their scientific endeavors owed more to his successors in the fifth and fourth centuries (Tatarkiewcicz 1970, 80).

10. For an account of this Orphic theory of music see Tatarkiewcicz 1970, 82–83.

11. See Tatarkiewcicz 1970, 218 for a schematic diagram of Aristoxenos's concept.

12. See periodization of Aign 1963, 359 and discussion of the evidence for these instruments in Aign 1963, 30ff.

13. The *krotala* was used to keep the dance rhythm, especially in ceremonies in honor of Cybele and Dionysius (Michaelides 1978, 179).

14. Aristotle also called the *kithara* a "professional" instrument in his *Politics* (8.6.1341A).

15. For discussions on the social role of musical instruments as revealed in Hellenic sonnets and iconographic sources, see Sachs 1924, Sendrey 1974, and Quastens 1930.

16. Much older panpipes have been found outside Greece; for example, one dated about 2000 BCE was found in the southern Ukraine (Aign 1963, 298).

17. Nicomachus, for example, mentioned in a treatise written in the first century of our era that the human speaking voice constituted "continuous sound" (Hickmann 1971, 26).

18. See Tatarkiewcicz 1970, 222, 223, 227, for a discussion of Aristides' historical-musical views. According to Anderson (1980, 585–86), Aristides' treatise, which has been termed "the musical encyclopaedia of antiquity," is heavily derivative, "with nothing by way

of content or organisation that can safely be attributed to Aristides himself"; thus he probably presented "a genuine tradition, possibly handed down in an incomplete form."

> 19. Of instruments, those fitted together of strands closely resemble the ethereal, dry, simple region of the cosmos and part of spiritual nature, being more without passion, immutable, and hostile to wetness . . .; the wind instruments closely resemble the windy, wetter, changeable region, making the hearing overly feminine. . . . The better instruments are similar to the better things, and the lesser instruments are the others. (Aristides 1983, 36)

As Aristides explains, the superiority of the *kithara* to the *aulos* is also established by a legend in which Apollo had a *kithara* and Marsyas an *aulos:*

> These things also demonstrate the legend, they say, that esteemed the instruments and mele of Apollo over those of Marsyas. The Phrygian [Marsyas], having been hung over the river in Celenae after the manner of a wineskin, happens to be in the aerial, full-windy, and dark-colored region, since he is on the one hand above the water and on the other hand suspended from the ether; but Apollo and his instruments happen to be in the purer and ethereal essence, and he is the leader of this essence. (Aristides 1983, 155)

20. Nichomachus also perpetuated the division of instruments into those used to illustrate musical theory and those used for musical practice (Hickmann 1971, 30).

21. Among the percussion *(cruomena)* instruments listed were the *lyra, kithara, barbiton, psalterion,* and *sambyke,* while the winds included the *syrinx, salpinx,* and *hydraulis* as well as the *aulos.*

CHAPTER NINE

1. Translated in Shiloah 1979a.

2. This Arabic legend is mentioned in a number of sources, including one attributed to Hishām ibn al-Kalbī (d. 819) that was reported by his contemporary Mufaddal ibn Salama in his *Kitāb al-malāhi* (Robson 1938, 9–10). Also quoted in Shiloah (1979b, 400–401).

3. Throughout its long history, the *ʿūd* was held in Near Eastern countries to be the king of musical instruments. Many poets extolled its merits, theorists and philosophers used it as a pivot for their theories and cosmological speculations, and some historians and litterateurs thought its creation marked the beginning of music itself (Shiloah 1979b, 395).

4. A verse by al-Hamdūni reads as follows: "He (the *ʿūd*) speaks a language without intimate thoughts. He looks like a thigh annexed to a leg" (quoted in Ibn Khurdādhbih's *Kitāb al-lahw* (see Shiloah 1979b, 402).

5. The *Arab world* in the title of this chapter refers to all areas where the lingua franca is Arabic. Because the Koran is in Arabic, Muslims everywhere are expected to know the language; thus, the Arab world covers a large geographical area. *Arabic* is also used in this chapter, however, to refer in a broader sense to the languages of science in the Muslim world, that is, Arabic, Persian, and Turkish (Shiloah 1981, 20).

6. Shiloah notes that Arab treatises of the ninth and tenth centuries (the earliest surviving Arab writings on music) that contain "scattered references to the musical past . . . may have been partial and tendentious . . . as their authors are simply reiterating what has been handed down . . . by oral tradition" and are "remote in time and spirit from the reality" (Shiloah 1986, 110).

7. Al Khwārizmī, for example, who died in 997, enumerated twenty-two kinds of instruments in his *Mafātīh al-ʿulūm* (The keys of sciences), which included mostly strings but also some winds and some percussion, as well as the organ (the full list is given in Shiloah 1979a, 251). He discussed the manufacturing of instruments as well as their tuning and gave

an especially detailed account of the *'ūd.* A list of sixteen kinds of instruments was given by the Ikhwān al-Ṣafā, a group of "brethren of purity" in their work *Risāla fi'l-mūsīkī* (Tract on music) of the second half of the tenth century (Shiloah 1979a, 231–32). In it they mentioned percussion, winds, and strings, without classifying them as such: *tabl* (cylindrical drum), *duff* (frame drum), *nāy* (flute), *ṣunūdj* (cymbals), *mizmār* (double clarinet), *surnāy* (oboe), *ṣaffāra* (whistle), *salbak* or *khilyāk* (harp or lyre), *shawshal* (fiddle?), *'ūd* (short-necked lute), *tunbūr* (long-necked lute), *djank* (harp), *rabāb* (fiddle), *maāzif* (zither or lyre), *urghān* (organ), and *armūnīkī* (panpipes).

8. The following reading of al-Fārābī's text was given in a personal communication from Amnon Shiloah.

9. Al-Fārābī's inclusion of dance among musical instruments was because of its capacity in common with instruments for producing durational units (in the form of body movements).

10. "The link between music, musical instruments and depravity may be traced back to the sons of Cain in the Bible. The descendants of Seth attempted to extract Cain's sons from their depraved indulgements but alas they themselves fell into the trap of beautiful women, music and intoxicating liquors" (Shiloah 1979b, 398).

CHAPTER TEN

1. The source of this quotation is Praetorius's *Syntagma Musicum,* vol. 2: *De Organographica* (1619) 1980, pt. 1, p. viii.

2. "Haec vero administratur aut intentione ut nervis, aut spiritu ut tibiis, vel his, quae ad aquam moventur, aut percussione quadam, ut in his, quae in concava quaedam aerea feriuntur, atque inde diversi efficiuntur soni" (Boethius 1867, 187) (see translation in Strunk 1950). Apart from the monochord, Boethius gave no examples of strings, but he named the *tibia* and *hydraulis* as examples of winds and described the *acetabula* as an example of percussion without actually naming the instruments (Hickmann 1971, 35).

3. "Percussionalia, ut sunt acitabula aenea & argentea, vel alia, quae metallico rigore percussa, reddunt cum suavitate tinnitum" (Cassiodorus [1784] 1931, 16). Under the percussion category Cassiodorus listed the metal *acetabula,* bells, and small cymbals; strings included various kinds of *cithara,* and the winds the *tibiae, calami, organa,* and *panduria.*

4. The relevant section of the 150th Psalm in the standard 1611 edition reads: "Praise him with the sound of the trumpet, praise him with the harp and the lyre, praise him with tambourine and dancing."

5. Cassiodorus's words were "Flatus in tuba, pulsus in cithara, tinnitus in cymbalis, vox in choro, spirituali harmonia dulcissimus ille concentus, qui non auribus carneis auditur, sed contemplatione purissimae mentis advertitur" (*Expositio in psalterium,* Psalm 150).

6. See relevant quotation from Gundissalinus's *De divisione philosophiae* in Hickmann 1971, 70.

7. See quotations in Aurelianus Gerbert 1931, I: 34.

8. Hickmann (1971, 348) suggested that early authors who put percussion first in their classifications were influenced by this legend, which is referred to in chap. 8.

9. Isidore of Seville also discussed instruments in the order of winds, strings, and percussion in his *Etymologiarum* (see quotation in Pietzsch 1929, 54, n. 7) but this was not his main classification.

10. "To produce every sound, which is the substance of song, there are in fact three means. The first is harmonic, which consists in the singing of the voice. The second is organic, which comes from a stream of air. The third is rhythmic, which achieves musical proportions by striking with the fingers. For sound is produced either by the voice coming from the throat; or by blowing, as with the trumpet or pipe; or by striking, as on the cithara

or any other instrument which sounds when it is struck" (*Etymologiarium*, Isidore of Seville 1980, 14).

11. "Instrumental music consists partly of striking, as upon tympans and strings; partly in blowing, as upon pipes or organs; and partly in giving voice, as in recitals and songs" (Hugh of St. Victor 1961, 69–70).

12. In the thirteenth century, Magister Lambertus divided instruments into the human voice, winds, and percussion as follows: "Nam aliquando voce, aliquando flatu, aliquando tactu exercentur. Voce vero ut hominis, flatu ut tibia, tactu ut psalterio, vel cythara et similia" (Magister Lambertus 1864, 253).

13. Very few writers used schemes other than the Porphyry, Boethian, or Pollux models. However, Ramos de Pareja in the fifteenth century presented a classification comprising only strings and winds (see Hickmann 1971, 83).

14. "Si est ex collisione tunc est musica instrumentalis, cuius instrumenta sunt percussionalia . . . , vel tensilia . . . , vel inflativa" appears in Bacon's *Opus tertium* (1267) (Bacon 1859, 230).

15. Regino of Prüm's terms were *tensible, inflatile,* and *percussionabile* ([1784] 1931, 236).

16. Johannes de Muris's terms were *chordalia* (strings), *foraminalia* (from L. *forare,* meaning "bore") (winds), and *vasalia* (from L. *vas,* meaning "vessel") (percussion) (de Muris [1784] 1931, 114).

17. de Brossard's categories were named *enchorda* or *entata* (a category comprising only instruments with several strings), *pneumatica* or *empneousta* (winds), and *krousta* or *pulsatilia* (percussion) (1703, 116–17).

18. Majer's categories were named *pneumatica* (winds), *pulsatilia* (percussion, including plucked strings), and *chordata* or *fidicina* (bowed strings) (Majer [1732] 1954, 29). *Fidicina* derives from the Old High German word *fidula,* meaning "fiddle."

19. Eisel named his categories *fidicinia, pulsatilia,* and *pneumatica* (1738, 23).

20. "The Lord fashioned man a beautiful, breathing instrument. . . . The instrument of God is loving to men" (translation of passage from Clement's *Exhortation to the Greeks;* van Deusen 1987, 4).

21. Earlier, however, St. Augustine had classified "musical sounds" à la Pollux into those produced by wind instruments (which resulted in "organic music"), those produced by the human voice (which resulted in "harmonic music"), and those produced by percussion and stringed instruments (which resulted in "rhythmic music"). This traditional threefold division of musical sounds, which appeared in St. Augustine's early treatise *De ordine* (2.14, Migne, ed., 32:1014), was also referred to more explicitly by later writers, including the Late Roman Isidore of Seville in his *Sententiae de Musica* ([1784] 1931, 21) and Marchetto of Padua in his *Lucidarium* in the early fourteenth century ([1784] 1931, 64–121; see also H. M. Brown 1984, 27).

22. "Nam musica mundana quae maxime in ipsorum caelorum motibus vel elemento-rum connexione seu temporum varietate conspicitur in suo silenti velocique cursu revolutis caelorum corporibus quam resonantem generat melodiam, ex ea caelesti recipit participatam cuius dulcissimae suavitatis immensitas." (Ugolino of Orvieto 1959, 16).

23. Isidore's instrumental examples were more numerous than those of Cassiodorus. Under wind instruments he included *tubae, calami* (trumpets), *fistulae* (reed instruments), *organa,* and *pandora* (panpipes). Under his percussion category he named a greater number of strings than drums or self-sounding percussion instruments. Strings included the *cythara, psalteria, lyrae,* etc., and the drums included the *tympanum* and *symphonia,* while other percussion instruments included the *cymbalum, sistrum, acitabula,* etc. ([1784] 1931, 22–23).

24. Material in this paragraph is derived from Salmen 1960, 92; see also Bowles 1958, 155–69, and 1954, 115–40. Steven Blum drew my attention to this matter.

25. The copper instrument had three names: *psalterion, cheirorganon,* and *kabithakanthion* (Hickmann 1971, 59).

26. Daniel, chap. 3, mentions the *tubae, fistulae, citharae, sambuccae, psalterii,* and *symphoniae,* omitting percussion instruments. Contemporary instruments mentioned elsewhere in Aegidius's text include the *guitarra, tympanum, lyra, cymbala,* and *sistrum* (Aegidius of Zamora [1784] 1931, 388).

27. "Instruments are divided by some people on the basis of artificial sounds generated by them. They say that sound on instruments is made by the breath, as in trumpets, reed instruments, flutes and organs; or by striking, as in strings, drums, cymbals, and bells. But if all these things are considered more carefully, they are discovered to happen by striking, since every sound is caused by striking" (Grocheo 1967, 18).

28. The drawing is from a manuscript book now held in the Österreichische Nationalbibliothek in Vienna (Cod. S.n. 2639, fol. 4) (H. M. Brown 1984, 25). Brown's method of investigating the fourteenth-century musical instrumentarium by means of iconographical sources is exemplified in his 1984 article. A method of classification by means of iconographical sources is expounded in Brown and Lascelle 1972.

29. String playing was the privilege of King David, and it is therefore not surprising that precedence was given to them, especially in Psalm 33:2, 3; 57:9; 71:22; 92:4; 98:5; 108:3; 144:9; and 147:7 (Hickmann 1971, 90).

30. "Tympanu vil eynander ding muß gewesen sein das man zu dem dienst gottes gebraucht hatt" (Herpaucken, Trumeln und dem päucklin section, Virdung 1931, 23).

31. The *sinfonia* had a wooden wheel that was rotated by a crank and acted as a bow.

32. Hickmann noted this lack of progress in her survey of eighteenth-century classifications of instruments, observing that organological treatises went under in a flood of general literature on music that was being produced for the growing bourgeois musical culture of the time, some of which had a pedagogical purpose and some of which was devoted to monographs on individual instruments (1971, 342).

33. de Brossard's dictionary referred to various bowed and plucked strings (1703, 320), and it divided multistringed instruments into those "plucked with the fingers" (e.g., the lute, theorbo, and harp), those with "sound excited through a stretched string" (e.g., the violin and the hurdy-gurdy), and those with "sound excited by a mechanical agent" (as in the spinet and harpsichord). Eisel grouped the strings in the order of the bowed and then the plucked, without making a formal classificatory distinction between them.

34. The fourteenth-century drawing referred to in H. M. Brown's n. 30a shows Lady Music playing a portative organ. As Brown (1984, 41) pointed out, the choice of this instrument in the work needs no explanation in view of the respect attached to it in the fourteenth century.

CHAPTER ELEVEN

1. Sometimes Sachs called Mahillon's scheme logical. Yet at other times he pointed out that "a completely logical classification is an impossibility because instruments are the artificial contrivances of man. They do not lend themselves to a consistent system as do plants and animals" (1940, 455).

2. Hornbostel and Sachs's regard for logical structure is evident in their expressed approval of the logic of Mahillon's scheme (1914, 6–7) and their criticism of the three-category classification into strings, winds, and percussion, where the first category is governed by a different character from the last two (1914, 6).

3. At the second step, idiophones were divided into the struck, plucked, friction operated, and blown; membranophones were divided into struck and plucked drums, etc.; chordo-

phones were divided into the single and the composite; and aerophones were divided into those with vibrating air confined in the instrument and those with nonconfined vibrating air.

4. Galpin distinguished a category of "electrophonic instruments" in 1937.

5. That is, "their sound vibrations are transformed into electrical vibrations corresponding to the acoustical vibrations amplified by means of vacuum tubes and their associated circuits, and then transformed back again into sound by means of a loudspeaker" (Sachs 1940, 447).

6. Ellingson's objection that sounds produced by electricity (as by lightning bolts or spark gaps) are not used in music is not tenable, but his point about the logical inadmissibility in Sachs's electrophone category of mechanically sounded instruments whose sounds are processed electronically is a valid one (see Ellingson 1979, 544).

7. Linguaphones were a fifth category distinguished by A. E. Cherbuliez, exemplified also by the jew's harp and the plucked chordophone called *kowongan* in Java (see Kunst 1974, 60).

8. Die Beschreibung hat so vorzugehen, dasz sie von funktionell wichtigen Teilen zu den akzessorischen fortschreitet. Die ein Musikinstrument als funktionierendes Gerät ausmachenden Konstruktionsmerkmale sind bestimmt durch die physikalische Beschaffenheit des primär in Schwingungen zu versetzenden Stoffes, dessen Formgebung und Montage, die angewendete Spieltechnik, das Material des primär in Schwingung zu versetzenden Stoffes und schliesslich den zur Erzeugung der Schwingung benutzten Erreger. Das Ideal einer Systematik wäre, diese Elemente so in Relation zu bringen dasz bei gleicher Fragefolge jedes Instrument in seinem ihm allein zukommenden Platz neben dem ihm zunächst verwandten stehen wurde. Da diese Verwandtschaft aber von den verschiedensten Momenten bestimmt sein kann, ist dieses Ziel nicht erreichbar (Dräger 1957, 1290).

9. Picken felt that the objections to the Hornbostel and Sachs scheme were not well founded, that their well-known scheme does not depend on the memorizability of the numerical designations, and that it may be adjusted when the need arises to accommodate any and all purposes (1975, 561, 569). While some of Picken's points are convincing in part, Montagu and Burton are not alone in their belief that the Hornbostel and Sachs scheme cannot always be adapted to new needs.

10. Although Mahillon's use of terms such as *class, subclass, order,* and *suborder* was rejected by Hornbostel and Sachs, a few other organologists have used similar terms, including not only Montagu and Burton but also Norlind (1936), who used the terms *group, sort (Gattung), kind (Art), family,* and *variant.*

11. Minor difficulties of Ramey's faceted system include the fact that it does not discriminate well between double-headed drums and sets of two drums (Ramey 1974, 149–50).

12. Heyde, however, referred in the course of his writings to the threefold division into stringed, wind, and percussion instruments, as well as to Hornbostel and Sachs's four categories of instruments (1975, 121–27).

13. Heyde's scheme has been applied in the wind instrument catalogue in the Karl Marx University's Museum of Musical Instruments in Leipzig (Heyde 1975, 7).

14. n = *nervales Steuerelement,* MS = Energiemengensteuerung, A = *Anreger,* V = *Vermittler,* and W = *Wandler.*

CHAPTER TWELVE

1. Since 1961, members of the International Council for Traditional Music's Study Group on Folk Music Instruments have been debating the meaning of this term, which is still often used in European context. As Stockmann argued (1961), the criterion that ultimately distinguishes a "folk music instrument" from an "art music instrument" is its social function.

A folk music instrument does not necessarily have different ergological or musical characteristics from an art music instrument, nor is it necessarily less perfect technically or found
only in a rural environment. Some art music instruments eventually become folk music
instruments and vice versa; thus the social context is crucial. Elschek (1976, 13), however,
argued that folk and art music instruments are separable in their artistic, consciously
intellectual, and functional aspects, as well as their level of technical development. A. Berner
thought that the use of the two terms should be dispensed with altogether because the
systematic differences between them cannot be firmly delineated, while E. Emsheimer,
F. Hellwig, and I. Macák suggested that the proper classification of folk instruments is
possible only if their uses and functions or social relations are considered, thus returning to
Stockmann's 1961 view (Elschek 1976, 13). Ling discussed the changing concept of folk
music instrument in contemporary industrial society (1981, 53–57).

   2. An article by Becker (1972) in *Studia Instrumentorum Musicae Popularis (SIMP)* deals
with the acoustics of instruments; other articles on acoustics include those by Holy in volume
1; Droysen, Graf, Jost, Meyer, and Tjernlund et al. in volume 2; and Picken in volume 3.

   3. Atanassov, Dević, Trojanowicz, Taari, Mauerhofer, Reinhard, and Traerup wrote
articles about the playing techniques of instruments in volume 6 of *SIMP*.

   4. Instrumental ensembles are the main subject of articles in volume 2 of *SIMP* by
authors including Kumer, Macák, Marcel-Dubois, Markl, Sárosi, Strajnar, and Todorov.

   5. Sound documentation was a main topic of volume 1 of *SIMP* (1969). Volumes 3 and
5 of *SIMP* contain a large number of historical, sociohistorical, or archeological articles, and
volume 4 is devoted to methods of historical research (e.g., Kaden 1976). The only article
on an orally transmitted instrument taxonomy (by Leisiö in volume 5) takes a historical
approach. Vertkov's article in volume 1 deals with the history of a Russian folk instrument
while Harrison's in volume 4 gives a chronology of Celtic folk instruments. Becker 1976
deals with the reception of folk music instruments by the music historian, and Elschek's
article in volume 4 discusses historical source-critical methods. See also Becker 1966 for a
well-known historical study of antique and medieval double-reed instruments.

   6. The ergological approach to classification, the importance of which Elschek,
Stockmann, and others emphasized, takes account of "the qualities showing the degree of
craftsmanship needed to fabricate" (an instrument) (Kunst 1974, 62).

   7. Anthropological or sociological articles are included by such authors as Rhodes in
volume 3 and Baumann, Brandl, Emsheimer, and Geiser in volume 5. Archeological articles
are included in volume 5; they were predated by Kunst's important study of archeological
sources of Hindu-Javanese instruments (1927).

   8. Articles on the player-instrument-music communication system include those by
Koning on the left-hand techniques of Irish fiddles (vol. 6, 80–84) and Ledang on the
Norwegian *Langleik* (vol. 3). A large number of articles on the amateur and professional folk
musicians are included in volumes 3 and 7. Also see Elschek 1970, 41–56.

   9. These scholars were (in decreasing order of number of articles contributed) from the
German Democratic Republic, the Federal Republic of Germany, Czechoslovak Socialist
Republic, Yugoslavia, Sweden, Hungary, Norway, Poland, Bulgaria, Denmark, Austria,
Switzerland, Rumania, the United States, Holland, and France. One article appeared from
each of the following countries: Great Britain, Republic of Ireland, Albania, Finland, and the
USSR. The most prolific of these writers include Sárosi (Hungary), Macák (CSSR), Dević
(Yugoslavia), Atanassov (Bulgaria), Markl (CSSR), Habenicht (Rumania), Sevåg (Norway),
Ling (Sweden), and Benggston and colleagues (Sweden), with theoretically important
articles by Reinecke (GDR), Becker (GDR), and Kaden (GDR). Though they wrote mainly
about instruments in Europe, ranging from Spain and Greece to the Balkans and Scandina-
via, some of them did write articles on instruments in Japan, Nepal, India, Tibet, Persia,

Afghanistan, and North America. Many of the authors share the opinion that the understanding of individual instruments depends on knowing their place in the whole European scene; for example, Emsheimer begins his study of the Swedish wooden trumpet (1969, 87) with the comment that the instrument is found all over Europe wherever the archaic shepherd culture is found. Articles dealing with instruments in the whole European environment are by Moeck in volume 1 and Salmen in volume 2.

10. The problem of mutual comprehensibility between English- and German-educated people is not just one of language and language contrasts but also culturally based differences in discourse structure expectations, as in all interlinguistic communication (see Clyne 1986).

11. See also Elschek's study (1978) of archaic types of holeless overtone flutes in the northern Gemer area.

12. Elschek and Elscheková first adopted a typological approach in their studies of Slovak folk tunes in the 1940s, publishing articles on their findings (see especially those by Elscheková, 1975 and 1981). Elschek then applied a typological method to instruments.

13. "Any apparent inadequacies in the existing Hornbostel/Sachs system are to be remedied by empirical adjustment as and when the need arises. This is the way in which the systematics of biological and other objects has advanced. No difficulties, flowing from the increased volume of material to be mastered, should be allowed to foster ideas of jettisoning the Hornbostel/Sachs system in favour of some ideal system yet to be devised" (Picken 1975, 569). Picken's comment about the way biological systematics has advanced is not supported by Mayr's book (1982) on the subject; on the contrary, Mayr clearly demonstrates that microtaxonomic biological research increasingly replaced the macrotaxonomic approach from the eighteenth century.

14. This point was first made not by Elschek and Stockmann, as Picken intimates (1975, 558), but by Dräger in 1947. Picken argues that the antithesis posed by Elschek and Stockmann between systematics and typology is not as significant as they claim. To him, systematics is not only partly empirical, in that its preliminary sorting is based on an act of perception or intuition, but it may also reflect historical relationships (1985, 558, 563, 565). But Picken's objections are only partly convincing. Systematics is not necessarily devoid of empirical observation or historical implication, it is true, but any preliminary sorting by perception is soon taken over by logically based ordering, as the aim of abstracting generalizations begins to be realized. Indeed, systematics is not designed to depict the complex details of variable forms of instruments or historical change.

15. Elschek chose the various forms of flute as objects of typological research because of their relative morphological and ergological simplicity, and because their theoretical, technical, and historical aspects were (to date) the most thoroughly researched of all instruments (Elschek 1969a, 26).

16. The complementary aspect was explained to me in a communication from Elschek. The study of an instrumentarium may begin with identifying and sifting the instruments into groups with the help, say, of the Hornbostel and Sachs scheme. At the second stage, each instrument is studied in detail and classified typologically into variants, groups of variants, types, and groups of types. (apart from *type,* these names of classificatory steps are to be regarded primarily as working terms [Elschek and Stockmann 1969, 21].) At the third stage, the low-level groupings may then be compared with—and thus either endorse or correct— those of the Hornbostel and Sachs scheme. This procedure can continue to alternate between the macrotaxonomic and microtaxonomic methods in order to clarify any problems that may still remain.

17. Instrumental ensembles are the main subject of articles in volume 2 of *SIMP* by Kumer, Macák, Marcel-Dubois, Markl, Sárosi, Strajnar, and Todorov, among others.

CHAPTER THIRTEEN

1. The groups are the Mandailing, Angkola, Pakpak (Dairi), Toba, and Simelungun, and they are situated around and to the southwest of Lake Toba. The Angkola group is sometimes regarded as having the same culture as the Mandailing. Indeed they are culturally very similar, but the Angkola musical repertoire and style are different from those of the Mandailing. All the groups have similar instruments, on the whole, but their construction, size, arrangements in ensembles, and hierarchy differ considerably in each, as do the rituals, belief system, and history of foreign contact of these peoples. Regional cultural variation also occurs within the groups. Data referred to about these groups were collected by myself and H. Kartomi in four field trips between 1973 and 1985.

2. The only Batak bowed instruments are the spiked bowl lute *(arbab, murbab)* and the necked bowl lute *(hapetan),* both of which are virtually obsolete.

3. Formerly, when jew's harps were widely used, the Batak may also have had a category of "pulled" instruments, like some of their neighbors. The Petalangan Malay in mainland Riau, for example, still play jew's harps by tugging at the strings attached to them, and they call the category *alat nan ditarik* ("pulled instruments"). The other four categories of instruments distinguished in the language are the "beaten instruments" *(alat nan dipukul),* "bowed instruments" *(alat nan digesek),* "blown instruments" *(alat nan ditiup),* and "swung instruments" *(alat nan digoyang),* where the last refers to suspended bells *(gento)* (personal communication from Ashley Turner).

4. A fuller account of the cosmological and socioreligious belief system and its relation to the arts is given in Kartomi 1981, having been elicited from elders, musicians, famous storytellers, and others in the Mandailing villages of Pakantan, Tamiang, Huta Godang, Maga, Muara Soma, and Panyabungan in 1975 and 1978.

5. Instruments that sometimes serve as substitutes for the regular instruments in the main ritual ensembles, however, may be given dualistic attributes, such as the pair of tube zithers called *gondang buluh* ("bamboo drum"); the lowest of its three strings is called "female," and the highest "male" (Simon 1985, 139). The distinction made between female and male flutes *(suling boru* and *suling jantan)* (see Simon 1985, 141) is probably due to their once having been used in a ritual context.

6. According to Simon *jangat* means "cow skin" (1985, 137). My informants gave the former meaning.

7. Another name is *kudong-kudong.* Several of these terms have alternative names or versions of names (see Simon 1985, 134).

8. The reason why female drums are slightly larger than male drums in Mandailing and many other cultures in Southeast Asia may be related to a connection made in ancient thought between pairs of instruments and the *linga-yoni* dichotomy. As Róheim puts it (1972, 325), "The penis is the small part of the body that penetrates deeper into Mother Earth . . . than any other part of the body."

9. Lévi-Strauss exemplifies these structures in territorial and social-structure terms. In his examples of diametric dualism, two phatries occupy the two hemispheres of a village (as in the case of the Great Lakes tribe the Winnebago). In his examples of concentric dualism, a sacred inner circle is surrounded by a profane outer circle (as in the case of the Badui in West Java), which in turn is surrounded by uncleared land. This concentric dualistic structure is actually a triad disguised as a dyad (Lévi-Strauss 1963, 133–39).

CHAPTER FOURTEEN

1. Data referred to in this chapter were collected by myself and H. Kartomi during five field trips to West Sumatra between 1971 and 1986.

2. The Minangkabau sentence translated at the head of this chapter reads "Mahindang manampeh bareh bapiliah atak ciek-ciek." According to legend, the Minangkabau frame drum *indang* was traditionally played at harvest festivals when rice was winnowed; indeed it derived its name from the word *mahindang* ("to winnow") as used in the above saying. The instrument called *indang* is now associated with a Muslim art form of the same name. This frame drum therefore links the Muslim cultural stratum to the pre-Muslim one, which was typified by agricultural and other rites, with their associated musical practices.

3. In the three main upland regions of Minangkabau, gongs were used mainly to mark a royal entry or departure (either in real life or at a theatrical presentation), but since the institution of royalty disappeared centuries ago, the importance of gongs has declined (according to a verbal communication from the late Rasjid Manggis Dt. Rajo Panghulu of Bukit Tinggi).

CHAPTER FIFTEEN

1. Materials for the chapter were kindly supplied by Manolete Mora, who carried out fieldwork among the T'boli in the mid-1980s. His Ph.D. dissertation (1990) discusses T'boli concepts and classification of instruments at some length.

2. Other terms also used in female-male differentiation are *lemnek,* meaning "tiny," and *lembang,* meaning "large," respectively (Mora, personal communication). The same terms also distinguish the moon and the sun and classes of objects. The Javanese distinguish between the "gentle" *(alus)* and the "strong" or "rough" *(kasar)* styles of human character, theatrical roles, and music and dance.

3. Gongs are not native T'boli instruments but have been bartered from neighboring Muslim Magindanaos.

4. Mora discovered that paired barbet birds, which sing antiphonally, are metaphorically linked by the T'boli to the concept of *utom* and *tang.*

CHAPTER SIXTEEN

1. Translated text of a Kpelle song performed by a multiple bow-lute player addressing his instrument before and after an instrumental interlude, which he interprets as his instrument's personal response to him. A *konin* is a triangular frame zither (Stone 1982, 90).

2. The myths referred to in figure 16.1 were collected by Zemp in early 1960. The classification tabled is not known in toto by individual Dan people. Each person knows only a few myths and is therefore not able to present a complete classification (letter from Hugo Zemp, March 1987).

3. Kpelle myths and variants of myths about the origins of instruments (sometimes with several myths or myth-variants attached to an instrument) are very similar to the ones collected by Zemp among the Dan (Stone, personal communication).

4. Personification of instruments also occurs in some other cultures, such as the Javanese (cf. the anthropomorphic/zoomorphic names of parts of the bowed stringed instrument *rebab* in Falk 1978, 59). However, this is not necessarily based on the view of instruments as performers (see fig. 7.4).

5. A taxonomy based on folk conceptions and terminology in the East African kingdom of Ankole in Uganda is similarly based on the character of playing action though not necessarily the playing method of an instrument. The scheme was pieced together by van Thiel (1977), who discussed it with the local people and gained their approval. It has as many steps of division as there are verbs for the different modes of playing action in common linguistic usage, though one term—*okuteera* ("to beat," "hit")—can also be applied to all other playing actions, including plucking, shaking, beating, blowing, and bowing (cf. the

Javanese term *tabuh*, which similarly means "to beat" or "to play" any kind of instrument). Categories are headed by such terms as *okuhonda* ("to stamp," "hit forcibly") and *okushungura* ("to sift," "winnow"), which denotes the playing action for the hand-shaken, flat reed-box rattle.

6. Categories B, C, and D somewhat resemble the ancient Indian *tāta* (stretched string) category, the *avanaddha* (covered instrument) category, and *suṣira* (hollow or tubular) category.

7. The Kpelle share this practice with some other peoples, such as the Toba Batak of North Sumatra, who may, for convenience, substitute a metal can or bottle tapped with a metal rod for the percussion plaque called *hesek-hesek*. I have witnessed such substitutions.

CHAPTER SEVENTEEN

1. Each settlement had a single slit drum; and owning an ensemble was and still is the privilege of a big man *(aaraha)*. The single slit drum is used to send messages concerning daily life, while the ensemble is employed in ceremonial feasts. Magic plays an integral part in the fabrication of an ensemble and intervenes each time the instruments are prepared for playing, while the single slit drum is carved and beaten without magic ritual (Zemp 1978, 54).

2. The equiheptaphonic second is the basic interval in the musical system of 'Are'are panpipe ensembles. The 'Are'are language has words for four intervals: the equiheptaphonic second *(rapi'au)*, the octave *(suri'au)*, the third *(hoami'au)*, and the major second *(hari'au)* (Zemp 1979, 6).

CHAPTER EIGHTEEN

1. The information in the first three paragraphs of this chapter was based on a letter written by Timo Leisiö to me in February 1987.

2. The term *torvi* may have reached Finland in the Neolithic Age along with the birch-bark trumpet (Leisiö, personal communication, 1987).

3. In Estonia the meaning of *pilli* broadened even further and now means "a musical instrument" or even "a piece of sound equipment" (Leisiö, personal communication, 1987).

4. The word *kello*, which is of German origin, means a bell or a jingle. It may once have denoted iron cowbells and the like. Leisiö suggests that it dates back to the Iron Age (0–1000 CE) (personal communication, 1987). The term *kantele* is of Baltic (Litho-Latvian) origin. A type of zither is called *kantele* in the region stretching from Estonia to Karelia as well as in the Veps area of northwest Russia (Leisiö, personal communication, 1987). In the nineteenth century the *kantele* was proclaimed the national instrument of Finland.

5. The word *huilu* dates back to the Bronze Age, being a loan word from early Proto-German culture. *Huilu*, which is related to the German *Schwegel*, may once have denoted a bark flute; that is, its original meaning was probably "flute." However, it has been used only in Finnish, not in Karelian (Leisiö 1985b). The word *sarvi* dates back to the Mesolithic Stone Age (Leisiö, personal communication, 1987).

Bibliography

Aegidius, Johannes, of Zamora. [1784] 1931. *Ars musica*. In *Scriptores ecclesiastici de musica sacra potissimum*, ed. M. Gerbert, vol. 2:369–93. Milan: Bollettino Bibliographico Musicale. Reprint, Milan.

Aign, Bernhard. 1963. *Die Geschichte der Musikinstrumente des agäischen Raumes bis um 700 vor Christus*. Ph.D. diss., Johann Wolfgang Goethe-Universität, Frankfurt-am-Main.

Amaradeva, W. D. 1971. Sinhalese music through the ages and its modern trends. In *The musics of Asia*, ed. J. Maceda. Manila.

Ames, David, and A. V. King. 1971. *Glossary of Hausa music and its social contexts*. Evanston: Northwestern University Press.

Amiot, Joseph Marie. 1780. *Mémoires concernant l'histoire, les sciences, les arts, les moeurs et les usages des chinois, par les missionaires de Pékin*. Vol. 6, *Mémoire sur la musique des Chinois tant anciens que modernes*. Paris.

Ananthapadmanabhan, C. S. 1954. *The veena*. Bangalore: n.p.

Anderson, Warren. 1966. *Ethos and education in ancient Greek music*. Cambridge: Harvard University Press.

———. 1980. Aristides Quintilianus. In *The new Grove dictionary of music and musicians*, ed. S. Sadie, vol. 1:585–86. London: Macmillan.

Aristides Quintilianus. 1983. *On music in three books*. Trans. with introduction, commentary, and annotations by Thomas J. Mathiesen. New Haven and London: Yale University Press.

Aristoxenos of Tarent. 1968. *Harmonikon ta sozomena.*In *Die harmonischen Fragmente des Aristoxenos*, ed. with German translation by P. Marquard. Berlin.

Atwood, Kathy Scholz. 1980. Sri Lanka. In vol. 18 of *The new Grove dictionary of music and musicians*, 32–35, S. Sadie (ed.). London: Macmillan.

Augustine of Hippo. *De ordine* 2.14, in *Patrologiae cursus completus*, 1: *Series latina*, J. P. Migne (ed.). Paris: 1844–64, (1877): 1014.

Bachmann, Werner. 1980. Bow (i). In *The new Grove dictionary of music and musicians*, ed. S. Sadie, vol. 19:825. London: Macmillan.

Bacon, Roger. 1859. *De musica*. In *Opus tertium*, ed. J. S. Brewer, 228ff. London.

Bake, Arnold A. 1930. *The mirror of music: Bydrage tot de Kennis der Voor-Indische muziek*. Paris: Paul Geuthner.

Banerji, Sures Chandra. 1976. *Fundamentals of ancient Indian music and dance*. Ahmedabad: L. D. Institute of Indology.

Barker, Andrew, ed. 1984. *Greek musical writings.* Vol. 1, *The musician and his art.* Cambridge: Cambridge University Press.

Barnickel. 1737. Kurtzgefasstes musicalisches Lexicon; worinnen eine nützliche Anleitung und gründlicher Begriff von der Music enthalten, die Termini technici erkläret, die Instrumente erläutert und die vornehumsten Musici beschrieben sind, nebst einer historischen Beschreibung von der Music Nahmen, Eintheilung, Ursprung, Erfindung, Vermehrung und Verbesserung . . . Alles aus derer besten und berühmtesten Musicorum ihren Schriften mit fleiss zusammen gesucht. . . . Chemnitz. John. Christoph and Joh. David Stössel.

Becker, Heinz. 1966. *Zur Entwicklungsgeschichte der antiken und mittelalterlichen Rohrblattinstrumente.* Hamburg: H. Sikorski.

———. 1972. Historische und systematische Aspekte der Instrumentenkunde. *SIMP* 2:184–96. (See Emsheimer and Stockmann 1969–85.)

———. 1976. Das Volksmusikinstrument in der Rezeption des Musikhistorikers. *SIMP* 4:30–38. (See Emsheimer and Stockmann 1969–85.)

Becker, Judith O. 1980. *Traditional music in modern Java.* Honolulu: University of Hawaii.

———, ed. 1984. *Karawitan: Source readings in Javanese gamelan and vocal music,* vol. 1. Ann Arbor: Center for South and Southeast Asian Studies, University of Michigan.

Berlin, B. 1972. Speculation and the growth of ethnobotanical nomenclature. *Language in Society* 1:51–86.

Bessaraboff, A. 1941. *Ancient European musical instruments.* Cambridge: Harvard University Press.

Bharata-Muni. 1961. *The Nāṭyaśāstra. Trans. M. Ghosh. Calcutta: Asiatic Society.*

Bhattacharya, Arun. 1987. *A treatise on ancient Hindu music.* Calcutta: Bagchi.

Bloch, Maurice. 1977. The past and the present in the present. *Man* 12:278–92.

Boethius, A. M. S. 1867. *De Institutione Musica Libri V,* I, viii. Ed. G. Friedlein. Leipzig, 1867.

Bonanni, Filippo. 1722. *Gabinetto armonico pieno d'istromenti sonori.* . . . Rome.

Bowles, Edmund A. 1954. Haut et bas: The grouping of musical instruments in the Middle Ages. *Musica disciplina* 8:115–40.

———. 1958. La hiérarchie des instruments de musique dans l'Europe féodale. *Revue de musicologie* 42:155–69.

Brown, Howard Mayer. 1984. St. Augustine, Lady Music, and the gittern in fourteenth-century Italy. *Musica disciplina* 38:25–63.

Brown, Howard Mayer, and Joan Lascelle. 1972. *Musical iconography: A manual for cataloguing musical subjects in Western art before 1800.* Cambridge: Harvard University Press.

Brown, Robert E. 1965. The *mṛdanga:* A study of drumming in South India. Ph.D. diss., University of California at Los Angeles. University Microfilms, Ann Arbor.

Bulmer, R. 1967. Why is a cassowary not a bird? A problem of zoological taxonomy among the Karam of the New Guinea highlands. *Man,* n.s. 2:5–25.

_____. 1968. Worms that croak and other mysteries of Karam natural history. *Mankind* 6:621–39.

_____. 1970. Which came first, the chicken or the egghead? In *Echanges et communications,* ed. J. Pouillon and P. Maranda. The Hague: Mouton.

Butcher, S. H. [1911] 1951. "Imitation" as an aesthetic term. In *Aristotle's theory of poetry and fine art, with a critical text and translation of the Poetics.* 4th ed., New York: St. Martin's Press. Reprint, New York: Dover.

Cassiodorus, M. A. 1877. *Expositio in psalterium.* J. P. Migne (ed.), *Patrologia Latina,* vol. 70, col. 1053, Psalm 150.

_____. 1980. *Institutiones.* Book 2, chap. 5, *Cassiodorus, Isidore of Seville.* Trans. H. D. Goode and G. C. Drake. Colorado Springs: Colorado College Music Press, 1980.

Cassiodorus, M. A. [1784] 1931. *Institutiones Musicae.* chap. 5, De musica, in *Scriptores ecclesiastici de musica sacra potissimum,* ed. M. Gerbert, vol. 1:14–19. Milan: Bollettino Biblographico Musicale. Reprint, Milan.

Castellino, G. R. 1972. *Two Sulgi hymns (BC).* Studi Semitici, no. 42. Rome: Istituto di Studi del Vicino Oriente, Universita di Roma.

Clyne, Michael. 1986. Discourse expectations and discourse structures. In *Discourse structures across cultures,* ed. L. Smith. Oxford: Pergamon.

Committee of Editors. 1980b. *Ci Hài* (Dictionary). Volume on art. Shanghai: Publisher of *Ci shu* (Dictionary and encyclopedia).

_____. 1980a. Instrumental music, revised by Fu Jin-rei, chapter in *Minzu yin yue gailun* (Survey of national music). Beijing: Peoples Music Publisher, Institute of Music, Academy of Literature and Art.

Conklin, Harold C. 1954. The relation of Hanunóo culture to the plant world. Ph.D. diss., Yale University. Microfilm.

_____. 1962. Lexicographical treatment in folk taxonomies. In *Problems in lexicography,* ed. F. W. Householder and S. Saporta, 119–41. Folklore and Linguistics Publication no. 21. Bloomington: Indiana University Research Center in Anthropology. Reprinted in Tyler 1969, 41–59.

_____, ed. [1964] 1969. Ethnogenealogical methods. In *Explorations in cultural anthropology,* ed. W. H. Goodenough. New York: McGraw Hill. Reprinted in Tyler 1969, 93–122.

Crossley-Holland, Peter. n.d. *The music of Tibetan Buddhism.* Record 1. Kassel: Bärenreiter-Musicaphon BM 30L2010.

de Brossard, Sebastien. 1703. *Dictionnaire de musique, contenant une explication des termes Grecs, Latins, Italiens, et François.* Paris.

de Muris, Johannes. [1784] 1931. *Summa musicae.* In *Scriptores ecclesiastici de musica sacra potissimum,* ed. M. Gerbert, vol. 3:189ff. Milan: Bollettino Biblographico Musicale. Reprint, Milan.

Dennler, J. G. 1939. Los nombres indigenas an guarani. *Physis* 16 (Buenos Aires).

d'Erlanger, R. 1930. *La musique arabe.* Vol. 1, al-Fārābī—Kitāb l'mūsīqī al-kabīr. Books 1–2. Paris.

de Silva, Lynn A. 1980. *Buddhism: Beliefs and practices in Sri Lanka.* 2d ed. Colombo: Wesley Press.

Deva, B. C. 1977. *Musical instruments.* New Delhi: National Book Trust.

———. 1980. Classification of Indian musical instruments. In *Indian music: A perspective*, ed. G. Kuppuswamy and M. Hariharan, 127–40.

Dharmarama, Dharmakirti, ed. 1951. *Dharmapradipika*. Colombo.

Douglas, Mary. 1966. *Purity and danger: An analysis of concepts of pollution and taboo*. London: Routledge and Kegan Paul.

Dräger, Hans Heinz. 1947. *Prinzip einer Systematik der Musikinstrumente*. Kassel und Basel: Bärenreiter.

———. 1957. Instrumentenkunde. *Die Musik in Geschichte und Gegenwart* 6:1288ff.

Eichborn, Hermann Ludwig. 1881. *Die Trompete in alter und neuer Zeit: Ein Beitrag zur Musikgeschichte und Instrumentationslehre*. Leipzig: Breitkopf und Härtel.

Eisel, Johann P. 1738. *Musicus autodidactos*. Erfurt: Funcken.

Ellingson, Terry. 1979. The mandala of sound: Concepts and sound structures in Tibetan ritual music. Ph.D. diss., University of Madison-Wisconsin.

Elschek, Oskár. 1969a. *System of graphical and symbolic signs for the typology of aerophones* (in Czech, German, and English). Bratislava: Vydatelstvo Slovenskej Académie Vied.

———. 1969b. Typologische Arbeitsverfahren bei Volksmusikinstrumenten. *SIMP* 1:23–40. (See Emsheimer and Stockmann, 1969–85.)

———. 1970. Mensch-Musik-Instrument: Funktionelle Schichtung der Primärformen. In *Musik als Gestalt und Erlebnis: Festschrift Walter Graf zum 65. Geburtstag*, 41–56. Vienna: Böhlhaus.

———. 1978. Archäische Typen von grifflochlosen Obertonflöten im nördlichen Gemer-Gebiet (Instrumente, Musikalisches Repertoire, Instrumentalstil) (in Czech with German summary). *Gemer, Národopisné Štúdie* 3.

Elschek, Oskár, and Erich Stockmann. 1969. Zur Typologie der Volksmusikinstrumente. *SIMP* 1:11–22. (See Emsheimer and Stockmann 1969–85.)

Elscheková, Alicia. 1975. Systematisierung, Klassifikation, und Katalogisierung von Volksliedweisen. In *Handbuch des Volkslieds*, vol. 2:549–82. Munich: Fink.

———. 1981. Vergleichende typologische Analysen der vokalen Mehrstimmigkeit in den Karpaten und auf dem Balkan. In *Statigraphische Probleme der Volksmusik in den Karpaten und auf dem Balkan*, ed. A. Elscheková, 159–258. Bratislava: Slovak Academy of Science.

Else, Gerald F. 1958. "Imitation" in the fifth century. *Classical Philology* 53:73–90.

Emsheimer, Ernst. 1969. Zur Typologie der schwedischen Holztrompeten. *SIMP* 1:87–99. (See Emsheimer and Stockmann 1969–85.)

Emsheimer, Ernst, and Erich Stockmann, (eds.) 1967–86. Handbuch der europäischen Volksmusikinstrumente, series 1, parts 1–5. Leipzig: VEB Deutscher Verlag für Musik; Llubljana: Slovenska akademija znanostie in umetnosti, Inštitut za slovensko narodopisje.

———, eds. 1969–85. *Studia instrumentorum musicae popularis (SIMP)*, vols. 1–8. Stockholm; Musikhistoriska Museet.

Eysenck, H. J., et al., eds. 1972. *Encyclopedia of philosophy*. New York: Herder and Herder.

Fa-hsien, [1886] 1965. *A record of Buddhistic kingdoms*. Trans. James Legge. New York: Paragon and Dover.

Falk, Catherine. 1978. The tarawangsa—A bowed stringed instrument from West Java. In *Studies in Indonesian music*, ed. M. Kartomi. Clayton: Centre of Southeast Asian Studies, Monash University.

Farmer, H. G. [1929] 1973. *A history of Arabian music to the thirteenth century*. London: Luzac and Co. Reprint.

————. 1965. *The sources of Arabian music*, second edition, Leiden. First edition: Bearsden, 1940.

————. 1966. *Islam: Musikgeschichte in Bildern*. Vol. 3, *Musik des Mittelalters und der Renaissance*. Leipzig: VEB Deutscher Verlag für Musik.

Feld, Steven. 1982. *Sound and sentiment: Birds, weeping, poetics, and song in Kaluli expression*. Philadelphia: University of Pennsylvania Press.

Finnegan, Ruth. 1980. *Oral poetry*. Cambridge: Cambridge University Press.

Flora, Reis. 1983. Miniature paintings: Important sources for music history. In *Performing arts in India*, ed. Bonnie Wade. Lanham: University Press of America.

Frake, Charles D. [1962] 1969. The ethnographic study of cognitive systems. In *Anthropology and human behaviour*. eds. Thomas Gladwin and William C. Sturtevant, Washington, D.C.: Anthropological Society of Washington. Reprinted in Tyler, 1969, 28–40.

Galpin, Francis. [1910] 1965. *Old English instruments of music: Their history and character*. London: Shenval.

————. 1937. *A textbook of European musical instruments: Their origin, history, and character*. London: Williams and Nowgate.

Geertz, Clifford. 1973. Person, time, and conduct in Bali. Reprinted in *The Interpretation of Culture*. New York: Basic Books.

Gerbert, Martin. 1931 [1963]. *Scriptores ecclesiastici de musica sacra potissimum*. St. Blasien, 1784/R 1963, 3/1931.

Ghosh, Manomohon, trans. 1961. *Nāṭyaśāstra*. Calcutta: Asiatic Society.

Gimm, Martin. 1966. *Das Yüeh-fu Tsa-Lu des Tuan An-Chieh. Studien zur Geschichte von Musik, Schauspiel, und Tanz in der T'ang-Dynastie*. Wiesbaden: Harrassowitz.

Gitosaprodjo, Sulaiman. 1984. Ichtisar teori karawitan dan teknik menabuh gamelan (Theory and technique of gamelan playing). In *Karawitan*, ed. J. Becker, vol. 1:335–88. Ann Arbor: University of Michigan.

Grame, Theodore C. 1963. Review of the Baines/Wachsmann translation of Hornbostel and Sachs's "A Classification of Musical Instruments." *Ethnomusicology* 7 (1):138.

Grocheo, Johannes de. 1967. *Concerning music (De musica)*. Trans. A. Seay. Colorado Springs: Colorado College Music Press.

Haavio, Martti. 1952. Väinamöinen's kantele music. In *Väinamöinen: Eternal sage. Folklore Fellows Communications* 61 (144): 140–73.

Hall, Edward T. 1984. *The dance of life: The other dimension of time*. New York: Anchor Press, Doubleday.

Hanslick, Eduard. [1854] 1957. *The beautiful in music*. First German edition, 1854. Indianapolis, New York: Liberal Arts Press.

Hariharan, M. 1979. Dikshitar and Hindustani music. In *Readings on Indian music,* ed. G. Kuppuswamy and M. Hariharan, 172–77. Trivandrum: College Book House.

Hartmann, Hildegard. 1978. "Kinderinstrumente"—Versuch einer Bestimmung aus (volks)musikinstrumentenkundlichen Sicht. In *Beiträge zur Volksmusik in Tirol,* ed. W. Deutsch et al, 107–14. Innsbruck.

Heyde, Herbert. 1975. *Grundlagen des natürlichen Systems der Musikinstrumente: Beiträge zur musikwissenschaftlichen Forschung in der DDR.* Leipzig: VEB Deutscher Verlag für Musik.

———. 1977. Eine indische Klassification der Musikinstrumente. *Archiv für Musikwissenschaft,* 34 (2):48–152.

Hickmann, Ellen. 1971. *Musica instrumentalis: Studien zur Klassifikation des Musikinstrumentariums im Mittelalter.* Baden-Baden: Valentin Koerner.

———. 1981. Der Spieler in Tiergestalt. *SIMP* 7:58–64. (See Emsheimer and Stockmann 1969–85.)

Hipkins, Alfred James. 1896. *A description and history of the pianoforte and of the older keyboard stringed instruments.* Edinburgh: A. and C. Black.

Honko, Lauri O. 1979. Finno-Ugric religion. *Encyclopaedia Britannica* 7:310–13.

Hood, Mantle. 1954. *The nuclear theme as a determinant of paṭet in Javanese music.* Groningen and Djakarta: J. B. Wolters.

———. 1971. *The ethnomusicologist.* New York: McGraw Hill.

Hornbostel, Erich M. von. 1933. The ethnology of African sound instruments. *Africa* 6:129.

Hornbostel, Erich M. von, and Curt Sachs. [1914] 1961. Systematik der Musikinstrumente: Ein Versuch. *Zeitschrift für Ethnologie* 45:3–90, 553–90. Translated by A. Baines and K. Wachsmann, under the title "A classification of Musical Instruments." *Galpin Society Journal* 14:3–29.

Hugh of St. Victor. 1961. *The Didascalicon.* Trans. with introduction and notes by Jerome Taylor. New York and London: Columbia University Press.

Husmann, Heinrich. 1938. Olympos: Die Anfänge der griechischen Enharmonik. *Jahrbuch Peters* 44 (for 1937): 29–44.

———. [1784] 1931. *Sententiae de musica.* In *Scriptores ecclesiastici de musica sacra potissimum,* ed. M. Gerbert, vol. 1:21. Milan: Bollettino Bibliographico Musicale. Reprint, Milan.

———. 1962. *Isidori Hispalensis Episcopi Etymologiarium sive Originum Libri XX.* Ed. W. M. Lindsay. London, Glasgow, New York, etc:

Isidore of Seville. 1980. *Etymologies Book III, Chapter 15–23,* in *Cassiodorus, Isidore of Seville.* Trans. H. D. Goode and G. C. Drake. Colorado Springs: Colorado College Music Press, 1980.

Izikowitz, Karl G. 1935. *Musical and other sound instruments of the South American Indians.* Göteborg: Wettergren and Kerber.

Jain, J. C. 1985. *Life in ancient India: As depicted in the Jain canon and commentaries, sixth Century BC to seventeenth Century AD,* (second revised and enlarged edition 1985). New Delhi: Munshiram Manoharlal.

Jaini, P. S. 1979. *The Jain path to purification.* Berkeley and Los Angeles: University of California Press.

Kaden, Christian. 1976. Methoden der graphischen Modellierung sozialhistorischer Prozesse als Hilfmittel bei der Erforschung instrumentaler Volksmusik. *SIMP* 4:39–44. (See Emsheimer and Stockmann 1969–85.)

Kapadia, Hiralal. 1970. Jain data about musical instruments: A monograph on music, Parts I and II. *Sangeet Kala Vihar English Supplement* 3:44–60, 4:36–50. (First published in *Journal of the Oriental Institute* 2 [3] [1953]: 263–392.)

Kaplan, Abraham. 1964. *The conduct of inquiry.* San Francisco: Chandler Publishing Co.

Kartomi, Margaret J. 1973. Music and trance in Central Java. *Ethnomusicology* 17(May): 163–208.

_____. 1976. Performance, music, and meaning of Reyog Ponorogo. *Indonesia* 22:85–130.

_____. 1980. Musical Strata in Sumatra, Java and Bali. In *Musics of many cultures,* ed. E. May, 111–33. Berkeley and Los Angeles: University of California Press.

_____. 1981. Lovely when heard from afar: Mandailing ideas of musical beauty. In *Five essays on the Indonesian arts,* ed. M. Kartomi. Clayton: Centre of Southeast Asian Studies, Monash University.

_____. 1983. *The Mandailing people of Sumatra, Angkola.* Bärenreiter Record, BM 30 SL 2567, Musicaphon, Kassel.

_____. 1985. *Musical instruments of Indonesia.* Melbourne: Indonesian Arts Society.

_____. 1986. Tabut—A Shi'a ritual transplanted from India to Sumatra. In *Nineteenth and twentieth century Indonesia,* ed. D. P. Chandler and M. C. Ricklefs, 141–62. Clayton: Centre of Southeast Asian Studies, Monash University.

Kassler, Jamie C. 1984. Organon: Musical and logical instrument. In *Problems and solutions: Occasional essays in musicology presented to Alice M. Moyle,* ed. J. C. Kassler and J. Stubington. Sydney: Hale and Ironmonger.

Kaufmann, Walter. 1975. *Tibetan Buddhist chant: Musical notations and interpretations of a song book by the Bkah Brgyud Pa and Sa Skya Pa sects.* Bloomington and London: Indiana University Press.

Kay, Paul. 1966. Comments on Colby. *Current Anthropology* 7 (1):20–23. Reprinted in Tyler 1969, 78–90.

_____. 1975. Synchronic variability in diachronic change in basic color terms. *Language in Society* 4:251–70.

Kinkeldey, Otto. 1910. *Orgel und Klavier in der Musik des 16. Jahrhunderts: Ein Beitrag zur Geschichte der Instrumentalmusik.* Leipzig: Breitkopf und Härtel.

Kishibe, I. 1980. China. In *The new Grove dictionary of music and musicians,* ed. S. Sadie, 251–52. London: Macmillan.

Koerner, Stefan. 1979. Classification Theory. *Encyclopaedia Britannica.* 15th ed. *Macropaedia* 4:691.

Koning, Jos. 1979. "That old plaintive touch," On the relation between tonality, in Irish traditional dance-music and the lefthand technique of fiddles in East Co. Clare. *SIMP* 6:80–84. (See Emsheimer and Stockmann 1969–85.)

Kothari, K. S. 1968. *Indian folk musical instruments.* New Delhi: Snageet Natak Akademi.

Krickeberg, Dieter. 1975. The documentation of musical instruments. *CIMCIM* (*Bulletin du Comité International des Musées et Collections d'Instruments de Musique*). *Newsletter* 2:25, 28.

Krishna Murthy, K. 1985. *Archaeology of Indian musical instruments.* Delhi: Sundeep Prakashan.

Kun dga' bsod nams. [1624] 1969. *Rig pa'i gnas las bzo rig pa'i bye brag Dpal Sa skya Paṇḍita'i gsung Rol mo'i bstan boos kyi rnam par bshad pa 'Jam dbyangs bla ma dgyes pa'i snyan pa'i sgra dbyangs blo gsal yid 'phrag 'phrin las yangs khyab.* Dharamsala: Bod gzhung chos don Lhan khang.

Kunst, Jaap. 1939. Music in Nias. *Internationales Archiv für Ethnographie* 38:1–92.

———. 1949. *Music of Java—Its history, its theory and its technique.* 2d ed. 2 vols. The Hague: Martinus Nijhoff. (First Dutch edition, 1934.)

———. 1968. *Hindu-Javanese musical instruments.* 2d ed. The Hague: Martinus Nijhoff. (First Dutch edition, 1927.)

———. 1969. *Ethno-musicology.* The Hague: Martinus Nijhoff.

———. 1974. *Ethnomusicology: A study of its nature, its problems, methods, and representative Personalities, to which is added a bibliography.* The Hague: Martinus Nijhoff.

Kvifte, Tellef. 1981. On variability, ambiguity, and formal structure in the Harding fiddle music. *SIMP* 7:102–7. (See Emsheimer and Stockmann 1969–85.)

Lambertus, Magister. 1864. *Tractatus de musica.* In *Tractatus de musica.* In *Scriptores de musica medii aevi,* ed. E. de Coussemaker, vol. 1:182ff. Paris.

Ledang, Ola Kai. 1972. On the acoustics and the systematic classification of the Jew's-Harp. *Yearbook of the International Folk Music Council* 4:94–103.

Legge, James. 1966. *The Chinese classics.* Vol. 4, *Shih ching* (The book of poetry) IV, i(I), 9. Vol. 5, *The* Ch'un ts'ew *with the* Tso chuen. London: Trubner, 1871–72. 18th reprint, Taipei: Wen-hsing shu-tien.

Leisiö, Timo. 1977. The taxonomy and historical interpretation of the Finnish pastoral aerophones. *SIMP* 5:45–50. (See Emsheimer and Stockmann 1969–85.)

———. 1983. *Suomen ja karjalan vanhakantaiset torvi-ja pillisoittimet* (Finnish and Karelian *torvi-* and *pilli-*instruments). Kaustinen.

———. 1985a. Gedanken über die Beziehungen von finnischen und europäischen Trompeten, Flöten, und Klarinetten in der Frühgeschichte. *SIMP* 8:147–56. (See Emsheimer and Stockmann 1969–85.)

———. 1985b. *Rapapallit ja Lakuttimet (Ancient Finnish musical instruments)* (in Finnish and English). Kansanmusiikki-instituutin julkaisuja, Kauhava.

Levin, Flora R. 1967. Nicomachus of Gerasa, *Manual of harmonies:* Translation and commentary. Ph.D. diss. Columbia University, New York.

Lévi-Strauss, Claude. 1963. Do dual organisations exist? In *Structural Anthropology.* New York: Basic Books. (First French edition, 1958.)

———. 1966. *The Savage Mind.* Chicago: University of Chicago Press. (First French edition, 1962.)

Liang, David. 1972. *The Chinese Ch'in.* San Francisco: Chinese National Music Association and San Francisco Conservatory of Music.

Ling, Jan. 1967. *Studier i ett folkligt musikinstrument* (The keyed fiddle: Studies on a folk instrument). Musikhistoriska museets skrifter 2. Stockholm.

———. 1981. Spielen von Volksmusikinstrumente in der Industriegesellschafts Schwedens. *SIMP* 7:53–57. *(See Emsheimer and Stockmann 1969–85.)*

Lund, C. 1980. Methoden und Probleme der nordischen Musikarchäologie. *L'arte musicale in Italia* 52, Fasc. I., Jan–July: 1–13.

Lysloff, René T. A., and Jim Matson. 1985. A new approach to the classification of sound-producing instruments. *Ethnomusicology* 29 (2):213–36.

McNeil, Adrian. The Expression of Authority in Musical Development: A Study of the Sarod in Hindustani Music. Ph.D. thesis in progress, Monarch University.

McPhee, Colin. 1966. *Music in Bali.* New Haven: Yale University Press.

Mahillon, Victor-Charles. 1893[1880].*Catalogue descriptif et analytique de Musée Instrumental du Conservatoire Royal de Musique de Bruxells*, vol. I, second edition. Paris: Gand (1–5: 1893–1922).

Majer, Joseph F. B. C. [1732] 1954. *Museum musicum.* Ed. Heinz Becker. Kassel und Basel: Bärenreiter.

Malalasekara, G. P., ed. 1935. *Vamsatthappakasini.* London: Pali Text Society.

Malm, W. P. 1967. *Music cultures of the Pacific, the Near East, and Asia.* Englewood Cliffs, N.J.: Prentice-Hall.

———. 1974. A computer aid in musical instrument research. *SIMP* 3:119–22. (See Emsheimer and Stockmann 1969–85.)

Mansukhani, Gobind Singh. 1982. Musical instruments. In *Indian classical music and Sikh Kirtan*, 49–65. New Delhi: Oxford and Indian Book House.

Marcel-Dubois, Claudie. 1941. *Les instruments de musique de l'Inde ancienne.* Paris: Presses Universitaires de France.

———. 1983–84. Typology and classification in musical organology: A museum perspective. Trans. H. La Rue. *CIMCIM Newsletter* 11:36–52.

Marchetto of Padua. [1874]. 1931. *Lucidarium.* In *Scriptores ecclesiastici de musica sacra potissimum*, ed. M. Gerbert, vol. 3:64–121. Milan: Bollettino Bibliographico Musicale. Reprint, Milan.

Martopangrawit, Raden Lurah. 1984. Catatan-catatan pengetahuan Karawitan (notes on gamelan playing). In *Karawitan*, ed. J. Becker, vol. 1:1–244. Ann Arbor: University of Michigan.

Mathiesen, Thomas. 1974. *A bibliography of sources for the study of ancient Greek music: Music indexes and bibliographies.* Vol. 10. Hackensack, New Jersey: Boonin.

———. 1984. Harmonia and ethos in ancient Greek music. *Journal of Musicology* (3):264–79.

Matthieson, Johann. 1713. *Das Neu-Eröffnete Orchestre, oder Universelle und gründliche Anleitung wie ein Galant Homme einen volkommen Begriff von der Hoheit und Würde der edlen Music erlangen möge.* Hamburg.

Mayr, Ernst. 1982. *The growth of biological thought: Diversity, evolution, and inheritance.* Cambridge, Mass., and London: Belknap Press.

Mersenne, Marin. 1636–37. *Harmonie universelle, contenant la théorie et la pratique de la musique.* Ed. F. Lesure. 3 vols. Paris.

Meyer, Leonard B. 1956. *Emotion and meaning in music.* Chicago: University of Chicago Press.

———. 1957. *Music, the arts, and ideas.* Chicago: University of Chicago Press.

Michaelides, Solon. 1978. *The music of ancient Greece: An encyclopaedia.* London: Faber and Faber.

Mitani, Yoko. 1980. *A study of long-zithers and their music in the Far East.* Tokyo: Zenongakufu.

Moeck, Hermann A.. 1951. Ursprung und Tradition der Kernspaltflöten des europäischen Volkstums in der Vorzeit und die Herkunft der musikgeschichtlichen Kernspaltflötentypen. Dr. Phil. diss., University of Göttingen.

Montagu, Jeremy, and John Burton. 1971. A proposed new classification system for musical instruments. *Ethnomusicology* 15 (1):49–70.

Montandon, George V. 1919. La généalogie des instruments de musique et les cycles de civilisation. Etude suivie du catalogue des instruments de musique du Musée ethnographique de Genève. *Archives Suisses d'Anthropologie Générale* 3:1–120.

Moorer, James A. 1977. Signal processing aspects of computer music: A survey. *Proceedings of the Institute of Electrical and Electronics Engineers* 65 (8):1108–37.

Mora, Manolete. 1987. The sounding pantheon of nature: T'boli instrumental music in the making of an ancestral symbol. *Acta Musicologica* 65:187–212.

———. 1990. Interpreting *Utom:* An ethnographic account of the musical instrumental practice of the T'boli of Mindonao, Philippines. diss., Monash University.

Nārada. 1920. *Sangitamakaranda.* Trans. M. R. Telang. Gaekwad Sanskrit Series. Baroda.

Needham, Joseph, and Kenneth Robinson. 1962. Sound (acoustics). In *Science and civilisation in China. Vol. 4, Physics and physical technology,* vol. 1: *Physics.* Cambridge: Cambridge University Press, 126–228.

Nicomachus. 1895. *Enchiridion harmonikes.* In *Musici scriptores Graeci,* ed. Carl Jan.

Norlind, Tobias. 1932. Musikinstrumentensystematik. *Svensk Tidskrift for Musikforskning* 14:95–123.

———. [1936] 1939. *Systematik der Saiteninstrumente* I-II. Stockholm: 1936. Hanover: 1939 (translation).

Odo. [1784] 1931. *Dialogus de musica.* In *Scriptores ecclesiastici de musica sacra potissimum,* ed. M. Gerbert, vol. 1:251–303. Milan: Bollettino Bibliographico Musicale. Reprint, Milan.

Olson, Dale A. 1986. Note on "corpophone." *Newsletter of the Society for Ethnomusicology* 20 (4):5.

Ong, Walter J. 1971. *Rhetoric, Romance, and Technology.* Ithaca: Cornell University Press.

Palisca, Claude V. 1980. Theory, theorists. *The new Grove dictionary of music and musicians,* ed. S. Sadie, vol. 18:740–62. London: Macmillan.

Parker, Ralph Halstead. 1979. Dewey decimal classification, Library science. *Encyclopaedia Britannica.* 15th ed. *Micropaedia* 3:508. *Macropaedia* 10:869.

Pian, Rulan Chao. 1967. *Sonq dynasty musical sources and their interpretation.* Cambridge: Harvard University Press.

Pian, Rulan Chao, S. Kishibe, and Bell N. Yung. 1981. China, sec. 1–4. In *The new Grove dictionary of music and musicians,* ed. S. Sadie, 4:245–62. London: Macmillan.

Picken, Lawrence E. R. 1975. Postscript. In *Folk musical instruments in Turkey,* 557–70. London: Oxford University Press.

Pietzsch, Gerhard. 1929. Die Klassifikation der Musik von Boetius bis Ugolino von Orvieto. Halle (Saale): Karras, Kröber, and Nietschmann.

Pigeaud, Theodore. 1960, 1970. *The literature of Java.* Vol. I, Vol. III. The Hague: Martinus Nijhoff.

Poerbapangrawit, Kodrat. 1984. Gendhing Jawa (Javanese gamelan works). In *Karawitan,* ed. J. Becker, vol. 1:409–38. Ann Arbor: University of Michigan.

Powers, Harold, and Kapila Vatsayan. 1980. India. In *The new Grove dictionary of music and musicians,* ed. S. Sadie, vol. 9:69–141, 158–66. London: Macmillan.

Praetorius, Michael. 1980. *The syntagma musicum.* Vol. 2, *De organographica,* first and second parts. Trans. H. Blumenfeld. Reprint, New York: Da Capo Press.

Prajanananda, Swami. 1979. Music in the Ramayana, Mahabharata, and Harivamsa. In *Music of the South-Asian peoples: A historical study of music of India, Kashmere, Ceylon, and Bangladesh and Pakistan,* 182–208. Calcutta: Ramakrishna Vedanta Math.

Quastens, J. 1930. *Musik und Gesang in den Kulten heidnischen Antike und der christlichen Frühzeit.* Munster.

Raman, V. P. 1979. The music of the ancient Tamils. In *Readings on Indian music,* ed. G. Kuppuswary and M. Hariharan, 80–99. Trivandrum: College Book House.

Ramey, Michael. 1974. A classification of musical instruments for comparative study. Ph.D. diss., University of California at Los Angeles.

Regino of Prüm. [1784] 1931. *Epistola de harmonica institutione.* . . . In *Scriptores ecclesiastici de musica sacra potissimum,* ed. M. Gerbert, vol. 1:230–47. Milan: Bollettino Bibliographico Musicale. Reprint, Milan.

Reinecke, Hans-Peter. 1974. Einige Bermerkungen zur methodologischen Basis instrumentaler Forschung. *SIMP* 3:176–79. (See Emsheimer and Stockmann 1969–85.)

Reinhard, Kurt. 1960. Beitrag zu einer neuen Systematik der Musikinstrumente. *Die Musikforschung* 13:160–64.

Risset, Jean-Claude, and David L. Wessel. 1982. Exploration of timbre by analysis and synthesis. In *The Psychology of Music,* ed. Diana Deutsch. New York: Academic Press.

Robinson, Kenneth. 1980. *A critical study of Chu Tsai-Yü's contribution to the theory of equal temperament in Chinese music.* Wiesbaden: Steiner.

Robson, J. 1938. *Ancient Arabian musical instruments as described by Muffaḍḍal ibn Salama, the Unique Manuscript of the Kitāb al-malahī* (text in facsmile and translation). Glasgow.

Róheim, Géza. 1972. *Animism, magic, and the divine king.* New York: International Universities Press. (First edition, 1930.)

Sachs, Curt. [1913] 1964. *Reallexikon der Musikinstrumente.* New York: Dover.

———. 1924. *Musik des Altertums: Griechenland und Rom.* Breslau: Jedermanns Bücherei, Joh. Wolf.

———. [1929] 1965. *Geist und Werden der Musikinstrumente.* Reprint, Berlin: Hilversum.

———. 1940. *The history of musical instruments.* New York: Norton.

Sakurai, Tetsuo. 1980. An outline of a new systematic classification of musical instruments (in Japanese with English summary). *Journal of the Japanese Musicological Society* 25(1):11–21.

———. 1981. The classification of musical instruments reconsidered. *Kokuritsu Minzokuyaku Hakubutsukan,* 6 (4):824–31.

Salmen, Walter. 1960. *Der fahrende Musiker im europäischen Mittelalter.* Kassel: Johann Philipp Hinnenthal-Verlag.

Sambamoorthy, P. 1967. *The flute.* Madras: Indian Music Publishing House.

Sarmadee, Shahab, ed. 1978. *Ghunyat-ul-Munya: The earliest known Persian work on Indian music.* Bombay: Asia Publishing House.

Sárosi, Bálint. 1967. *Die Volksmusikinstrumente Ungarns. Handbuch der europäischen Volksmusikinstrumente,* vol. 1 (1). Leipzig: VEB Deutscher Verlag für Musik.

———. 1976. Instrumentale Volksmusik in Ungarn. *SIMP* 4:115–41. (See Emsheimer and Stockmann 1969–85.)

Sastri, K. S. Ramaswamy. 1966. *Indian aesthetics—Music and dance.* Madras: Sri Venkaleswara University.

Schaeffner, André. 1932. D'une nouvelle classification méthodique des instruments de musique. *Revue Musicale* (Sept.–Oct.): 215–31.

———. [1936] 1968. *Origine des instruments de musique.* Paris. Reprint, New York: Johnson Reprint.

Sedaraman, J. E. 1959. *Nrtyaratnakaraya.* Colombo.

Sendry, Alfred. 1974. *Music in the social and religious life of antiquity.* Rutherford: Fairleigh Dickinson University.

Seneviratna, Anuradha. 1979. Pancaturya Nada and the Hewisi Puja. *Ethnomusicology* 23 (1):49–56.

Shakuntala, K. V. 1968. Martial musical instruments of ancient India. *Sangeet Natak* 10.

Shastri, K. Vasudeva. 1973. Dance in Sanskrit literature. *Journal of the Indian Musicological Society* 3:19–54, 4:36–50.

Shiloah, Amnon. 1979a. *The theory of music in Arabic writings (c. 900–1900): Descriptive catalogue of manuscripts in libraries of Europe and the USA.* Répertoire International des Sources Musicales, ser. B10. Munich: G. Henle.

———. 1979b. The ʿūd and the origin of music. In *Studia Orientalia: Memoriae D. H. Baneth Dedicata.* Jerusalem: Magnes.

———. 1981. The Arabic concept of mode. *Journal of the American Musicological Society* 34 (1):19–42.

————. 1986. Music in the pre-Islamic period as reflected in Arabic writings and the first Islamic centuries. *Jerusalem Studies in Arabic and Islam* 7:109–20.

Simon, Artur. 1985. The terminology of Batak instrumental music in northern Sumatra. *Yearbook for Traditional Music* 13:113–45.

Singh, Thakur Jaideva. 1979. Samadevic music. *Readings on Indian Music,* 19–25.

Sisodia, V. N. R. 1966 A note on the classification of the musical instruments of the Varlis. *Ethnos* 31:120–30.

Sivaramamurti, C. n.d. *Bulletin of the Madras Government Museum. IV.* Madras.

Snellgrove, David. 1967. *The nine ways of Bon.* London: Oxford University Press.

Snellgrove, David, and Hugh Richardson. 1968. *A cultural history of Tibet.* New York: Praeger.

Steszewski, Jan. 1970. Z zagadnień teorii i metod polskich badań folkloru muzycznego (Sytuacja i tendencje w okresie po 1945 r.). *Muzyka* 15 (2):11–26. (Problems of the theory and method in Polish research on folklore in music [The situation and tendencies since 1945]. *Polish Musicological Studies* 1 (1977): 237–60.)

Stockmann, Erich. 1961. Zum Terminus Volksmusikinstrument. *Forschung und Fortschritte* 35 (11):337–40.

————. 1964. Die europäischen Volksmusikinstrumente: Möglichkeiten und Probleme ihrer Darstellung in einem Handbuch. *Deutsches Jahrbuch für Volkskunde* 10:238–53.

————. 1965. Volksmusikinstrumente und Arbeit. *Deutsches Jahrbuch für Volkskunde* 11:245–59.

————. 1972. Internationale und interdiziplinäre Zusammenarbeit in der Volksmusikinstrumentenforschung. *SIMP* 2:11–23. (See Emsheimer and Stockmann 1969–85.)

————. 1974a. Interethnische Kommunikationsprozesse und die Verbreitung von Musikinstrumenten. *Beiträge zur Musikwissenschaft* 3:189ff.

————. 1974b. Das Musikinstrument als Gegenstand anthropologischen und historischen Forschung. In *Kongress-Bericht of the Study Group on Folk Music Instruments of the IFMC in Kopenhagen, 1972,* 131–35. Copenhagen.

Stone, Ruth. 1982. *Let the inside be sweet: The interpretation of music event among the Kpelle of Liberia.* Bloomington: Indiana University Press.

Strunk, Oliver. 1950. *Source readings in music history from classical antiquity through the Romantic Era.* New York: Norton.

Subramanian, Karaikudi S. 1985. An introduction to the Vina. *Asian Music* 16 (2):7–82.

Sumarsam. 1975. Inner melody in Javanese gamelan music. *Asian Music* 7 (1):3–13.

————. 1984. Gamelan music and the Javanese Wayang Kulit. In *Aesthetic tradition and cultural transition in Java and Bali,* ed. S. Morgan and L. J. Seares Center for Southeast Asian Studies, monograph 2. Madison: University of Wisconsin.

Sutton, R. Anderson. 1984. Change and ambiguity: Gamelan style and regional identity in Yogyakarta, in *Aesthetic Tradition and Cultural Transition in Java and Bali,* S. Morgan and L. J. Seares (eds.). Madison: Center for Southeast Asian Studies, University of Wisconsin, monograph 2.

Sweeney, Amin. 1987. *A full hearing: Orality and literacy in the Malay world.* Berkeley and Los Angeles: University of California Press.

Tambiah, Stanley J. 1970. *Buddhism and the spirit cults in northeast Thailand.* Cambridge: Cambridge University Press.

———. 1985. The galactic polity in Southeast Asia. In *Culture thought, and action: An anthropological perspective,* S. J. Tambiah, 123–68. Cambridge: Harvard University Press.

Tatarkiewcicz, Wladislaw. 1970. *History of aesthetics. Vol. 1, Ancient aesthetics.* The Hague, Paris, and Warsaw: Mouton and Polish Scientific Publishers. (First Polish edition, 1962.)

Tinctoris, Johannes. c.1446-c.1511. *Concerning the nature and propriety of tones (De natura et proprietate tonorum).* Trans. Albert Seay, (1967) 1976. Colorado Springs: Colorado College Music Press.

Turner, Ashley. n.d. Musical Identity of the Petalangan Malays of Riau. Ph.D. diss., Monash University.

Tyler, S. R. 1979. *The said and the unsaid: Mind, meaning, and culture.* New York: Academic Press.

Tyler, Stephen A., ed. 1969. *Cognitive Anthropology.* New York: Holt, Rinehart and Winston.

Ugolino, Blasius, ed. 1767. *40 Schriften über Musik.* Vol. 32 of *Thesaurus antiquitatum sacrarum.* 34 vols. Venice.

Ugolino of Orvieto. 1959. *Declaratio musicae disciplinae.* Vol. 1. ed. Albert Seay. Rome: American Institute of Musicology.

van der Kroef, J. M. 1954. Dualism and symbolic antithesis in Indonesian society. *American Anthropologist,* n.s. 56 (5):847–62.

van Deusen, Nancy. 1987. Mediaeval organologies: Augustine vs. Cassiodor on the subject of musical instruments. In *Augustine and Music,* ed. R. de la Croix. New York: Mellen Press.

van Thiel, Paul. 1977. *Multi-tribal music of Ankole: An ethnomusicological study, including a glossary of musical terms.* Musée Royal de l'Afrique Centrale Annales, ser. in-80, Sciences Humaines, no. 91. Tervuren.

Villoteau, G. A. 1823. Déscription historique, technique, et littéraire des instruments de musique des orientaux. In *Description de l'Egypte.* Paris: Commission des Monuments d'Egypte.

Virdung, Sebastian. 1931. *Musica Getuscht.* Facs. and commentary by Leo Schrade. Kassel and Basle: Bärenreiter.

Wachsmann, Klaus P. 1980. Instruments, classification of. In *The new Grove dictionary of music and musicians* ed. S. Sadie, vol. 9:237–41. London: Macmillan.

Westphal, R. 1883. *Aristoxenos von Tarent: Melik und Rhythmik des klassischen Hellentums.* Hildesheim: George Olm.

Willard, N. Augustus. 1875. Treatise on the music of Hindustan. In *Hindu music from various authors,* ed. S. M. Tagore. Calcutta: Babu Punchanun Mukerjea.

Willis, R. 1974. *Man and beast.* London: Hart-Davis McGibbon.

Winnington-Ingram, R. P. 1980. Greece, ancient. In *The new Grove dictionary of music and musicians,* ed. S. Sadie, vol. 7:659–72. London: Macmillan.

Wright, Owen. 1980. Arab music. In *The new Grove dictionary of music and musicians,* ed. S. Sadie, vol. 1:4. London: Macmillan.

Yamaguchi, Osamu. 1969. Introduction to a taxonomy of musical instruments (in Japanese with English summary). *Bulletin of Musashino Academia Musicae* 3:187–97.

Yang Jia-luo, ed. 1975. *Zhongguo Yinyue Shiliao* (Historical sources on Chinese music). In *Zhongguo Shiliao Xibian* (Compilation of Chinese historical sources). 6 vols. Taipei: Dingwen Bookstore.

Yang Yin-Liu. 1952. *Chung-kuo Yin-yueh Shi-kang* (Outline of the history of Chinese music). Shanghai: Wan-yeh Book Co.

————. 1980. *Zhongguo Yinyue Shiliao* (Manuscript of Chinese ancient musical history). 2 vols. Beijing: Peoples Music Publishers.

Zarlino, Gioseffo. 1588. *Sopplimenti musicali* III. Venice: Chapters 33–34: 218–220.

Zemp, Hugo. 1971. *La musique dans la pensée et la vie sociale d'une société africaine.* Cahiers de l'Homme, Ethnologie-Geographie-Linguistique, n.s. 11, pt. 2, Conceptions et verbalisations 69: The Hague and Paris: Mouton.

————. 1978. 'Are'are classification of musical types and instruments. *Ethnomusicology* 22 (1):37–68.

————. 1979. Aspects of 'Are'are musical theory. *Ethnomusicology* 23 (1):6–48.

Glossary of Terms Used in Classification Theory

This glossary is based partly on Mayr 1982, Tyler 1969, and Brown 1972.* Words set in SMALL CAPS are defined elsewhere in the glossary.

aerophone Musical instruments that produce sound by using the air in a tube as the primary element of vibration or, as in the case of a free aerophone (such as a bull-roarer), the air surrounding the instrument.

artificial classification A classification imposed on a body of data rather than emerging naturally from it. Opposite of NATURAL CLASSIFICATION.

asymmetrical classification Grouping with close subdivisions in some taxa and broad ones in others.

broad classification Grouping in only one or a few steps. Opposite of CLOSE CLASSIFICATION.

category A class or level distinguished at the highest or most abstract step of classification.

character of division The distinguishing feature of a STEP of division.

chordophone Musical instruments that produce sound by exciting stretched strings.

classification The assigning to a proper class; the ordering of objects or organisms into taxa on the basis of their similarity and relationships as determined by their taxonomic characters; the division of an ensemble or other body of collected data into its component parts.

close classification Grouping in a substantial number of steps. Opposite of BROAD CLASSIFICATION.

concept of instruments A view of what an instrument is and means.

downward classification Grouping by logical division. Moving from a highly abstract level downward to a more specific level. The highest classes are broken down into their subclasses until the individuals that are their members are reached. Downward classification is based on any arbitrary viewpoint that disregards historical factors.

---

*A cataloguing system with standardized terms (e.g., "s-shaped trumpets") has been developed for the classification of instruments in iconographical sources in Howard Mayer Brown and Joan Lascelle, *Musical Iconography: a Manual for Cataloguing Musical Subjects in Western Art before 1800,* (Cambridge: Harvard University Press, 1972).

essentialism A philosophy that emphasizes regularity and constancy, seeing variation among specimens not as historically explainable phenomena but merely as an imperfect form of the underlying essence.

facet A sharply defined aspect of an object, a feature.

faceted grouping See UPWARD CLASSIFICATION.

idiophone Musical instruments on which sound can be produced by exciting the substance of the instrument itself, being sufficiently solid or elastic not to need stretched membranes or strings.

index The simplest form of catalogue listing, occurring in a sequence in alphabetical order or some other arbitrary method of ordering.

instrument (1) An implement used to produce music (as defined in the relevant culture), especially as distinguished from the human voice (based on Webster's Dictionary entry, 1976, ed.). (2) Any object from which sound may be produced intentionally (a much broader definition by Hornbostel 1933, 129).

instrumentarium The sum total of instruments in a particular context, culture, or period of a culture's history.

key An arrangement of dichotomous oppositions imposed on a body of data by application of one CHARACTER OF DIVISION per step, in order, for example, to locate or identify entities in a collection or set. Resembles ARTIFICIAL CLASSIFICATION.

lexeme A label of a cognitive category; a lexical unit having several levels of meaning.

logical division A classification method using one CHARACTER OF DIVISION per step.

macrotaxonomy Methods and principles by which kinds of objects are arranged in forms of classification.

membranophone Musical instruments that produce sounds from tightly stretched membranes.

microtaxonomy Methods and principles by which kinds of objects are recognized and delimited.

morphology A branch of ORGANOLOGY that deals with the structure, relations, and metamorphoses of instruments, apart from their functions. The term is similar, to the term anatomy in a medical context.

natural classification A classification that emerges naturally from a body of data rather than being imposed on it. Resembles TAXONOMY. Opposite of ARTIFICIAL CLASSIFICATION.

organogram A symbolic taxonomy presented in graphic form (Hood 1971, 124ff.).

organography The body of knowledge covering the classification of instruments and the principles on which it is based.

organology The scientific inquiry into musical instruments, concerned especially with structural detail.

paradigm The grouping of objects by application of more than one dimension simultaneously, as opposed to the sequential application of CHARACTERS OF DIVISION (as in a TAXONOMY).

population thinking The method recognizing the importance of individual specimens, stressing their uniqueness and rejecting the idea of the typical individual; view of classes as populations of changing individuals.

step A stage of subdivision of a CATEGORY, a level.

symmetrical classification A grouping based on an equally thorough investigation of all members of a body of objects; that is, the same question or series of questions is asked of all objects in a class, even if these questions yield nonsensical answers.

systematics Any ordered investigation into a body of objects; the scientific study of kinds and diversities of organisms and of all relationships among them.

taxon A group of characteristics of any taxonomic rank that is sufficiently distinct to be named and assigned to a definite CATEGORY.

taxonomy (1) A set of TAXA that are given by the culture or group that created it rather than being imposed on or manipulated intellectually by the observer. A grouping of objects by sequential inclusion of reference or application of CHARACTERS OF DIVISION, resulting in a hierarchy of contrasting division, as opposed to the application of more than one dimension simultaneously (as in a PARADIGM). Thus, items presented at the same level are related by inclusion, while items at different levels contrast with each other (Tyler 1969,7). (2) The study of the general principles of scientific classification; the systematic distinguishing, ordering, and naming of groups in a subject field (see MICROTAXONOMY, MACROTAXONOMY).

tree Classification in the form of a branch diagram using the method of a KEY.

type (1) A group of objects linked together by similarities of internal structure or similar processes of change. The term is not used in the sense of a paragon or archetype, nor in the sense of a "kind" of entity. It means a bundle or combination of attributes (Conklin 1969, 108). (2) A model with variable realizations, subject to constant change; a collection of VARIANTS or a group of qualitatively different but essentially similar objects.

typology (1) A multidimensional or multicharacter form of arranging objects according to the simultaneous intersection of CATEGORIES, as opposed to the sequential application of CHARACTERS OF DIVISION (as in a TAXONOMY). Investigation usually proceeds from the inspection of detailed attributes to a grouping of them in increasingly higher levels of generality. (2) A method of upward classification based on scanning the totality of the data and isolating VARIANTS, groups of variants, and TYPES; special graphic symbols may be used (Elschek 1969a, 33).

upward classification A method of grouping that begins at a low, more specific level and moves upward to increasingly more abstract levels. After detailed inspection of individual objects or species, they are sorted into groups of similar objects, which are grouped in turn into higher TAXA. Upward classification may take historical genesis and development into account. Similar to classification by faceted grouping (see TYPOLOGY).

variant One of two or more entities that exhibit slight differences from each other. See TYPE.

Index